THE
MONEY SUPPLY
AND THE
EXCHANGE RATE

EDITED BY

W. A. ELTIS AND P. J. N. SINCLAIR

CLARENDON PRESS · OXFORD

1981

Oxford University Press, Walton Street, Oxford OX2 6DP

London Glasgow New York Toronto
Delhi Bombay Calcutta Madras Karachi
Kuala Lumpur Singapore Hong Kong Tokyo
Nairobi Dar es Salaam Cape Town
Melbourne Auckland

and associate companies in
Beirut Berlin Ibadan Mexico City

Published in the United States
by Oxford University Press, New York

British Library Cataloguing in Publication Data

The money supply and the exchange rate.
1. Money supply — Great Britain
2. Foreign exchange
I. Eltis, W. A.   II. Sinclair, P. J. N.
332.4'0941   HG939.5
ISBN 0-19-877168-1

Printed in Northern Ireland
at The Universities Press (Belfast) Ltd.

CONTENTS

LIST OF CONTRIBUTORS

W. A. ELTIS, Fellow of Exeter College, Oxford.

G. D. N. WORSWICK, Director, National Institute of Economic and Social Research, London.

W. M. CORDEN, Professor of Economics, Australian National University, Canberra.

M. FG. SCOTT, Fellow of Nuffield College, Oxford.

D. LAIDLER, Professor of Economics, University of Western Ontario, London, Ontario.

M. BEENSTOCK, A. BUDD and P. WARBURTON; Professor of Finance, The City University, London; Director, Centre for Economic Forecasting at the London Business School; Senior Lecturer in Economics, London Business School.

P. MINFORD, Professor of Economics, University of Liverpool.

W. H. BUITER and M. H. MILLER, Professor of Economics, University of Bristol and Professor of Economics, University of Warwick.

M. H. ARTIS and D. A. CURRIE, Professor of Economics, University of Manchester and Reader in Economics, Queen Mary College, London.

G. HACCHE and J. TOWNEND, Economists, Bank of England.

D. A. HAY and D. J. MORRIS, Fellow of Jesus College, Oxford; Economic Director, National Economic Development Office, London and Fellow of Oriel College, Oxford.

M. J. BRECH and D. K. STOUT, Economist, National Economic Development Office, London; Tyler Professor of Economics, University of Leicester, and formerly Economic Director, National Economic Development Office, London.

J. F. WRIGHT, Fellow of Trinity College, Oxford.

N. H. DIMSDALE, Fellow of the Queen's College, Oxford.

P. J. N. SINCLAIR, Fellow of Brasenose College, Oxford.

THE FUNDAMENTAL PROBLEM

By W. A. ELTIS

I

IN MARCH 1980 the Editors of Oxford Economic Papers sent the following note to the contributors to the present Symposium.

The money supply and the exchange rate

It has become conventional wisdom in a number of countries that the rate of growth of the money supply must be controlled. The authorities state money supply targets which broadly correspond to the inflation rate plus the rate of growth of productivity which they are aiming for, and steps are then taken to achieve those targets through policies to control the level of government borrowing and, if necessary, high interest rates. It is hoped that the target inflation rate will be achieved after a time lag of between one and three years. A planned reduction in the rate of growth of the money supply rather than an immediate slow rate is one obvious variant of these new policies. They started to be implemented in Britain in 1976 as a result of the experience of the loose monetary policies of 1972–4. It is widely believed that the extra rapid increase of the money supply in that period was a factor in Britain's exceptional rate of inflation (among developed countries) in 1973–6. Britain is not, of course, the only country that has adopted policies to implement money supply targets, and this approach to the control of inflation has taken hold in several countries and may do so in more if it appears successful.

An older element in the British conventional wisdom is the effect of the exchange rate on profitability and employment. Keynes criticised Churchill's decision to return to the gold standard at the pre-war parity in 1925 which involved a 10 per cent revaluation of sterling.[1] In 1925–9 Britain had around 10 per cent unemployment when other developed economies were far closer to full employment. There was no 1920s boom in Britain, and the attempts of trade unions to resist the money wage cuts needed to restore British wage costs to their former international value led to the General Strike of 1926. Despite the failure of the General Strike, and a higher ratio of earnings of those at work to social security benefits than is the case today, money wages failed to fall significantly, and some believe that British wage costs only adjusted to internationally competitive levels after the fall of sterling in the 1930s. These events seemed to confirm Keynes's analysis, and to suggest that the exchange rate rather than money wage adjustment is the appropriate tool to maintain international competitiveness. This is still widely believed in Britain today, and in certain other countries.

[1] J. M. Keynes, *The Economic Consequences of Mr Churchill*, 1925. Reprinted in *The Collected Writings of John Maynard Keynes*, IX. *Essays in Persuasion*, pp. 207–30.

It might be naively supposed by some that it is possible to go along with monetary targets and to believe at the same time that a competitive exchange rate should always be maintained. There are, let us suppose, two objectives, a moderate rate of inflation and a high employment-balance of payments equilibrium. The money supply could then be used to control the rate of inflation after the appropriate time lags and the exchange rate to produce the desired high employment-balance of payments equilibrium. If balance of payments equilibrium is achieved at higher employment the lower the exchange rate in relation to domestic costs, there will always be a particular exchange rate at each level of domestic costs at which a high employment-balance of payments equilibrium is achievable.

A difficulty with this naive approach is the monetary theory of the balance of payments. It is believed by international monetarists that money will flow into a country where the money supply rises more slowly than the national product, and out of a country where the money supply grows faster than the national product. A country which seeks to reduce its rate of inflation by raising its money supply more slowly than its national product will therefore experience monetary inflows, and these will have a tendency to raise the exchange rate. A country with tight monetary policies can therefore expect to experience rising exchange rates. Conversely, a country with loose monetary policies can expect to have a falling exchange rate.

If this is accepted, a country which, like Britain, decides to increase its money supply more slowly than its national product can expect to move towards an overvalued exchange rate as a necessary consequence of its decision to adopt tight monetary policies. If alternatively it decided to give priority to lowering its exchange rate, it might need accompanying fiscal and interest rate policies which would involve a loosening of money supply constraints. So it appears that a country in this position may get either its exchange rate or its money supply wrong. It may therefore need to choose between the dangers of an overvalued exchange rate, or a rate of growth in the money supply faster than the rate appropriate to its inflation targets.

The difficulty would disappear if domestic wage costs per unit of output could adjust to internationally competitive levels despite the maintenance of a high exchange rate. There are several ways in which this could occur, and two in particular. First, if productivity is far lower than in other comparable countries, wage costs per unit could fall if productivity rose substantially, and international competition might force productivity upwards. Second, the high unemployment accompanying an overvalued exchange rate could so moderate the rate of increase of money wages that these would gradually come into line with what is required for international competitiveness. The difficulties with these possibilities are that productivity does not ordinarily rise rapidly while output stagnates. The Verdoorn relationships which see productivity rising with output have been quite commonly observed. As for the possibility of money wage adjustments, if high unemployment can produce these on a sufficient scale, why did it fail to do so in the 1920s?

There is certainly published evidence that in recent years wages have adjusted upwards to cancel out some of the hoped-for benefits for competitiveness of devaluations, but is there equal evidence of wages adjusting downwards to correct for the adverse effects on competitiveness of revaluations?

The dilemma policy makers may face between the adoption of the money supply targets they believe to be right to control inflation and the exchange rate policies that favour competitiveness could well be faced by Britain in the early 1980s. The trade weighted exchange rate of sterling rose 12 per cent between March 1979 and March 1980, and money wages rose at an annual rate of 20 per cent over this period. The real revaluation of sterling in this period was therefore far greater than in 1925. With money growth targets of 11 per cent or less while earnings are rising at almost 20 per cent, there should be shortages of money in Britain tending to cause monetary inflows in the early 1980s. The high income predicted from North Sea oil should reinforce the upward pressure on the exchange rate. There are therefore two particular reasons why the non-oil sector of the British economy may be unable to maintain profitability and employment: the effect of monetary stringency may produce an exchange rate that is too high for the non-oil sector to live with, and the favourable balance of trade in oil may produce an exchange rate which necessarily forces the non-oil sector to contract.

A number of questions are raised in this statement which economists will wish to discuss further:

1. How strong is the line of argument which suggests that tight monetary conditions will produce a rising exchange rate?
2. Are there satisfactory technical means by which a competitive exchange rate can be maintained while the authorities are simultaneously pursuing tight monetary policies?
3. Are profitability and employment closely associated with international competitiveness?
4. By what means should any possible tendency of North Sea oil to raise the exchange rate be neutralized, if this tends to reduce the profitability of the rest of the British economy?
5. Were Britain's relatively high unemployment and labour difficulties in the 1920s attributable, as Keynes believed, to the overvaluation of sterling, and were the relatively favourable developments in the later 1930s attributable to the lower exchange rate?
6. What light does the experience of other countries throw on these policy dilemmas?

II

These questions raised issues of fundamental importance for both theory and policy which are relevant to the problems of many countries. They are of course especially important for Britain. In March 1980 when we sent out our invitations to contribute, the trade weighted exchange rate of sterling had risen 12 per cent in twelve months. At the time of going to the press in February 1981 it has risen a further 5 per cent. In the intervening 11 months British wages in the production of tradables have been rising at an annual rate of about 18 per cent, while those in almost all other industrial economies have been rising more slowly than this. In consequence, the real revaluation of sterling has increased by perhaps a further 10 per cent. The problems which were worrying in March 1979 have therefore become still more acute.

It is a little reassuring that several of those who responded to our invitation outline and make use of a model where the real exchange rate rises over-sharply in a period where the economy is adjusting to a slower rate of growth of the money supply, and falls again once full adjustment is complete. If Britain is under the influence of deflationary monetary policies to which adjustment is still incomplete—and that is rather obviously the case[2]—then according to the analysis of several of these contributions, part of the enormous rise in the real exchange rate of sterling should be reversed in due course.

Most of the present contributors see the problem of the real exchange rate in a far longer time perspective than we did in our note of March 1980. We spoke then of the danger that a country might find that its money supply targets were incompatible with the real exchange rate that it needed for international competitiveness. Several contributors agree that this will immediately be the case, but base their full argument on a model where all will come out as it should in the end. Before they read these very illuminating and helpful articles some readers may find it useful to keep the following very simple theoretical framework in mind as a starting point. Elements of it are to be found in the contributions from the London Business School, Professors Buiter and Miller, Professor Corden, Professor Laidler, Professor Minford and Mr Scott, who do not of course present it in the very simple and perhaps oversimplified form which follows.

Suppose that a country's international current and capital accounts balance at a particular price level and exchange rate when its labour market is also in equilibrium. Suppose that its price and wage costs per unit of output then rise 10 per cent relative to those of other countries, and that its exchange rate falls 10 per cent at the same time. Suppose that while this is occurring there is no fundamental change in its relative level of output, or in the products it produces compared to those of other countries, so that after its prices and wage costs have risen 10 per cent its labour market is still in equilibrium and its current and capital accounts still balance. In that situation one would say that its *real* exchange rate was unaltered and that the 10 per cent fall in its *nominal* exchange rate had merely compensated for its 10 per cent of extra inflation.

Monetarists would say that the 10 per cent rise in prices was associated with excess growth in the money supply of about 10 per cent, and that this will have had the effect of causing a 10 per cent depreciation of the nominal exchange rate without affecting the real exchange rate.

Reversing the story, it can be argued that a 10 per cent reduction in the money supply in relation to what it would otherwise have been will produce a situation in the end where prices are 10 per cent lower than they otherwise would have been, where the nominal exchange rate is 10 per cent higher and the real exchange rate is unchanged. It can be argued that changes in the money supply will only affect nominal values like the price level, the nominal exchange rate and the money rate of interest, and cannot in the long term affect the real level of output, real competitiveness, and the real rate of interest.

What occurs immediately after the rate of growth of the money supply is reduced? In the first instance this will tend to reduce money effective demand in relation to money wages, and hence the level of output and employment. The labour market will then be out of equilibrium with fewer jobs available than the number of workers actively seeking employment. At this lower real national income there will be two effects on the *real* exchange rate. First imports will be reduced relative to exports, because these are more sensitive than exports to the level of the real national income. This fall in imports relative to exports will tend to raise the real exchange rate. Second, monetary tightness will tend to raise the real rate of interest. This will in part be a response to a scarcity of money relative to the transactions that need to be financed: it will also be a consequence of the techniques the monetary authorities use to reduce the rate of growth of the money supply. The higher real interest rate will attract capital to the country that is pursuing a policy of monetary deflation, and this will tend to produce a favourable balance of payments capital account, which will also temporarily raise the real exchange rate.

During the period of transition to a new equilibrium where the price level is lower than it otherwise would have been, the country that pursues these policies will find that its real exchange rate is raised both because of the influence of a lower real national income on its current account and because of the influence of higher real interest rates on its capital account.

In due course, it can be argued, the excess of the supply of labour seeking employment over the demand for labour, and the shortage of money, will reduce the rate of increase of wages and prices until the demand for labour is once again in line with the numbers seeking employment. Once employment has risen sufficiently to restore equilibrium in the labour market, the exchange rate will return to its appropriate real long-term level, which will be the real rate from which it set out in the absence of underlying structural changes. The pound will therefore lose some of its recent gains if this model applies to Britain.

The authors who base their analysis on propositions like those outlined above, and those mentioned subscribe to some of them, also take account of the fact that the exploitation of a new natural resource, North Sea oil in Britain's case, will raise the real exchange rate by increasing the capacity to export and reducing import requirements. They therefore attribute part of the increase in Britain's real exchange rate since 1977 to North Sea oil.

Professor Corden's article includes a full and careful analysis of the influence of this on Britain's exchange rate. He suggests that there are ways of taking advantage of oil which do not involve a large reduction in the profitability of the tradable sector of the economy, for instance by using the revenues from North Sea oil to repay debt.

But North Sea oil will obviously, on balance, raise the exchange rate. There are therefore three reasons for the rise in Britain's real exchange rate. First the influence of North Sea oil, second the influence of a lower real National Income in a period of monetary contraction, and third the influence of a favourable capital account in a period of monetary contraction. The first effect will not be reversed but the second and third will be as soon as wages fall sufficiently to restore the equilibrium in the labour market that is appropriate to the new lower monetary growth rate.

For Professor Minford the period in which unemployment exceeds the natural rate to produce this temporary fluctuation in the real exchange rate is happily brief. In his model there are rational expectations, a labour market where unemployment is voluntary, and strong portfolio balance effects on spending. As a result, while there is a significant period in which real interest rates and the real exchange rate are high, putting pressure on the non-oil tradables sector, unemployment and the national income are only. modestly and transitorily disturbed because of the countervailing pressures. Professors Buiter and Miller, in contrast, assume that while the exchange rate responds immediately to current and anticipated future policy changes, domestic costs and prices adjust more slowly, so that unemployment can exceed the natural rate for a time: they see the transition as prolonged and uncomfortable in the extreme. The paper from the London Business School analyses the transition carefully, making a variety of assumptions about expectations etc., and finds it uncomfortable but inescapable. Complete adjustment of domestic wages and prices to a change in monetary policy may require several years. The econometrics of the London Business School suggests that the effect on the exchange rate of a favourable capital account due to high interest rates has been slight, and that the effect of North Sea oil has been very considerable.

Mr Worswick does not find a monetarist framework of analysis helpful. He believes that the period of transition between the equilibria where the labour market is in equilibrium and the real exchange rate is unaffected by monetary policy are so long that irreversible structural deterioration may occur in the interim. If wages respond only slowly to high unemployment, there will be many years in which the supply of labour exceeds the employment opportunities available, the real exchange rate exceeds the one appropriate to full employment equilibrium, and prices are so low in relation to wages that the real level of output is adversely affected.

In this context Mr Wright's article about the 1920s and the 1930s, when Keynesian thinking evolved, is especially interesting. He argues that the excess unemployment of the 1920s was partly structural, and partly a result of increased unemployment benefits in the 1920s, and that Mr Churchill's revaluation of the exchange rate in 1925 added only slightly to unemployment. By 1929 relative prices had fallen sufficiently to negate the effects of Mr Churchill's 10 per cent revaluation. Mr Dimsdale believes however that a *devaluation* was in fact needed in the 1920s to counteract the structural weaknesses which emerged after the War. He surveys the literature on these issues and on balance agrees with Keynes. He believes that wage flexibility was slight after 1923, and that there would have been substantially less unemployment in the 1920s if the exchange rate had been lower, which is also Mr Worswick's view. Mr Dimsdale believes that the relative prosperity of the 1930s was partly due to tariffs and the depreciation of sterling, and also to the far lower interest rates which became feasible once the exchange rate no longer needed to be defended. Balanced budgets throughout most of the 1930s meant that there was no upward pressure on interest rates from government borrowing which made a 2 per cent bank rate possible.

Mr Hay and Dr Morris examine the association between the real exchange rate and British industrial profitability in the 1960s and the 1970s, and they find that in the very short run a 20 per cent rise in the real exchange rate cuts export profitability by as much as 40 per cent, and profits as a whole by only 2 per cent. There is thus an extremely sharp fall in the relative profitability of exporting, but very little direct influence on aggregate company profits. Company profits as a whole did not react especially favourably to the frequent reductions in the real exchange rate from 1967 to 1976, and it may be that the rise in sterling since then has had an equally neutral effect. Mr Hay and Dr Morris stress however that they have only estimated very short term responses. Different results may occur as the process of adjustment continues. Mr Brech and Professor Stout find that at a higher real exchange rate some British exporters move up market. This may reflect the deaths of low value-added products, or extra births of high value-added products. If the latter effect is significant, a period of deflation with an over-high exchange rate may actually produce some favourable effects on the economy in the period of transition.

It may be that the adjustment the monetarists seek is attainable, and that it will involve less social cost than many now believe, but there must be some significant disadvantages from a large and prolonged fluctuation of the exchange rate. Some of the contributions consider deeply the question of whether there are ways in which adjustment can be achieved more smoothly and at less social cost. The simple story outlined so far has the real exchange rate rise sharply in the period immediately after the rate of growth of the money supply contracts, and then come down again once adjustment is complete and prices and wages have fallen enough to restore unemployment to the natural rate. Mr Scott believes that there are practicable policies to intervene in the foreign exchange market to reduce the fluctuation of the exchange rate, but that these would not lessen the welfare cost of reducing the rate of inflation, which is the ultimate objective of the policies in question. Professors Buiter and Miller consider the possibility of taxing the interest receipts of foreign sterling holdings to lessen the fluctuation of the exchange rate. They also consider the possibility of a once-for-all increase in the money supply to ease the costs of transition to a new equilibrium where *the rate of growth* of the money supply and therefore the long-term inflation rate is slower.

Professor Artis and Dr Currie consider the advantages of attempting to attain economic objectives by controlling the exchange rate rather than the money supply. This would in effect link a country's inflation rate to that of the country or countries against which its exchange rate is fixed. This can have the advantages of avoiding the extreme fluctuations that may result from pursuing independent and changing money supply targets, while the inflation rate achieved will be no worse provided that other countries are successfully controlling inflation. Professor Artis and Dr Currie argue that better policy results are on balance attainable with alternative targets to simple money supply control. Mr Hacche and Mr Townend of the Bank of England underline the difficulties involved in any policies to intervene to manage the exchange rate of sterling by showing that this did not conform to any simple model of exchange rate behaviour from 1972 to 1980.

In the end one comes back to the question of how prolonged and uncomfortable the monetarist transition to a lower price level and a higher nominal exchange rate is liable to be. If it is as brief as Professor Minford believes, it can readily be borne. If it is long and uncomfortable, then we may indeed be faced with the choice as Mr Worswick sees it between intolerable inflation and the unacceptable unemployment which is needed to reduce it in the absence of successful incomes policies. If the cost of the monetarists' transition lies between Professor Minford's optimism and Mr Worswick's pessimism, then those of the present articles which are concerned with the technical problems of minimising the economic costs involved make especially valuable contributions.

THE MONEY SUPPLY AND
THE EXCHANGE RATE

By G. D. N. WORSWICK

Introduction

IT IS little more than a dozen years since devaluation was being urged as a major change in order to remove the brake of the balance of payments constraint on the British economy. The introduction to the Brookings study of the British economy published in 1968 observed that: 'Statistical evidence now firmly supports the view that devaluation should improve the British current account, and indeed that the 14.3 per cent change of 1967 should at least restore equilibrium, even allowing for the adverse effects of higher import prices on the domestic price level.'[1] The strongest consideration in the case for devaluation was the desire to avert the need for recurrent bouts of deflation and unemployment, but some economists went further, arguing that devaluation would set off a virtuous circle whereby higher exports would induce higher investment, thereby raising productivity and lowering costs, which would induce yet further rises in exports.

Two years ago, when the possible accession of Britain to the new European Monetary System, was under active consideration, the British government published a Green Paper[2] which also offered a virtuous circle, only this time it was to be started off by *raising* the exchange rate. A rise in the exchange rate would mean British goods and services becoming dearer to foreigners, but it would make imports cheaper. This should lead to smaller rises in nominal incomes, notably wages, without loss to living standards. The pressure to keep down costs would stimulate cost-saving and thus, efficiency. 'Once a virtuous circle of exchange rate stability, lower costs, greater stimulus to efficiency has been established, the effects of any initial loss of price competitiveness may be removed.'[3]

How has such a dramatic reversal in policy prescription for the exchange rate been possible in such a short time? No-one should under-rate the element of fashion. The reversal may well represent no more than a swing in the pendulum of influence in Whitehall, where Green Papers are written. Whatever the progress of the economy itself, there has been no lack of innovation in economic policy in the post-war period. Mr Blackaby and his colleagues have recently documented the 'great many changes, and indeed frequent reversals, in policy'.[4] If pulling the string will not move it, try pushing the string for a change!

Nevertheless, it is possible to enumerate more substantial explanations than a mere change of fashion. First of all there is the change in attitudes

---

[1] *Britain's Economic Prospects*, George Allen and Unwin, 1968, p. 11.
[2] Cmnd 7405, November 1978.
[3] Ibid. para. 39.
[4] *British Economic Policy* 1960–74, Cambridge University Press, 1978, p. 652.

which has been taking place towards the objectives of full employment, growth and price stability. In the sixties and early seventies the dislike of inflation was still subordinate to the desire for growth and more especially full employment. Since then the balance has tilted so that today, in Britain, and in many other countries, the reduction of inflation has become overriding, and government policy explicitly accepts that production may stagnate or fall and unemployment rise for a time until inflation is 'under control'. The primary objective of devaluation was to avert unemployment and to accelerate growth, it being recognised that prices would rise. The primary objective of the Green Paper policy of raising the exchange rate was to slow down the rise in prices, although little was said in that particular place about the costs in terms of output foregone, and it was hoped that in the longer run output might even increase. Although such a change in priorities could suffice to explain the change in attitudes towards policy, there have also been changes in ideas about how the economy works. The devaluation of 1967 was a step-wise move of sterling within the essentially fixed exchange rate system of Bretton Woods. The exchange rate increases of today are in the context of an essentially floating rate regime. Thus even if the framework of theoretical analysis had remained the same, it could be argued quite plausibly that the responses of different economic variables, such as output or prices, to an alteration of the exchange rate would be different in a flexible system than in a system of fixed rates.[5] While the institutions have been changing, the framework of analysis has also been modified in important respects. The monetary approach to the balance of payments is formally distinct from 'monetarism', but it has come to the fore at roughly the same time, and in some hands at least, seems to lead to similar conclusions about the unwisdom of governments attempting to influence real output and employment.

Thus the change in attitude towards the exchange rate in recent years is the outcome of changes on three planes:

1. A change in economics;
2. A change in institutions;
3. A change in priorities.

1. Changes in economics

What later became known as 'demand management' dates from the acceptance in the White Paper on *Employment Policy* of 1944 of the government's responsibility for maintaining a high and stable level of employment. The implication was that, left to itself, a capitalist economy might get stuck with high, and possibly persistent levels of unemployment,

[5] The contrast between fixed and floating rates systems is not one of polar opposites. Had Britain joined EMS, sterling would have been fixed, within a certain band, with respect to other EMS currencies, and would have continued to float jointly with them against other currencies such as the dollar and the yen.

which could be alleviated by appropriate policies. Throughout the post-war years the main weight of regulating aggregate demand and employment rested on fiscal policy, with monetary policy being either accommodating or being more actively managed in relation to the external balance.

It was always recognised that exchange rate changes might be needed to ensure external equilibrium if a policy of full employment was being pursued; this was most clearly seen in the devaluation of 1967 and again when sterling was allowed to float in 1972. After 1960 it was also increasingly accepted that a high employment policy was likely to entail chronic inflation, and if that were thought to be unacceptable some means of influencing nominal incomes directly, through some kind of incomes policy, would have to be added to the armoury of instruments. The modelling of the economy, both inside and outside the Treasury, which was being developed throughout this period reflected this approach. Simulations with the models of the Treasury, the National Institute and the London Business School, reported as late as 1978, showed that in all three an increase of public expenditure or a cut in taxes would generate increases in real output and employment, in different degrees in different models and also according as the exchange rate was fixed or floating. There were, however, greater differences between models in what they said about the effects of devaluation; the Treasury and the National Institute both showed some increases in output and ultimately in the current balance, while the LBS showed little output effect and larger prices and earnings responses.[6]

Central to the monetarism of the early 1970s is the equation $MV = PT$. The resurrection of the equation itself would not have caused a very great stir. The equation is a truism, and any objection would be on the grounds of its undue narrowness as a framework for reasoning about the economy. The impetus to the revival was given by two ultimately empirical claims, namely that the velocity of circulation is stable and there exists a 'natural' rate of unemployment. Governments might, by budgetary policy, push the level of unemployment below the natural rate, but if they did, not only inflation, but accelerating inflation, would be the inevitable consequence. It was also implied that the economy is self-righting and will always find its own way back to the natural rate of unemployment. More recently, the idea of 'rational expectations' has been seized upon by some monetarists to reinforce the argument that demand management must be ineffective.

The earlier monetarists stressed the long and variable lags which existed between changes in the quantity of money and consequential changes in the rate of inflation, and they also acknowledged that reducing inflation by

[6] See *National Institute Economic Review*, Feb. 1978, pp. 52–72. An earlier version of the LBS model gave a somewhat different answer. Their estimate was that the devaluation of 1967 both caused an increase in activity—with unemployment being eventually 500,000 less than would otherwise have been the case—and an improvement in the current balance by 1970 of £470 million. On a comparable basis this last estimate 'was much larger than that of NIESR' made in 1972. (Ball, Burns and Miller, Simulations with the LBS Macroeconomic Model, in *Modelling the Economy*, Heinemann, 1975, p. 207.)

monetary restriction entailed 'transitional' increases in unemployment. Some monetarists went so far as to argue that temporary incomes policies might be justified as a means of averting excessive transitional unemployment. In purely analytical terms, this reduced the gap between monetarists and Keynesians almost to vanishing point.[7] Many of the latter have always accepted that the achievement of full employment by fiscal policy would entail chronic cost-inflation and that the money supply would have to expand to accommodate this. For non-inflationary full employment an incomes policy would be needed. Thus the residual issue between Keynesians and monetarists became one of whether an acceptable level of unemployment once reached, could be maintained without some form of continuing restraint upon money wages, whether imposed by statute or reached by agreement in some form of social contract.

According to one application of the rational expectations argument, the cost-inflation persisted precisely because economic agents, notably trade union leaders, knew that if they secured 'excessive' wage increases there would be consequential monetary accommodation. Once they realised that the authorities would no longer adjust the money supply, they would promptly modify their claims to correspond to the new situation. The response of inflation to changes in monetary targets would thus be quick and relatively painless. This difference in the speed of response in the two versions of monetarism needs to be kept in mind.

The monetary approach to the balance of payments is most simply seen as the extension to more than one country of the quantity theory of money. For a single country it is possible to imagine that the absolute price level is uniquely determined by the quantity of money. But this is no longer possible for two countries if there is trade between them, for the absolute price levels of any goods which can be traded cannot move independently. Consequently the simplest kind of quantity theory will no longer do and a modification is required. This modification does not apply only to the oversimplified models like the quantity theory but to more complex ones as well. Until recent years the modelling of the balance of payments and the exchange rate in nearly all British models was conceived in terms of flows of trade and payments. But besides a flow equilibrium there is also a question of stock equilibrium. People do not only acquire dollars to spend on travel or imports: they also acquire them to purchase financial or real assets in the United States or elsewhere which they wish to hold.

The point can be seen clearly in one of the current paradoxes concerning the relation between the PSBR and the exchange rate. What would be the effect upon the exchange rate and the balance of payments of a cut in taxes?

---

[7] For Keynesians there is a level of unemployment below which there is inflation, for monetarists a level below which there is accelerating inflation. If the current rate of inflation is already considered too high, the question whether it is also accelerating may not seem all that important. The real issue is whether either of these 'critical' unemployment levels can actually be measured.

One answer is that lower taxes would mean increased private expenditure, part of which would go on imports, the balance of payments would worsen and the exchange rate fall. The lower exchange rate would promote exports and lead to import substitution. Nevertheless the most likely outcome is that national income and output would be higher, both because of increased production of consumer goods and of exports. Imports also would be higher and on balance by more than exports, so that in the final situation the trade balance would be worse and the exchange rate lower than in the initial position. At the end of the day the PSBR would be higher.

The other answer is that lower taxes would increase government borrowing which would put up interest rates. The UK would become more attractive to investors, there would be a net inflow of funds into the UK which would raise the exchange rate. This would set in motion a process of reduced exports and increased imports, thus worsening the current account. The net outcome would be that the lower taxes have increased the PSBR but raised the exchange rate.

The resolution of the paradox lies in the fact that each answer omits one strand of the argument which appears in the other. Thus, in the first case there is no mention of the possibility that the higher budget deficit would, if the money supply were not changed, tend to push up the rate of interest, induce a net inflow of funds across the exchanges and thus push up the rate of exchange as well. In the second answer, nothing was said about the effect of lower taxes on private net income and expenditure which would mean higher imports, pulling the exchange rate down, and higher savings, damping the rise in interest rates.

One suspects that the different answers are related to different standpoints in economic analysis. In the one the primary concern is with long run equilibrium and the question of whether the economy is actually in equilibrium, and, if not, how it will find its way there is ignored. In particular, it is frequently assumed that the economy is at full employment, which is maintained by complete flexibility of wages and prices. In the other approach we start from where the economy actually is and ask where it can be expected to go next, and next again. As to the long run, that is when we are all dead.

Which standpoint is superior, or whether some synthesis would be better still, ought, in principle, to be answerable by a well conducted appeal to the facts. Yet notwithstanding a huge volume of econometric work, the residue of established truth is comparatively meagre, as must be evident to anyone who has waded through a sample of equations for wages, imports or for the demand for money, to mention only three of the more important variables.[8]

The 'natural rate' of unemployment has not fared too well. Friedman's

[8] A good example of how much light has been shed on problems of this kind by econometric evidence can be found in the chapter on monetary policy by M. J. Artis in *British Economic Policy* 1960–74, Edited F. T. Blackaby, Cambridge, 1978.

famous phrase that it was 'the level that would be ground out by the Walrasian equations of general equilibrium...' is suggestive of something like the average age or of the average height of the population, which changes only slowly through time. Early British estimates put it at less than 2 per cent.[9] But as unemployment has risen from 2 to 3 to 5 to 7 per cent, with inflation sometimes accelerating and sometimes slowing down, the 'natural rate' has been puffing and panting trying to keep up.[10] But the more volatile it is, the less value it retains as a guide to policy. On the question of whether the demand for money is stable, American economists appear to have had some success using American data, while the great majority of British economists have had none using British data.

The same contrast between the long term tendencies and shorter term behaviour arises in the international field with the so-called 'law of one price'. The price predictions of the elasticity and monetary theories of balance of payments adjustments have been compared with actual price behaviour by Kravis and Lipsey.[11] Their conclusion is: 'price behaviour differs more from the relatively demanding monetary approach in that price levels and price movements for GDP as a whole and for specific types of export goods vary substantially, even among major industrial countries. As for the elasticity approach, price levels tend to rise with appreciations and fall with depreciations as expected.' In some cases it is plain that a mistake is being made. What is postulated, at best, as a long run relationship is then written into a model as though it operated instantaneously.

Where a proper distinction between postulated long run behaviour and actual short run behaviour is maintained the results can be very interesting. At a recent symposium[12] Burns and Beenstock presented a new econometric model with impeccable 'monetary theory of the balance of payments' credentials in that in the long run it was postulated that there was a 'natural' rate of unemployment, and the domestic price level varied with the world money supply and inversely with the exchange rate; and the model had other *long term* properties as well. However, if disturbed, the model was allowed to take time to find its way to the new long term equilibrium, and it was asked what would happen if the exchange rate were to be five per cent higher. Exactly the same question was put to the National Institute model of 1979 which is a mongrel, lacking the pure pedigree which would enable it to enter any high theory Crufts show. Table 1 shows the answers given by the two models as percentages of divergence from the control solution in the two cases. The two simulations were not exactly comparable: nevertheless

[9] Cf D. Laidler in Institute of Economic Affairs *Occasional Paper*, 44, 1975, p. 45.

[10] Mr Samuel Brittan has recently argued (*Financial Times*, 30 October 1980) that: (a) the natural rate (which he calls CIR, for constant inflation rate, and others call NAIRU, for non-accelerating inflation rate of unemployment) is **very** important; (b) it is impossible to measure; and, (c) his own 'extremely wild guess' is $1\frac{1}{2}$ m to **2 m**, or 'just below the present rate'.

[11] Kravis, I. B. and Lipsey, R. E. 'Price behaviour in the light of balance of payments theories', *Journal of International Economics*, May 1978.

[12] *Britain's Trade and Exchange Rate Policy*, ed R. L. Major, Heinemann, 1979, chapter 5.

TABLE 1
Effects of 5 per cent appreciation

End year	Wholesale prices (%)		Average earnings (%)		Real GDP (%)		Current balance (£b)		Competitiveness (%)	
	LBS	NIESR	LBS[1]	NIESR	LBS	NIESR	LBS[2]	NIESR	LBS	NIESR
1	−2.0	−1.1	−0.9	−0.1	+0.1	−0.4	+0.7	+0.3	−3.0	−3.3
2	−2.9	−2.7	−2.1	−1.1	+0.1	−0.2	−0.8	−0.1	−1.9	−1.6
3	−3.6	−3.2	−3.4	−1.9	−0.2	−0.1	−1.2	−0.2	−1.2	−1.3
4	−4.3	−3.5	−4.5	−2.6	−0.1	+0.1	−1.3	−0.4	−0.4	−0.9
5	−4.9	−3.8	−5.4	−3.0	−0.1	+0.2	−1.2	−0.4	+0.2	−0.6

[1] Manufacturing only.
[2] Balance of Official Financing.
Source: *Britain's Trade and Exchange Rate Policy* ed Robin Major, HEB 1979, pp. 113 and 127.

they both showed the same direction of change for wholesale prices and average earnings, competitiveness and the external balance, with a *J* curve in the first year. The output profile is different, the changes in the LBS case being very small. I have elsewhere given objections to both these simulations,[13] but for what they are worth, they do indicate that exchange rate appreciation may reduce inflation but only at the expense of the current balance and in the NIESR case at the expense of a loss of output in the first two or three years. Both agree that competitiveness deteriorates and the gap is not closed for some years. This conclusion is important. Burns and Beenstock postulate that exchange rate changes have 'no lasting balance of payments effects' but in their model the cumulative worsening of the balance of official financing over five years was £3.8 billions; thus a succession of 5 per cent appreciations—and the effective exchange rate did in fact rise by over 20 per cent in the past two years—could have powerful affects for some years. No doubt it is important to observe that if an economy is disturbed it will have certain tendencies to move in a certain direction. If the adjustment process is slow the question arises whether in the intervening 'disequilibrium' some important, and irreversible, changes, whether favourable or unfavourable, may occur.

2. Changes in institutions

Four changes have occurred in the economic environment since 1967 which compel the re-examination of almost every proposition previously taken for granted. They are the crumbling of the Bretton Woods fixed exchange rate system, which has given way to a predominantly floating rate system, in which some currencies float, with varying degrees of management, and others are pegged to other currencies, to the SDR or to some composite

[13] Op. cit. pp. 128 *et seq.*

of currencies. While most currencies remain pegged, most trade takes place between countries whose currencies float. Secondly there was the abandonment in 1979 by the UK of all forms of exchange control, which is having effects upon monetary policy which are still not fully appreciated. Thirdly, there is the new oil price regime, inaugurated by the fourfold increase in the price at the end of 1973. Contrary to the hopes and expectations of some economists, the OPEC cartel has held together well enough to allow a substantial push, from time to time, to the real price of oil. The cartel plays a role in inflation internationally not unlike that played by Trade Unions domestically, sometimes leading and sometimes trailing, but always trying to keep up with the rate of inflation. In addition it creates recurrent problems for the rest of the world of the unspent current payments surplus. Finally, there has been the development of North Sea oil itself with profound implications for the British balance of payments and for the economy at large.

3. Changes in priorities

In the spring of 1980 the Treasury and Civil Service Committee of the House of Commons sent a questionnaire on monetary policy to a number of institutional and academic witnesses. The Treasury's reply contained the following sentences:

'The main objectives of the government's economic strategy are ... to reduce inflation and to create conditions in which sustainable economic growth can be achieved.

There is no fundamental difference between these objectives and those of previous governments, but there is an important shift of emphasis. The government is looking at these objectives in a medium term context; its policies are designed to be conducive to their achievement on that time scale. This means no longer giving pride of place to short term stabilisation of output, employment and the external current account that dominated economic policy making in the 1950s and 1960s ...

In present circumstances this involves giving overriding priority to reducing inflation and to strengthening the supply side of the economy.'[14]

The government strategy is to fix targets for the money supply and the PSBR, as a ratio of GDP on declining paths for the next four years; the rest of the economy will then be allowed to adapt itself to these targets. The belief is that this will be sufficient to bring about a reduction in the rate of inflation. 'But the process of reducing inflation almost inevitably entails some losses of output initially, though it promises a better growth of output in the long term.[15]

These statements do in fact represent a change in priorities, giving

---

[14] House of Commons, Treasury and Civil Service Committee, Memoranda on Monetary Policy, July 1980, HMSO 720.
[15] Financial Statement and Budget Report, March 1980, HMSO 500.

overriding priority to reducing inflation, but they also involve a change in the government's view about how the economy works, along the lines discussed in Section 1 above. It is very difficult to know how far any particular policy is being adopted simply because of a change in priority (getting inflation down being now seen as more urgent than keeping unemployment down) and how far because of a change in belief about the economy. For instance, when they came into office many ministers clearly believed that fixing the money supply would be enough and that wages could be allowed to determine themselves. There was no need for an incomes policy, a social contract or even for lectures about moderation. Now the idea of leaving wages to market forces and collective bargaining has been abandoned. There are lectures from ministers almost every day and it is clear that long standing practices for determining pay in the public sector are going to be changed.

The six questions

The editors of this symposium list six questions on which they invite further comment. My answers come under three headings.

    (a) The high exchange rate in the twenties and the eighties.
    (b) Demand management and the exchange rate.
    (c) Money and the exchange rate.

(a) *A high exchange rate*

The story on which my generation was brought up is that in 1925 Britain returned to the Gold Standard at a rate which Keynes said was too high. (See *The Economic Consequences of Mr Churchill.*) That precipitated the miners' strike and the General Strike of 1926 and kept unemployment high in the 1920s. Then came the Great Depression. Britain left the Gold Standard, which helped. Keynes wrote the *General Theory*, which was not in time to help much before the war, but helped a lot after—until everything was spoiled by inflation, though we do not agree exactly how. Some say it came from neglect of money, others say it was all the fault of the Unions and the Sheikhs.

There seems no need to revise the story of the 1920s. At the restored rate of exchange, British export prices were too high and British exports did not do well. By 1929 the volume of British exports of manufactures was still only 93 per cent of the 1913 level, whereas for Germany it was 107, for France 132 and for the United States 245.[16] Unemployment remained high. Pigou later wrote of the 1920s as the Doldrums and of the 'intractable million of unemployed.'[17] D. H. Aldcroft has noted that 'it has been estimated that in 1929 unemployment in the six leading export trades

---

[16] Cf. A. Maizels, *Industrial Growth and World Trade*, CUP 1963, Table A6, p. 435.
[17] *Aspects of British Economic History*, A. C. Pigou, Macmillan, 1947, pp. 42 *et seq.*

caused by a fall in exports since 1913 amounted to no less than 700–800,000 workers, or pratically the whole of the core of unemployment.'[18]

In the Depression unemployment rose much further. But in 1931 Britain left the Gold Standard and devalued with respect to the dollar and the franc. Although world trade had collapsed, the volume of British exports of manufactures in 1937 was back to 78 per cent of the 1929 level, compared with 80 per cent for USA but only 68 per cent for Germany and a mere 42 per cent for France.

In the 1920s the world was in the main on a Gold Standard and this was a case of the sterling parity being fixed too high and thereafter being defended by a restrictive monetary policy, so that exports and employment suffered. By contrast, the critics in the 1980s are arguing that a floating rate is being allowed to rise to such an extent as to inflict serious damage on British manufacturing industry.

The most durable economic theory relating to exchange rates is the doctrine of purchasing power parity. Nevertheless antiquity does not confer exactitude. Now, as ever, purchasing power parity, or to use a modern expression international 'competitiveness', is only one, albeit an important one, of the factors influencing exchange rates. In a fixed exchange rate regime an upward deviation of the national price level from the rest of the world will have unfavourable effects on reserves: but these may be offset if output contracts, or interest rates differ, and for a host of other reasons, including expectations about future developments of the economy or of the policies likely to be pursued by governments or central banks.

For much of the post-war period the intensity of pressure to preserve the fixed exchange rate under Bretton Woods, and the actual movement of the subsequently floating exchange rate have been broadly consistent with a purchasing power parity interpretation. In the Bretton Woods period British consumer prices and export prices as a rule rose a bit faster than the average of principal competitors, up to the devaluation of 1967, which purchased some leeway for export prices. From 1970 to 1976 also British prices rose considerably faster than those of principal competitors. Thereafter the story breaks down, for although British inflation has continued to outstrip that of others, the effective exchange rate has been rising strongly. Most people considered that the effective exchange rate for sterling had been driven 'too low' in the panic at the end of 1976, and the movement up to 1978 could be considered as a rectification. Of course, it is inevitably arbitrary what value of relative absolute prices, or 'competitiveness', is chosen as right. Certainly a number of economists thought it was about right in 1978, and virtually all economists who at the end of that year expressed opinions to the House of Commons Committee were against Britain joining the European monetary system because of the fear that it would be unwise to be committed to a

---

[18] *Economic Growth in Twentieth Century Britain*, edited by D. H. Aldcroft and P. Fearon, Macmillan, 1969, p. 52.

fixed rate (albeit with respect to only some currencies) as Britain was so inflation prone, so that in all probability the exchange rate ought to be allowed to fall. Britain did not join the EMS but equally the exchange rate did not fall.

One measure of competitiveness is the IMF index of relative unit labour costs. This measures labour cost per unit of output in UK, divided by an average of similar costs in competitive countries and adjusting for exchange rate changes. From the end of 1978 to October 1980 this index deteriorated by 45 per cent, about 25 percentage points reflecting the rapid rise in relative UK labour costs, and about 20 percentage points the rise in the exchange rate itself, the latter becoming the more significant factor during 1980. In other words, the exchange was 45 per cent higher than it would need to have been to preserve 1978 competitiveness, as measured by unit labour costs. This must appear an astonishing development for anyone thinking simply in terms of purchasing power parity.

A rise in the exchange rate is normally expected to worsen the balance of payments on current account, *J* curve effects apart. Yet such trend as can be discerned in the current balance in 1978–80 is one of improvement. Of course, with the exchange rate floating the line of causality between the exchange rate and the current account runs both ways, and one should look therefore for reasons why the current account might have been expected to improve. First there was the increase in production of North Sea oil. Then apart from 1978, the *ex ante* impact of the weighted high employment budget balance has been restrictive in every single year since 1976. Similarly the stance of monetary policy has been restrictive, notwithstanding the fact that the corset appears to have been exerting a weaker contractionary effect than was imagined at the time. The contractionary impact of monetary and fiscal policy is reflected in the course of total demand and output. Such a contraction could be expected to improve the current balance, mainly through a reduction in the demand for imports. If we postulate that the effects of changes in the effective exchange rate on the volume of exports come through rather slowly, while those on imports come through rather more quickly, the events of recent years fall into a fairly consistent pattern.[19] Output growth was stopped and went into reverse. There was a big increase in imports and services in 1979 which might be attributed to the high exchange rate, but that has now been stopped. On the other hand, export volume has held up quite well so far, possibly the delayed response to the low value of sterling in 1976–7. Should exports of manufactures fall in 1981–82, as some surveys suggest, that would be in conformity with this general picture.

---

[19] The estimation of price coefficients on imports has a chequered history. Following the 1967 devaluation, neither the National Institute nor the London Business School were initially able to find a significant influence of the relative price of imports. Later on, with experience of more widely fluctuating exchange rates and relative prices, the majority of researchers, though not all, have been able to obtain significant coefficients of the right sign, although of varying magnitude.

There is another, more direct route from a monetary contraction to a higher exchange rate and that is through the higher rate of interest. If this achieves a differential against other rates, UK investors lend less abroad and foreign investors are attracted here, both changes raising the exchange rate.

There are three quite separate factors to be taken into account. First, there is North Sea oil. If fiscal policy is not adjusted to take special account of the large new revenues being generated by North Sea oil, not only will the balance of payments improve from the ending of the need to import so much oil but also the non-oil economy may contract as well, reinforcing the mechanism for raising the exchange rate described above.[20] There may in addition be an independent upward influence arising from the expectation of further growth in oil output and revenues. Secondly, there has lately been another very large rise in OPEC prices creating, once more, huge OPEC surpluses on current account. Some of these new funds will be attracted by the interest differential and some may come from a preference for UK as such. At the end of 1979 UK exchange control was completely abolished for residents as well as non-residents, and by conventional reasoning this would be a factor making for lowering the exchange rate, as, for instance, UK lenders diversified their portfolios abroad.

It has not been difficult to list four more or less independent factors influencing the exchange rate—the restrictive stance of fiscal and monetary policy, North Sea oil, OPEC surpluses and the ending of exchange control— the first three of which certainly tended to raise the rate and only the last might have been expected to lower it. But it would be much more difficult to apportion the very large rise in the rate among the different factors. Yet this apportionment is important since the different factors involve different policy responses.

The question of the OPEC surpluses is essentially international. The danger is well known. OPEC surpluses entail correspondingly 'exceptional' deficits somewhere in the rest of the world. Competition among deficit countries to restore their own balances may simply pass the parcel. Besides uncovenanted increases in the oil price, there are other unpredictable events which may lead to large capital flows from one centre to another which may well have disruptive effects on output and trade. Only international action could succeed in wholly offsetting them. Nevertheless, there is still room for national policies to make things worse, or, one might hope, to make them better.

It will be apparent that in saying this I am slipping round the formidable road-block which nowadays stands in the way of rational policy analysis. If one believes that: (a) fixing the quantity of money is a necessary and sufficient condition to fix the price level; (b) there is a one to one correspondence between the quantity of money and the PSBR; (c) once inflation has been 'squeezed out' it will be gone for good so that when output expands and unemployment falls in the future inflation will not return; and (d) any easing of policy before inflation has been 'squeezed out' will only mean worse inflation in the long run, then discussion stops here, and we take the consequences. But if, like the author, one does not believe some or all of these things the discussion may continue.[21]

The most direct way to get the exchange rate lower is for the central bank to buy foreign currencies with its own. Depending on the institutional set-up this will normally increase whatever monetary aggregate is being used as a target variable. A less direct way is through fiscal expansion, by tax reduction or increased expenditure, generating a rise in demand dividing itself between home output and imports according to the amount of excess capacity in various parts of the economy. The third way is to increase the quantity of money itself inducing a fall in interest rates, a capital outflow and later a domestic expansion which will spill over into imports. Are there means whereby either of the first two routes might be followed *without* increasing the relevant monetary aggregate? This is a question of importance to those who, without being 'road-block' monetarists, nevertheless think that changes in the quantity of money affect prices more and output less, while changes in the budget affect output more and prices less. Such devices may well exist and should be exploited. The economy is not rigidly structured; there is a good deal of tolerance at most of the joints and good policy will take advantage of the discretion given by this tolerance.

There are suggestions for the imposition of specific controls such as a control over the inflow of capital. Controls can, of course, be evaded, as has been made apparent by the recent history of the corset. It should not be concluded that such controls have no effects of the desired kind but rather that they may leak and so have a weaker effect than originally intended. However, neither the exploitation of loose joints in the economy nor the imposition of financial controls are likely to reconcile large inconsistencies in the economy.

The famous Questionnaire on Monetary Policy addressed by the Treasury and Civil Service Committee of the House of Commons to a number of economists and central banks, included a question whose second part read: 'Can the exchange rate be controlled without undesirable loss of control over the appropriate monetary target?' The Swiss National Bank answered as follows: 'The Swiss experience indicates that the exchange rate cannot be controlled without losing control over the appropriate monetary target. For this reason we do not believe that it is feasible to combine in some way monetary and exchange rate targets. The practice of the Swiss National Bank has been to handle monetary targets in a flexible manner. If the foreign exchange market is seriously disrupted—as was the case in the summer of 1978—we are prepared to abandon temporarily the money stock target and replace it by an exchange rate target.'

[21] On money and PSBR, for instance, see Cuthbertson, Henry, Mayes and Savage in National Institute *Economic Review*, November 1980, pp. 19 *et seq*.

In fact the Swiss, whose M1 annual target of the time was 5 per cent in 1977–78, allowed M1 to increase by 17 per cent in that year in order to prevent the exchange rate from rising, without triggering a subsequent price explosion, bearing out the observation of the National Bank that 'in Switzerland we do not find a one to one relationship between the money supply and the exchange rate'.

It used to be believed in the 1950s and the 1960s that there was a trade-off between 'tolerable inflation' and 'tolerable unemployment'. Then, in the 1970s, it was argued that there was no such trade-off. Today's experience suggests that there is still a trade-off, but it is between intolerable inflation and intolerable unemployment, and that this is the choice which will remain so long as we insist on maintaining 'free collective bargaining'. Monetarism had seemed to suggest that either directly, or through the agency of a rising exchange rate, there was an escape from this dilemma. But there is none, and so long as the nettle of reform of pay bargaining is not grasped, we are left with a choice between the intolerable and the unacceptable.

THE EXCHANGE RATE, MONETARY POLICY AND NORTH SEA OIL: THE ECONOMIC THEORY OF THE SQUEEZE ON TRADEABLES*

By W. M. CORDEN

THE starting point of this paper is the squeeze on the tradeables sector of the British economy in 1980 brought about by the combination of nominal appreciation of sterling and continuous increase in nominal wages. I shall call this the *tradeables squeeze*. The aim of the paper is to provide a theoretical framework for analysing this type of phenomenon. It would appear that there have been two distinct causes which happened to come together. (1) First there was a *monetary squeeze*, namely a monetary contraction in real terms designed to moderate inflation along Friedmanite lines. (2) Secondly there was the *North Sea oil effect*, namely the actual and anticipated effects of North Sea oil revenues. At the time of writing the relative importance of the two factors is unclear. There is some indication that the nominal money supply actually grew much faster than intended, so that factor (2) may have been the main cause of the tradeables squeeze in 1980. This paper will analyse both causes. It will show how the effects of the two are related. The analysis of the monetary squeeze will emphasize particularly the differential effect on the tradeables and the non-tradeables sector, something which is rarely done rigorously. The analysis of the North Sea oil effect will stress the importance of (i) fiscal policy and (ii) real wage behaviour.

Sections I and II deal with the effects of a monetary squeeze first in a closed and then an open economy. Section III introduces the more interesting two-sector model. Section IV deals with the short-run macro-economic effects of North Sea oil and Section V with the longer-run structural effects. This last section discusses the important "Dutch disease" issues and could be read independently of the rest of the paper.

I. Monetary squeeze: closed economy

The following analysis of the closed economy could also be applied to the open economy if it is regarded as representing the effects on the non-tradeables sector only.

A simple static diagram gives an insight into the main considerations. The results will subsequently be translated into rates-of-growth terms. Figure 1 is drawn in aggregate price-output space. D is the aggregate demand curve (drawn for a given nominal money supply) in the original equilibrium. A

* This paper was written at the Centre for Banking and International Finance of The City University and at the Australian National University. I am indebted to extensive discussions with and comments from Patrick de Fontenay and Geoffrey Wood.

contraction of the nominal money supply will shift it to the left. Similarly a
fiscal contraction would do so (by reducing the interest rate and hence the
velocity of circulation). S is the initial aggregate supply curve *drawn for a
given nominal wage*; it is upward-sloping because of diminishing returns to
labour with a given capital stock. The initial price is OP and output OR,
with equilibrium at Q. The monetary contraction to be considered shifts the
aggregate demand curve from D to D'.

We can now imagine the following process. The nominal money supply is
gradually reduced, shifting demand from D to D'. For the time being the
nominal wage stays constant, so that the S curve does not change. Furthermore, at first the product price does not fall. This is the stage from Q to A
in Fig. 1. Then the product price starts falling, and hence the real wage rises.
At first the product price falls more slowly than nominal money is falling, so
that real expenditure keeps on falling. This stage comes to an end at C.
From then on the product price falls more and real expenditure increases.
Hence deflation in real terms has come to an end. The money supply stops
falling at C'. When the system is at E there is product market equilibrium at
the new level of the money supply represented by the curve D'. This is the
General Theory equilibrium with product price flexibility and downward
rigidity of the nominal wage. The monetary contraction has been associated
with a rise in the real wage.

The advocates of Friedmanite contractionary policy do not believe that
the system will rest there. Assuming that the labour market was initially in
equilibrium and that trade unions (or individuals in the labour market able
to determine their wages) expect the monetary contraction to last, the
nominal wage will fall. The hope or belief is that it will fall until the original

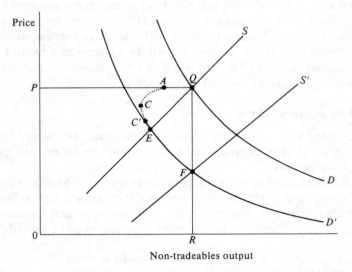

Non-tradeables output

FIG. 1

levels of output and employment are restored. Thus the S curve will move downwards, and as it does so the price will fall, possibly lagging behind. Thus the movement will be from E to F. Finally the aggregate supply curve will be S'. Real expenditure and the real wage will be the same as at Q, but the process has brought about a reduction in the product price and in the nominal wage.

All this can be restated in rates-of-growth terms. In Fig. 2 rates of change are on the vertical axis and time on the horizontal. Initially the nominal money supply, the product price and the nominal wage are all increasing at a rate OA. This is the equivalent of the initial equilibrium Q in Fig. 1. The rate of monetary growth is then gradually reduced until it reaches the lower growth rate of FT. This is the equivalent of the shift from D to D' in Fig. 1. After a time (from point B) the rate of price inflation declines until it has reached the rate of monetary growth at C. Up to this point real expenditure, output and employment are falling. After that the rate of price inflation has to be less than the rate of monetary growth if real expenditure is eventually to recover again. Thus, as in Fig. 1, up to point C real expenditure falls and after that it rises.

The rate of wage inflation stays constant longer than the rate of price inflation. Eventually wage inflation also slackens but until point E wages are still increasing faster than prices so that the real wage is rising. After that the real wage has to fall for a period if at time T it is to be at the same level as it was at the beginning—i.e. if employment is to be restored. At time T there is a new steady state situation, with the same real expenditure and real wage as originally. It is the equivalent of point F in Fig. 1.

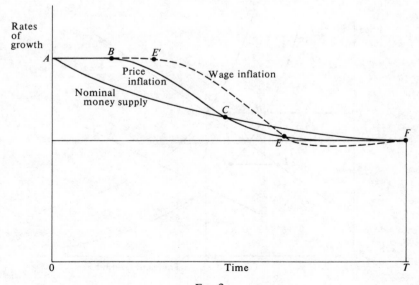

Fig. 2

The effects of productivity changes have been disregarded, but these could easily be superimposed on the analysis. It should also be noted that at the later stages some rise in the rate of increase of prices and of wages may be required if these are to grow at rates less than monetary growth for a time while finally settling eventually at the identical steady state rate of growth of *FT*. If we suppose that the product market is in equilibrium at *E* and stays there after that, then *E* is the *General Theory* equilibrium (equivalent to *E* in Fig. 1). Alternatively one might argue that the equivalent of the static *General Theory* equilibrium is anywhere between *B* and *E'*, this being the range where wage inflation has stayed unchanged while real expenditure is falling and the real wage is rising.

II. Monetary squeeze: open economy with one sector

(1) *Simple model*

We now turn to the open economy with a floating exchange rate. For the moment we assume also that (i) all goods are traded, with their prices determined in world markets, (ii) the terms of trade are externally given (small country assumption), and (iii) there is zero international capital mobility.

Consider Fig. 3. The given product price level abroad and the initial exchange rate together fix the initial domestic price-level at *OP*. It is important to stress the assumption that the world price-level is held constant. The nominal wage is given initially, yielding the supply curve *S*. Hence output is *OR*. The aggregate demand curve at the initial money supply is *D*,

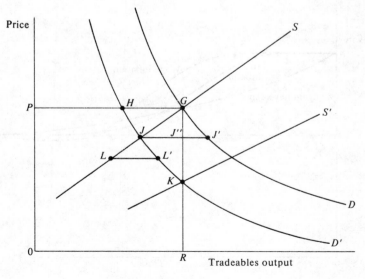

Fig. 3

and with the given price-level this determines real expenditure (absorption) at *OR*. Since expenditure is equal to output, the current account is assumed to be initially in balance.

A monetary contraction then shifts the aggregate demand curve to *D'*. If the exchange rate stayed fixed, expenditure would fall to *H* while output stayed at *G* (because the nominal wage does not change), a current account surplus of *HG* being the result. But we are assuming complete absence of intervention in the foreign exchange market and also (for the moment) zero capital mobility. The exchange rate must thus appreciate, instantaneous balance of payments equilibrium being maintained. With the given nominal wage (and hence given supply curve *S*), equilibrium will thus be attained at *J*. This is the equivalent of the *General Theory* equilibrium of Fig. 1. In the closed economy model this result depended on domestic product price flexibility. In the open economy model it hinges on the combination of domestic product price flexibility (prices determined by import and export prices) and exchange rate flexibility. This simple analysis thus brings out the key role of exchange rate flexibility when there is a monetary contraction in an open economy.

The further story is the same as in our closed economy case. If output and employment are to recover to their initial levels the nominal wage must fall until the supply curve reaches *S'* and a new equilibrium is attained at *K* where real expenditure and the real wage are the same as at *G*, the price-level and the nominal wage are lower, while the exchange rate—which determines the price-level—has appreciated.

The analysis can, again, be converted into rates-of-change terms. Initially, with the exchange rate fixed, there will have been a domestic rate of inflation equal to the given rate of inflation abroad. As soon as the rate of monetary growth is reduced the domestic rate of inflation will slacken and there will have to be not just once-for-all, but continuous appreciation. Thus at *K* a continuous appreciation is needed to convert the new lower rate of domestic price inflation into the initial and constant rate of inflation in foreign currency terms.

Let us now return to the simple comparative static diagram of Fig. 3.

(2) *Departure from one-price assumption*

The simplicity of the analysis represented in Fig. 3 has hinged on the two assumptions that (i) all goods are traded and (ii) the terms of trade are given. Removal of these two assumptions does not alter the main arguments but slightly complicates the story. When domestic import-competing goods are not perfect substitutes for imports (so that, strictly, import-competing goods are not actually traded) an appreciation will not necessarily lead to a fall in the prices of import-competing goods to the same extent. If there is some downward rigidity of the prices of import-competing goods, product market equilibrium will not be attained instantaneously when the money supply falls. In Fig. 3 the price may not fall completely to *J*, in which case output would be on *D'* but to the left of the supply curve.

Terms of trade effects also mean that the average domestic price-level change may not coincide exactly with the exchange rate appreciation. Suppose, initially, that foreign exchange market intervention keeps the exchange rate fixed when the money supply is reduced. Exports will rise and imports will fall and this may cause world prices of both to decline somewhat, especially export prices. Thus the average domestic price-level falls even with a fixed exchange rate. The appreciation required to restore balance of payments equilibrium will be less than before. But normally some appreciation and hence further fall in the domestic price-level will be needed. The essentials of our story need not be changed, even though it will be slightly complicated by a relative price change betwen exportables and importables.

(3) *Capital mobility*

Capital mobility will alter the analysis in a number of ways. Firstly, it will lead to more appreciation for a given monetary contraction. Secondly it will lead to a speedier movement towards the new equilibrium both because capital flows respond more rapidly to interest changes than investment expenditures, and for expectational reasons. Lastly, it may lead to "over-shooting"—i.e. a greater initial appreciation than is required for the final equilibrium—this having, again two possible reasons.

(a) *More appreciation and speedier movement towards the new equilibrium*

Let us first focus on the *General Theory* equilibrium situation represented by point *J* in Fig. 3. The nominal wage has not changed but the exchange rate has appreciated. We assume for the moment that no further appreciation is expected (expectations are static), which means that the nominal wage is not expected to fall nor the money supply to fall further. The extent of the appreciation depends on the size of the fall in nominal expenditure (MV), which depends in turn on the given fall in *M* and—in the absence of capital mobility—on the partially offsetting rise in *V* resulting from the rise in the domestic interest rate. Capital mobility means that the domestic interest rate will rise less than before, and if all bonds were traded, the world interest rate were given and there were perfect capital mobility it would not rise at all. Thus velocity will rise less and in the limiting case would not rise at all. It follows that the fall in *MV* for a given fall in *M* will be greater with capital mobility than without; there will be a greater appreciation than before.

This conclusion does not apply to the Friedman equilibrium at *K*. At this point even *without* capital mobility the interest rate, and hence velocity, would be back at the same level as at the initial position at *A*, the point being that everything *real* in the economy—including the real money supply—is the same at K as at G. Hence capital mobility makes no difference to the extent of the appreciation at K.

Let us now assume that the D' curve in Fig. 3 is the aggregate demand curve when capital is mobile and expectations are static. With perfect capital mobility (V constant) it is a constant nominal expenditure (MV) curve.

Capital mobility not only increases the extent of the appreciation for a given monetary contraction and given nominal wage level (other than at the Friedman equilibrium K) but also speeds up the movement towards the new equilibrium, wherever it is. This point, which plays an important role in understanding the events of 1980, is well-known. In the absence of capital mobility the appreciation would depend on the fall in expenditure resulting from the rise in the interest rate, and hence on the interest-elasticity of investment. If this response is slow or delayed a fall in M will be offset by a rise in V and there will be little or no deflation and appreciation. Once capital mobility is introduced this slow mechanism is by-passed. The reduced money supply, acting partly through a rise in the interest rate, leads to incipient capital inflows which quickly appreciate the exchange rate directly.

(b) *Temporary capital inflow*

The situation at J in Fig. 3 just described is a new stock equilibrium and there will not be any actual capital movements. (This conclusion would have to be amended if the analysis were embedded in a growth model.) But there is a possibility of temporary capital inflow resulting from the monetary contraction. The exchange rate will then appreciate temporarily beyond J—a form of "over-shooting". The reason why such an inflow—i.e. a current account deficit—might be expected will be discussed in a moment. First, let us show its effects in Fig. 3. Suppose the inflow is LL'. Thus the current account deficit has to be LL' and real expenditure must exceed output by LL'. It follows that (when the aggregate demand curve is D') the exchange rate has to appreciate until the domestic price-level is down to L. For a given monetary contraction, output and employment will fall by more than before and real expenditure will fall by less.

Let us now turn to the question of whether an actual capital inflow and hence a current account deficit are to be expected. Assuming the budget balance stays unchanged, say at zero, a current account deficit means that the private sector has gone into financial deficit. Why should it? On the one hand there may be a fall in investment owing to the lower level of output and higher interest rate. On the other hand, the private sector may to some extent wish to exchange money for goods rather than for bonds when the decline in income reduces the demand for money. If the latter effect outweighs the former there will be a financial deficit. This would be a once-for-all adjustment and thus in flow terms only a temporary deficit.

An alternative, more Keynesian, approach is to argue that reduced income will naturally be associated with reduced savings, or with dissavings, designed to moderate the decline in real expenditure, and this will manifest itself as a current account deficit. In addition, government expenditure and tax rates might be kept constant (rather than the budget balance staying unchanged), so that the fall in incomes would lead to a budget deficit financed by official bond sales, and hence to an even greater current account deficit.

(c) Expectations and the exchange rate[1]

Once a contraction of the money supply is expected, and hence a new equilibrium with an appreciated exchange rate is foreseen, the spot exchange rate will be affected by expectations. As expectations shift about, the exchange rate will also. We shall now assume perfect capital mobility, with all bonds traded, so that the interest parity condition must be satisfied at all times. The main point is that the spot exchange rate will move rapidly towards its expected equilibrium value even before the actual equilibrium conditions—especially the new expenditure level—have been established.

Suppose for the moment that there has been no actual contraction of the money supply, but only an announcement of a contraction. Expenditure is unchanged so far, and hence the domestic interest rate is unchanged. If the equilibrium exchange rate is expected to appreciate (say to K in Fig. 3, or alternatively to J), the spot rate will have to appreciate to the same extent to satisfy the interest parity condition. But this appreciation in itself will lower the price-level even if, in the short-run it does not change output (the supply elasticity being zero). Departing for the moment from the assumption that all goods have their prices fixed in world markets, domestically-produced goods can be allowed to have rigid prices, but prices of imports in domestic curency will still fall. The lower price-level will reduce the demand for money and tend to lower the domestic interest rate and so moderate the spot appreciation required for the sake of satisfying the interest parity condition.

Once the contraction of the money supply actually takes place the domestic interest rate will tend to rise, though the more the price-level and output fall, the less this will be so. But insofar as the domestic interest rate does rise—rising above the world rate—depreciation of the exchange rate must be expected to satisfy the interest parity condition. This would seem to be a surprising result, since we know that the equilibrium exchange rate is expected to appreciate. The only way to reconcile this is to assume that the exchange rate overshoots its equilibrium value once the money supply contraction takes place. There will thus be a large appreciation, leading to expectations of depreciation as the new equilibrium is approached.

---

[1] This section is much influenced by Rudiger Dornbusch's "Expectations and Exchange Rate Dynamics", *Journal of Political Economy*, vol. 84, no. 6, December 1976, pp. 1161–76. I have attempted to reconcile the analysis in this much-cited but rather difficult article with the present model, and have been helped in doing so by studying an unpublished paper by George Fane and Ted Sieper.

This "overshooting" result also raises a problem. The domestic interest rate only rises because the domestic price and output levels have not yet fallen to their equilibrium values. It would appear that in the movement from the initial "over-shooting" outcome towards the new equilibrium at K (or J) the price-level will fall and yet the exchange rate will depreciate. This is inconsistent with our simple model.

The matter can be resolved in three ways. Firstly, the assumption of our simple model that the domestic price-level and the exchange rate always move together can be maintained. The spot exchange rate will then have to appreciate instantaneously to the equilibrium rate, with no further change expected; there is then no "over-shooting". The price-level has to fall sufficiently (and instantaneously) for the resultant fall in nominal expenditure to generate a reduction in the demand for money equal to the reduced supply at the given world interest rate. Secondly, the assumption that all goods are traded, with prices fixed in world markets, can be modified, so that the average price-level can fall even though the exchange rate depreciates. Thirdly, the extreme assumption of perfect capital mobility can be modified to eliminate the need for over-shooting: some short-run rise in the domestic interest rate can then be compatible with expectations of further appreciation.

III. Monetary squeeze: open economy with two sectors

We now introduce the open economy with a non-tradeable and a tradeable sector. The distinction between the two sectors is, of course, arbitrary, and just a heuristic device. The aim is to distinguish between those parts of the economy where prices and profitability are very directly influenced by the exchange rate (even though the goods produced need not be perfect substitutes for imports) and those parts where the relationship is much more indirect. The latter include the public services. In practice there is a continuum of products and industries from this point of view. Figure 1 represents the non-tradeable sector and Fig. 3 the tradeable sector. Capital is assumed to be specific to each sector, so that the two supply curves are quite distinct. The nominal wage is held constant here (the supply curves are fixed) so as to bring out the "squeeze" effects—effects which would be temporary if Friedmanite expectations that the nominal wage would eventually fall sufficiently (or that wage inflation would decline) were justified.

At this point there is a difficulty if one wishes to keep the analysis simple. In the subsequent exposition it will be assumed that the D curve in one diagram is independent of the equilibrium in the other diagram. This depends on two subsidiary assumptions. (1) Aggregate nominal expenditure does not change as the price of either good changes. Hence V is constant, which would strictly only be true if the interest rate stayed unchanged. (2) The price elasticity of demand for each of the two goods is unity. Thus the share of expenditure on each of the two goods is independent of relative prices. If the price of tradeables falls because of appreciation, while total *nominal* expenditure and the price of non-tradeables are both constant, a substitution effect will switch spending away from non-tradeables and the rise in *real* expenditure will raise spending on non-tradeables, the net effect leaving spending on non-tradeables unchanged.

It has to be noted that while assumption (2) may be a reasonable simplification, assumption (1) presents a real problem if there is any change in the interest rate. As the price of either good falls, the real money supply rises and hence V may rise. The D curve in one sector would thus depend on the price outcome in the other sector. This complication is ignored below.

(1) *Nature of the fall in demand*

We suppose that there is a decline in the money supply, leading to declines in expenditures on each of the two goods, and shifting the demand curve in each diagram from D to D'. In the absence of capital mobility the expenditure decline is initiated by the reduction in investment induced by a rise in the interest rate, and this factor may also be operative to some extent when capital is mobile. With capital mobility the exchange rate appreciates through the rapid mechanism of incipient capital inflows generated by monetary contraction. A fall in incomes in tradeables then results, which in turn generates a fall in aggregate expenditures. Thus, even when the interest rate remains unchanged, so that investment does not fall, demand for non-tradeables as well as for tradeables falls because of the lower incomes in tradeables.

There will be a tradeables squeeze acting through exchange rate appreciation and represented in Fig. 3 by a movement from G to J if there is no actual capital inflow, and further if there is. The essence of the squeeze is that the domestic price-level falls more than the nominal wage-level (which here is assumed not to fall at all). But there will also be a non-tradeables squeeze represented in Fig. 1 by a movement to some point on the dotted curve QE.

(2) *Which sector's squeeze will be greater?*

It is highly likely that the squeeze on tradeables would be greater, at least in the short-run. Nevertheless it is useful to spell out the assumptions under which the squeeze would actually be the same, so that the outcome from the point of view of output, prices and profits would be identical in proportional terms. This would be so (i) if there were perfect product price flexibility in non-tradeables, so that the outcome were at the *General Theory* equilibrium E (Fig. 1), (ii) if there were no actual capital movements generated, so that the tradeables outcome was at the similar equilibrium J (Fig. 3), (iii) if the two supply elasticities were identical, and (iv) if the proportional declines in expenditure were identical.

Let us consider each of these assumptions.

(i) The less flexible downwards the non-tradeables product price the greater the fall in output and employment but the less the fall in profits. This is for a given fall in nominal expenditures on non-tradeables. Short-run profits are approximately described by the area between the supply curve and the price line (*PQ* originally). Assuming—as seems reasonable—that there *is* some degree of downward sluggishness of the non-tradeables price, the squeeze would, on this account, be greater than in tradeables when it is defined in tems of output or employment, but would be *less* when it is defined in terms of effects on profits.

(ii) Actual capital inflow will (other things equal) make the squeeze greater in tradeables through the additional appreciation it brings about (which is likely to be a temporary effect).

(iii) There seems to be no general presumption to expect one elasticity of supply to be greater than the other, bearing in mind that each curve is an aggregate curve for a large sector consisting of many firms.

(iv) There may be some presumption that a monetary squeeze acting mainly on private investment (including investment in consumer durables) would reduce expenditure on tradeables proportionately more than on non-tradeables, bearing in mind that a large part of non-tradeables output consists of publicly-supplied services. But it must also be remembered that building and construction are essentially non-tradeables or at least have a large non-tradeable content, so that the nature of the reduction in private investment (whether affecting fixed capital equipment spending, consumer durables or building and construction) is relevant.

One major short-term consideration remains. Suppose that investment is not at all interest-elastic in the short-term, so that expenditure does not fall on that account even though the interest rate may have risen. The only effect of the monetary contraction is that it causes the exchange rate to appreciate, possibly very considerably—perhaps even overshooting its equilibrium value—through the mechanism of incipient capital flows. Hence there is a squeeze on tradeables, leading to reduced output and incomes there. But the resultant fall in expenditures is delayed as tradeables producers seek to maintain their spending. In Fig. 3 the exchange rate and output move to J but nominal expenditure stays at D, with real expenditure now J', the deficit being financed by borrowing (capital inflow of JJ'). There is thus no fall in expenditure on non-tradeables, and hence no squeeze there at all. One might alternatively suppose that output of tradeables does not decline in the short-run, so that there is a temporary output equilibrium at J''.

We thus have a limiting case where the whole of the squeeze, whether only on prices and profits or also on output, is felt in the tradeables sector, while non-tradeables are temporarily protected from the consequences of monetary contraction. More generally, because of the rapid effects of incipient capital flows on the exchange rate and the slower response of expenditure to interest rate and income changes, it is reasonable to expect the squeeze on tradeables to be greater than on non-tradeables—as was evident in Britain in 1980.

(3) *The real exchange rate*

The real exchange rate is usually defined as the ratio of the domestic price of tradeables to the price of non-tradeables (or the ratio of the former to an average of the two). It is also usually presumed that a tradeables squeeze would be associated with a real appreciation and that, in the short-run, a monetary contraction would yield both. While it is clear from the preceding analysis that in theory there could be a monetary contraction and a tradeables squeeze *without* a real appreciation (the proportional price effects being the same for the two sectors) the association of tradeables squeeze with real appreciation does seem justified. On the other hand, the actual extent of a tradeables squeeze cannot be measured by the extent of real appreciation because non-tradeables prices do not necessarily remain constant relative to nominal wages as a result of monetary contraction.

(4) *Fiscal contraction: removing bias against tradeables*

It would be possible to reduce nominal expenditure without a bias against tradeables. This could be brought about by combining monetary contraction with some fiscal contraction (reducing the public sector borrowing requirement). This was a clear policy alternative in 1980, with well-known difficulties.

In the absence of capital mobility, if private investment expenditure is tradeable-intensive while government expenditure is non-tradeable-intensive, some combination of monetary contraction and government expenditure reduction can obviously bring about a balanced contraction. Allowing for capital mobility, the key point is that fiscal contraction tends to reduce the domestic interest rate, and so on this account lead to depreciation, offsetting the adverse effects on the tradeables sector of monetary contraction (though full offsetting is not required).

It has to be stressed that a fiscal contraction need not inevitably have this effect. If the contraction is brought about by a reduction in government spending that makes possible a retirement of debt, the issue is how a shift from goods purchases to bond purchases affects the exchange rate. If the goods purchases foregone were all tradeable while the bonds were non-tradeable, the exchange rate would actually tend to appreciate. But the more reasonable assumption is that there is a large non-tradeable element in government purchases, while bonds are highly tradeable, so that the rate would *de*preciate.

The same issues apply to fiscal contraction brought about by raising tax rates. It is likely that private expenditure reduction induced by lower disposable incomes would involve a substantial reduction in spending on non-tradeables. An additional consideration (returned to in Section V below) is that tax increases may lead to nominal wage increases designed to maintain, or moderate a decline in, post-tax real wages.

IV. North Sea oil: the short run effects

The preceding analysis was short-run. Wages were rigid or sluggish in nominal terms and the employment and real wage outcomes were incidental by-products of the monetary contraction policies. If the actual monetary contraction had been fully anticipated, if the actors in the product and labour markets fully understood the economic system, if they approached their price and wage decisions rationally—making the best use of their anticipations about monetary policy and of their understanding of the system—and if there were no costs to adjustments in nominal values, there would have been no real changes. But these assumptions did not hold.

Let us now stay within this short-run framework and specifically assume (i) fixed nominal wages and (ii) a fixed nominal money supply. The last assumption, when translated into rate of growth terms, fits in with the monetary target approach. It is likely that in the longer-run a monetary target would be adjusted to allow for real shocks, so this analysis can only be regarded as short-run. The objective is now to show the effects of North Sea oil within the framework used in the preceding parts of this paper. These effects must then be superimposed on the effects of monetary contraction already analysed.

The short-run North Sea oil effect has three aspects: the capital inflow designed to finance North Sea development itself, the speculative capital inflow anticipating sterling appreciation, and the effects of the actual revenues from North Sea oil.

(1) *Investment for North Sea oil development*

Capital flows in to finance North Sea development. Suppose that extra investment expenditures were exactly equal to capital inflow and that the whole of the extra expenditures went directly on tradeables, for example imported capital equipment. This is the limiting case. The exchange rate would then not alter. If the extra investment were substantially domestically financed the extra demand for tradeables might exceed capital inflow; on the other hand, if some part of the extra expenditures go on non-tradeables, including domestic labour services, the net result could go the other way. Since the oil investment is primarily foreign-financed and there must be a considerable non-tradeable content, it seems likely that capital inflow would, on balance, exceed additional demand for tradeables. Ignoring one complication, this case is represented in Fig. 4, where the aggregate demand curves D and D'' are drawn, as usual, for a constant money supply. Capital inflow is ZZ', additional expenditure on tradeables is $Z''Z'$, and the exchange rate thus appreciates to Z.

The complication is that higher expenditure will increase the demand for

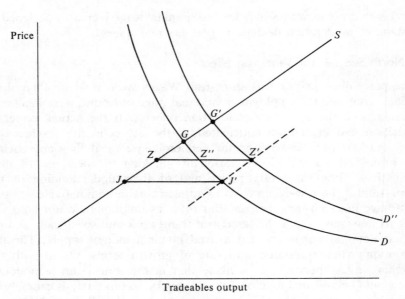

Fig. 4

money for a given interest rate and given price-level. With the money supply fixed the interest rate will tend to rise, crowding-out non-oil investment. So expenditure will finally not rise as far as D'', and the appreciation will go beyond Z. Of course increased expenditures out of foreign currency funds directly on imported goods may not significantly affect the demand for domestic money, so this effect may not be important if the direct import content of extra investment is high. Nevertheless, one might just note the limiting case. Suppose capital mobility were perfect and the interest rate were given. Suppose further that the demand for money function did not shift. Thus the ratio of nominal expenditure to money would have to stay constant, and with the money supply fixed, nominal expenditure could not increase. The increase in oil investment would then be fully offset by extra domestic hoarding. The appreciation would go as far as J, where $JJ' = ZZ'$.

(2) Speculative capital inflows

Foreigners seek to buy sterling-denominated bonds because they expect sterling appreciation to result from the forthcoming flow of North Sea oil revenues (effect (3) discussed below). This speculative effect was prominent in 1980 and brought about appreciation in anticipation of the fundamental underlying forces. The effect is similar to the effects of an anticipated monetary contraction that was discussed earlier.

There need not be any actual net capital inflow as a result of this. But if there is, it must mean that a private sector financial deficit (or a reduction in a surplus) has resulted. This can be explained as follows. The increased demand for sterling-denominated bonds has raised the bond price and induced British holders of bonds to part with bonds in exchange for goods. In addition, investment may increase because of the lower interest rate, though this possible effect was obviously outweighed by other factors in 1980.

(3) North Sea oil revenues

Finally we come to the effects of the North Sea oil revenues themselves. I shall assume that there are net exports of oil, the gain in revenues being initially both from import-replacement and from exporting. A situation *with* North Sea oil is set against one *without*, where the world price and the domestic price of oil are unchanged. Thus the various effects of the rise in the oil price at a time when Britain was still a net importer are not considered, nor are the effects considered of a subsequent change in the price or of the tax rate on that part of North Sea oil which is sold domestically.

If nominal expenditure on tradeables were held constant the story would be straightforward. Assuming for the moment zero net capital flows, the exchange rate would appreciate sufficiently to generate a non-oil current account deficit equal to the net oil surplus. Output and employment in tradeables would fall. This is represented in Fig. 4 where the net oil surplus is *JJ'*, nominal expenditure stays at *D*, and the exchange rate appreciates to *J*, yielding a non-oil current account deficit of *JJ'*. The North Sea oil effect thus re-enforces the effects of a monetary contraction.

Complications ensue once the nominal money supply, rather than nominal expenditure, is held constant, and once capital movements are allowed for. I shall now assume that net revenues accruing to domestic residents are wholly taxed away—which may be about 80 per cent of the truth. Consider two cases:

(a) Debt is retired

The extra revenue is wholly used to retire debt. If all bonds were traded and there were a perfect capital market, with the interest rate remaining unchanged, bonds would be imported equal in value to the oil revenues. The non-oil current account would stay in balance and the exchange rate would not alter (i.e. the system would stay at *G* in Fig. 4). On the other hand, when there are non-tradeable bonds or the capital market is not perfect, capital outflow may be less than the oil revenues, so that there would be some appreciation. In that case the domestic interest rate would steadily fall as the stock of bonds in the hands of the public falls. This will increase expenditure and might eventually bring about depreciation.

Before going on to the next case the following two reversals in processes might be noted. (i) Speculation in anticipation of the oil revenues may lead to capital inflows (as discussed earlier), while the actual revenues themselves lead to capital outflows. Thus at first the current account deteriorates and then it improves. (ii) The direct effect of North Sea oil revenues is to appreciate the exchange rate, but the induced expenditure increase brought about by a continuing retirement of debt and interest rate decline (in the absence of perfect capital mobility) has the opposite effect, an effect that might eventually dominate if the revenues are indeed continually used for debt retirement.

(b) *Tax reductions*

Next, assume that the oil revenues cause the government to reduce other taxes so as to leave the net budget balance unchanged. The disposable income of the public thus rises to the extent of the oil revenues. We may first consider two extreme cases. (i) The whole of the extra disposable income is spent on tradeables, and investment spending does not change. In that case a non-oil current account deficit is generated equal to the oil income, and the exchange rate does not alter. (ii) The whole of the extra income is used by the public to purchase tradeable bonds, so that expenditure does not change at all. A capital outflow then matches the oil income and (with investment constant) again the exchange rate does not alter.

The key point is that when the extra income is spent wholly on tradeable goods and bonds the exchange rate will not alter. If the spending is partly on tradeable goods and partly on tradeable bonds—so that nominal expenditure does increase but falls short of the rise in oil income—the extra oil revenues will be matched partly by a non-oil current account deficit and partly by capital outflow.

Of course, it is again inevitable that part of the extra spending will be on non-tradeables. Hence there will again be need for appreciation. In addition, possible effects on investment through changes in the rate of interest need to be taken into account. Assuming that domestic bonds are not perfect substitutes for foreign bonds, the increased flow demand for bonds will tend to continually lower the rate of interest, hence raise investment and expenditure, and so moderate the appreciation, conceivably even leading eventually to depreciation. On the other hand the increased demand for money associated with the higher expenditure will tend to raise the rate of interest, this offsetting effect being once-and-for-all.

The general conclusion is simple. The various effects of North Sea oil will all tend to appreciate the exchange rate, at least at first, and this will re-enforce the *tradeables squeeze* resulting from monetary contraction. The coincidence of these two causes of the squeeze was a central theme of economic policy discussion in Britain in 1980. But it has to be added that the tendency for the exchange rate to appreciate could be modified (and eventually even negated) through capital outflows and through expenditure increases generated indirectly by North Sea oil revenues.

V. North Sea oil: structural effects

So far we have assumed that neither the nominal wage, the budget deficit nor the money supply are varied to maintain the total level of employment in spite of the various repercussions of North Sea oil. The effects on aggregate employment have thus been endogenous. Such rigidities can surely only be short-term, though they may come close to describing the behaviourial reactions of 1980. We shall now make a crucial switch of assumptions for medium-term analysis, namely that aggregate employment in the two sectors combined is to stay constant. This could be brought about either by nominal wage flexibility or by demand management policy. We shall assume the latter here, hence staying thoroughly Keynesian. The nominal wage is rigid and demand management (i.e. management of nominal expenditures) maintains a constant overall employment level. (Employment in North Sea oil production is assumed to be negligible.) An assumption of flexible (Keynesian) demand management policy would seem to be more reasonable for medium-term analysis than the assumption of rigidity in the previous section. But the central conclusions below would also apply if the Friedman model applied: if the nominal wage were flexible and nominal demand (or the money supply) were fixed or growing at some rigid rate. At this stage the real wage will be endogenous. Later, real wage rigidity will be introduced.

(1) *Demand management and North Sea oil: two extreme cases*

Fig. 5a refers to non-tradeables and Fig. 5b to tradeables. Both supply curves are drawn on the assumption of a constant nominal wage, and this

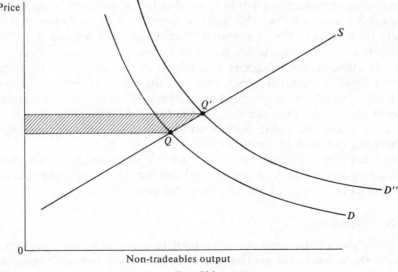

FIG. 5(a)

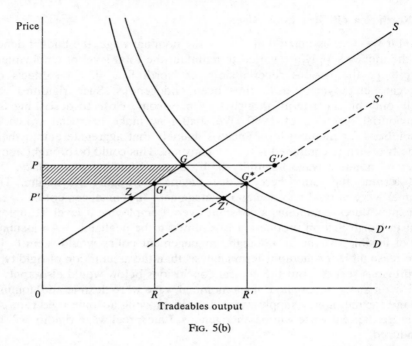

FIG. 5(b)

assumption will be maintained throughout. It would be easy to transform the analysis to allow for an exogenously given rate of nominal wage inflation, one which may, of course, vary over time. As before, each supply curve is drawn on the assumption of a fixed capital stock in the relevant sector. Considerable complications would result if either intersectoral capital mobility or capital accumulation (the fruits of investment expenditures that have already been allowed for as a source of demand) were introduced. Finally, the supply curve for tradeables, S, refers to non-oil production only.

The D curve in each diagram is assumed in this section to represent a constant level of nominal expenditure on the relevant good. The curves could, alternatively, be interpreted as constant-M curves, with V varying in response to interest rate changes. In the latter case there is the difficulty mentioned earlier that each curve's position depends, among other things, on the price outcome in the other diagram.

The initial pre-oil equilibria are Q and G respectively. North Sea oil yields foreign exchange revenues of GG'' and thus shifts the supply curve for total tradeables output to S'. Now consider two extreme cases.

(a) *Zero impact case*

If the whole of the revenues were used to accumulate foreign exchange reserves there would be no change in the exchange rate or employment. This is the *zero impact case*. Nominal expenditure would stay at D. This result could be brought about in the following way. The Exchange Equalisation Account buys dollars and sells Treasury Bills to the same extent—i.e. the extent of the oil revenues. The Treasury uses the oil revenues (all of which are assumed here to go in tax) to buy Treasury Bills (retire debt). There will thus be no change in Treasury Bill holdings by the public, no change in the money supply and no change in any element of public or private expenditures. The key point is that zero impact requires the government *not* to spend the oil revenues nor to reduce non-oil taxes.

(b) *Current account kept in balance*

Alternatively, assume no intervention in the foreign exchange market and no change in capital movements (which, for this purpose, are assumed to be zero initially). Thus imports must rise and non-oil exports fall to offset the oil revenues. If nominal expenditure stayed constant the exchange rate would appreciate to yield a tradeables price-level of OP' (Fig. 5b), real expenditures at Z' and non-oil output at Z. At this stage there is no change in non-tradeables output, so that, with employment in tradeables reduced, total employment has fallen. In order to maintain a constant aggregate level of employment, expenditure must thus be increased (to the D'' curves), output in non-tradeables rising to Q' and in tradeables being partially restored to G'. The rise in employment in non-tradeables resulting from the output increase from Q to Q' must be equal to the net fall in employment in tradeables resulting from the net decline in output from G to G'. The fall in output and employment in tradeables—incidentally involving a fall in profits there—is the "Dutch disease".

The non-tradeables price-level has risen and the tradeables price-level has fallen. But total real expenditure (absorption) has clearly increased: absorption of non-tradeables has risen to Q' and of tradeables to G^*. This is an obvious conclusion, but needs stressing when the focus is on the fall in output and profits in tradeables. If the "Dutch disease" is to be avoided, the increase in real expenditure, whether public or private, consumption or investment, has to be foregone. In 1980 there was much focus on the prospective losers from the Dutch disease. But it needs stressing that, when total employment is kept constant, there are also gainers, namely the beneficiaries from the extra spending.

The simplest mechanism by which the rise in expenditure could be brought about is through the government spending its oil tax revenues or remitting other taxes to maintain the initial fiscal balance. But this may not bring about precisely the right increase in expenditure—it would not do so, for example, if taxpayers saved some part of their higher disposable incomes—and it may be necessary to go into fiscal deficit or have some supplementary monetary expansion—always assuming that none of the funds are to be lent abroad, whether through accumulation of reserves or indirectly through private capital outflow.

(2) Income distribution effects

It is possible to use Figs 5a and 5b to show rather simply the principal sectional income effects of the North Sea oil revenues when the revenues go wholly in tax and the budget balance is kept unchanged. The analysis is conducted in nominal terms. With both the nominal wage and employment constant, pre-tax wage income will be unchanged. The gain in profits in the non-tradeables sector can be approximately represented by the shaded area in Fig. 5a and the loss in profits in the tradeable sector is (approximately) the shaded area in Fig. 5b. The initial gain to the government in tax revenue is the area $RG'G^*R'$. It should be noted that the appreciation of the exchange rate has reduced this gain by lowering the domestic currency value of the oil revenues. If the whole of the extra expenditure had gone on tradeables (so that output of non-oil tradeables would have stayed at G) appreciation would not have been necessary. Hence the more of the extra spending goes on non-tradeables, the less the initial gain goes to the government.

The initial tax revenue gain will be distributed to the community through the benefits derived from higher government expenditures or through remissions of non-oil taxes. In the latter case, while pre-tax nominal wages have stayed constant, post-tax wages will have risen provided tax remissions benefit wage-earners. Furthermore, post-tax profits of tradeables producers may also have risen even though pre-tax profits must have fallen. When the community as a whole has more income there are clearly possibilities of compensating losers from the process. The manner in which the gain is distributed determines the precise expenditure effects. For example, if the oil tax revenue is used to increase government services, extra spending is likely to go largely on non-tradeables. On the other hand, if taxes on profits are reduced or investment allowances increased, so that investment in fixed capital equipment increases as a result, extra spending will go largely on tradeables.

This income distribution analysis has been in nominal terms. With the price of non-tradeables higher and of tradeables lower there are further possible effects through different spending patterns. In addition we have made the small country assumption, hence ruling out terms of trade changes. The reduction in non-oil exports may improve the terms of trade, which would have further effects—in particular making the rise in real expenditure even greater. But the small country assumption might be quite reasonable for Britain when the analysis is medium or longer-run.

(3) Capital outflow

It is likely that one effect of North Sea oil revenues would be to lead to some private capital outflow. This was already mentioned in Section III. Two processes can be envisaged.

(i) The oil tax revenue is used to retire debt, but this time bonds are bought from the public, not the Exchange Equalisation Account. Again, the rate of interest falls and capital flows out. If all bonds were traded and there were a perfect capital market, there would be no change in the rate of interest and (as already pointed out in Section III) the capital outflow would be exactly equal to the oil revenues. Thus, with these extreme assumptions, this would be another route to *zero impact*. In this case the extra foreign assets are privately owned while, with intervention in the foreign exchange market, the monetary authority (the Exchange Equalisation Account) is accumulating foreign assets.

(ii) Fiscal balance is maintained through remission of non-oil taxes, so raising private disposable income. Some part of the extra disposable income is used for the purchase of financial assets, lowering the rate of interest and leading to capital outflow. Appreciation of the exchange rate would need to be less in this case than if the whole of the extra income had been spent on goods and services. The result would be in between the *zero impact* and the *current-account balance* case.

(4) *The real wage and the Dutch disease*

It was noted earlier that, when the oil revenue is spent and a constant level of employment is maintained, the price of tradeables falls (owing to appreciation) and of non-tradeables rises (owing to higher spending). With a given nominal wage it cannot be said in general whether the pre-tax real wage rises or falls. This depends on the two supply elasticities, on the way in which the aggregate expenditure increase is distributed between the two types of goods, and on the spending pattern of wage-earners. But perhaps there is some presumption that the elasticity of supply of non-tradeables is rather high—or that there is some sluggishness in price adjustment in that sector—in which case it is likely that the real wage rises. It would normally be expected that an appreciation would raise the real wage. Nevertheless, it has to be stressed that, when the appreciation is combined with an expenditure policy designed to maintain employment, the real wage could rise or fall.

(a) *Pre-tax rigidity: ratchet effect*

Let us now suppose that a new equilibrium, with oil revenues being spent indirectly through remissions of non-oil taxes, has been reached. There is now a new, higher pre-tax real wage, and an even higher post-tax real wage. Of course, output, employment and profits in tradeables have all gone down, this being the Dutch disease. Let us also assume that the real wage solidifies in the new situation—that is, it becomes rigid downward. There is thus a ratchet effect: the real wage can rise but real wage resistance successfully avoids a fall, any rise in the price-level being quickly compensated by an appropriate rise in the nominal wage. We shall suppose first that this rigidity is in pre-tax terms, and later in post-tax terms.

We now imagine that in the new situation a government wishes to counter-act the Dutch disease. It wishes to restore the price and output of tradeables. If the pre-tax real wage is rigid it will then be necessary for the output of non-tradeables to fall sufficiently for their price decline to offset the price rise of tradeables. In our earlier analysis the maintenance of a constant level of employment required a fall in output of one sector to be offset by a rise in the other; now the maintenance of the pre-tax real wage requires a similar offsetting process. Thus a depreciation that raises employment and prices in tradeables must be associated with an expenditure reduction that reduces employment and prices in non-tradeables sufficiently.

Let us now assume realistically that prices of non-tradeables are somewhat sluggish downwards or the elasticity of supply is relatively high. A given shift in employment out of non-tradeables into tradeables brought about by the combination of depreciation and expenditure reduction will then lower prices of non-tradeables very little but raise prices of tradeables quite a lot, and so lower the real wage for a constant nominal wage. If in fact there is a tendency to real wage rigidity such a movement will not be sustainable. To keep the real wage constant while raising employment in tradeables it will be necessary to have a large movement of labour out of non-tradeables and a relatively small movement into tradeables. In other words aggregate employment will have to fall.

It follows that the effort of raising employment in tradeables to counteract the Dutch disease will not only require total expenditures to be reduced— with all the sacrifices this implies—but will also involve a fall in total employment. It is even conceivable that a fall in the pre-tax real wage in the process of counteracting the Dutch disease cannot be avoided at all. This would be so if the prices of non-tradeables were completely rigid downwards so that a rise in the price of tradeables resulting from depreciation could not be offset by any fall in the prices of non-tradeables.

(b) *Post-tax rigidity*

Finally, suppose that (i) the *post*-tax real wage is rigid downwards, rather than the *pre*-tax real wage, and that (ii) expenditure can only be reduced by raising taxes (government expenditure and investment being held constant). There is a depreciation designed to restore the output of tradeables which, on its own, lowers the real wage on the basis of the preceding analysis. It is then associated with a reduction in expenditure, as before.

This time the expenditure reduction has two opposing effects. On the one hand, by reducing demand for non-tradeables and so lowering their prices it will raise the pre-tax real wage and, for given tax rates, also the post-tax real wage. On the other hand, by requiring higher tax rates it will tend to lower the post-tax real wage. It follows that expenditure may need to be reduced (taxes raised) or increased (taxes lowered). It is even possible that the two effects just offset each other, so that a post-tax real wage fall owing to the depreciation cannot be avoided by an expenditure adjustment even though a pre-tax fall could be. Real wage rigidity would then prevent a cure of the Dutch disease.

(5) *Exchange rate protection*

Let us return to the case where the real wage is flexible and expenditure adjustment is used to maintain a constant level of employment. In that case one can imagine a deliberate policy of curing the Dutch disease by bringing about a shift out of non-tradeables back into tradeables, hence raising output, employment and profits in the latter. This was widely advocated in Britain in 1980. The mechanism of such a policy is a depreciation of the exchange rate combined with expenditure reduction. The incidental result will be to generate a current account surplus. If the objective is to protect the tradeables sector even at the cost of accumulating more foreign financial assets than are required by optimal savings and portfolio balancing considerations, then the policy can be described as *exchange rate protection*.

The cost of exchange rate protection is the net cost of accumulating excess foreign assets. The lower the real rate of interest received on these assets and the less secure they are, the higher this cost. If the real wage is rigid and a movement out of non-tradeables into tradeables requires some net fall in employment (as explained above), there is an additional cost, namely the loss of output resulting from the reduced employment.

VI. Conclusion

There have been three strands in this paper, namely (1) the short-run effects of a monetary squeeze, (2) the short-run effects of North Sea oil, and (3) the medium-run effects of North Sea oil.

(1) The essential and obvious effect of a monetary squeeze is that it affects both the tradeables and the non-tradeables sectors adversely, the extent of the effects depending above all on the degree of downward flexibility of nominal wages. The adverse effect on tradeables works through nominal appreciation. As discussed in Section III, there is some presumption that the effect on tradeables would be relatively more adverse, and also that the real exchange rate would appreciate, but these results are not inevitable.

(2) The various short-run North Sea oil effects tend also to be adverse for tradeables through nominal appreciation, but this could be offset by expenditure increases, at least to some extent. The short-run is assumed to have a given nominal money supply and nominal wage. Thus, in general the North Sea oil effect and the monetary contraction both tend to appreciate the exchange rate and together create a *tradeables squeeze.*

(3) In the medium-run, when expenditure is adjusted to maintain employment (or perhaps is partially adjusted for this purpose), North Sea oil involves a structural shift from tradeables to non-tradeables, at least if the whole of the revenue is not used for the purchase of foreign financial assets.

The extent of this structural effect depends crucially on the fiscal policy response: to what extent is the oil revenue used to retire debt and to what extent is it spent, directly or indirectly? While undoubtedly the tradeables squeeze of 1980 reflected some of the short-run effects of North Sea oil, there may also have been elements of a medium-run effect, with at least a relative shift from tradeables to non-tradeables, and a greater squeeze on the former than the latter.

Finally, it has been stressed that attempts to reverse the tradeables squeeze—i.e. the Dutch disease—in the medium-run context would require a reduction in real expenditure, and, insofar as there is a tendency to real wage rigidity downwards, might lead to unemployment. Further, such "exchange rate protection" might involve an accumulation of foreign financial assets above the optimum from a non-protectionist point of view. But this paper has been positive, not normative. It provides only some of the positive theory required for a full normative analysis of policies leading to a tradeable squeeze.

HOW BEST TO DEFLATE THE ECONOMY[1]

By M. FG. SCOTT

SINCE it took office in May 1979, the Conservative Government has pursued a policy of limiting the rate of growth of the money supply in order to reduce the rate of inflation. Given this objective, one may ask (as do the editors in their note) exactly how control of the money supply affects inflation, and whether there are not more efficient means of attaining the same objective. The policies appear to have resulted in a very high exchange rate. Might it not be better to pursue policies which lead to a lower exchange rate, thereby putting less of the burden of adjustment on the traded goods sector of the economy and, in particular, on manufacturing? A similar point is made by Blackaby (1980, p. 14):

'Once the Government accepts the proposition that it is simply deflating the economy, then it can at least take the first, limited step towards a more sensible strategy. There is no law which says that a deflationary policy has to fall particularly heavily on the foreign trade sector, which is what has been happening during the last two years. It is perfectly possible to devise a deflationary strategy which raises unemployment by the same amount as present policies, and therefore has just as big an effect on prices and earnings (whatever that may be), but is not biased against industries which compete with foreign suppliers'.

The object of deflating the economy is to reduce the rate at which prices are increasing. In the past, both Conservative and Labour Governments have sought to achieve this objective without reducing output and employment by means of incomes policies of various kinds, but, for one reason or another, these policies have all broken down and/or been abandoned. It is not my intention here to discuss whether some alternative incomes policy could be devised with better chances of success, or whether some means of reforming our system for fixing wages could be found which would reconcile low unemployment, reasonably high profits, and moderate wage increases (see Blackaby (editor) 1980). Nor do I wish to question the objective of reducing the rate of inflation (as does, for example, Hahn, 1980). All these are very important issues, but they are not those which I take to be the concern of this Symposium.

It is, rather, the efficiency of macroeconomic policy as a means of reducing the rate of inflation, and of monetary policy in particular, which seems to me to be the issue. One would like to minimise the economic welfare cost of achieving a given reduction in the rate of inflation. Does that require a different mix of macroeconomic policies from those presently being used with, in particular, less emphasis on monetary policy and with a lower exchange rate?

[1] A. S. Courakis, J. S. Flemming, C. A. E. Goodhart, D. Helm, S. Maitra & A. Simpson provided some very helpful comments and corrections, but are not responsible for any mistakes which remain, and do not necessarily agree with the views expressed.

Different macroeconomic policies

To make the discussion manageable, it is convenient to simplify macroeconomic policies so that they consist of the following four activities:

1. Fixing the public sector financial deficit. Broadly speaking this equals
   current expenditure on goods and services and social security and
   other current transfers and debt interest by the public sector less
   current receipts (tax receipts plus net receipts from sales of goods and
   services) plus gross domestic investment, less net capital transfer
   receipts. A complex of policies is involved, of which fixing the level of
   public expenditure, and fixing tax rates, are the two main components.
2. Fixing the net sale of foreign assets by the public sector. The largest
   components of this are usually the net decrease in official foreign
   exchange reserves and transactions with the International Monetary
   Fund and foreign central banks.
3. Fixing the net sale of public sector securities, excluding those mentioned in 2 above or 4 below.
4. Fixing the net issue of money by the public sector. This includes notes
   and coin as well as an increase in the deposit liabilities of the Bank of
   England (included here within the public sector) to the private sector
   banks (but excluding 'special deposits').

These four items, all of which have the dimensions of a money flow, must
sum to zero. The financial deficit is equal to, or financed by, the sale of
foreign assets, the sale of securities and the issue of money. Consequently,
only three of the items can be determined independently.

What is monetary policy?

Again for simplicity, I shall *define* monetary policy as item 4, the fixing of
the net issue of money by the public sector. This is unconventional since the
money so issued does not equal the change in either M_1 or M_3 (or Sterling
M_3), which are the stocks of money to which attention is conventionally
given. Instead, it equals the change in the total stock of notes and coin in the
hands of the private sector plus the deposit liabilities of the Bank of England
to the private sector banks (which we shall call just 'banks' for short). This
stock may be called M_0.[2] It can be divided into two parts, that held by the
'public' excluding the banks, and that held by the banks. Let us call these
M_{01} and M_{02}. There is evidence that M_{01} is closely related to the value of
consumers' expenditure, and that its velocity of circulation with respect to
consumers' expenditure has an upward trend of about 2 per cent per annum

---

[2] It is the same as what is usually referred to as the 'monetary base'. However, as will become
apparent, I differ from advocates of monetary base control in some important respects, and, in
particular, do not regard M_0 as an intermediate target for the control of some wider monetary
aggregates.

and is not much responsive to interest rates.[3] M_{02} consists of the cash reserves of the banks, and the demand for it is likely to be responsive to interest rates, since it is known that the demand for bank deposits is responsive to them, and since cash ratios are likely to rise when interest rates are low, and vice-versa, so that, for example, a fall in interest rates is likely to increase M_{02} proportionately more than it increases deposits. This means that the velocity of circulation of M_0, the sum of M_{01} and M_{02}, with respect to consumers' expenditure, will respond to changes in interest rates, but not very much, since M_{02} (the responsive part) is only about 17 per cent of the total.

The close relationship of M_{01} to consumers' expenditure, the fact that it is not much responsive to interest rates, together with the fact that by far the greater part of M_0 consists of M_{01} and the fact that the government can closely monitor and control changes in M_0, seem to me to constitute a strong case for making it, rather than sterling M_3, the chief target of monetary policy.[4] The demand function for sterling M_3 is not stable in the short run, and, since most of it earns interest, it is not necessarily or always the case that a rise in interest rates will tend to reduce the demand for it. That depends on how the pattern of interest rates is changed. Recent experience indeed suggests that the Authorities have difficulty in controlling £M_3.

Andersen and Karnosky (1977), writing in the influential Review of the Federal Reserve Bank of St. Louis, have suggested two questions which are relevant to the choice of a monetary aggregate for the implementation of monetary policy. '(1) Which monetary aggregate projects future patterns of economic activity with the smallest error? (2) Which monetary aggregate can the Federal Reserve control with the smallest error . . . . The appropriate monetary aggregate for achieving a desired pattern of economic activity would be the one with the smallest probability of error—*projection error* plus

---

[3] The regression equation $\ln M_{01} = a + b \ln C + ct$, where C is the current value of consumers' expenditure and t is time in years was fitted to annual data for the years 1958–79. $\bar{R}^2 = 0.999$, $b = 0.956$ and $c = -0.018$, both b and c being highly significant. A similar equation, but with t replaced by the natural logarithm of the annual average yield on $2\frac{1}{2}$ per cent Consols, gave a slightly worse fit and a fairly low value for the elasticity of demand for notes and coin with respect to interest rates. In this equation, $\bar{R}^2 = 0.997$, $b = 0.833$, $c = -0.115$, both b and c being significant at the one per cent level. Replacing the yield on Consols by the average rate on Treasury Bills worsened the fit and resulted in an interest elasticity not significantly different from zero. Since we are concerned here with fairly short-term policies, and since long-term rates of interest respond much less to these than short-term ones, these equations support the statement in the text. In making its forecasts of demand for notes, the Bank of England uses an equation which contains consumers' expenditure as an explanatory variable, but not interest rates (see *Bank of England Quarterly Bulletin*, September 1978, p. 363). The Bank of England model of the U.K. economy contains an equation in which the stock of notes and coin in circulation is explained by consumers' expenditure and a long-term interest rate term. However, the latter implies a small interest-elasticity, and the term is not very significant (see Bank of England, September 1979, p. 88).

[4] This is not a novel proposal, of course. The Bank Charter Act of 1844 can be said to have enshrined it in one particular form. More recently, Wilson (1957) advocated control of the note issue, making many of the points repeated here, and drawing attention to the relative stability of the velocity of circulation of the note issue.

control error. The controversy can only be settled by taking into consideration both types of error.'

Without undertaking a full econometric study, which would in any case be beyond my capability, I hazard the guess that M_0 would, judged by this criterion, be a better aggregate than M_3 or $£M_3$. Its projection error is probably as good as theirs, or better, and its control error should be smaller. The projection error should be low because notes and coin are mainly used for transactions in goods and services, whereas M_1 and M_3 are also used, to an important extent, for financial transactions which are not closely related to transactions in goods and services. Bank deposits are also used as a store of value to an extent which notes and coin probably are not. The control error should be less because it is possible to monitor the issue of notes and coin closely.

To avoid misunderstanding it needs to be stated that the proposal here is not that there should be a *quantitative rationing* of notes and coin. The demand for them would be brought into equality with the supply by interest rate changes. *Essentially, it is the Government's freedom to finance itself by printing money which is constrained by the adoption of M_0 as a monetary target.* There would be no new constraint on the ability of members of the public, or the banks, to convert other financial assets into notes and coin.

There would therefore be no reason to expect recourse to substitutes for notes and coin to result from the adoption of this target any more than from the adoption of M_1 or $£M_3$. This does imply, however, that the Government accepts whatever interest rate levels are necessary for this purpose. I assume that there is always *some* level of interest rates at which the required volume of Government securities can be sold to satisfy the pre-determined money supply target. This assumption may be questioned, but I do not wish here to enter into controversies about the problem of selling securities on a falling market. In my scheme the Government does not seek to determine interest rates, it merely determines three out of the four items listed on p. 48 of which one will generally be the change in M_0. There may be occasions when the Government will deem it wise to override its monetary target in the interests of preserving stability in financial markets. The classic case would be a financial panic when the Bank of England must play its role of lender of last resort. This does not materially alter the analysis.

It might be feared that the adoption of M_0 as a target rather than $£M_3$ would itself be a cause of instability. Suppose, for example, that (contrary to the experience of the past 20 years or more, see footnote on p. 49) there was a sizeable shift in the demand function for M_0 leading to x per cent less notes and coin being held by the public. The excess would then be absorbed by the banks, who might commence a multiple expansion of bank deposits. However, this could not expand consumers' expenditure by more than x per cent, since then the public would reabsorb all the notes and coin they had previously disgorged. Exactly the same x per cent rise in consumers' expenditure would occur if there were an x per cent shift in the demand function for $£M_3$, and if the arguments in that function were consumers' expenditure and interest rates, and if expansion continued until the previous interest rates were restored. While these conditions may not all be fulfilled, there does not seem to be any reason to expect that the adoption of M_0 as a target should cause more instability than that of $£M_3$. Even if it did so initially, the financial system could be expected to adapt itself accordingly (e.g. the banks might increase their cash reserves), and, as suggested above, the target could be overridden if necessary for a time.

Although in what follows I adhere to the definition of monetary policy and money supply, M_0, given above, I doubt whether my main conclusions would be greatly altered if $£M_3$ were substituted for M_0. The official view is, in any case that, as well as $£M_3$:

> 'it is important to take account of growth in other measures of the money stock and to direct policy to a progressive and substantial reduction in the rate of growth of them all'.
>
> (H.M. Treasury, 1980, p. 2)

One might reasonably ask why the Government should adopt a target rate of increase for any monetary aggregate. Would it not be better, as Meade has argued (Meade, 1975, p. 34), to set the rate of increase of some carefully chosen price index as the target, or else the rate of growth of the money value of national income? I find Meade's argument persuasive, but will nevertheless proceed on the assumption that the Government does fix a target rate of increase for M_0. In my view, one would do this as a means of constraining the Government's macroeconomic policies so that they resulted in a certain rate of growth of the *demand* for money. If the demand for money is closely linked to the level of consumers' expenditure (or total final expenditure, for that matter), as does seem to be the case for M_0, this is an indirect way of constraining macroeconomic policies so that they result in a certain rate of growth of the current value of consumers' expenditure, or aggregate demand. There is a case for adopting this indirect method: information on M_0 is more up to date; and the psychological impact of a monetary target may be greater than that of a national income target. People may believe that the Government can control M_0, but not the national income. The ultimate purpose presumably would be to convince both employers and employees that faster price and wage increases would, *ceteris paribus*, tend to reduce output and employment. One would hope thereby to break inflationary expectations and change price- and wage-setting behaviour. U.K. Governments in recent years have in fact adopted monetary targets whether for this reason or for others, and it is therefore interesting to analyse the consequences.

By confining macroeconomic policy to the four items listed on p. 48 we omit a number of other controls and policies which are commonly included, for example, controls over liquidity ratios, special deposits, hire-purchase, bank advances, or outward capital movements. We also ignore the fixing of the Bank of England's Minimum Lending Rate (MLR), assuming it to be adjusted consistently with, and as a result of, the other macroeconomic policies. Despite these simplifications, it is thought that the most important points can still be made and emerge with greater clarity.

It is clear that the same monetary targets can, in principle, be hit in a variety of ways: the same net issue of money by the public sector can be arrived at with different values for items 1, 2 and 3. If, then, monetary policy is defined as securing a given rate of increase in the quantity of money, this definition is inadequate. It is quite possible that the same rate of increase in the quantity of money will have different effects on prices, output and employment depending on how it is achieved, i.e. by which combination of items 1, 2 and 3, and one must search for the most efficient combination. Furthermore, since items 1, 2 and 3 may have direct or indirect effects on prices of their own, independently of their effects via changes in the quantity of money, one may be able to achieve a given effect on prices with different monetary targets. It may be possible, for example, to trade off a more restrictive fiscal policy (item 1) for a more restrictive monetary policy, and once again the most efficient combination of policies needs to be found.

The components of price changes

No deflationary policy can succeed until it has reduced the rate of increase of money wages (used, for short, to include all incomes from employment). The reason for this is that they form the largest component of prices. However, one must not lose sight of the other components, viz profits, taxes, and imports. Their relative importance is shown in Table 2.[5] *Changes* in prices can, statistically, be analysed into changes in each of these four components: wages, profits, taxes and imports per unit of output. In principle, changes in each of these four components can, in turn, be sub-divided into two further changes: a quantity and a 'price'. Thus changes in wages per unit of output consist of a change in the quantity of labour per unit of output (i.e. a change in labour productivity), together with a change in wage rates (i.e. a change in the price of labour). Likewise, changes in profits per unit of output divide into a change in capital productivity and a change in the rental of capital; changes in taxes per unit of output into changes in the quantity of public expenditure per unit of output and changes in its 'price' (and this must include changes in the public sector surplus or deficit since 'price' for this purpose equals public sector receipts per unit of quantity of public expenditure); and changes in imports per unit of output into changes in the quantity and prices of imports. It is often helpful to consider the effects of various deflationary policies on each of these subdivisions of price changes.

[5] Only indirect taxes and subsidies are shown in the Table, and not direct taxes. In principle, one would like to show profits and wages net of direct taxes, which would reduce their relative importance and increase the importance of taxes as a component of prices, but I am unable to estimate the amounts involved. The point is important when there is a large shift from direct to indirect taxation, such as was made in the Budget of June 1979, and we return to it subsequently.

Three phases of deflation

One more preliminary point must be made before we can begin our comparison of the efficiency of different policies, and this relates to the phases of deflation, of which three may be considered. There is, first, the phase *before* wage rate increases have been materially affected. In this phase the other components of price increases are being reduced. Thus, profits per unit of output fall and, if the exchange rate appreciates, imports per unit of output also fall. If there are public expenditure cuts, it is also possible for taxes per unit of output to fall. My assumption is that, at least in the U.K. economy at the present day, most of the initial impact of deflationary policies falls on these components of prices, while wages per unit of output are initially not much affected. In fact, in so far as deflation initially causes a drop in output (below what it would otherwise have been), it is very likely that wages per unit of output will rise, since output tends to fall by more than employment in the short run, so labour productivity falls. But even if one corrects for this effect, which means that one ignores the effect on labour productivity and looks only at the effect on wage rates, there may be little initial effect. It is true that, if the deflationary measures alter price expectations held by employers and employees, this will tend to moderate wage rate increases. But this requires a past history in which such measures have been pursued far enough actually to reduce prices (again, compared with what they would otherwise have been). In the century or more up to 1938 this past history existed, and the cyclical behaviour of wage-rates is well-attested, and produced the data for Phillips's famous study. Since then, however, the memory of all this has steadily faded away, so that the credibility of deflation has been much reduced, while the credibility of inflation has increased. Consequently, the stage has now been reached in which, as Sir Bryan Hopkin has put it, 'if inflationary expectations are to be got down, *actual* inflation has to be got down first' (Hopkin, 1980).

It should be noted that the first phase can only work in so far as *some* domestic factor payments are flexible downwards, as compared with what they would otherwise have been, or in so far as the terms of trade can be improved or tax rates be cut. Consider each in turn. Clearly, deflation is not going to improve either labour or capital productivity appreciably—rather the reverse, at least in the short run. Consequently, neither wages nor profits per unit of output can be reduced without falls in the prices of labour or capital. For the reasons given, it is thought that, at present, it is a fall in the rental of capital rather than labour which is likely to be most important in phase one. Now consider the terms of trade. If there were no improvement in these, a fall in import prices would require an equal proportionate fall in export prices, and that, in turn (and in the absence of productivity improvements) would require downward flexibility in domestic factor prices. Hence for prices to fall there must be either this downward flexibility in domestic factor prices, or else there must be an improvement in the terms of trade.

This is an important point, since attention is often concentrated on import prices, neglecting the fact that, apart from productivity gains, these cannot be reduced unless there is a fall in domestic factor prices or an improvement in terms of trade. Finally, consider cuts in tax rates. Deflation will tend to reduce the tax base, and so reduce the yield of given tax rates. Consequently, a given public sector financial deficit can only be maintained by cutting public expenditure or increasing tax rates. Since a high proportion of public expenditure consists of wages, which we assume are not much reduced in phase one, it seems likely that tax rates will have to be increased unless public expenditure is cut. By this I mean a cut in, for example, the numbers of teachers, hospital staff, police, civil servants, or in purchases of goods and services by the public sector or in social security benefits and similar transfers. Some so-called public expenditure cuts have really been increases in tax-rates (e.g. when local authorities have increased rates on property) or similar to them (e.g. increases in rents for council houses, increases in charges by nationalised industries), and have thus tended to increase, not decrease, prices directly.

So much for the first phase. In the second phase, wage rate increases are moderated, while most of the changes in the other components are reversed. The extent to which they are reversed depends upon the initial starting point. If, in a sense to be defined below, the situation was 'normal' with regard to profit margins and the terms of trade before the deflation started, and if the level of public expenditure and the surplus or deficit were also 'normal', then, before the third and final phase can be reached, profits, import prices and tax rates must all be restored to normal. They cannot permanently be squeezed. Hence wage rates must be moderated despite this restoration of profits, imports and taxes to normal levels. The main factors moderating wage rate increases in this phase must be revisions, downwards, of expectations of future price and wage increases resulting from the moderation in price increases already experienced, *plus* the squeeze on profits resulting from the first phase, *plus* higher levels of unemployment. The stronger and more prevalent is collective bargaining as opposed to atomistic bargaining, the more importance attaches to the first two of these forces. This is because unemployment presents less of a threat to workers who are collectively organized than it does to workers who are not. If the rule is 'one out all out', employed workers may feel the threat of a shut-down of the whole works, due to bankruptcy or loss-making, but, short of that, it may not matter to them greatly how long is the queue of job applicants outside the works gates. Their chief concerns will then be profits, rises in the cost of living, and the increases other workers are getting. Nevertheless, even collectively organized workers will be affected to some extent by the general level of unemployment. Their employers will, for a start, be less willing to concede wage increases if recruitment of new workers becomes easier. Workers' confidence is also likely to be affected and, in so far as they compare themselves with other groups, including those not collectively organized, they will feel it less necessary to press for large wage increases.

The third, and final, phase is an analytical abstraction. We assume that inflation has been brought down in the first two phases to some tolerable constant rate, and that it stays there. The economy is then assumed to grow at a constant rate, with the shares of wages, profits, taxes and imports in prices all constant. If inflation is strictly zero, this requires that wage rates rise only as fast as labour productivity, that capital and output grow at the same rate, with a constant rate of return, that tax rates and the share of public expenditure are constant, and that imports per unit of output are constant which, in the simplest case, could be secured by no change in import prices and 'import productivity'. If export prices are also constant, this implies no change in the terms of trade. No economy ever maintains such a steady state, but, in the long run, it is probably a reasonable approximation to the trend behaviour of many economies, except that we should superimpose upon it some average rate of price increase which would simply affect all the components of prices *pro-rata* without altering any real magnitudes or relativities. In reality there will be fluctuations, but we are not concerned with these here. What we are concerned with are the conditions which have to be satisfied if inflation is to be moderated in the long-run, and they are sufficiently described by the above analytical abstraction.

It should now be clear why profits, taxes and the terms of trade have to recover to normal levels in the second phase. A certain share of profits is needed in a predominantly private enterprise system (and even in a public enterprise system) to secure sufficient investment, and *sufficiently labour-using investment* (see Scott with Laslett, 1978, ch. 5), to make the demand for labour grow as fast as the supply in the long run. For an open economy, this share of profits will obtain only if the traded goods sector is sufficiently competitive, and that implies that the 'right' exchange rate must obtain. If, in phase one, the exchange rate has appreciated, and the competitiveness of the traded goods sector has declined, then, in phase two, this must be reversed sufficiently to restore profits and competitiveness. Likewise, in a steadily growing economy there will be some level and rate of growth of public expenditure which the political process will require. It may be politically feasible, as part of a set of temporary crisis measures, to cut public expenditure and so tax rates to bring prices down. But once inflation has become tolerable, some normal level of public expenditure and tax rates must be restored. It seems likely that profits were below 'normal' when the Conservative Government took over, so that a large reversal will be required there. On the other hand, it is less clear how far depreciation of the exchange rate will be required in view of the continuing increase in North Sea Oil production (and prices) expected. Rather different views on this are put forward by Forsyth and Kay (July, 1980) and Matthews and Reddaway (Autumn, 1980).

We may thus summarise the deflationary process as follows. Measures are taken which squeeze some or all of profits, taxes and imports per unit of output, thus reducing the rate of inflation. This is phase one. In phase two, wage rates react to the fall in the rate of inflation, the squeeze of profits and the rise in unemployment. It is then possible for profit margins, tax rates and import prices to be restored to 'normal' levels without inflation accelerating again because of this moderation in wage rates. This means that the economy can emerge from phase two into phase three, in which wages, profits, taxes and imports fluctuate around long-term trends in which the conditions of steady growth are satisfied *and* inflation is at a permanently lower rate. Unemployment must then be at its so-called 'natural' level, that is, a level consistent with no acceleration of inflation. All this is highly schematic. The actual course the economy takes will always be subject to outside shocks (such as the world commodity price increases of 1972–3) and special influences (such as the miners' strikes of 1972 and 1974). Nevertheless, we must abstract from these if we want to obtain a usable analysis of the efficiency of different deflationary policies, and for that purpose our somewhat artificial division into three phases will serve. In the conclusion to the paper we compare theory with the reality of the last two years.

Deflation 'purely' through monetary policy

A 'purely' monetary deflation could be defined as consisting only of items 3 and 4. That is, the government could fix the public sector financial deficit, item 1, and could (let us say, for simplicity) avoid intervening in the foreign exchange market, thus setting net sales of foreign assets at zero, item 2, and could them procure deflation by achieving certain rates of increase in M_0 (i.e. item 4) by means of appropriate net sales of securities, item 3. We shall take this as our 'base' policy for comparison with other policies. It is an exaggeration to say that the present government's policies are purely monetary in this sense, but perhaps one can say that it is their degree of purity which distinguishes them most sharply from the policies of their predecessors.

A purely monetary deflation starts with increased sales of securities and a reduction in M_0 (all as compared with what would otherwise have occurred) which drive up interest rates. In so far as the value of transactions does not at once fall (and there is likely to be some lag), and in so far as the velocity of circulation of notes held by the public does not respond very much to higher interest rates (and some believe that there is unlikely to be much response), the cut in M_0 must fall on the banks' cash reserves. The banks will then curtail their lending, and attempt to sell government securities, thus further pushing up interest rates. They will also seek to attract notes from the public by raising interest rates paid on deposits, perhaps even by paying interest on current accounts (as in the U.S.A. to an increasing extent through various devices in recent years). Some of the initial sales of securities by the Government will be made to foreigners, or to U.K.

residents who would otherwise have invested abroad, and the same is true of subsequent sales by the banks. So, in the absence of government intervention in the foreign exchange market, the exchange rate will tend to appreciate which, in turn, is likely to improve the terms of trade. The deflationary policy will also improve the current account of the balance of payments, which, in turn, must tend to raise the exchange rate. In what follows, however, we shall neglect this so far as phase one is concerned. We assume that phase is short enough for the exchange rate to be dominated by capital movements which depend on interest rates and expectations. In any case, the exchange rate rises and the terms of trade improve and this, together with the rise in interest rates, is likely to reduce profits, investment, and exports, and so the value of transactions will tend to fall. The fall in rates of profit and the improvement in the terms of trade will tend to reduce prices. On the other hand, unless the volume of public expenditure is cut,[6] tax rates will have to rise (because of the shrinkage of the tax base) to prevent the public sector deficit increasing. There will then be some fall in prices (compared with what would otherwise have happened), although the extent of the fall will depend quite heavily on the extent to which real public expenditure is cut. There will also be a fall in the volume of transactions, partly because of the fall in exports, production of import substitutes and investment (including less stockbuilding and less purchases of consumer durables), and partly because of real public expenditure cuts. Thus output will fall and unemployment will increase.

In what follows, we assume that the optimum mix of expenditure cuts and tax-rate changes is selected. Public expenditure cuts, accompanied by cuts in tax rates, are obviously helpful in reducing the rate at which prices increase. Furthermore, cuts in public expenditure can help to spread the burden of adjustment more evenly (and those who are most vociferous in deploring the impact of deflation on the traded goods sector should presumably welcome them on that account). On the other hand, large cuts may be neither feasible nor desirable, for reasons which are sufficiently obvious. We assume that whatever can be done is being done, whatever alternative mix of macroeconomic policies is chosen. Hence, while selecting the optimum size of the cuts (always matched by tax cuts, it must be remembered) is of great importance, it is not a problem which is discussed any further here.

This brings us to the end of phase one. In phase two the fall in prices, the squeeze of profits and the rise in unemployment moderate wage rate increases. The total loss of economic welfare which occurs may then be regarded, roughly speaking, as depending on three magnitudes: the reduction in real income, its distribution, and its duration. The loss is greater the greater is the average reduction in real income during phases one and two, the more heavily is its impact concentrated on lower income groups or on

---

[6] In fact, public expenditure will tend to increase, both because of higher interest payments on public sector debt and because of an increase in social security payments as unemployment rises.

particular sectors of the economy, and the longer is the duration of phases one and two. There may be longer-term effects on output as investment falls in phases one and two, and this reduces the level of capacity below what it might otherwise have been in later years. However, this loss is included in the loss of *income* in phases one and two, so long as the present value of investment equals its cost. The alternative way of measuring the loss of welfare would be to estimate the fall in *consumption*, rather than income, in which case falls in later years would have to be brought into account. While this would be theoretically preferable, it is sufficient for our purposes to make the above assumption and to consider only income.

There are several reasons for wanting an evenly spread impact of deflation as opposed to one concentrated on a few sectors of the economy. The law of diminishing marginal utility suggests that small losses widely spread are less painful than the same total loss narrowly concentrated. Customary wage differentials may be disturbed if, for example, particular groups in the private sector suffer wage cuts which are much larger than comparable groups in the public sector, and this may cause trouble later on in phase three. It has been said that one reason why the very heavy unemployment of the 1930's had such a small impact on wage rates was that it was very heavily concentrated in particular industries and regions. The more prosperous industries and regions were comparatively unaffected. This is a consequence of the curvature of the Phillips' curve—high unemployment is less effective in cutting wages than low unemployment is in increasing them.

One must then ask how concentrated deflation 'purely' through monetary policy will be? The answer, perhaps surprisingly, is 'not very'. The point has already been made that public expenditure should be cut (along with tax rates) to the optimum extent. The traded goods sector is affected by the high exchange rate, and this is a very large part of the whole economy. Some make the mistake of thinking it is more or less equivalent to manufacturing industry, but that is very wide of the mark. In 1972, for example, if one excludes the import content of U.K. exports of goods and services, only about a half of the remainder is accounted for (directly or indirectly) by value-added in manufacturing.[7] Furthermore, high interest rates deflate demand for housing and other building and construction. The multiplier also sees to it that private consumers' expenditure is cut quite widely. Banking, it is true, positively benefits from high interest rates, but this is largely because of insufficient competition, which results in no interest being paid on current accounts, and it should be possible to find a suitable remedy for that. The more competitive U.S. banks have not been especially profitable in recent years, despite high interest rates.

What is the alternative outcome with which deflation is being compared? Implicitly, in the preceding paragraphs a comparison is being made with a continuation of past trends of real income and employment but this is

---

[7] See Department of Industry, 1976, Table H.

misleading. It is, indeed, a criticism which can be levelled at a great deal of contemporary discussion—and attacks on government policy—that the realistic alternatives which should be compared are concealed or forgotten. The comparison should be with what would happen if no deflationary policies were introduced 'now', and the true alternative may be deflationary policies introduced later on, when inflationary expectations have become more deeply embedded, and when there is less North Sea Oil available to cushion the economy. However that may be, we need not concern ourselves with the point here, since we are not considering the costs and benefits of deflation in any absolute sense, but only the relative costs and benefits of different kinds of deflation. Hence what we need to know are the *differences* made by other deflationary policies to our three magnitudes: real income, its distribution, and the duration of phases one and two. Strictly speaking, it is the net present value of these differences that we should measure, but, since we are unable to estimate this, the point is academic. The following analysis makes no claims to precision. Let us now consider some of the alternative deflationary policies.

Same monetary targets, but emphasis on fiscal policy

One alternative would be to place more emphasis on deflation through fiscal policy. The government would achieve a smaller public sector financial deficit (or larger surplus), item 1, and would therefore need to sell less securities, item 3, in order to issue the same quantity of money M_0, item 4. The difference this would make depends on how far the deficit is reduced by public expenditure cuts and how far by tax rate increases. Consider each in turn.

Greater public expenditure cuts than in our 'base' deflationary policy, unaccompanied by tax rate reductions but accompanied, instead, by smaller sales of securities, would mean that there would be a bigger drop in this component of real final expenditure and lower interest rates. There would also be a lower exchange rate, and so production of traded goods and services would fare better, and there would be less improvement of the terms of trade. Would output fall more or less? If the velocity of circulation of M_0 is at all sensitive to interest rates that velocity would be lower, since interest rates would be lower. With worse terms of trade, and the same tax rates, prices would be higher if profit margins were the same. This must imply a lower volume of transactions (since M_0 is the same and V is lower and P is higher) and so, probably, a lower volume of output. That would probably imply somewhat lower profits per unit of output, which would modify, but probably not upset, this conclusion. Finally, with real output lower and worse terms of trade, real income must be lower.

Can one say anything about the likely duration of phases one and two? Phase one ends with real output lower but prices higher than in the 'base'. Profits are probably a bit lower, since real income is lower. Hence much will depend on whether wage rates respond faster to lower prices or to lower profits combined with higher unemployment (higher because output is lower). In other words, if a given fall in PT is secured more by a fall in T than by a fall in P, will this accelerate or retard the moderation of wage rate increases? I would be inclined to back retardation, with the implication that phases one and two would be longer than in the 'base', but this is a mere guess and a more thorough investigation should be made. My guess is based on the fact that econometric studies of wage rates generally show that prices are an important determinant, but are more equivocal about the effects of profits and unemployment.

It is far from clear that the distribution of the burden would be improved as compared with the 'base'. In the latter, public expenditure is cut to whatever extent is deemed optimal when the cuts are matched by tax cuts. Why should it be possible to improve the distribution by further cuts in expenditure matched by less sales of securities?

To sum up, therefore, it is far from clear that placing more emphasis on fiscal policy in the form of bigger public expenditure cuts would achieve a more efficient deflation. Indeed, the reverse seems likely since the fall in real income in phases one and two would probably be bigger, last longer, and might have a distribution no better than in the 'base'. What, then, of the other alternative of higher tax rates?

First, consider higher indirect taxes. These must tend to increase prices as compared with public expenditure cuts. The preceding conclusions are then strengthened as regards the fall in output and real income and, if one believes that wage moderaton is retarded by the smaller fall in P than in T, the duration of phase two is increased. Hence both the fall in real income and its duration may be increased. It is arguable that the distribution of the burden would be improved as compared with public expenditure cuts, but it is less clear that it would be improved as compared with the 'base'. Presumably, consumption would fall rather more, and exports and investment rather less, but it is not clear that this would be better for the real incomes of the poor, or that the impact would be spread much more evenly.

Next consider higher direct taxes. These do not directly affect prices as do indirect taxes, but they may affect them indirectly. Both profits taxes and income taxes may be 'passed on' to a greater or lesser extent and, in so far as they are, the difference between direct and indirect taxes tends to disappear. It is only if there is some sort of 'tax illusion' that higher direct taxes are likely to lead to a better result than with higher indirect taxes. And even if this illusion exists, the result may still not be preferable to the 'base'.

Of course, the government could attempt to place most of the burden on the rich by raising direct taxes mainly or entirely on those with higher incomes. We must assume that this is an extra burden, over and above the tax rates deemed best in the long run, since we do not want to confuse a discussion of short-term measures by long-run considerations of equity and efficiency. The problem then is that not much deflationary mileage can be gained by taxing the rich more heavily in the short run. Since the rich are wealthy, they can defend their consumption standards in the short-run by cutting saving, or by dissaving. Indeed, it is possible that the lower interest rates (compared with the 'base') may do more to sustain the consumption of the rich (by increasing their wealth) than the higher income tax rates do to cut it.

Alistair Simpson has pointed out to me that the argument in this section constitutes a case for a policy of greater tax cuts matched by greater sales of securities (all as compared with the 'base'). This should result in lower prices at the end of phase one, accompanied by higher real income, less unemployment, and a higher exchange rate (because of higher interest rates). We may not have found the right balance between taxation and borrowing, so that if higher taxes with less borrowing are harmful, lower taxes with more borrowing could be beneficial up to a point.

Same monetary targets, but greater purchases of foreign assets

The government could achieve the same increase in M_0, item 4, but combine it with greater purchases of foreign assets, item 2, financing these by larger sales of securities, item 3. Item 1, the financial deficit, is assumed to be the same as in the 'base'. The main objective of this policy variant would be to keep the exchange rate lower than in the 'base', and so to place less of the 'burden' of deflation on the traded goods sector.

Is this alternative possible? In 1977 the government kept the exchange rate down and accumulated large stocks of foreign exchange, but it eventually abandoned this policy and 'uncapped' the exchange rate, which rose sharply, though only temporarily. At the time, it was argued that a policy of keeping the exchange rate down was inconsistent with a policy of restricting the rate of growth of the stock of money. The low exchange rate encouraged an inflow of foreign capital which tended to increase the stock of money.

Congdon (1978), for example, asserts that 'any active exchange rate management is incompatible with a money supply rule' (p. 48). The argument he gives to support this assertion makes no mention of the possibility of 'sterilising' capital inflows by sales of securities. It is, in fact, essentially a long-run argument, and rests on the proposition that, in the long-run, changes in the money supply are directly proportional to changes in domestic prices (apart from some exogenous trend in the velocity of circulation), while changes in domestic prices must bear a fixed relation to changes in foreign prices corrected by changes in the exchange rate. Hence, in the long-run a given rate of growth of the money supply is compatible with only one possible change in the exchange rate, since changes in foreign prices are exogenous. Even if this argument is accepted, it relates only to the long-run (as do so many monetarist arguments), and says nothing about different possible routes by which the same long-run equilibrium may be reached. In our terms, it relates to a comparison of phase 0 with phase 3, and says nothing about phases 1 and 2. It is quite consistent with Congdon's long-run argument to assert that, in phases 1 and 2, different exchange rates are compatible with the same monetary targets, especially since, as has already been pointed out, the exchange-rate will be dominated by capital movements in the short-run.

If attention is confined to phases one and two, it does seem that greater purchases of foreign assets by the Government financed by greater sales of securities must normally be expected to depress the exchange rate and raise interest rates. The extent to which it will do so is hard to predict, since much will depend on how portfolio managers, both U.K. and foreign, react to such measures. In 1976, it is often said, intervention like this to push the exchange rate down led to a flight from sterling, so in that case the reaction apparently exaggerated the initial effect greatly. However, the view taken instead might be that the authorities were trying to maintain an unrealistically low exchange rate (just as in 1964–6 they tried to maintain an unrealistically high one), and so portfolio managers might respond in such a way as to prevent either the exchange rate or interest rates changing very much at all.

A general objection to intervention of this kind in the foreign exchange market is that it may be unprofitable for the government. The interest earned on foreign assets purchased may be less than that paid out on securities sold, which implies a running loss. A capital loss may also result if, in the end, the exchange rate rises and so the foreign assets depreciate in relation to the sterling securities sold. Of course, a capital gain could equally be made if the exchange rate were to fall. However, the risk of loss must be borne in mind if large-scale intervention is contemplated, and, as we have seen, the intervention might have to be large-scale to depress the exchange-rate very much.

Let us now compare our 'base' policy with the intervention policy, assuming that the latter would raise interest rates and lower the exchange rate by an appreciable amount. Higher interest rates should tend to increase V, so that, with M_0 the same (by assumption), $M_0 V$ and so PT would be higher. Since the lower exchange rate would tend to worsen the terms of trade, this would tend to raise P, hence the outcome for T is unclear. However, if we can assume that the demand for M_0 is not very responsive to interest rates, so that V does not increase very much, the higher P implies a lower T. Presumably, interest rates would have to rise enough to lower investment, and purchases of consumer durables, so that these would fall by more than in the 'base', and real output would be more depressed despite the lower exchange rate and higher output of tradeables.

Hence the total fall in output, and *a fortiori* (since the terms of trade would be worse) real income, would probably be greater, and would be concentrated more heavily on investment and consumer durables and less on tradeables than in the 'base'. The duration of phase two would be longer if I am right in assuming that a given fall in PT moderates wages more the more is P affected. On these assumptions, the option seems worse than the 'base' since the distribution seems no better and the magnitude and duration of the loss of total income worse.

Relaxing monetary policy

A last policy option which is considered here[8] is that of allowing the money stock M_0 to grow faster (i.e. increasing item 4), while securing the same fall in prices in phase one by means of a tougher fiscal policy (item 1). No intervention in the foreign exchange market is assumed, so item 2 is set at zero, as in the 'base'. Sales of securities, item 3, are smaller than in the base for two reasons: the smaller financial deficit and the bigger increase in the money stock.

As compared with the 'base', this option *ex hypothesi* results in the same fall in P in phase one, but M_0 is bigger. Interest rates must be lower, so V must be lower too, but we shall assume that the change here is small. Hence T must be bigger. With a lower exchange rate (because of lower interest rates), and higher T, profits are likely to be bigger, and the terms of trade worse. How, then, can P have fallen as much as in the base?

Higher productivity due to higher T could be advanced as a possible reason, but it is unlikely to be so. The higher T means that profit mark-ups (i.e. the ratio of price to 'normal' cost, adjusting for cyclical variations in productivity, and hence adjusting for the higher productivity in this case) will, if anything, be higher. Since wage-rates are, as yet, unaffected, the implication is that prices must be, if anything, higher, despite the higher productivity. Hence, so long as the higher productivity is regarded by price-fixers as a temporary fluctuation, it will not depress prices and, in fact, the higher level of demand is likely, if anything, to raise them.

The only remaining possibility is that prices are reduced by a fall in tax rates. If, as we have assumed thus far, the financial deficit is also reduced, the fall in tax rates must result either from the enlarged tax base (as PT is bigger) or from cuts in public expenditure, or both.

In several respects this is an attractive option—if it is feasible. Prices are reduced in phase one as much as in the 'base' with less of a squeeze on profits, with less of a fall in output and with less of an increase in unemployment. Because the terms of trade are worse, one cannot be sure that real income is higher than in the base, but let us assume that it is for the sake of argument. Thus far, then, this option is better than the 'base'.

However, there are some serious disadvantages. First, if public expenditure has to be cut severely to secure a sufficient fall in tax rates, this may have unwelcome distributive effects. True, there will be some fall in public

---

[8] Other policy options can be constructed by considering different combinations of the ones we have considered.

expenditure due to the fall in payments to the unemployed, since employment will be higher, but this may not be sufficient, and the cuts must then be more severe than the optimum which is assumed for the 'base'. Secondly, phase two must be longer than in the 'base', since the forces making for wage moderation are weaker. There is the same price fall, but there is a smaller profits squeeze and less unemployment. Hence the total cost of this option could exceed that of the 'base'. One might seek to reduce the length of phase two by securing a bigger price fall through bigger tax cuts, while allowing T to be bigger as well, on the assumption that the net result of this would be to moderate wage increases by more. Even so, this would require bigger public expenditure cuts with more adverse distributive effects. The feasibility of very large public expenditure cuts is also questionable.

Conclusion on the policy options

When objections are made to deflation, they generally amount to objections to all forms of it—to the loss of output and higher unemployment which inevitably accompany it, as well as to the public expenditure cuts which usually do as well. From the standpoint of this essay such objections are beside the point, since my concern is with the efficiency of deflation, and not with the question of its desirability as compared with some alternative policy. Some may be inclined to brush the analysis aside, since they are opposed to any forms of deflation whatever. To them I would say that, however desirable it may be to find a better way of reducing inflation, the fact remains that successive governments, both Labour and Conservative, have felt compelled to adopt deflationary policies from time to time. Is it not then a little arrogant to assert that they have all been wrong, and that some manifestly better alternative, avoiding the admitted costs of deflation, lies at hand? All the same there still remains an important question which has not been considered here, and that is the extent to which inflation should be reduced in a given period. Whatever policy option is deemed more efficient, there is still the question of how vigorously it should be pursued. It would be nice to have a rapid cure, but not if it kills the patient. Some of the objections made to government policy are to its vigour rather than to its nature.

The reader may complain that the analysis given here lacks rigour and empirical backing. These points are well taken, and the only defence offered is that to meet them properly would require, not an essay, but a book. I am not seeking to provide definitive answers here, only to put forward a method of analysis and to provoke further thought.

The main conclusion is, then, very tentative. I wish to show only that the 'purely monetarist' method of deflating the economy is by no means obviously inferior to other possible methods. To the objection that it results in an exchange rate which is 'too high' I answer that this is, indeed, an advantage, since it tends to improve the terms of trade, and this enables prices to be reduced in phase one without the necessity for any fall in either profits or wage rates or tax rates. In so far as this advantage is lost when other methods of deflation are adopted, they have to secure cuts in domestic factor payments or cuts in tax rates, and these are likely to require more painful measures. As a corollary of this point, it follows that the bonanza of North Sea Oil really is a bonanza, since it enables tax rates to be cut, and so prices, without cuts in public expenditure. In addition, it improves our terms of trade.

The main point can be driven home if the reader will perform the following thought-experiment. Imagine that, for some extraneous reason, confidence in the existing exchange rate is lost, capital flows out, and the rate falls fairly drastically, so that import prices rise sharply, as do profits in the traded goods sector. Suppose that, in these circumstances, the Government pursues a deflationary policy which is sufficiently powerful to reduce prices and wages to the same extent as the present policy in present circumstances. Is the outcome likely to be more or less painful?

What has happened in the U.K.

It is of some interest to confront this theoretical analysis with reality. In Tables 1 and 2 a comparison is thus made between the last year of the

TABLE 1

Indicators of macroeconomic policy in the U.K.

	2Q 1978 to 2Q 1979	2Q 1979 to 2Q 1980
A. *Percentage increase during year in*		
1. M_0	15.6[a]	8.6[b]
2. $£M_3$	10.4[a]	11.3[b]
3. Consumers' expenditure	18.5	14.6
4. Final expenditure	16.6	14.2
	Year ending 2Q 1979 incl.	Year ending 2Q 1980 incl.
B. *£ millions*[c]		
5. Net acquisition of financial assets by public sector, of which:	−8214	−9435
6. overseas assets,	1778	571
7. other securities	−8957	−9062
8. notes & coin[d]	−1035	− 944

[a] Change from level at May 17 1978 to May 16 1979

[b] Change from level at May 16 1979 to May 21 1980

[c] A minus sign indicates e.g., net sales of securities or issue of notes and coin.

[d] This is not precisely equal to the (negative of the) increase in M_0, since changes in bankers' deposits at the Bank of England are excluded.

Sources: Lines 1, 2, 5, 6, 7, 8, *Financial Statistics* C.S.O., October 1980 and earlier issues Lines 3, 4, *Economic Trends*, C.S.O., October 1980

TABLE 2

Changes in costs and prices in the U.K. 1978–80

A. *Percentage change at annual rate in 'costs' per unit of final*
   expenditure (seasonally adjusted).

	2Q 1978 to 2Q 1979	2Q 1979 to 2Q 1980	Weight in 1979
1. Income from employment	9.4	22.4	46.8
2. 'Profits', adj. for oil & gas	4.4	12.9	20.1
3. Imports	17.7	11.7	10.7
4. Net indirect taxes	21.2	28.0	22.4
5. Total final expenditure, adj. for oil & gas	11.2	18.6	100.0
6. Direct and indirect taxes	13.5	19.0	

B. *Percentage changes in prices etc.*

	2Q 1978 to 2Q 1979	2Q 1979 to 2Q 1980
7. Retail prices	10.6	21.5
8. Tax and price index	12.9	18.1
9. Average earnings, whole economy	13.5	21.4
10. Imports of goods, unit value	8.4	17.8
11. Exports of manufactures, unit value	9.2	12.7
12. Imports of manufactures, unit value	6.0	7.5
13. Terms of trade, all goods	1.7	−3.7
14. Terms of trade, mfrs. only	3.1	4.8
15. Sterling effective exchange rate	9.6	9.0

Sources: *Economic Trends*, C.S.O., October 1980; *Monthly Digest of Statistics*, September 1980

Note: For Part A, index numbers of costs were calculated by dividing the current value of each cost component by the value of total final expenditure at constant 1975 prices. 'Profits' include all factor incomes other than income from employment. Both 'profits' and final expenditure were reduced by half the value of gross trading profits of North Sea oil and gas as a rough adjustment for depletion of capital; this adjustment did not alter the price index of final expenditure in line 5, but reduced line 2 while increasing lines 1, 3 and 4. A further adjustment is in principle required to include appreciation of the value of oil and gas stocks at some expected trend rate, but this would have affected the percentage changes only marginally, although it would have raised the weight of 'profits' in 1979 appreciably. In principle it would also be desirable to exclude direct taxes from lines 1 and 2 and add them to line 4. Line 6 was calculated by dividing total direct and indirect taxes and social security contributions by final expenditure at 1975 prices. Lines 11, 12 and 14 are for all manufactures excluding ships, N. Sea oil installations, aircraft and precious stones (SNAP).

Labour Government and the first year of the new Conservative one which took office in May 1979. For statistical convenience, the change-over is assumed to have taken place in the middle of 1979.

Table 1 shows that the new Government increased the public sector financial deficit slightly in nominal terms (line 5) although not in real terms, bearing in mind that inflation, measured by the retail prices index, was 19 per cent from 1978–9 to 1979–80. The main changes in the financing of the deficit were smaller acquisitions of foreign assets (line 6) and less recourse to the printing press (line 8) leading to a slower rate of growth of M_0 (line 1). Sales of other securities were slightly greater in nominal terms in 1979–80 than in 1978–9, though less in real terms. Short-term interest rates rose sharply, but not long-term rates. To the surprise of some (including the writer), but quite explicable with hindsight, the pound appreciated considerably against other currencies (Table 2, line 15). Although the rate of appreciation was about the same as in 1978–9, the real effective appreciation was much more because it was accompanied by much faster inflation in the U.K. relative to inflation in the main competitor countries.[9] Hence the impact of the policy, together with developments in the world economy (notably, the very big oil price increase which enlarged the OPEC surplus, and the value of the U.K.'s oil and gas output), was heavily on the exchange rate.

It is remarkable, by way of aside, that the credit squeeze was accompanied by a slightly faster growth of sterling M_3 in 1979–80 than in the previous year (Table 1, line 2) and even more remarkable when this faster growth is related to the slower accompanying growth in the value of consumers' expenditure and total final expenditure, and when it is remembered that the 'underlying' growth of sterling M_3 was probably higher, since it was restrained by the 'corset'. As a simple monitoring device, M_0 seems to have come out rather better than sterling M_3 in this period, since the behaviour of interest rates and the economy generally suggests that there was indeed a tightening credit squeeze.

In Table 2 it can be seen that both 'profits' and imports rose more slowly than total final expenditure, but that the average price of final expenditure rose faster than before at 18.6 per cent in the year to 2Q 1980 compared with 11.2 per cent in the year to 2Q 1979. The main explanation for this acceleration was the much faster growth in income from employment (line 1). With the switch from direct to indirect taxation in the June 1979 Budget, net indirect taxes continued to rise much faster than final expenditure (line 4). However, if direct and indirect taxes are taken together, there was little change in their share whereas this had risen over the previous year (line 6).

In the lower part of the Table, the same point is made by the slower growth in the 'tax and price index' (which allows for changes in the direct tax burden of the typical tax-payer) than in the retail price index (lines 7 and 8). Lines 10 and 13 show that import prices rose much faster in the year ending 2Q 1980 than in the previous year, and that the UK's terms of trade deteriorated, whereas they had previously improved. The explanation is that world commodity prices rose much faster.[10] Appreciation of the exchange

[9] Thus, according to the O.E.D.C. (*Economic Outlook*, July 1980 p. 44) consumer prices in the UK in the year to April 1980 rose at 21.8 per cent p.a. as compared with 13.9 per cent for the weighted average of O.E.C.D. countries. Comparing the year 1978 with 1979, the two rates of increase were 13.4 and 9.9, and comparing 1977 with 1978, there was a very small difference between them.

[10] The UN index of world commodity prices in sterling terms rose by 36% 2Q 1979 to 2Q 1980, as compared with only 9% in the previous year (*Economic Trends*, October 1980, p. 44).

rate did, all the same, improve the terms of trade compared with what would otherwise have happened (i.e. with no appreciation) as is indicated by the continuing improvement in the U.K.'s terms of trade in manufactures of about 5 per cent in 1979–80, following on an improvement of 3 per cent in 1978–79 (line 14).

To sum up. There was a monetary squeeze, as measured by M_0 and short-term interest rates but not sterling M_3, policy switched from heavy purchases of overseas assets to little intevention, and the pound continued to appreciate, and much more strongly in relative real terms (but not all of this could be attributed to the monetary squeeze, since some was due to the rise in oil and gas prices). As was to be expected, the squeeze reduced profits' share of final expenditure. Furthermore, compared with what would otherwise have happened, the terms of trade probably improved a bit. All this, however, was not enough to stop the rate of growth of prices accelerating, since wage rates, commodity prices and tax rates all accelerated. To a great extent one must attribute these unfortunate developments to factors outside the control of the Government. However, the switch from direct to indirect taxation in the June 1979 Budget probably aggravated inflation, since wage bargainers probably responded more to an increase in the retail prices index than they did to a cut in income taxes of equal value. There is also a question mark applying to the very large increase in public sector wage-rates. Although these were mainly the result of the previous Government's incomes policy and promises, which the new Conservative Government was pledged to honour, some greater restraint might have been possible.

During 1980 inflation slowed down remarkably. World commodity prices in sterling actually fell after April and this was reflected in wholesales prices and, with a lag, in retail prices. Wage rate increases here and there began to react to the deflation, indicating a beginning of phase two. The squeeze on profits, which had lasted for a considerable time, led to growing pressure on the Government to relax its monetary policy. Profit margins had to be restored if growth was to be resumed. The main uncertainty at the time of writing is whether, when they are restored, wage rate increases will have been appreciably moderated, whether moderation can be maintained, and what level of unemployment will remain.

REFERENCES

ANDERSEN, L. C. and KARNOSKY, D. S., 1977, 'Some considerations in the use of monetary aggregates for the implementation of monetary policy', *Federal Reserve Bank of St. Louis Review*, September.

BANK OF ENGLAND, September 1979, *Bank of England model of the UK economy*, Discussion Paper No. 5.

BLACKABY, F., (Editor) 1980, *The Future of Pay Bargaining* N.I.E.S.R., Heinemann, London.

CONGDON, T., 1978, *Monetarisim: An Essay in Definition*, Centre for Policy Studies, London.

DEPARTMENT OF INDUSTRY, 1976, 1972 Input-output tables for the United Kingdom, *Business Monitor* PA1004, H.M.S.O.

FORSYTH, P. J. and KAY, J. A., July, 1980, 'The Economic Implications of North Sea Oil Revenues', *Fiscal Studies*

HAHN, F., 1980, Memorandum to the House of Commons Treasury and Civil Service Committee, Session 1979–80, *Memoranda on Monetary Policy*., 17 July, No. 720, H.M.S.O.

H.M. TREASURY, 1980, 'Monetary policy and the economy', *Economic Progress Report*, July.

HOPKIN, Sir Bryan, 1980, *The Times*, 15 April, p. 19.

MATTHEWS, R. C. O., and REDDAWAY, W. B., Autumn 1980, 'Can Mrs. Thatcher do it?', *Midland Bank Review.*

MEADE, J. E., 1975, *The Intelligent Radical's Guide to Economic Policy*, Allen and Unwin, London.

SCOTT, M. FG with LASLETT, R. A., 1978, *Can we get back to full employment?* Macmillan, London.

WILSON, T., 1957, 'The Rate of Interest and Monetary Policy', *Oxford Economic Papers*, October.

SOME POLICY IMPLICATIONS OF THE MONETARY APPROACH TO BALANCE OF PAYMENTS AND EXCHANGE RATE ANALYSIS

By DAVID LAIDLER*

I. An outline of the monetary approach

THE monetary approach to balance of payments and exchange rate analysis is in some respects a modern version of the once predominant English Classical approach to the same problem area, and it is sufficiently different from the one usually taken towards such problems during the 1950s and 60s, that it would be as well to begin this paper with a brief outline of its salient characteristics.[1]

First and foremost, the monetary approach is macroeconomic rather than microeconomic in nature. It seeks to explain the behaviour either of the overall balance of payments, or of the exchange rate, by focussing directly on the interaction of simple aggregate relationships, rather than attempting to build up to such an explanation by way of modelling individually the determination of the various component accounts of the balance of payments. It has nothing specific to say about those component accounts, and if their details are important for particular policy issues, then the monetary approach is not an appropriate tool for their analysis. The monetary approach starts from the accounting identity which tells us that the liabilities of the consolidated banking system are equal to the sum of that system's domestic assets and its foreign assets, and notes that any divergence between the non-bank public's demand for banking system liabilities and that system's willingness to acquire domestic assets must result either in reserve changes or in exchange rate changes. From a purely logical point of view, there is no incompatibility between the monetary approach and that which builds up from the individual components of the balance of payments accounts. Where it does differ from them is in making a number of empirical assertions.

The most important of these assertions is that the non-bank public's demand for banking system liabilities is a stable function of a few arguments. In this respect the monetary approach to balance of payments theory represents a working out of the implications for an open economy of the characteristically monetarist proposition that there exists a stable demand

*This paper has grown out of work that I have been carrying out on the interaction of exchange rate regimes and domestic policy with the aid of a grant from the Social Sciences and Humanities Research Council of Canada, to whom I am extremely grateful.

An early draft was presented at the Bank of England, April 27, 1979, where it benefitted from many helpful comments, particularly from Christopher Dow, Brian Griffiths, Robin Matthews, Patrick Minford and Sir John Hick

[1] For a useful survey of the historical origins of the monetary approach to balance of payments theory see Frenkel (1976). For an extensive survey of recent literature see Whitman (1975), and for an excellent brief survey see Parkin (1977).

for money function. However, in its simplest—perhaps most extreme is a better term—form, it goes further than this. It postulates that two of the arguments of such a function—real income and the real interest rate—may be taken as given, and that, under a fixed exchange rate so may the general price level. Given these further propositions, the balance of payments must depend upon the behaviour of domestic credit expansion relative to that of the arguments of the demand for money function. Under a flexible exchange rate, instead of the price level, it is the behaviour of the foreign component of the banking system's assets that is tied down. In that case the interaction of the domestic money supply with the other two arguments in the function determines the domestic price level, and simultaneously, given the behaviour of the supply and demand for foreign currencies, the exchange rate as well.

In the literature on the monetary approach the proposition that real income may be taken as given is usually justified by assuming the economy to be operating at "full" (or "natural") employment, under which circumstances "productivity and thrift" on a worldwide basis determine the real interest rate, and perfect commodity arbitrage is usually invoked to ensure that the "law of one price" ties down either the domestic price level or the exchange rate. When matters are put this way it is easy to recognize the "Classical" pedigree of this approach, and to understand why the label "Global Monetarism" is sometimes attached to it. It is also easy to understand why many have found it so hard to swallow: pure theorists have found nothing new in the approach (and from a strictly logical point of view they are correct as I have already suggested) while the more empirically inclined find it severely deficient in the problems to which it can usefully be applied.[2]

Now there is no doubt that an approach to balance of payments analysis that postulates at the outset the existence of Classical long-run equilibrium leaves a lot of questions unanswered, but that is not the same thing as saying that it is irrelevant. The long run is not, after all, just a series of short runs. In a relatively closed economy, if variations in monetary expansion had no effects at all within twelve months, it would not follow that a stabilization policy carried out with regard to a one-year horizon could safely ignore the long-run interaction of money and prices; nor in an open economy would it be safe to overlook the forces to which the monetary theory of the balance of payments directs attention. One can go further than this in defending it, because the academic literature now abounds with dynamic models, whose long-run steady state properties are such as would be predicted by "global monetarism" but whose short-run behaviour may be extremely "Keynesian". Such models permit fiscal policy and other real shocks to influence real income and employment, make the real interest rate partially

---

[2] For pure theorists' views on the monetary approach to balance of payments theory see Hahn (1977). Note that Whitman (1975) criticizes the monetary approach on the grounds of its relatively limited empirical applicability. Whitman is particularly concerned that the approach has nothing to say about component accounts of the balance of payments.

a monetary phenomenon, allow devaluation to change the terms of trade, and so on.[3] Such effects are temporary of course, but that is not to say that they are necessarily of such short duration that they can be ignored. How far and for how long an economy may deviate from its long-run steady state are empirical questions whose answers might well vary from time to time and place to place. The same may be said of the question whether that steady state represents a stable equilibrium in the first place.

There is no space here to discuss the empirical evidence on these matters in detail: a series of assertions about what I believe to be the case as far as the majority of economies (including the United Kingdom) are concerned must suffice as a basis for the discussion of Policy issues that follows. First, and most important, virtually every economy does seem to be characterized by a reasonably stable long-run demand for money function.[4] Secondly, even the United States seems to be open enough, and sufficiently well integrated into international capital markets, for the "long run" linkages between domestic monetary policy on the one hand and the balance of payments and the exchange rate on the other to be important, at least as important as those between monetary variables and purely domestic variables such as income and employment. Thirdly, though something like the "law of one price" might operate for the world economy on average over rather long time periods, there is ample scope for domestic price levels and exchange rates to diverge from their long-run equilibrium values for periods that are better measured in years than in months.[5] Finally, though economies probably do tend to approach a full employment equilibrium in the long run, deviations from such equilibrium can be of long duration and can be influenced by the traditional tools of Keynesian stabilization policy.

II. Activist policies

In the first section of this paper, I have argued that the Monetary Approach to balance of payments and exchange rate analysis tells us that, if we returned to a system of fixed exchange rates, prices in the world economy *would* be predominantly determined in international markets, and the balance of payments between various countries *would* be dominated by the behaviour of domestic credit expansion rates. It also tells us that, if flexible exchange rates are maintained, then their long-run behaviour, as well as that of domestic prices, *will* mainly respond to domestic monetary

[3] See such models as those contained in Laidler (1975, Ch. 9), Laidler (1978), Bilson (1978), Jonson (1976) and Kingston and Turnovsky (1978). This list is by no means exhaustive.

[4] The stability of the demand for money function has been questioned in a number of countries recently. The reader's attention is drawn to the fact that I am here talking about the *long-run* function. I believe that stability problems have largely arisen from misspecification of the dynamics of the *short-run* relationship. On such matters see Artis and Lewis (1976), Lewis (1978) and Laidler (1980).

[5] Myhrman (1976), and Ball and Burns (1976), both contain empirical evidence relevant to this characterization of the operation of the law of one price.

policies. However, these propositions are about the long run. As I have also noted, empirical evidence suggests that, in the short run, prices, output and exchange rates are susceptible to all manner of other disturbances. Therefore domestic policymakers do, *in principle*, have considerable room for manoeuvre in the face of such disturbances.

The qualification "in principle" is all important. In my view there is ample evidence to justify the proposition that conventional Keynesian demand management policies, both fiscal and monetary, *can* influence income, employment, prices and so on for sufficiently long for their effects to matter. However that evidence in no way implies that out knowledge, either theoretical or empirical, is sufficiently accurate to enable such policies *actually* to be deployed with any confidence that they will in fact end up having the effects that they were designed to have. An economy that is always in, or on the verge of, Classical full employment equilibrium has no need of demand management policies. It is only if private sector adjustment mechanisms are characterized by rigidity and sluggishness that active policy intervention has any scope for improving matters. However it is well-known that the very same rigidity and sluggishness which make active policy intervention potentially worthwhile usually cause the dynamics of the private sector's adjustment towards long-run equilibrium to be complex and prone to generate cycles in key variables. Although it is reasonably easy at any time, with the benefit of hindsight, to design a policy that would have coped with past problems better than the one actually implemented, designing a policy for the present or future is altogether more difficult. When an actual economy, as opposed to an econometric model in a simulation exercise, is out of equilibrium it is extraordinarily difficult to judge where it is, and where it is ultimately heading, and even slight mis-calculations in the design of activist policy can lead to its effects making matters worse rather than better. Although effective activist policies can, in principle, be designed, in practice given the current state of knowledge it is next to impossible to do so.[6]

It is not well enough understood that, among those commonly called "monetarists", although there is almost universal hostility to activist policies, there is considerable disagreement about the grounds for such hostility. Some argue that, in practice, the world is always sufficiently close to Classical equilibrium, and that agents in the private sector are in a position sufficiently quickly to anticipate the ultimate effects of activist policy on prices, and hence offset their systematic effects on output and employment, that there is no point in the authorities trying to influence real variables.[7]

[6] Although views such as those expressed in this paragraph are usually associated with monetarism, and particularly with Milton Friedman, it is worth remembering that a considerable amount of the work of A. W. Phillips was devoted to analyzing just such problems. The practical conclusions that emerge from Phillips' work were very much the same as those stated by Friedman. See, for example, Phillips (1954).

[7] This is the essential implication of the theoretical work of Lucas (1975) and Sargent and Wallace (1975) to give two examples.

Others take the view that, although the world is frequently far away from such an equilibrium, we understand so little about the dynamics inherent in such a state of affairs as to make the risk that an activist policy will make things worse rather than better unacceptable high. As will be apparent, I would put myself among the latter group, particularly as far as debates about activist monetary policies are concerned. The well known fact that these policies operate with long and variable time lags seems to me to present an overwhelming objection to their use for activist stabilization policies. When it comes to fiscal policies, which do act more rapidly, and at least in the British case, can be deployed quickly as well, I am more ambivalent. Such policies do seem to have been useful in the past, and though I have doubts about their feasibility in current circumstances, a situation in which they could again be useful might well be re-established in the future, as I shall now argue.

In the 1950s and 60s Keynesian fiscal policies were used for stabilization purposes in Britain, and though at the time it was fashionable to express disappointment at the limited nature of their success, the performance of the economy in those years looks much better than it did, now that we have begun to digest the experience of the 1970s. The economy *was* managed over those years; largely by fiscal fine tuning; income and employment targets *were* on the whole attained; and by comparison with later experience inflation never *was* more than a minor irritant. Only the balance of payments gave problems.[8] The very same monetary approach to balance of payments theory which now yields pessimistic conclusions about policy can, I believe, explain this earlier "success".

In the 1950s and 60s the United Kingdom was linked by a fixed exchange rate to a word economy dominated by the United States. Until the mid-1960s, US macro policies were extremely conservative and that country experienced virtual price stability. The monetary theory of the balance of payments implies that, under such circumstances, the "law of one price" would also have kept Britain largely inflation free, though the version of it to which I adhere would certainly not rule out variations in domestic demand pressures leading to fluctuations in the domestic inflation rate around an average rate in the main determined abroad. Moreover, the proposition that conventional fiscal fine tuning is likely to be effective in an economy in which the behaviour of prices is mainly exogenously determined surely needs little defending. As to the balance of payments problems, though conventional wisdom usually attributes these to the UK having a pathologically high marginal propensity to import, the monetary approach suggests, rather, that they were due to variations in the domestic credit expansion rate which in turn stemmed from attempts to maintain interest

[8] For a useful study of the relationship between policy goals and policy actions in Britain over this period, see Kennedy (1973).

rate stability while financing the fluctuating deficit produced by those same fiscal fine tuning policies.[9]

The monetary approach tells us that the United Kingdom could continue to implement fiscal stabilization policies successfully for just so long as price stability characterized the world economy, and for just so long as the maintenance of a fixed exchange rate was ultimately accorded priority over other policy goals. For reasons that there is no need to belabour here, these two preconditions have now vanished. The world economy is far from inflation free, and exchange rate flexibility is likely to remain a fact of life into the foreseeable future. Thus the consequences of policy for the exchange rate and prices must now be taken into account in its design. However it is precisely the dynamics of price-exchange-rate-output interaction, which were largely irrelevant in the 1950s and 60s, that are particularly badly understood. That is why despite the advances in knowledge that the last two decades have produced, and the monetary approach is surely one of these, an approach to policy which in the UK was viable twenty years ago no longer is. However, once price stability is restored to the economy, then if monetary policy is assigned the role of maintaining it, a role for fiscal policy as a short run stabilizer might re-emerge.

III. The "locomotive" and "convoy" approaches to macroeconomic stability

Whatever might be the case once price stability is restored, there can be no doubt that the most pressing current policy problem, not just for Britain, but for the other industralized countries as well, is its restoration while simultaneously re-establishing high employment levels. In this context the negative implications of the monetary approach are more obvious than the positive ones. In particular it suggests that OECD's "locomotive approach" and its later variant the "convoy approach" to achieving macroeconomic stability among the advanced industrial nations by way of internationally co-ordinated policies are seriously flawed.[10]

Although there has been little discussion of these policy proposals over the last two or three years, the onset of a now-worldwide recession in 1980 will undoubtedly produce a revival of interest in them, so they are worth dealing with here in some detail. Both approaches start from at least one

---

[9] The model presented in Laidler (1978), and further developed in Laidler and O'Shea (1980), attributes a strong influence on the balance of payments to domestic monetary policy. Certain experiments carried out with that model since the above-mentioned papers were prepared have been able to find no direct influence either of fiscal policy or of the level of income on the balance of payments. These latter results are of course tentative.

[10] The most accessible source for these policy recommendations is the McCracken Report. See McCracken *et al.* (1977). Not all members of the Committee agreed with all aspects of the Report's policy proposals, and the following account of the theoretical underpinning of this approach should therefore not be attributed to any individual member of that Committee. I hope however that I have not merely erected a "straw man" in the following few paragraphs.

correct premise, namely, that, under a system of flexible exchange rates, any one economy's response to expansionary domestic policy, if that policy is undertaken in isolation, is not going to be that which we would expect of a closed economy. In a closed economy the price formation process is prone to stickiness and sluggishness, not least in the labour market which is the archetypical "fix-price" market, to borrow Sir John Hicks's phrase. If prices do not respond to changes in the level of aggregate demand, then quantities do: hence in a closed economy it is possible to use expansionary demand management policies secure in the belief that, at least in the short run, they will have their major impact upon income and employment, rather than prices.

In a flexible exchange rate open economy, expanding aggregate demand spills over into the foreign sector, putting immediate downward pressure on the exchange rate. Since the foreign exchange market is the archetypical "flex-price" market, such pressure will immediately be converted into a depreciating exchange rate, rising import prices, and thence to rising money wages and general inflation. Hence, under flexible rates the authorities of an individual economy cannot act alone to expand domestic income and employment without also having to pay an unacceptably high price in terms of inflation. The "locomotive" and "convoy" approaches are schemes to coordinate demand management policies between countries in such a way as to achieve the benefits of expansion without paying the inflationary price. As I have already noted, the monetary approach to balance of payments analysis implies that both are flawed, the former variant more obviously so than the latter.

The "locomotive" approach seems to be based on the view that some countries have "strong" currencies and that they can therefore expand at less risk of exchange depreciation than others. If they expand, their "weaker" trading partners will experience an increase in demand for exports which in turn will lead to real expansion without exchange depreciation. The monetary theory of the exchange rate tells us that whether a currency is "strong" or "weak" depends upon the rate at which monetary assets denominated in it are being created, relative to the rate of growth of demand for such assets. Hence it warns that the major consequences of one or two countries attempting to expand alone will be to convert their strong currencies into weak ones, to generate for them both a falling exchange rate and domestic inflation. Though the monetary approach would not deny the existence of income effects that might benefit the exports of non-expanding countries, the significance of such effects is ultimately an empirical matter, and the distinctly non-monetarist models of Project Link suggest that they are minor.[11] The experience of the United States dollar from late 1977 onwards, both in foreign exchange markets and domestically, may be cited as an illustration, and indeed a confirmation, of the predictions of monetary

---

[11] On this matter I draw on the work of Pieter Korteweg (1978).

analysis about the consequences of monetary expansion in a country with an initially "strong" currency.

As I understand it, the "convoy" approach to expansion is an attempt to avoid the problems discussed in the last paragraph. It proposes that, instead of one or two countries taking the lead in expansion, with others being pulled along behind, all countries attempt to expand together. The reasoning here seems to be that if all countries expand together, the pressures of monetary expansion are taken off the "flex-price" foreign exchange market, and no one country can suffer a significant depreciation relative to the others. Instead the pressure of expanding demand will be transmitted to "fix-price" markets, including labour markets, and hence will result in quantity changes rather than price changes. In effect, the "convoy" approach seeks to turn the world into something like one large closed economy. The monetary theory of the balance of payments points to a number of problems with it.

First of all the "convoy" approach seems to presume that the authorities of various countries are sufficiently skillful, and in sufficient agreement with one another, to be able so to coordinate their domestic policies as to put no undue pressure on exchange rates. In short, implicit in the proposal is the assumption that we know enough about the dynamics of the interaction of domestic policies, output, prices, and exchange rates to be able to design an array of measures that will effectively lead to a return to exchange rate stability, not as the eventual outcome of an internationally coordinated stabilization program, but as a precondition for such a program . Though the advocates of the "convoy" approach would flinch from being called "global monetarists" they seem to me to be committing a very similar error to certain of the advocates of European monetary union among the latter group in believing that exchange rate stability can be treated, if not as an instrument of policy then at least as an intermediate target. In my view, the monetary approach to balance of payments analysis tells us that such stability should be looked upon at best as a by-product of each country individually achieving a long-run price stability goal, not as a tool whereby such a goal can be achieved and maintained.[12]

The argument of the last paragraph in and of itself perhaps provides sufficient reason to cease taking the "convoy" approach seriously, but there is another deeper flaw in that approach that merits some discussion. As I have already pointed out, it rests on the proposition that what no one country acting alone can accomplish, all countries acting together can accomplish, namely achieve a significantly higher level of economic activity without generating an unacceptably high inflation rate in the process. This proposition stems from the belief that the inflationary pressures which are transmitted through the foreign exchange market in the single country case will be absorbed into higher output when all countries expand together. The

---

[12] See Fratianni and Peeters (1978) for material on these issues.

monetary approach to balance of payments analysis tells us that when policies are arranged so that exchange rates are stable, prices are determined on a worldwide basis as if the world economy were one closed system.[13] Thus, closed economy monetarist analysis becomes relevant, and that analysis warns that the expansion of output achieved by the "convoy" approach will, if it is too rapid and taken too far, simply be a prelude to accelerating worldwide inflation. In effect, the monetary approach predicts that expansion coordinated across countries is likely at best to delay the onset of inflation rather than prevent it. This prediction follows from a belief that price rigidity in such "fix-price" markets as those for labour is not absolute, that such markets display a sluggishness on the part of prices to respond to excess demand rather than a complete absence of such a response.

Of course, if expansion is not "too rapid" and is not taken "too far" it will not lead to an accelerating inflation. However this qualification leads us back to the question of how much we know about the structure of the economy. If we do not know how rapid is rapid enough, or how far is far enough in the context of the world economy and I do not believe we do, then we cannot design an activist policy for it.[14]

IV. Some current British problems

If an internationally coordinated attack on high unemployment and rapid inflation is impractical as I believe it is, then we are reduced to facing up to such issues on a piecemeal country by country basis. What then does the monetary approach have to say about current British problems? Once more, it has more to say about what is unlikely to help, than about what will help. In particular it suggests that both wage and price controls and import controls are in large measure beside the point, for reasons that by now are surely well known. It also tells us that monetary and exchange rate policy can do nothing to ameliorate the problems caused for the rest of the economy by North Sea oil.

Let us first of all deal with wage and price controls. If the time path of prices and exchange rates is, in the long run, dominated by the interaction of the supply and demand for money then a policy which ignores the strategic role of money is going to fail. One lesson at least of 1972–74 is now widely accepted: namely that controls are bound to break down if an attempt is made to use them to offset the consequences of an otherwise inflationary policy. At best therefore, they can perhaps be deployed in order to damp down the consequences for income and employment of contractionary demand management policy, either because of some beneficial effects on

---

[13] Parkin (1977) gives a particularly clear account of this matter. Note also that the empirical work of Duck et al. (1976) and Gray et al. (1976) may be cited in support of this basic proposition.

[14] I believe that it is this issue above all which undermines the McCracken Report.

inflation expectations or because they can somehow lead to a pattern of wages and prices that is closer to that which will clear markets than that which market mechanisms left to themselves would produce. One cannot rule out either possibility *a priori*, unless one believes that the private sector forms its expectations "rationally" by observing monetary policy and un-biasedly predicting its consequences. In that case agents would set the structure of relative prices so as to conform to such predictions and a structure of market clearing prices would always prevail in any event. I would not wish to attack controls on these grounds. Rather I would yet again raise the matter of our ignorance of the economy's structure and point to the relevant implication of that ignorance: namely that if controls do help to get prices closer to a market-clearing structure, it is going to be more by accident than by design.[15]

One can push the argument further than this. If controls are effective in the sense that they make money wages and prices lower than they otherwise would be given the conduct of monetary policy, then the excess supply of money that in their absence would have been absorbed in higher domestic prices must make its presence felt elsewhere. Monetary analysis would tell us that, unless by some happy accident output rose to absorb this excess supply of money, extra downward pressure on the exchange rate would result, and that overall, the general price level would be much as it would have been in the absence of controls. Their primary effect would be on the structure of relative prices between what we are usually termed the "domestic" and "foreign" components of the price index, and on the level of real wages. If controls did generate, and then did maintain, lower real wages that would probably eventually lead to higher employment but the history of those wage-price control experiments which have initially produced real wage cuts does not make one optimistic on this score. This experience suggests that a breakdown of controls with subsequent catch-up effects seems the more likely outcome in the longer run, with a renewal of all the political tensions that usually accompany such a sequence of events.

In short, what we know about the economy's structure is insufficient to enable us to design a helpful wage-price control scheme except by accident, and the monetary approach tells us that an unhelpful scheme rather than being merely irrelevant is likely to be actually damaging. The monetary approach casts a similarly unfavourable light upon import controls schemes. To the extent that import controls are effective, and remove pressure from the trade account, the monetary approach tells us that such pressure will simply manifest itself in the capital account instead, producing much the same effect on the exchange rate as would have been generated in their absence given the conduct of monetary policy. Not quite the same effect, however, because, the demand for money depends partly upon income, and

---

[15] And of course there is also the matter of the wide variety of empirical evidence, none of which to my knowledge points to any systematic long-term effects of wage and price controls on the behavior of money wages and prices.

to the extent that import controls influence this they will also influence the exchange rate. And none of this is to mention the other well-known problems, in the main associated with the slowing down of desirable structural change and the protection of inefficiency, to which import controls give rise.

The last few paragraphs have ignored the fact that uncomfortably high inflation and unemployment in Britain are now (1980) thanks largely to North Sea oil, accompanied not by a falling but by a rising exchange rate. One of those "other things" usually assumed constant when the monetary approach to exchange rate analysis is employed has in this case changed with a vengeance in the last few years, and the equilibrium exchange rate has shifted up markedly. At the moment, certain sectors of the economy, particularly import substitute and export manufacturing, are finding things difficult, and there is a strong tendency to argue that if only the exchange rate could be held at a lower rate than it is now taking, such difficulties would be alleviated.

The first thing to be said here is that not all of British industry's problems should be laid at the door of North Sea oil. In the 1970s problems of structural readjustment, for example in steel and car production, were faced only slowly, and are now being tackled with inevitably disruptive effects. Moreover, the world economy is moving into a sharp recession in 1980. Both of these factors would have caused difficulties for large segments of British Industry regardless of the behaviour of the exchange rate. Furthermore, it seems to most observers that, perhaps as a result of the sharp tightening of monetary policy that took place in the winter of 1979–80, the exchange rate has actually moved above its equilibrium level. If that is true, the effect in question will be temporary, and ought not to be the cause of anything other than temporary inconvenience.

Nevertheless, setting aside all these other factors, the equilibrium exchange rate has certainly risen, and is associated with grave difficulties for certain segments of the economy. However, the monetary approach tells us that, genuine though these problems may be, to treat the exchange rate's behaviour as their cause rather than as an associated effect of something more fundamental is a mistake. What has happened is that a new and extremely productive industry in the shape of North Sea oil has been developed, and certain decisions have been taken about its scale of operations. Given those decisions that industry competes with the rest of the economy for resources and the currently higher exchange rate is in part at least an indirect manifestation of that competition. Sectors which cannot maintain their scale of operations at the current equilibrium exchange rate are forced to release resources to those that are expanding.

However, because North Sea oil is much less labour intensive than much manufacturing, because labour market rigidities prevent wages adjusting quickly, and because of the many barriers to geographical as well as occupational mobility of labour, much of the labour that is being released is ending up unemployed rather than redeployed, and the fact that this is a "short run" problem of adjustment does not mean that it is going to disappear quickly. The key question, though is whether policies designed to lower the exchange rate can alleviate the problem, and the monetary approach yields a negative answer. The exchange rate could certainly be moved to a lower level if the authorities were to create money at a more rapid rate than they are now doing. Such a policy would drive the exchange rate down, but it would also drive domestic money wages and prices up more rapidly, leaving the rest of the economy in much the same real competitive position.

Thus, to the extent that industry's difficulties and the associated unemployment stem from the factors discussed here, attempts to alleviate them by driving down the exchange rate would not have the desired effects. It is the *real* exchange rate, the terms of trade, that has moved against British manufacturers, and except perhaps temporarily, the *real* exchange rate cannot be changed by changing the *nominal* exchange rate.

The development of North Sea oil, and whatever other factors may be at work on the real exchange rate, create genuine problems for the British economy having to do with resource allocation and income distribution but no solution to these problems can be found by manipulating the nominal exchange rate and the money supply. The latter are monetary variables and the problems in question are problems of the real economy. That does not mean that the problems are insoluble, or that the solutions to them cannot be influenced by policy. However, it does mean that guidance for their solution must be sought from the economic theory of allocation and distribution and not from the theory of money and prices. The monetary approach to balance of payments and exchange rate analysis belongs to the latter category and hence has nothing to say about these important problems.

V. Concluding comments

It is easy enough to give a brief summary of the arguments presented in this paper. The monetary approach to balance of payments theory is essentially an extension to the problems of the open economy of the most fundamental postulates of closed economy monetarism, namely that there exists a stable long-run aggregate demand for money function, and that, in the long run there is no money illusion. As with closed economy monetarism, the most basic policy implications of the monetary approach to balance of payments theory amount to an injunction not to ignore these two factors. In the first instance then, the approach provides a blueprint, not for getting out of trouble, but for staying out of it in the first place, and once an economy is in trouble, that is not the most attractive blueprint that an academic economist can offer the policymaker.[16]

---

[16] In putting matters this way I am reiterating a point which I first made in Laidler (1971). Thus this conclusion is not based solely upon hindsight.

However, I have argued that the monetary approach is by no means irrelevant to the diagnosis and treatment of the problems of an economy in trouble. At the very least it offers a framework in terms of which policy proposals based upon more activist preconceptions can be analyzed, and though a body of doctrine that suggests that policy activism is likely to be unsuccessful is not going to be popular, that does not mean that it is not useful. Even so, the uncommitted policymaker is entitled to ask for more than negative policy implications from a theoretical approach, and the monetary approach to balance of payments analysis does yield some, albeit not too original, positive advice.

To begin with, it tells us that, given the wide disparity of inflation rates in the international economy, whether or not a system of fixed exchange rates is desirable, it is not viable. Thus, it implies that policies should be designed on the assumption that exchange rate flexibility is going to persist into the foreseeable future. That in turn suggests that the exchange rate should not in any sense be made a policy target; its behaviour is going to be influenced by events abroad, over which domestic policymakers can have no control, as much as by their own policies. In such circumstances, domestic policies can be devoted to pursuing price level and employment targets. Given the position that I have taken in this paper about the state of our knowledge of the structure of the economy, the implication here is that, *as far as macro policy is concerned*, the best that can be done about employment is to pursue price stability and let employment take care of itself.

Let it be explicitly noted, though, that this in no way rules out the use of micro policies designed to enhance labour mobility, to deal with particular structural or regional problems, and so forth. To say that macro policies should not be geared to achieving employment targets in no way precludes the use of micro policies to that end.

As to how price stability should be pursued, unless the "new classical" economics, which in its extreme form says that the economy is always save for random disturbances in long-run equilibrium, is taken seriously, the answer yielded by the monetary approach is one word: "gradually". Such a conclusion is certainly not a novel one.[17] Nevertheless, in the field of economic policy, novelty is surely not a relevant criterion for judging a proposal. Therefore I offer no apology for concluding that monetary gradualism which carries with it no promise of rapid success in restoring macro equilibrium is the fundamental policy implication of the monetary approach to balance of payments and exchange rate analysis for the British Economy. The turn around in monetary policy that took place in 1979/80 was anything but gradual, coming as it did on top of a four percent upward push imparted to the consumer price index by the switch from direct to indirect taxation implemented in the 1979 Budget. Moreover I find it hard

---

[17] Again this conclusion is the same as that which I draw in (1971), and in a number of subsequent articles.

to defend the government's rigid pursuit of restrictive public sector borrowing targets at a time of deepening depression. That being said, the money supply growth targets which have been adopted for the next few years are more in keeping with gradualist principles. *If they are adhered to*, the next five years will provide something of a practical test of the basic policy implications of the monetary approach, a crude test, to be sure, but perhaps as clear cut as an economist has any right to expect the political process to generate.

REFERENCES

ARTIS, M. J. and LEWIS, M. K. (1976), "The Demand for Money in the United Kingdom 1963–1973," *Manchester School*, June, 147–181.

BALL, R. J. and BURNS, T. (1976), "The Inflationary Mechanism in the U.K. Economy," *American Economic Review* 66, September, 467–484.

BILSON, J. F. O. (1978), "A Dynamic Model of Devaluation," *Canadian Journal of Economics* 11, May, 194–209.

DUCK, N. W., PARKIN, J. M., ROSE, D. and ZIS, G. (1976), "The Determination of the Rate of Change of Wages and Prices in the Fixed Exchange Rate World Economy 1956–1970," in PARKIN J. M. and ZIS, G. (eds.), *Inflation in the World Economy*, Manchester, Manchester University Press.

FRATIANNI, M. and PEETERS T. (1978), *One Money for Europe*, London, Macmillan.

FRENKEL, J. A. (1976), "A Monetary Approach to the Exchange Rate: Doctrinal Aspects and Empirical Evidence," *Scandinavian Journal of Economics* 78, 200–224.

GRAY, M. R., WARD R. and ZIS G. (1976), "World Demand for Money," in PARKIN J. M. and ZIS G. (eds.), *Inflation in the World Economy*, Manchester, Manchester University Press.

HAHN, F. H. (1977), "The Monetary Approach to the Balance of Payments," *Jounal of International Economics* 7, August, 231–249.

JONSON, P. D. (1976), "Money and Economic Activity in the Open Economy, The United Kingdom 1880–1970," *Journal of Political Economy* 84, September/October, 979–1012.

KENNEDY, M. C. (1973), "Employment Policy—What Went Wrong?" in ROBINSON J. (ed.), *After Keynes*, Oxford, Basil Blackwell.

KINGSTON, G. H. and TURNOVSKY S. J. (1978), "A Small Economy in an Inflationary World: Monetary and Fiscal Policy Under Fixed Exchange Rates," *Economic Journal* 88, March, 18–43.

KORTEWEG, P. (1978), "Towards Full Employment and Price Stability: An Assessment and Appraisal of the OECD's McCracken Report," paper read at the Carnegie-Rochester Conference, Pittsburgh, November 1978, Erasmus University mimeo.

LAIDLER, D. (1971), "Monetarism, Stabilization Policy and the Exchange Rate," *The Bankers Magazine*, September.

—— (1975), *Essays in Money and Inflation*, Manchester, Manchester University Press, Chicago, University of Chicago Press.

—— (1976), "Inflation in Britain—A Monetarist Perspective," *American Economic Review* 66, September, 485–500.

—— (1978), "A Monetarist Viewpoint," in POSNER M. (ed.), *Demand Management*, London, Heinemann Educational Books for the SSRC.

—— (1980), "The Demand for Money in the United States Yet Again," in Brunner K. and Meltzer A. H. (eds.), *The State of Macroeconomics*, Amsterdam, North Holland.

LAIDLER, D. and O'SHEA P. (1980), "An Empirical Macro Model of an Open Economy Under Fixed Exchange Rates: The United Kingdom 1954–1970," *Economica* 47 (May) 141–158.

LEWIS, M. (1978), "Interest Rates and Monetary Velocity in Australia and the United States," *Economic Record*, April, 111–126.

LUCAS, R. E. JR. (1975), "An Equilibrium Model of the Business Cycle," *Journal of Political Economy* 83, November/December, 1113–1144.

MCCRACKEN, P. *et al.* (1977), *Towards Full Employment and Price Stability* (The McCracken Report), Paris, OECD.

MYHRMAN, J. (1976), "Experiences of Flexible Exchange Rates in Earlier Periods: Theories, Evidence and a New View," *Scandinavian Journal of Economics* 78, 169–196.

PARKIN, J. M. (1977), "A Monetarist Analysis of the Generation and Transmission of World Inflation, 1958–1971," *American Economic Review* 67, Papers and Proceedings, May.

PHILLIPS, A. W. (1954), "Stabilization in a Closed Economy," *Economic Journal* 64.

SARGENT, T. J. and WALLACE N. (1975), "Rational Expectations and the Theory of Economic Policy," Research Development, Federal Reserve Bank of Minneapolis, Studies in Monetary Economics 2.

WHITMAN, M. V. N. (1975), "Global Monetarism and the Monetary Approach to the Balance of Payments," *Brookings Papers on Economic Activity* 3, 491–536.

MONETARY POLICY, EXPECTATIONS AND REAL EXCHANGE RATE DYNAMICS*

By MICHAEL BEENSTOCK, ALAN BUDD and PETER WARBURTON

Introduction

THIS paper presents a general theoretical framework within which the role of the exchange rate in economic policy may be discussed. We believe that a general approach is necessary since much of the current policy debate is based on partial analysis or on ad hoc empirical assertions.[1]

The theoretical analysis is presented in Section I in which we use a small model of an open economy to explore the response of output, inflation and the exchange rate to a change in monetary policy. Since the results depend critically on the nature of expectations we consider the implications separately of adaptive and rational expectations.

In Section II we report the results of our empirical studies of exchange rate determination. We develop a general model of the exchange rate which incorporates the "structural" and "portfolio balance" approaches as well as the "purchasing power parity approach". We also examine the role of interest rate changes and North Sea oil in determining the level of sterling.

In Section III we conclude with a discussion of the policy issues arising from the paper as a whole. We distinguish between real shocks (such as the discovery and exploitation of North Sea oil) and nominal shocks (such as 'balanced' changes in the money supply). The former will have real effects on the economy in the long term; the latter will not. The real effects may include changes in the real money supply. Nominal shocks may also affect the real exchange rate in the short term. We argue that it is wrong to attempt to offset these real effects either in the short term or the long term. If intervention is thought desirable it should not be directed at the exchange rate, which is determined in an efficient market, but at those sectors of the economy—particularly labour markets—which operate inefficiently.

I. The model

In this section we discuss a general model of the economy and present the results of simulations following a policy shock, (Full details of the model are presented in the Appendix.) The model specifies the markets for goods, money, bonds, labour and foreign exchange and jointly determines output, employment, inflation, the exchange rate and financial aggregates through time. Since the dynamic behaviour of the model depends on the nature of expectations we consider specifications in which expectations about inflation

* The authors gratefully acknowledge the support of the SSRC.
[1] This is the case, for example, in the model presented by Dornbusch (1976) which has been influential in the debate about counter-inflationary policy in an open economy.

and the exchange rate are formed rationally and in which they are formed adaptively.

It transpires that even under the simplest of specifications the model is non-linear so that solutions have to be obtained numerically. This contrasts with the alternative procedure where implausibly simple models are specified which produce results which are analytically tractable but insufficiently general.

In the long run when expectations are fulfilled and portfolios are balanced the model implies that

(i) Output is equal to its 'natural' level which is inelastic in supply,
(ii) Real wages and unemployment are at their 'natural' levels,
(iii) The price level is proportionate to the stock of money and interest bearing bonds,
(iv) The rate of interest varies directly with the share of bonds in portfolios, and
(v) The exchange rate reflects purchasing power parity and so varies inversely with money and bonds for given world variables.

In the short term changes in monetary policy may affect output through real balance effects on consumption and through trade balance effects. These effects occur if prices do not adjust immediately. The real balance effect may be reinforced by a reduction in wealth caused by a temporary increase in interest rates. The trade balance effect occurs because the exchange rate may adjust more rapidly than domestic prices and export prices. These output effects in turn bring about an adjustment of prices through an augmented Phillips curve relationship.

Expectations

Expectations about the exchange rate and prices affect expenditure and pricing decisions throughout the model. We consider both adaptive and rational expectations. In the case of adaptive expectations the expectation formed in the current period (for the next period) rises in proportion to the current forecast error. For example, for the exchange rate:

$$_tS^e_{t+1} = S_t + \lambda(S_t - _{t-1}S^e_t)$$

where $_tS^e_{t+1}$ is the expectation formed in period t of the value of the exchange rate in period $t+1$.

Our second alternative is to assume that expectations are rational. In this case we postulate

$$_tS^e_{t+1} = \hat{S}_{t+1}$$

where $\hat{S}_{t+1}$ is the one period ahead solution generated by the model itself.

Since the simulations we present are deterministic rational expectations are equivalent to perfect foresight.

We simulate the model under three assumptions about the generation of expectations.

(i) Exchange rate and price expectations are rational
(ii) Exchange rate and price expectations are adaptive
(iii) Price expectations in the labour market are adaptive while all other expectations are rational.

We describe the first case as "rational"; the second as "adaptive" and the third case as "mixed". The third case is included because it has a fairly obvious intuitive appeal. In this case rational agents must take into consideration the irrational expectations of agents in the labour market. In the "rational" case we also explore the response of the economy under two conditions: where the policy change comes into effect immediately, and where it is announced in advance.

Policy simulations[2]

We use the model to simulate the consequences of a policy designed to reduce the rate of inflation. The policy change consists of a monetary contraction accompanied by a tightening of fiscal policy. This mirrors the intention of the Medium Term Financial Strategy introduced in the Budget of March 1980. It also reflects the main features of the policies introduced in the autumn of 1976 following the IMF 'Letter of Intent'.

Since the money supply is an endogenous variable in our model we do not set specific monetary targets. To do so would require the use of optimal control methods or a similar technique to provide solutions for the policy instruments through time. Although the Medium Term Financial Strategy does specify targets for the money supply we believe that our simulations capture the spirit of the strategy which relies on a progressive reduction in the ratio of the PSBR to GDP.

The actual policy change in the simulations is a 10 per cent reduction in public expenditure. (Our model does not allow for changes in tax rates but the use of public expenditure as an instrument corresponds to the intentions of the MTFS.) Our central assumption is that the fiscal contraction is accompanied by a balanced reduction in money supply and government bonds. (We call this case 'balanced finance'.) Under balanced finance the initial ratio of money to bonds is kept constant. However we also consider the case of unbalanced finance, i.e. where the ratio of money to bonds is changed. We believe that in practice there are bounds to the ratio of money to

[2] We are extremely grateful to Sean Holly and Andrew Longbottom for their assistance in running these simulations. Full details of the simulations are available on request.

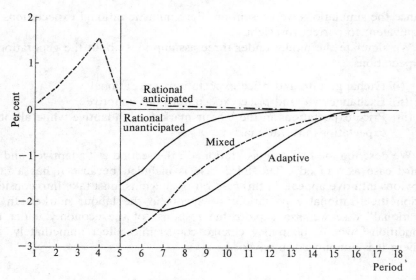

CHART 1. Deviations of output from its natural level

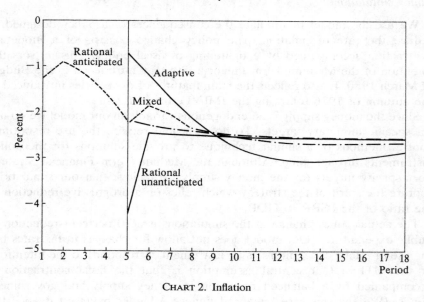

CHART 2. Inflation

bonds for otherwise interest rates would tend to zero or infinity along the lines discussed e.g. by Minford (1980). Nevertheless, for a temporary period bond finance may be feasible.

The simulation model is stationary and starts from a position of zero inflation. The shock involves a reduction of approximately 2 per cent *per period* in the money supply. Thus the relevant long term results are in terms

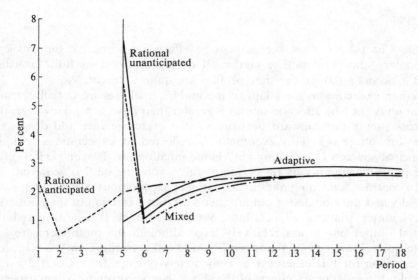

CHART 3. Rate of nominal exchange rate appreciation

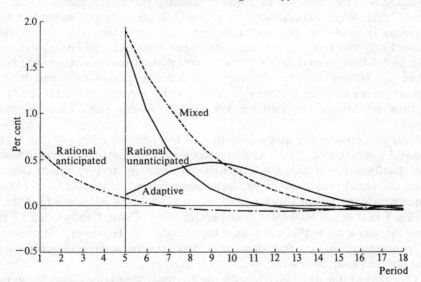

CHART 4. Deviations of the real exchange rate from its starting value

of the *level* of output, the level of the real exchange rate, nominal exchange *appreciation per period*, and the rate of price decrease per period. It is not implied that current policies are designed to reduce prices, but the results can be interpreted as showing the effect on the inflation rate etc of reducing monetary growth starting from a point at which the economy had fully adjusted to a particular monetary growth rate.

Output

On Chart 1 we show the percentage effects on output of the shock to monetary and fiscal policy. Under all of the assumptions full "crowding out"[3] occurs although the time profiles are quite different.

When expectations are adaptive the multiplier effects are initially greater than unity (i.e. the effect on output is greater than 2 per cent). However, this excess supply puts upward pressure on the exchange rate and downward pressure on prices. This eventually is reflected in expectations and the principal source of "crowding out" is the inflation tax. Eleven periods after the policy change occurs (in period 5) full "crowding out" is achieved.

In contrast "crowding out" under rational expectations occurs much more rapidly and the cumulative output effects are but a fraction of their counterparts under adaptive expectations. When the shock is unanticipated the initial output effects are relatively large although the multipliers are less than unity. However, by the seventh period full "crowding out" is achieved. The reason for this difference is immediately obvious from Chart 2 where we plot the inflationary effects of the shock. Not surprisingly, when expectations are adaptive inflation falls slowly reaching just below minus 3% in the steady state. When expectations are rational agents cotton on to the fact that inflation is going to fall and that the exchange rate is going to rise. Accordingly the rate of exchange rate appreciation exceeds its equilibrium rate (see Chart 3) and the net rate of disinflation exceeds its steady state value too (Chart 2). This reaction lasts for one period only and by the second period the steady state rate of inflation is more or less achieved. This in turn accelerates the inflation tax and "crowding out" happens more rapidly.

Next we consider the case when the shock is announced in advance under rational expectations. The unanticipated shock suggested that 'persistence' was distributed over about 4–7 periods. Accordingly, to give agents time to react the shock was announced four periods ahead of the actual event. In other words the actual shock occurs in period 5 but it is known for sure in period 1 that it will happen in four periods' time. Chart 1 shows that by the time the shock takes place output is hardly affected. However, the presence of 'persistence' implies that there will in general be some non-neutral lead and lag effects as indicated.

The reason for this is not difficult to understand as Chart 2 shows. Inflation falls in anticipation of the shock so that by period 5 the steady state rate of inflation has been more or less achieved. As inflation falls in this way there is actually some "crowding in" in advance of the shock. It can be

---

[3] "Crowding out" has become rather a vague concept. In this paper "crowding out" refers to changes in demand which offset an initial demand stimulus i.e. there is "crowding out" if the multiplier is less than unity (starting from a position of equilibrium). "Full crowding out" means that the multiplier is zero. "Crowding in" means that the multiplier is negative, i.e. a fiscal expansion reduces output or a fiscal contraction expands it.

shown that the longer the announcement period the closer to super-neutrality is the out-turn once the shock has occurred.

Finally we consider what happens in the mixed model when labour market expectations are adaptive and when the shock is unanticipated. Chart 1 shows that the outcome is a blend of the adaptive and rational cases although at the beginning and end of the lag distribution the mixed case is more deflationary.

It is worth pointing out that the budget deficit depends upon the structure of the model. Because the deficit depends upon output and the "crowding out" effects differ it follows that steady state rates of inflation will vary. It turns out (Chart 2) that the largest drop in inflation occurs when expectations are adaptive and the smallest when the policy change is announced in advance and expectations are rational.

Exchange Rates

Our primary concern is with the real exchange rate and on Chart 4 we plot the real exchange rate[4] multipliers obtained under the assumption of 'balanced finance'. In all of the cases the real exchange rate rises but once again the time profiles vary quite considerably. The rise in the real exchange rate reflects the greater flexibility of the exchange rate relative to domestic wage-price setting. Not surprisingly these effects tend to vanish as wages become more responsive to deviations of output from its 'natural' rate and as capital flows become less responsive to interest rates and expected changes in the exchange rate. Since there are no a priori restrictions on these parameters there is no iron law about the nature of the real exchange rate adjustment path. Nevertheless, most econometric models (including the London Business School model) generate the qualitative profiles shown on Chart 4.

The striking feature about this chart is that initially the real exchange rate effects under adaptive expectations are less pronounced than their counter-parts under rational expectations. This seems odd because rational expectations usually imply greater neutrality. The essential point to note is that under adaptive expectations there is more inertia to expectations so that prices and exchange rates do not vary so much in the early stages as may be seen from Charts 2 and 3. Consequently the real exchange rate is not so sensitive. In contrast, when expectations are rational both exchange rates and prices adjust more rapidly but the former move more rapidly than the latter through the structure of the model. Accordingly the real exchange rate response is initially greater.

Chart 4 shows that although the initial effect is smaller the real exchange rate disequilibrium lasts much longer under adaptive expectations. For example in the case of anticipated rational expectations there is no dis-equilibrium at all by the time the shock occurs and the lead effects are small

----

[4] Defined as $PX_t \cdot S_t$

and short-lived. This underlines the lack of generality of the Dornbusch model and the critical role played by expectations in the adjustment process. In particular the real exchange rate effects of changes in fiscal and monetary policy can be softened by sufficient foresight on the part of policymakers.

A further lesson from this exercise is that what really matters is real output rather than the real exchange rate. Charts 1 and 4 together show that in the short run although under adaptive expectations the real exchange rate effects are less pronounced the output effects are more pronounced. It is important therefore to consider the economy as a whole instead of focussing narrowly on the real exchange rate as a measure of the real disequilibrium following a fiscal-monetary shock of the kind described.

The nominal exchange rate paths are shown on Chart 3 and indicate that in all cases the exchange rate eventually tends to a constant rate of appreciation. However, the initial responses differ. When expectations are adaptive the rate of appreciation adjusts to the actual rate of appreciation from below since agents only come to expect appreciation after the event. When expectations are rational (unanticipated) the opposite tends to happen, i.e. the rate of appreciation adjusts to its steady state from above. This reflects the discontinuities implicit in the unannounced policy shock. Since rational expectations are forward looking and since the market has been surprised the exchange rate has to catch-up with its underlying path. While this catch-up is taking place the rate of appreciation will exceed its steady state. Clearly this kind of catch-up phenomenon should not be confused with overshooting. It therefore is meaningless to talk of a "high" or "low" exchange rate. What matters instead is whether the current exchange rate embodies all the available information in the sense of the efficient markets paradigm. If it does not it is meaningful to speak of "high" or "low" exchange rates but this valid concept is altogether different from the one that is popularized in the media and elsewhere, e.g. Allsopp and Joshi (1980).

Unbalanced finance

So far we have assumed that finance is balanced in the sense that the reduction in the budget deficit leaves the ratio of money to bonds unchanged. We now go on to consider the effects of unbalanced finance, i.e. when this ratio is allowed to alter. We consider two cases. In the first, "bond finance," the money supply is unchanged and the fall in the deficit is reflected in a fall in bonds. In the second, "money finance", bonds are unchanged and the fall in the deficit is reflected in a fall in the money supply.

On Chart 5 we compare the effects on output of money finance and bond finance when expectations are adaptive. The qualitative effects do not depend on the nature of expectations. The chart shows that "crowding out" takes place more rapidly when the ratio of bonds to money is reduced since interest rates are driven down by a reduction in government borrowing. This generates three forms of "crowding out". Firstly, declining interest rates will

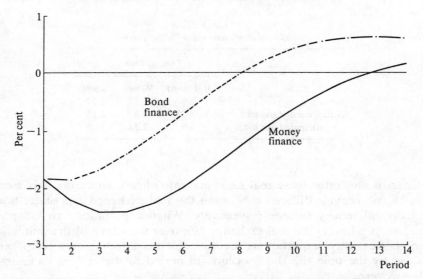

CHART 5. Deviations of output from its natural level following a 10 per cent reduction in government spending on the assumptions that the budget deficit is bond or money financed in model where expectations are adaptive

generate private expenditure increases along familiar lines. Secondly, as interest rates fall the market value of private sector wealth will rise and this will reduce saving and stimulate consumption. Thirdly, the real exchange rate may depreciate and the trade balance may rise. In other words the current account "crowds out" the capital account as lower domestic rates discourage foreign capital.

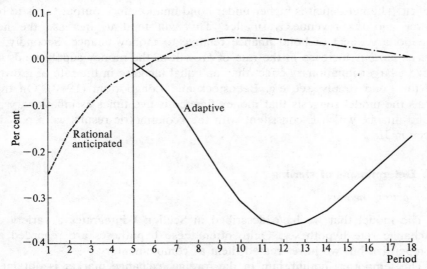

CHART 6. The difference between the responses of the real exchange rate to a 10 per cent reduction in government spending under the assumption of a bond-financed deficit relative to a money financed deficit

TABLE 1
Steady-state inflation rates (% per period)

| | Type of finance | | |
	Balanced	Money	Bonds
Adaptive	2.9	3.72	1.24
Anticipated Rational	2.57	3.3	1.13
Unanticipated Rational	2.6	3.38	1.06

Chart 6 illustrates these real exchange rate effects where the axis measures the percentage difference between the real exchange rate under bond finance and money finance respectively. When expectations are adaptive bond finance lowers the real exchange rate over the whole of the simulation period. But when expectations are rational this effect is only temporary. Indeed by the time the shock occurs (in period 5) the real exchange rate effect is zero.

As argued before, it is unreasonable to assume that the ratio of bonds to money can be changed without limit. Therefore, we do not believe that unbalanced finance can be used for very long.

Unbalanced finance will also alter the steady state rate of inflation when the demand for money is interest elastic. On Table 1 we summarize the steady state inflation rates for the various models under different financing assumptions. The table shows that money finance is about three times as inflationary as bond finance. However, Table 1 conceals two separate issues. First, different methods of finance will, as we have seen, affect the fiscal deficit. The net deficit is higher under bond finance since output tends to be lower and tax revenue is smaller. This will tend to increase the net inflationary effect of bond finance relative to money finance. Secondly, a *ceteris paribus* increase in the rate of growth of the money supply tends to have a larger inflationary effect than an equal increase in the rate of growth of the bond supply, see e.g. Beenstock and Longbottom (1980). On this basis the model suggests that money finance is five times as inflationary as bond finance which is consistent with the econometric results we report in Section II.

II. Determinants of sterling

Competing theories

The model that we have described in Section I integrates a variety of exchange rate hypotheses. Quite often these hypotheses are regarded as competitive but we have treated them as complementary.

The temporary equilibrium in the foreign exchange market is obtained according to the structural theory i.e. the exchange rate that satisfies the balance of payments identity. This equilibrium therefore embraces the trade elasticities model and the asset pricing or portfolio balance model e.g. Frankel (1979). Therefore the temporary equilibrium integrates a number of different strands of foreign exchange theory.

In addition the long run equilibrium exchange rate reflects purchasing power parity and the domestic price level and interest rate reflect internal and external portfolio balance. In the next section we show that under restrictive assumptions the monetary theory of the exchange rate is a special case of the generalized portfolio balance approach to macroeconomic analysis. We also integrate these theoretical approaches into an empirical model for the effective exchange rate for sterling.

In the foreign exchange market speculative factors are of paramount importance but they are extremely difficult to take account of in econometric estimation. This is particularly the case when expectations are rational and the parameters are not usually identified.[5] Most probably this suggests that our time would be better spent testing whether the foreign exchange market is efficient and that it is begging the question even to contemplate the estimation of predictive equations of the type that typically feature in econometric models. We therefore confess to an element of inconsistency which we justify by saying that we seek only to explain the past rather than to predict the future which is inherently impossible. We do no more than investigate basic trends in the exchange rate in the light of competing hypotheses and in so doing complement the efficient markets literature by identifying the main variables in the relevant information set.

Theory—Nominal

In what follows we seek to develop a theory about the long run determinants of the real and nominal exchange rates. The temporary equilibrium condition in the foreign exchange market is that the flow demand for foreign exchange must equal its flow supply as shown in the Appendix. The model as a whole implied that the real exchange rate was constant and since the domestic price level reflected the quantity of both money (M) and bonds (B) the long run equilibrium condition in the foreign exchange market required that S vary inversely with both M and B. We now propose to develop these issues.

We assume that the UK is a small open economy in the sense that it is affected by the world but is too small to significantly affect the rest of the world. The world demand for money function is assumed to vary inversely with the world interest rate, or

$$\ln M_w = \alpha_1 \ln Y_w - \alpha_2 \ln R_w + \ln P_w \qquad (1)$$

while the world demand for bonds varies directly with the world interest

[5] See Peseran (1980)

rate, or

$$\ln B_w = \beta_1 \ln Y_w + \beta_2 \ln R_w + \ln P_w \tag{2}$$

Both of these equations imply that asset demand functions are homogenous of degree one in prices.

Assuming that the world monetary authorities determine M_w and B_w we may solve equations (1) and (2) for P_w and R_w respectively as

$$\ln P_w = [\beta_2 \ln M_w + \alpha_2 \ln B_w - (\beta_2\alpha_1 + \beta_1\alpha_2) \ln Y_w]/(\alpha_2 + \beta_2) \tag{3}$$

$$\ln R_w = [\ln B_w - \ln M_w + (\alpha_1 - \beta_1) \ln Y_w]/(\alpha_2 + \beta_2) \tag{4}$$

The respective UK asset demand functions are written as

$$\ln M = \gamma_1 \ln Y - \gamma_2 \ln R + \ln P \tag{5}$$

$$\ln B = \delta_1 \ln Y + \delta_2 \ln R - \delta_3(\ln R_w - \dot{S}^e) + \ln P \tag{6}$$

i.e. external assets compete with domestic assets in portfolios.

Variable definitions

B: Stock of privately-held domestic bonds valued in nominal £
B_w: Stock of privately-held foreign bonds valued in nominal world currency
M: Stock of UK money, in nominal £
M_w: Stock of world money in nominal world currency
P: UK price level, sterling index
P_w: World price level, world currency index
R: UK interest rate, expressed as 1 plus % per annum/100
R_w: World interest rate, expressed as 1 plus % per annum/100
S^*: Long run equilibrium value of the index of the effective exchange rate for sterling
Y: UK index of Gross Domestic Product, in constant price £
Y_w: World index of Gross National Product, in constant price world currency.
$\dot{S}^e$: Expected change in exchange rate

The theory of Purchasing Power Parity (PPP), when applied to traded goods, implies that in the long run the real exchange rate is a constant, k. We shall defer consideration of the reasons why k may vary until the discussion below of the theory of the real exchange rate. Thus we define

$$\ln P + \ln S^* - \ln P_w = k \tag{7}$$

We may now solve this system for the long-run equilibrium exchange rate for given values of nominal asset stocks. Although in equilibrium Y and Y_w will be growing at their respective natural rates we must take account of their disparate levels. The equilibrium is thus defined as

$$\ln S^* = k + \left[\frac{\beta_2 \ln M_w + \alpha_2 \ln B_w}{(\alpha_2 + \beta_2)}\right] - \left[\frac{\delta_2 \ln M + \gamma_2 \ln B}{(\delta_2 + \gamma_2)}\right]$$
$$- \left[\frac{\delta_3 \gamma_2 (\ln B_w - \ln M_w)}{(\alpha_2 + \beta_2)(\delta_2 + \gamma_2)}\right] + \left[\frac{(\delta_1 \gamma_2 + \delta_2 \gamma_1)}{(\delta_2 + \gamma_2)}\right] \ln Y \qquad (8)$$
$$- \left[\frac{(\delta_2 + \gamma_2)(\alpha_1 \beta_2 + \alpha_2 \beta_1) + (\alpha_1 - \beta_1)\delta_3 \gamma_2}{(\alpha_2 + \beta_2)(\delta_2 + \gamma_2)}\right] \ln Y_w + \left(\frac{\delta_3 \gamma_2}{\delta_3 + \gamma_2}\right) \dot{S}^e$$

S^* varies inversely with M and B since the latter raise P. M_w raises S^* since it raises P_w as well as lowering R_w. However, the effects of B_w are ambiguous since it raises P_w and R_w. In the long run, S^* depends positively on Y and negatively on Y_w.

Equation (8) represents the long-run portfolio balance theory of the exchange rate since the exchange rate is generated by the balancing of portfolios in terms of money and bonds at home and abroad. However, when the demand for money is interest inelastic, i.e. when $\alpha_2 = \gamma_2 = 0$, it has a very familiar solution;

$$\ln S^* = k + \ln M_w - \ln M + \gamma_1 \ln Y - \alpha_1 \ln Y_w \qquad (9)$$

which is the relative money supply theory of the exchange rate. Thus the relative money theory is a special case of the portfolio balance theory.

Another special case arises when there is perfect capital mobility i.e. when $\delta_2 = \delta_3 = \infty$. In this case equation (8) simplifies to (ignoring terms in Y and Y_w):

$$\ln S^* = k + \frac{\beta_2 \ln M_w + \alpha_2 \ln B_w}{\alpha_2 + \beta_2} - \ln M - \gamma_2 (\ln R_w - \dot{S}^e) \qquad (9a)$$

i.e. the elasticity with respect to the domestic money stock is minus one and the domestic bond supply no longer affects the equilibrium exchange rate. However, external interest rates identify the domestic interest elasticity of the demand for money.

Therefore equation (8) may be used to test a number of hypotheses, including the monetary theory, the portfolio balance theory and the interest parity theory. If $\ln B$ enters the solution and the coefficient of $\ln M$ is less than unity the monetary and interest parity theories must be rejected in favour of the less restrictive portfolio balance theory.

Theory—Real

Equation (8) describes a theory of the long run nominal exchange rate. We now turn to the determinants of the real exchange rate in the long run. We propose to derive these determinants using the balance of payments flow equilibrium identity

$$CA + DK - \text{BOF} = 0 \qquad (10)$$

where CA and DK represent the current and capital accounts of the UK balance of payments and where BOF (balance for official financing) represents the government's spot market intervention. The current account depends on the real exchange rate but it also depends in the UK on exogenous factors such as the production of North Sea oil (NSO). In principle NSO need not affect the current account since UK beneficiaries might spend all their income on traded goods. In practice, however, this seems unlikely since they will wish to increase their consumption of non-tradeables which by definition cannot be provided through the balance of payments.

Whilst it is clear that an increase in domestic demand for goods will worsen the UK current account and that an increase in foreign demand for goods will have the opposite effect, it is unclear whether these effects will be permanent.

A more permanent influence on the current account is thought to be the differences in the supply characteristics of aggregate production at home and abroad which result in differential rates of productivity growth in the respective traded goods sectors. This phenomenon has been widely discussed since the contribution of Balassa (1964). In the absence of a series for world employment we approximate this productivity bias effect by relative GDP, thereby making the assumption that the ratio of UK employment to world is constant around a trend.

Since we observe neither the demand nor the supply of goods, we must regard the sign of the long-run relative output effect on the real exchange rate, through the current balance, as an empirical matter. However, our theory suggests that a short-run negative relative output effect may be followed by a positive long-run effect. Hence

$$CA = CA[\bar{k}, \overset{+}{N}SO, \bar{\Delta} Y, \Delta \overset{+}{Y}_w, \overset{+}{Y}, \bar{Y}_w] \tag{11}$$

where the signs above the variables refer to partial derivatives.

As noted in the Appendix, capital flows depend on changes in the uncovered interest rate differential and changes in the expected rate of exchange rate appreciation. There are particular factors which affect UK exchange rate expectations. For example when a North Sea oil discovery is made, or when the estimated existing stock of oil is revalued by an increase in the real price of oil, there is an expectation of a higher exchange rate underpinned by the larger implied value of future oil production. The variable which we use in the empirical section which follows is slightly more complicated than the basic concept of discoveries and deserves explanation. Its definition is given below.[6]

$$\Delta \text{OILRES}/_t = \frac{(\text{DISC}_t - \text{NSO}_t) \cdot \text{PNSO}_t}{\text{GDP } \pounds E_t} \tag{11a}$$

Thus current production of oil (in millions of tonnes) is subtracted from

---

[6] Data definitions are given in Table 2.

current discoveries of oil (DISC) before valuing the difference at current prices and dividing through by the nominal value of GDP. It is important to realise that ΔOILRES/ will actually fall if there are no discoveries and also if the relative price of oil in terms of other goods falls. It should be noted that the capital account effect of a discovery is shortlived; in order to cause a sustained capital account inflow, it would be necessary for the pace of discovery of new oil resources to increase. A further source of capital account disturbance is the demand for sterling denominated assets by OPEC following large current account surpluses as a result of sudden oil price increases. Again, the effect is expected to be temporary, and it would require the investment of some proportion of sustained OPEC surpluses to have a permanent affect on the UK capital account and thence the exchange rate. However, it is equally possible that, by depositing larger quantities of short-term money in other financial centres, sterling may effectively *depreciate*, and therefore the sign on BALOPEC, suitably normalised, is indeterminate. Hence we may write

$$DK = DK(\Delta \overset{+}{R}S, \Delta \bar{R}S_w, \Delta(_tS_{t+1}^{e+} - S_t)) \tag{12}$$

Combining equations (10) to (12) we can write a composite real exchange rate specification

$$k = k[\overset{-}{\text{NSO}}, \bar{\Delta} Y, \Delta \overset{+}{\bar{Y}}_w, \overset{+}{Y}, \bar{Y}_w, \Delta \overset{+}{R}S, \Delta \bar{R}S_w \ \Delta(_tS_{t+1}^{e+} - S_t), \text{B}\bar{\text{O}}\text{F}/] \tag{13}$$

where BOF/ is defined as BOF divided by the value of total exports. The principal determinants of ΔRS, ΔRS_w and $\dot{S}^{e7}$ are the relative asset stock growth rates while $\dot{S}^e$ will also depend upon changes in the expected rate of production of North Sea oil (reflecting depletion policy) and upon the pace of discoveries of new oil reserves. Thus,

$$\dot{S}^e = S(\Delta M, \Delta B, \Delta M_w, \Delta B_w, \Delta \text{NSO}, \Delta^2 \text{OILRES}/, \text{BALOPEC}) \tag{13a}$$

Integrating the arguments of equations (8) and (13) yields a rich theory of the determination of the equilibrium exchange rate which is represented below as a regression specification.

$$\ln S^* = a_0 + a_1 \ln M_w + a_2 \ln B_w + a_3 \ln M + a_4 \ln B + a_5 \ln Y + a_6 \ln Y_w$$
$$+ a_7 \ln \text{NSO} + a_8 \Delta \ln Y + a_9 \Delta \ln Y_w + a_{10}\Delta nRS + a_{11}\Delta nRS_w$$
$$+ a_{12}\Delta \text{OILRES}/ + a_{13}\text{BALOPEC}/ + a_{14}\text{BOF}/ \tag{14}$$

The determinants of $\dot{S}^e$ are omitted from this list but they consist of higher order difference terms in the asset stocks and North Sea oil variables. The actual effective exchange rate at time t, S_t, is assumed to adjust to S^* in equilibrium but its path to equilibrium will be disturbed by movements in $_tS_{t+1}^e$ reflecting new information available to the market. The adjustment

---

[7] For convenience we refer to $(_tS_{t+1}^e - S_t)$ as $\dot{S}^e$ in the text.

function can be written

$$\Delta \ln S_t = \lambda_1 \Delta \ln {}_t S_{t+1}^e - \lambda_2 \ln \left(\frac{S}{S^*}\right)_{t-1} + \varepsilon_t \qquad (15)$$

where ε_t is normally and independently distributed with zero mean and constant variance.

Empirical Results

In this section we summarize our empirical estimates of equation (14) with several objectives in mind. First we wish to test the monetary theory of the exchange rate (which implies that $a_1 = 1$, $a_3 = -1$ and $a_4 = a_2 = 0$) against the generalized portfolio balance theory (which implies $a_3 + a_4 = -1$). Secondly, we wish to test the sensitivity of the exchange rate to capital flows induced by interest rate changes. Of special interest in this context is the test for perfect capital mobility that is suggested by equation (9a). Thirdly, we seek empirical estimates for the sensitivity of the exchange rate to North Sea oil production (a_7) and the announcement of oil discoveries (a_{12}). Finally, we consider the sensitivity of the exchange rate to OPEC's current balance (a_{13}) and official intervention in the foreign exchange market (a_{14}).

Details of the econometric results are presented in Warburton and Beenstock (1980). The estimation methodology follows the procedures described in Davidson et al. (1978) and Mizon (1977) which enable us to disentangle dynamic responses from steady state solutions. In Table 2 we report the steady state solutions obtained from quarterly data over the period 1970Q1–1978Q4. The data definitions are provided below the estimates. Although the lag distributions from the estimated equations are important, space prevents their inclusion here.

1. The monetary theory

Case 1A in Table 2 is the familiar relative money supply model in which we find that the homogeneity restriction that $a_1 = 1$ and $a_3 = -1$ is not rejected by the data. This serves as our starting point and may be regarded as an unconstrained dynamic version of the equation previously reported by Ball, Burns and Warburton (1980). In case 1B we test the strict monetarist model by including B, the quantity of government debt held by the non-bank private sector. We find that the statistical performance of the model is improved by this modification and that the homogeneity restriction now applies to $\hat{a}_3 + \hat{a}_4 = -1$. However, the weight on $\ln M$ is four times larger than the weight on $\ln B$, a result which broadly corresponds with the analysis of inflation in Beenstock and Longbottom (1980) and which rejects the Quantity Theory in favour of the more generalized portfolio balance theory. However, attempts to replace world asset data by price data (P_w replaces M_w) in case 1C reduced the statistical performance of the model but still confirmed the portfolio balance model.

This result suggests that the asset theory of the exchange rate for which the monetarist model is a special case may be usefully extended to embrace government debt.

2. Interest rate effects

Case 2 integrates interest rate effects into the basic model. In every case the restrictions suggested by equation (9a) were rejected. Therefore we must reject the hypothesis of perfect capital mobility. Case 2A indicates that *changes* in external interest rates only exert temporary effects on the exchange rate, i.e. they are inherently short-lived. This is because they generate a once-and-for-all stock adjustment which puts temporary pressure on the capital account. Once this effect has passed the long run stock equilibrium prevails once more.

It will be noted that in Case 2 the exchange rate varies inversely with the *level* of domestic interest rates and positively with the level of foreign interest rates. This may appear to contradict the intuitive view that high interest rates attract capital inflows and raise the exchange rate. The result is however consistent with the monetary approach and with the broader portfolio balance approach to exchange rate determination. According to the monetary approach a rise in interest rates will reduce the demand for money and will therefore lower the exchange rate for a given relative quantity of money. Alternatively, the rise in domestic interest rates stands as a proxy for an increase in the supply of bonds, which lowers the exchange rate via the portfolio balance approach.

3. Oil effects

Cases 3A and 3B confirm the importance of both oil effects that we identified in theory. First the flow of North Sea oil production affects the real exchange rate as does the announcement of oil discoveries. The latter effect generates a speculative inflow on the capital account. Just as interest rates improved the basic model so do the two North Sea oil effects. However, in none of the cases was it possible to identify a systematic BALOPEC effect. The evidence therefore rejects the hypothesis that OPEC surpluses significantly affect the exchange rate.

4. Integrated model

Case 4 brings together all of the above elements into a comprehensive model. Unfortunately degrees of freedom are in short supply and the *LM* statistic in Case 4B suggests over-fitting. Nevertheless we shall adopt this result as representing the comprehensive model since it incorporates generalized portfolio balance effects, interest rate effects and oil effects. This equation suggests:

(a) by mid-1980 the steady state real exchange rate was 14 per cent

TABLE 2 *Steady state influences upon*

Case	$n\left(\dfrac{NSO£}{X£}\right)$	$\Delta_4\left(\dfrac{OILRES}{GDP£E}\right)$	$\ln(M/Y)$	$\ln(B/Y)$	$\ln(M_w/Y_w)$	$\ln(Y/Y_w)$	$\Delta\ln(Y/Y_w)$	$\ln P_w$
1								
A			−1.0		1.0	2.4	−1.22	
B			−0.88	−0.12	1.0	2.07	−0.87	
C			−0.68	−0.32		1.34	−1.08	1.0
2								
A			−1.0		1.0	2.12	−2.06	
B			−1.0		1.0	1.91	−2.33	
C⁺			−1.0		1.0	0.92	−2.37	
3								
A	7.13	0.035	−1.0		1.0	4.8		
B	1.71	0.017	−0.84	−0.16	1.0	2.63	−0.69	
4								
A	6.16	0.025	−1.0		1.0	4.63	−2.04	
B	4.43	0.026	−0.79	−0.21	1.0	3.51		
C	3.23	0.017	−1.0		1.0	3.24	−1.26	

Critical values for test statistics

[+] Equation 2C was estimated using two stage least squares. Elsewhere estimates are OLS

a) *Data Definitions and Sources*

B:	Total non-bank private domestic holdings of British government securities at nominal value £m
Source:	Bank of England Quarterly Bulletin annual article on the composition of the national debt. Quarterly values were obtained using the net acquisitions data as a guide to the quarterly pattern.
BALOPEC:	Exports (f.o.b.) minus imports (c.i.f.) of the oil exporting countries expressed in billions of US$.
Source:	IMF International Financial Statistics
BOF:	Balance for official financing, £m. Source: Financial Statistics
DISC:	The annual change in the Estimated Possible Reserves of North Sea oil in millions of tonnes.
Source:	Department of Energy Brown Books
GDP£E:	Gross Domestic Expenditure at Current Prices £m, SA. Source: Economic Trends
M:	Sterling M3 money stock index (1975 = 1) derived from the series provided in the Bank of England Quarterly Bulletin
M_w:	Index of World M3 money stock (1975 = 1) constructed from 17 individual country indices using geometric trade weights
NSO:	Production of North Sea oil in millions of tonnes per quarter.
Source:	Oil facts (Hoare Govett) and Department of energy
NSO£:	The value of North Sea oil production at current prices £m, derived as the product of NSO and PNSO£
OILRES:	The value of estimated North Sea oil reserves in the ground at current prices. Defined as on p. 98.
P:	Index of World Wholesale Prices in World currency (1975 = 1). Constructed from 17 individual country indices.
PNSO£:	Price of a typical tonne of North Sea oil in £. Constructed using $ prices and period average exchange rates.
RS:	Short term rate of interest (91 day Treasury Bill Rate) in % per annum
Source:	Bank of England Quarterly Bulletin
RS_w:	World* short term interest rate, % p.a., constructed as a weighted average of US, Japan, Germany & France.
RL:	Redemption yield on medium dated UK government stocks, % p.a. Source: Bank of England Quarterly Bulletin

the effective exchange rate for sterling (i.e. foreign currency per pound)

		Capital account effects						Test statistics		
nRS	ΔnRS	nRS_w	ΔnRS_w	n(RL − RL_w)	Constant	$\bar{R}^2$	SE	Q(8)	LM(5)	Chow(6, 20)
					−0.1	0.358	0.023	10.4	7.3	3.8
					−0.05	0.57	0.019	11.8	8.9	4.2
					−0.03	0.46	0.021	8.0	11.5	4.1
		−3.1	−0.51		−0.09	0.652	0.017	10.4	10.7	8.2
−0.79		0.79	−2.17		−0.09	0.651	0.017	13.2	14.9	10.8
−4.93	3.22	5.19	−1.45		−0.08	0.83	0.012	8.7	8.7	20.1
					−0.24	0.529	0.02	9.2	9.5	1.9
					−0.08	0.788	0.013	19.8	18.1	4.5
		−3.22			−0.26	0.761	0.014	7.9	8.3	4.7
	0.79	−0.79			−0.13	0.781	0.014	13.3	14.3	4.1
			(BOF/X£)							
			−2.22	−0.07	−0.15	0.83·	0.0121	19.8	14.9	7.3
								(15.5)	(11.1)	(3.6)

RL_w:	World* long term interest rate, derived as a weighted average of secondary market yields of securities of maturity greater than 10 years for US, Japan, Germany and France.
S:	Effective Exchange Rate Index (1975 = 1) in foreign currency per £. Source: B. of E. quarterly Bulletin.
$X£$:	Total UK exports of goods and services at current prices, £m. Source: Economic Trends.
Y:	Index of UK Gross Domestic Product at constant 1975 prices (1975 = 1). Source: Economic Trends.
Y_w:	Index of World* Gross National Product 1975 = 1. Constructed as a weighted average of the six largest non-UK countries' GNP

 * excluding UK

b) *Syntax of symbols used*

Δ:	First difference operator
Δ^2:	First difference of a first difference operator
$\ln x$:	Natural logarithm of x
$n(x)$:	$\ln\left[1+\left(\dfrac{x}{100}\right)\right]$

c) *Explanation of diagnostic statistics used*

$\bar{R}^2$:	Multiple correlation coefficient adjusted for degrees of freedom.
SE:	Estimated equation standard error.
$Q(X)$:	Small sample Box-Pierce statistic testing the null hypothesis of randomness of the residual correlogram to degree X. If the Chi-squared value in parenthesis (e.g. 15.5) is exceeded by the test statistic value which precedes it, then the null hypothesis may be rejected at the 95% confidence level.
$LM(Y)$:	A Lagrange-Multiplier test for the joint significance of the first Y autocorrelation coefficients. A test statistic which exceeds the bracketed chi-squared value indicates the presence of significant autocorrelation.
$Chow(Z_1, Z_2)$:	The Chow statistic tests the hypothesis that the residual sum of squares from the equation estimated over an additional Z_1 observations belongs to the same population as the residual sum of squares from the original equation estimated with Z_2 degrees of freedom. This statistic has an F-distribution and the 99% critical value is given in brackets. Again if this value is exceeded, the test fails.

higher on account of North Sea oil production than would have been the case without North Sea oil,

(b) a one percent increase in UK oil reserves raises the real exchange rate by approximately 2.5 per cent in the short run,

(c) an increase in the uncovered interest rate differential by one annual percentage point temporarily raises the exchange rate by 0.8 per cent,

(d) an increase in the domestic money stock by one per cent eventually leads to a depreciation of about 0.8 per cent,

(e) a one per cent increase in the stock of government bonds held outside the banking sector eventually leads to a depreciation of 0.2 per cent, and

(f) a one per cent increase in the world quantity of money eventually leads to a proportionate appreciation in the nominal exchange rate.

It should go without saying that these estimates only indicate broad orders of magnitude and should be treated with the usual caution accorded to econometric estimates. However, Table 2 suggests that the oil and portfolio effects are more robust than the interest rate effects. Finally, Case 4C shows that official exchange rate intervention has a temporary effect on the exchange rate. For intervention to have a permanent real effect infinite intervention would be necessary which is quite obviously beyond the capacity of the authorities to implement.

Identification of the Structural Parameters

It is interesting at this point to note that the framework developed earlier in this section, whilst overdetermined in terms of the parameters of the nominal exchange rate model and the equation dynamics, is nearly identified in the case of the steady states of the real variables.

Rewriting equations (10) to (12) as parametric functions and making certain simplifying assumptions we may write:

$$\frac{CA}{X\pounds} = -\alpha_1 \ln \left(S^* \cdot \frac{P}{P_w} \right) + \alpha_2 \ln \left(\frac{Y}{Y_w} \right) + \alpha_3 \left(\frac{NSO\pounds}{X\pounds} \right) \tag{16}$$

$$\frac{DK}{X\pounds} = \beta_1 \Delta n (RS - RS_w) + \beta_2 \Delta^2 \frac{OILRES}{GDP\pounds E} + \beta_3 BALOPEC \tag{17}$$

Thence:

$$k = \ln \left(S^* \cdot \frac{P}{P_w} \right) = \frac{\alpha_2}{\alpha_1} \ln \left(\frac{Y}{Y_w} \right) + \frac{\alpha_3}{\alpha_1} \left(\frac{NSO\pounds}{X\pounds} \right) + \frac{\beta_1}{\alpha_1} \Delta n (RS - RS_w)$$

$$+ \frac{\beta_2}{\alpha_1} \Delta^2 \left(\frac{OILRES}{GDP\pounds E} \right) + \frac{\beta_3}{\alpha_1} BALOPEC \tag{18}$$

In order to identify the structural parameters of (19) an assumption about α_3 is necessary. The parameter α_3 represents the proportion of North Sea oil production (and therefore income) that is not offset by expenditure on

TABLE 3
Long run structural parameters

Symbol	Meaning	Equation 4A	Equation 4B
α_1	Elasticity of exports relative to imports with respect to the real exchange rate	0.10	0.14
α_2	Effect of relative real GDP on the current account	0.47	0.50
	(Implied productivity bias effect	−0.85%p.a.	−0.91%p.a.)
α_3	Net effect of North Sea oil production on the current account	0.63*	0.63*
β_1	Elasticity of capital account credits relative to debits with respect to the interest rate differential	0.33	0.11
β_2	Elasticity of capital account credits relative to debits with respect to the pace of North Sea oil discoveries per unit of nominal GDP	0.0025†	0.0036†

* Assumed value
† This coefficient applies to a temporary, not a sustained capital inflow. The precise definition of (OILRES/GDP£E) is given on p. 98, equation 11a.

traded goods, in other words, α_3 is the net effect of North Sea oil on the current balance of payments. Using the analysis and assumptions of Forsyth and Kay we can deduce an implicit value of α_3, if we make the extra assumption that no more than half of UK primary production is exported. Thus the addition of £10b to net output results in an additional £3.7b of imports implying $\alpha_3 = 0.63$.

On this basis we show on Table 3 the implied long run structural parameters of the model for Cases 4A and 4B.

If $\hat{\alpha}_1 = 0.14$, we can deduce that the absolute value of the sum of the export and import real exchange rate elasticities is 1.14. This implies rather smaller overall trade elasticities than empirical studies from the 1950's and 1960's indicated, although more recent studies have found import elasticities of about a half, e.g. Whitley (1977). Since our entire estimation period spans only the 1970's, if the relative price elasticities of export and import demand functions have in fact declined then the estimate above seems quite plausible.

A value of 0.11 for $\hat{\beta}_1$ implies that a one per cent increase in the uncovered interest rate differential would generate a meagre capital inflow of £18 millions. Even allowing for a large degree of underestimation of $\hat{\alpha}_1$, the capital account response is unlikely to exceed £100 millions. Either way the interest elasticity is low and much removed from the estimates implied by perfect capital mobility.

Predictive performance

We retained 1979Q1–1980Q2 for predictive testing. For the most part Table 2 indicates that the various models failed the predictive Chow tests. In our view this is hardly surprising; in an efficient market models that describe average dynamic behaviour over the past are unlikely to explain dynamic responses outside the observation period. Our concern instead is with predicting the general trend in the exchange rate rather than the changes from one quarter to the next. We are not aware that appropriate test statistics exist for such purposes. Nevertheless in Table 4 we report the percentage prediction errors for the *level* of the effective exchange rate in 1980Q2, i.e. after the sharp appreciation up to that time. The table shows that Case 3 results raise the level of the exchange rate, a property which carries over to the Case 4 results.

TABLE 4
Percentage prediction errors for the exchange rate in 1980Q2

Equation	1A	1B	1C	2A	2B	3A	3B	4A	4B	4C
Error	−11.1	−13.8	−11.9	−8.4	−11.9	8	−0.1	11.1	6.7	6.7

Note: A negative sign indicates underprediction. Predictions assume that lagged endogenous and exogenous variables are known.

Thus the results imply that the rise in sterling was principally due not to interest rates but to oil. Of course these equations necessarily omit other speculative influences. For example the Medium-Term Financial Strategy published in March 1980 implied that the money supply in 1983/84 would be about 30% below what might have been previously expected (assuming expected monetary growth were 15% per annum). In an efficient market this 'news' would tend to raise the exchange rate by a substantial amount. If the 'news' were completely credible sterling would have appreciated by 30% more or less immediately.

III. The exchange rate and economic policy

In this section we consider the implications for economic policy of the theoretical studies presented in Section I and the empirical studies presented in Section II. Our conclusions may be summarised by re-stating the general rule of economics that nominal shocks to the economy have nominal effects and real shocks have real effects. It is therefore fruitless to attempt to produce real changes to an economy by manipulating nominal variables such as the exchange rate. This general rule clearly holds in the long term; but we argue that even if there appears to be some means (according to some models) for changing real variables in the short term this does not justify an interventionist exchange rate policy.

It is important to distinguish two separate issues which frequently become confused in the discussion of exchange rate policy. The first involves a debate about social welfare functions; the second involves a debate about the behaviour of the economy. Many who wish to intervene are in effect arguing that a lower priority should be given to price stability and a higher priority should be given to output. That argument is beyond the scope of this paper; we are concerned only with the technical trade-off between output and inflation. The important questions are how does it arise, what is its empirical value, and are there any policy measures which could alter it? We argue that the emphasis on the exchange rate in this regard is mistaken. The problem arises because markets for goods and labour (particularly the latter) operate inefficiently. It is in those markets that policy changes should be introduced, not in the market for foreign exchange.

Section I concentrated on the effects of changes in fiscal and monetary policy on the nominal and real exchange rate. Section II suggested that, in addition to monetary policy, North Sea oil has had significant effects. In this section we consider the policy debate that has arisen from both these sources. We consider them separately since there is an important distinction between them. The discovery, exploitation and changes in the prices of North Sea oil are all real developments while changes in monetary policy (provided the changes are 'balanced' in the sense defined in Section I) are, by contrast, nominal developments. The former will have long-term real effects; the latter will not. We consider monetary policy first.

Monetary policy and the exchange rate

Section I examined the response of the economy to "balanced" and "unbalanced" changes in monetary policy. The balanced changes involve a proportionate change in the growth of public sector debt and also imply a change in the fiscal structure through changes in taxation or public expenditure.

The simulations show that balanced changes in monetary growth change the rate of inflation and leave real output unaffected in the long run. This result holds under a wide range of model specifications and we would regard the conclusion as non-controversial. It is, of course, true that any change in policy, even if it is balanced in our sense, may have long-term structural effects. This point has been made, for example, by Hahn (1980) and Buiter (1980). Any change in taxation or public expenditure will have real effects. And even if a policy change could be devised which was intended to be wholly neutral, there might be transitional effects e.g. on the capital stock which changed the future history of an economy permanently. While we accept that view, we would not regard it as important in the present context. Since the government has a powerful armoury of weapons to change the economic structure, if it so wishes, it should not attempt to use monetary policy for this end.

The change in the price level comes about through domestic and international linkages. It is not part of the "international monetarist" case that the exchange rate provides the only mechanism linking money and prices. (We may have contributed to this misunderstanding ourselves). Movements in the exchange rate do however increase the responsiveness of prices to changes in the money supply through their effect on export and import prices.

The question that has dominated recent debate concerns the short run response of the economy to changes in monetary policy. It has been generally assumed that if monetary policy is tightened, the real exchange rate rises and real output falls (ceteris paribus). The theoretical analysis of Section I shows that neither of these results is inevitable. The simulations show that a balanced reduction in monetary growth does raise the real exchange rate and reduce real output in the short term. But this result depends on the imposed structure of the model. The loss of output is reduced if labour markets are more flexible and if capital markets are less flexible than we have assumed. Further the results are extremely sensitive to the assumption about expectations. The cost is much reduced if expectations in all markets are rational and, in the latter case, the cost can be avoided completely if the policy change is announced in advance.

We accept that domestic price inflexibility may have contributed to real exchange rate overshooting but we are sceptical about the claims that there has also been nominal exchange rate overshooting in response to interest rate movements. The model proposed (e.g. Dornbusch 1976) asserts that interest rates rise because of price stickiness and that this in turn causes a rise in the nominal exchange rate above its long-term equilibrium level. This implies that the foreign exchange market operates efficiently but that domestic financial markets do not, since interest rates rise even though they are expected to fall.

Since the empirical results in Section II are limited to exchange rate determination they cannot, on their own, answer questions about the behaviour of the economic system as a whole. (We have at any rate already stressed the dangers of extrapolating dynamic responses from estimated time series data). However we report the dynamic multiplier effects for the real exchange rate when the money supply is permanently cut by one per cent. To compute the nominal exchange rate profile we apply equation 2A in Table 2 and we assume that the nominal rate of interest initially rises by two percentage points after which it declines geometrically to its starting value over a period of six years as the price level adjusts. To compute the domestic price level we apply equation (10) reported by Beenstock and Longbottom (1980).

The result of this exercise is plotted on Chart 7. The striking feature of this chart is that apart from the initial quarter the real exchange rate declines, i.e. in marked contrast to the conventional view. The initial overshooting reflects the stock adjustment on the capital account which in

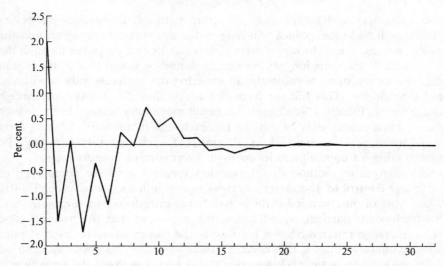

CHART 7. Impulse response of the real exchange rate to a 1 per cent permanent cut in the UK money stock on the assumption of a contemporaneous 2 per cent increase in domestic short interest rates

turn reflects arbitrary assumptions about the response of interest rates to the monetary disturbance as noted at the end of Section II. We do not cite this result as evidence of undershooting. We simply wish to draw attention to the theoretical and empirical point that overshooting is not inevitable.

Experience since 1977 does suggest that the announced tightening of monetary policy has raised the real exchange rate. It is clear that when policies are first changed a substantial reduction in monetary growth may catch the market unawares. We can describe this as a problem of "expectational inefficiency"; but once the new situation has been absorbed into agents' expectations this phenomenon should die away.

We emphasise that real exchange rate overshooting is not an inevitable fact of life. Further even if it does occur this does not necessarily indicate an increased cost in terms of lost output. If the real exchange rate rises the trade balance is likely to deteriorate but the fall in import prices will induce a domestic real balance effect and will speed up the disinflation of wages.[8] Policy proposals to intervene in the exchange market assume that real exchange rate overshooting occurs and that it has a net deflationary effect on output.

Two methods of intervention have been proposed. The first is direct intervention by the authorities in the exchange market. Such intervention will generally lead to a change in monetary growth. We shall therefore have

---

[8] Indeed Beenstock and Burns (1979) argue that the effects of the exchange rate on output are broadly neutral.

two influences which will alter the time path of disinflation—monetary growth will be higher, which will have a domestic impact on prices, and the exchange rate will be lower, which will have an impact on prices through the international transmission mechanism. It should be noted that to the extent that the intervention is successful in lowering the exchange rate it will also be unprofitable. This follows from the result that the market for foreign exchange is efficient. (We discuss this result more fully below). Even though the authorities may only be moving the exchange rate towards its long-term equilibrium, if they succeed in altering the exchange rate they will be undertaking an unprofitable investment given current interest rates.

An alternative method of intervention involves a tax or some type of exchange control to discourage overseas capital inflows (Dornbusch (1980)). This type of intervention, which has been introduced in Germany and Switzerland, is particularly related to the argument that the nominal (and real) exchange rate overshoots because of the rise in domestic interest rates when monetary policy is tightened. To the extent that this policy succeeds in reducing the rise in the exchange rate it will also slow down the reduction in the rate of inflation. However, for a given monetary policy, the proposal does appear to offer a lower cost in terms of output.

We object to this proposal on three grounds. The first is that it is derived from an entirely *ad hoc* model of the economy which makes special assumptions about the operation of different markets. In particular as mentioned earlier the market for foreign exchange is efficient whereas no other markets are. (The model goes further than efficiency and assumes interest rate parity, which we believe is inconsistent with the evidence). It is no doubt true that foreign exchange markets are more flexible than domestic markets for goods and labour. The model also implies that domestic financial markets are inefficient since interest rates rise even though rationally they must be expected to fall. It is easy to show that the Dornbusch effect disappears with slight adjustments to the model.

The second objection is that, in practice, as German experience shows such schemes are unlikely to be effective.

Our third objection is more fundamental. The empirical evidence discussed in Section II is consistent with the view that the market for foreign exchange is efficient. This result is also supported in a number of studies (e.g. Frenkel (1980)). It is efficient in the sense that it embodies all available information and exhausts all possibilities of profitable arbitrage subject to risk and transactions costs.

The Dornbusch proposal seeks nevertheless to alter the exchange rate by altering the return to overseas investors on UK financial assets (or by limiting access to them). The traditional ground for intervention of this type is that social costs and benefits differ from private ones. But it cannot be shown that this is true in exchange markets themselves. If there is a problem it arises elsewhere in the economy. In this case it arises in the markets for goods and labour because prices and wages do not change instantaneously in response to a change in monetary policy. This in turn can happen partly because of uncertainty about the future course of monetary policy, partly because of uncertainty about the implications for prices of any given change in monetary policy and partly because of institutional rigidities in wage and price fixing. The latter in turn may represent one way of coping with uncertainty. If, in addition, there have been real shocks to the economy (North Sea oil, for example) labour markets may be slow to adjust their behaviour.

Either in the case of a nominal shock or a real shock the first priority of policy should surely be to improve the operation of the labour market.

For nominal shocks, the difficulties arise from wage-setting behaviour and from the credibility of policy changes. Long-term wage contracts have particularly been emphasised as a source of difficulty. But long-term contracts are not an inevitable aspect of wage-setting. Since there are probably fixed costs to wage-setting, there is always likely to be some optimal period of wage contract; but the optimal length will depend on the variability of economic considerations. A long contract period will be particularly inefficient when monetary policy is in transition.

We have described the failure to recognise the consequences of a change in monetary policy as "expectational inefficiency". The problem is likely to be most acute when monetary restraint is first introduced. Any measures which improve economic understanding are valuable, as are clear indications in advance of the government's intentions. Finally it is important to increase not only the flexibility of wages and prices but also the perception of the need for such changes. Movements in the exchange rate are a valuable signal which should be left undistorted. Attempts to intervene in exchange rate markets should only be made if possibilities of improving the working of other markets have been exhausted.

We have become accustomed to wage inflexibility but that does not mean that we should be resigned to it. In all markets, price inflexibility places the burden of adjustment on quantities. Wage inflexibility places the burden of adjustment on employment. Those who are fortunate enough to maintain employment under conditions in which wages should fall have the dubious advantage of nominal wage certainty and also enjoy a temporary increase in real wages. Those who become unemployed (and there is virtually nothing they can do about it as individuals) experience a sudden fall in their real incomes. It is difficult to believe that this lottery system is socially optimal. In times of structural change or of attempts to change the underlying rate of inflation, wage flexibility is particularly desirable and there are very strong reasons for trying to extend the area in which price flexibility operates.

Even if one accepts that it may in theory be possible to offset the output effects of counter-inflationary policy that does not establish the case for doing so. It will be recognised that the problem is analogous to the question of whether it is possible to exploit the short-run Phillips curve. In fact it is part of the same story, set in the framework of an open economy. In each case the problem (or the opportunity) arises because labour markets react slowly to changes in monetary conditions.

Successful policies require that the dynamics of adjustment are known and stable. But the empirical analysis of Section II shows that it has not been possible to obtain stable equations which will successfully predict movements in the exchange rate. This result is not surprising; but it suggests that there is no empirical basis for successful intervention. It may be possible to control the nominal exchange rate but the government cannot know in advance what changes in policy will be required to maintain a particular path, nor can it know what the consequences will be for the real exchange rate. The exchange rate joins the list of variables, including real interest rates and the unemployment rate which governments have tried in vain to control by nominal macro economic policies. Attempts to intervene are subject to the critique directed by Lucas (1976) at attempts to exploit the Phillips curve. Policy changes themselves will change the behaviour of the economy. In particular labour markets will learn from experience. This cuts both ways. Just as attempts to "trick" labour markets by monetary expansion will progressively fail, so the costs of reducing inflation by contraction will progressively fall.

North Sea oil

We have suggested that the effects of North Sea oil on the real exchange rate are permanent. We accept the form of analysis set out by Forsyth and Kay (1980) which suggests that there will be a real exchange rate response to the extent that the increase in real income results in an increase in demand for non-traded goods.

In Section II we distinguished three means by which North Sea oil may raise the real exchange rate. First, there is a current balance effect. Second, capital account movements in anticipation of the current balance effect may bring the increase in the real rate forward. Finally there may be a portfolio shift towards sterling.

At no point can one talk of "overshooting". It is possible that the real exchange rate will rise further in the short run than in the long run. But the effect on the trade balance is the same in either case. It is also possible that the resources shifted out of the traded goods sector will not be immediately re-absorbed elsewhere; but as with the case of monetary policy that does not provide a case for intervening in the exchange market, even if such intervention were successful in offsetting the real exchange rate effect. It is better to leave the exchange rate alone and to introduce local subsidies (if they are thought necessary) to alleviate the transitional problems. Best of all are policies which increase the mobility of resources. (There are no grounds for believing that the exchange rate response to North Sea oil is irrational, given the evidence that the market operates efficiently).

Both the theory and the empirical evidence support the view that the advent of North Sea oil has raised the real exchange rate. Our estimates suggest, tentatively, that the North Sea oil raised the steady state value of the real exchange rate by about 14 per cent by mid-1980. Some commentators have suggested that the government should take steps to offset this effect. We have already argued that a change in nominal policy (e.g. a "balanced" change in the money supply) could not affect the real exchange rate in the long term. However it has been proposed, particularly by Forsyth (1980) that the government should use fiscal policy to reduce the real exchange rate.

The proposed mechanism is as follows. Fiscal policy should be tightened (using the North Sea oil revenues) and the PSBR should be reduced while the monetary growth policy was unchanged. This would be an example of an "unbalanced" change in monetary policy which would leave the private sector short of public sector debt relative to its holdings of money balances. The shortage would cause a fall in interest rates which would cause the capital account to deteriorate. To maintain the overall balance, the trade balance must improve. Equilibrium in the overall balance of payments will therefore require a fall in the real exchange rate. In principle there is some level of the PSBR which would leave the non-oil trade balance unaffected by the production of North Sea oil. The oil balance would be offset by a capital account deficit.

It is important to be clear about the time dimensions of the required changes. Our model assumes that long-run equilibria are in terms of stocks which depend, *inter alia* on interest rate levels. Therefore to maintain the desired level of capital flows a continuous fall in interest rates is required. Further, stock equilibrium will also depend on expected exchange rate changes. If the fiscal policy at the same time produces a fall in interest rates and changes the expected rate of depreciation of sterling, the capital flows may be multiplied. In brief, the policy can only work if the squeeze on holdings of public sector debt continues and if the squeeze is expected to continue. Since its continuation would require continuous falls in interest rates, expectations would soon build up that the policy would end. If people believed that monetary policy would be brought into line with fiscal policy, exchange rate expectations would change. The capital outflows could be modified or even reversed and the real exchange rate could rise.

Thus there must be serious doubts about the stability of such a system of altering the real exchange rate. But there must be even more serious doubts about the benefits of changing the rate even if it could be achieved. The general idea is to preserve the size of the traded goods sector. But why should this be done? We repeat our conclusion that the exchange market is efficient; why then should the public sector seek to divert resources to its own use in order to alter the exchange rate? One argument is that the exchange rate does not reflect the long term value of the traded goods sector. While North Sea oil is available, so the story goes, the real exchange rate rises and the size of the traded goods sector is reduced. When North Sea oil runs out, we find ourselves without an export industry.

If the exchange rate market is efficient, this fear is groundless. Just as the effects of rising North Sea oil production are reflected in exchange rate movements, so will the effects of falling production. The real exchange rate will anticipate the balance of payments effects and the traded goods sector will be restored. Over the period of time involved there is no reason to believe that the adjustment will be excessive. Nor is there any reason to believe that the government knows more about the future of North Sea oil than anyone else does.

There would not seem to be any valid grounds for attempting to offset the real exchange rate effects of North Sea oil either in the short term or in the long term.

If there are long term effects on the real exchange rate these should be regarded as favourable. They achieve, after all, the goal of classical trade policy—an improvement in the terms of trade. (It is always possible for the government to intervene if it does not like the distributional effects).

Conclusions

We may conclude this section on policy implications by re-stating our view that the market for foreign exchange is efficient. It is therefore meaningless to assert that the exchange rate is "too high" or "too low". If there are believed to be problems in the real economy, if for example a movement in the nominal exchange rate has raised the international price of UK labour and has raised unemployment, the solution should be sought in the labour market and not in the exchange rate market.

We have argued that, in the long term, nominal changes in policy will have nominal effects. It is not therefore possible to change the real exchange rate (or any other real variable) by "balanced" changes in monetary policy. A number of models have been put forward which suggest that a change in monetary policy will have short-run real effects. These models are *ad hoc*. It is easy to present models in which the short run real effects of a reduction in monetary policy are favourable. The Dornbusch model, which has been widely accepted, depends on a limited and artificial set of assumptions. It has no generality. The one policy conclusion which it is reasonable to draw is that policy changes should be announced well in advance.

If there is a short-run trade off between inflation and output this does not automatically lead to the conclusion that it should be exploited. That is a question of political choice. More importantly we would argue that behaviour is not sufficiently stable for the trade-off to be exploited with confidence. The experience of the early 1970s established that.

The emphasis on movements in the real exchange rate as a source of output loss is mistaken. Changes in the nominal exchange rate which anticipate domestic price changes may cause a deterioration of the trade balance; but the direct effects on domestic costs will help to reduce the fall in real balances. We cannot glibly classify the exchange rate as a villain in the counter-inflationary process.

The real exchange rate rose by 30 per cent between October 1976 and October 1980. Our empirical study suggests that both interest rate movements and North Sea oil played a part; but we cannot convincingly establish the quantitative role played by each of these factors and we would not expect to be able to. We would also assume that some part has been played by the announcement of the Medium Term Financial Strategy which has altered expectations about the future of inflation rates and hence of the future of the nominal exchange rate. This announcement, together with the development of North Sea oil has also much reduced the risks attached to investment in UK securities and we would expect this to raise the real exchange rate permanently.

Our theory suggests that part of the increase in the real rate is permanent and part is transitional but we have no basis for concluding that exchange rate intervention to reverse the increase is either feasible or desirable.

APPENDIX SIMULATION MODEL

The equations of the model are set out in Table 1 along with the assumptions about the parameter values.[9] A glossary of terms is provided in Table 2 which also indicates the initial steady state values that have been assumed for the variables. The model consists of 18 endogenous variables, 4 exogenous variables and 2 policy instruments.

For simplicity the model abstracts from economic growth so that the natural rate of output $(\bar{Y})$ is constant. Domestic private expenditure (C) is equal to disposable income (Y^d) when portfolios are balanced, i.e. when desired wealth equals actual wealth. Net saving takes place when portfolios are unbalanced and equation (2) assumes that desired real personal wealth is proportionate to real disposable income. Notice that in this context wealth is affected by capital losses and gains on bonds when interest rates change (equation (8)).

Exports (X) are proportional to the volume of world trade and vary with relative export prices. In the import equation imports (I) are proportional to domestic output and relative prices. The elasticities assumed are intended to broadly reflect empirical estimates for the UK.

We postulate a Keynesian demand function for money in equation (7) which is augmented by the expected rate of inflation and wealth. The other domestic financial asset in the model is government bonds (B) which bear a rate of interest (R). These bonds carry a fixed coupon of one unit of currency per time period and are perpetuities.

Equations (9) to (12) and (18) provide the link between fiscal and monetary variables. The change in the stock of money is the difference between the budget deficit of the government and sales of bonds to the private sector, i.e. for simplicity we assume there is no banking sector and because the exchange rate is freely floating external flows cannot affect the supply of

---

[9] The model draws heavily on Ball and Burns (1979). It has been augmented by Holly (1980) to allow for rational as well as adaptive expectations. The method of solution is described in Holly and Beenstock (1980).

TABLE 1
Model Equations

$$Y_t = C_t + G_t + X_t - I_t \tag{1}$$
$$C_t = \alpha_1 Y_t^d + (1-\alpha_1)Y_{t-1}^d + \alpha_2\{(W_t^*/P_t) - \alpha_1 Y_t^d - (1-\alpha_1)Y_{t-1}^d\} \tag{2}$$
$$I_t = \alpha_3 Y_t \cdot \{S_t \cdot P_t/P_{wt}\} \tag{3}$$
$$X_t = \alpha_4 WT_t \cdot \{P_{wt}/S_t \cdot PX_t\}^2 \tag{4}$$
$$PX_t = \alpha_5 P_t + (1-\alpha_5)\{P_{wt}/S_t\} \tag{5}$$
$$CA_t = X_t \cdot PX_t - I_t \cdot P_{wt}/S_t \tag{6}$$
$$M_d^t = \beta_0 P_t \cdot (W_t^*/P_t) \cdot R_t^{-\beta_1} \cdot \{_tP_{t+1}^e/P_t\}^{-\beta_2} \cdot Y_t \tag{7}$$
$$W_t^* = M_{t-1} + B_{t-1}/R_t \tag{8}$$
$$\Delta M_t = DEF_t - \Delta B_t/R_t \tag{9}$$
$$DEF_t = G_t \cdot P_t - T_t \tag{10}$$
$$T_t = \tau\{Y_t \cdot P_t\} \tag{11}$$
$$Y_t^d = (1-\tau)\{Y_t/P_t\} \tag{12}$$
$$K_t = \gamma_1\{_tS_{t+1}^e - S_t\} + \gamma_2\{R_t - R_{wt}\} \tag{13}$$
$$DK_t = -CA_t \tag{14}$$
$$DK_t = K_t - K_{t-1} \tag{15}$$
$$w_t = {}_tp_{t+1}^e + \theta_1\{Y_t - \bar{Y}\} \tag{16}$$
$$p_t = \theta_2 w_t + (1-\theta_2)\{P_{wt}/s_t\} \tag{17}$$
$$M_t = M_t^d \tag{18}$$

Notation

(i) e superscript indicates an expectation

(ii) subscripts before the variable indicate the time at which an expectation is formed

(iii) p_t, w_t and s_t are the rates of change of P_t, W_t and S_t.

Thus ${}_tp_{t+1}^e$ is the expectation for the inflation rate in period $t+1$ formed in period t.

$\alpha_1 = 0.5$	$\beta_0 = 0.00625$	$\theta_1 = 0.2$
$\alpha_2 = 0.25$	$\beta_1 = 0.25$	$\theta_2 = 0.75$
$\alpha_3 = 0.25$	$\beta_2 = 0.25$	$\gamma_1 = 100$
$\alpha_4 = 0.25$	$\tau = 0.2$	$\gamma_2 = 0.3$
$\alpha_5 = 0.5$		

money.[10] Alternatively, the government could issue bonds to finance the deficit in which case the control variable would be ΔB. However, because R is endogenous the government cannot directly control the cash revenues it obtains from debt issue. On the other hand we do not complicate the model further by adding debt interest payments on these bonds to the government's deficit. This omission will have a stabilizing effect because bond finance will not increase debt interest charges. Alternatively we assume that the authorities tax back these charges in the form of lump sum taxes. Otherwise tax revenue is proportionate to nominal income. In the initial steady state the budget is balanced so that M and B are constant.

The remaining equations complete the model by integrating the product and labour markets and the market in foreign exchange. Net holdings of foreign exchange (K) in equation (13) are a function of the expected change in the exchange rate and the uncovered interest rate

[10] Following Blinder and Solow (1973) we believe that it is important to include the government's budget constraint, since, as Turnovsky (1977) points out, this imparts to the model its own 'intrinsic' dynamics as the deficit alters the stocks of financial assets through time.

TABLE 2

Endogenous variables

		Imial steady state value
Y:	Output, constant prices	100
C:	Domestic private expenditure, constant prices	80
X:	Exports, constant prices	25
I:	Imports, constant prices	25
M^d:	Demand for money	50
W^*:	Stock of wealth	80
CA:	Current account	0
DEF:	Budget deficit	0
T:	Tax revenues	20
Y^d:	Disposable income	80
K:	Net foreign currency position	0
DK:	Capital flows	0
S:	Exchange rate	1
P:	Price level	1
W:	Wage index	1
R:	Rate of interest (index)	1
PX:	Export price level	1
Exogenous variables		
$\bar{Y}$:	Normal level of output, constant prices	100
WT:	World trade	100
P_w:	World price level	1
R_w:	World rate of interest	1
*Policy instruments**		
G:	Government expenditure, constant prices	20
B:	Stock of bonds	30
M:	Supply of money	50

* The policy instruments should be considered as G and the ratio of B to M. Thus at any one time only two of these three variables are policy instruments, the other being endogenous.

differential. International capital flows (DK) are defined as the change in these holdings. Note that a change in the interest rate differential has only a temporary effect on capital flows. (In this model we assume, for simplicity, that the entire adjustment takes place in a single period. Some kind of extended adjustment process might be more realistic, but it would still be true that the flow effect was only temporary).

The assumptions about γ_1 and γ_2 imply that the capital account is sensitive to exchange rate expectations while it is relatively insensitive to interest rate differentials. The empirical evidence upon these parameters is mixed, see Beenstock (1978, Chaps 6–7), and it should be noted that our specification does not accord with the interest parity condition which implies $\gamma_1 = \gamma_2 = \infty$, or

$$R_t + {}_tS^e_{t+1} - S_t = R_{wt}$$

It should further be pointed out that violation of the interest parity condition does not necessarily imply that the foreign exchange market is not efficient. In general both exchange risk and default risk will imply that internationally traded financial assets are imperfect substitutes in which case γ_1 and γ_2 will be finite and γ_1 may differ from γ_2. The issue of efficiency turns instead upon whether only non-diversifiable risk remains and whether exchange rate expectations are rational. This has nothing necessarily to do with interest rate parity.

The exchange rate is assumed to float freely so that we can ignore changes in the foreign reserve holdings of the government. The exchange rate must thus adjust to clear the market in foreign exchange with the flow on the capital account exactly offsetting the flow on the current account (equation 14). We can thus solve for the spot exchange rate as a function of the current account, the expected exchange rate, lagged holdings of foreign currencies and the uncovered interest rate differential.

Equation (16) is an augmented Phillips Curve in which wage inflation depends upon the expected rate of inflation and the disequilibrium in the labour market which for simplicity is assumed to be dependent upon the deviation of output from its natural level. This kind of specification introduces an element of wage-price stickiness into the model and plays a crucial role in the transmission mechanism. Behaviour of this type may be rationalized in a number of ways, e.g. search models, contract models and so on. However, at this stage we do not wish to attach any specific interpretations to the finite value of θ_1.

The model is closed by equation (17) which is simply a cost mark-up model for prices. This implies that demand pressures are entirely reflected in the labour market.

REFERENCES

ALLSOPP, C. and JOSHI, V. (1980) 'Alternative Strategies for the UK'. *National Institute Economic Review* (February) pp. 86–103.

BALASSA, B. (1964) 'The Purchasing Power Parity Doctrine: A Reappraisal' *Journal of Political Economy* (December).

BALL, R. J. and BURNS, T. (1979) 'Long-run Portfolio Equilibrium and Balance of Payments Adjustment in Econometric Models' in *Modelling the International Transmission Mechanism*' Sawyer, J. (ed), North Holland.

BALL, R. J., BURNS, T. and WARBURTON, P. (1980) 'The London Business School Model of the U.K. Economy: An Exercise in International Monetarism'. Chapter 4 in *Economic Modelling*, Omerod, P (ed) Heinemann, London.

BEENSTOCK, M. (1978) '*The Foreign Exchanges: Theory, Modelling and Policy*', Macmillan, London.

BEENSTOCK, M. and LONGBOTTOM, J. A. (1980) 'Portfolio Balance and Inflation in the United Kingdom', L.B.S. Econometric Forecasting Unit Discussion Paper No. 79.

BEENSTOCK, M. and BURNS, T. (1979) 'Exchange Rate Objectives and Macroeconomic Adjustment in the UK' in *Britain's Trade and Exchange Rate Policy* R. Major (ed), Heinemann, London.

BLINDER, A. S. and SOLOW, R. M. (1973) 'Does Fiscal Policy Matter?' *Journal of Public Finance*, Vol. 2 (November).

BUITER, W. H. (1980) 'The Macroeconomics of Dr. Pangloss: A Critical Survey of the New Classical Macroeconomics' *Economic Journal* Vol 90, (March) pp. 34–50.

DAVIDSON, J. E. H., HENDRY, D. F., SRBA, F. and YEO, S. (1978) 'Econometric Modelling of the Time Series Relationship Between Consumers Expenditure and Income in the United Kingdom' *Economic Journal* (December).

DORNBUSCH, R. (1976) 'Expectation and Exchange Rate Dynamics' *Journal of Political Economy* (December) pp. 1161–1176.

DORNBUSCH, R. (1980) Memorandum on Monetary Policy to the Treasury and Civil Service Committee, Session 1979–80, House of Commons Paper 720, HMSO.

FORSYTH, J. (1980) 'A Fiscal Policy for the 1980's ' *Morgan Grenfell Economic Review* (March).

FORSYTH, P. J. and KAY, J. A. (1980). 'The Economic Implications of North Sea Oil Revenues', *Journal of the Institute for Fiscal Studies* Vol 1 No. 3 (July) pp. 1–28.

FRANKEL, J. A. (1979) 'On the Mark: A Theory of Floating Exchange Rates Based on Real Interest Rate Differentials', *American Economic Review* (September).

FRENKEL, J. A. (1980) 'Flexible Exchange Rates, Prices and the Role of "News": Lessons from the 1970's' Conference on Exchange Rate Policy, The City University, May.

HAHN, F. H. (1980) 'Monetarism and Economic Theory', *Economica* Vol 47 (February) pp. 1–18.

HOLLY, S. (1980) 'An Anticipated Optimal Policy in a Perfect Foresight Model' L.B.S. Econometric Forecasting Unit Discussion Paper No. 84.

HOLLY, S. and BEENSTOCK, M. (1980) 'The Implications of Rational Expectations for the Forecasting and Simulation of Econometric Models' L.B.S. Econometric Forecasting Unit Discussion Paper No. 72.

LUCAS, R. E. (1976) 'Econometric Policy Evaluation: A Critique in "The Phillips Curve and Labour Markets", Brunner, K. and Meltzer, A. N. (eds), North Holland, Amsterdam.

MINFORD, A. P. L. (1980) 'Government Borrowing and Inflation', *Journal of Economic Affairs* Vol 1 No. 1 (October).

MIZON, G. E. (1977) 'Model Selection Procedures' in M. J. Artis and A. R. Nobay (eds) *Studies in Modern Economic Analysis*, Oxford, Blackwell.

PESERAN, M. H. (1980) 'Identification of Rational Expectation Models' mimeo, Trinity College, Cambridge, January.

TURNOVSKY, S. J. (1977) *Macroeconomic Analysis and Stabilisation Policy* Cambridge University Press.

WARBURTON, P. J. and BEENSTOCK, M. (1980) 'An Integrated Analysis of the Effective Exchange Rate for Sterling' London Business School.

WHITLEY, J. D. (1977) 'National Institute Model II: Imports of Goods', N.I.E.S.R. Discussion Paper No. 10B.

THE EXCHANGE RATE AND
MONETARY POLICY

By PATRICK MINFORD*

THE topic of this paper is nothing less than the macroeconomic behaviour of
an open economy under alternative policy regimes. As such it requires an
integrated treatment, in which labour, goods, money, bonds, and foreign
exchange markets are each accorded a place. This treatment must also take
account of Lucas' (1972) critique of econometric models, that their parameters should be invariant to changes in policy regime if they are to be used to
say anything about the effects of such changes in regime. The implication is
that any treatment must have a strong basis in economic theory, so that we
can as far as possible estimate the parameters of structural relationships; and
that we must interpret with the greatest caution any empirical evidence
which does *not* identify these parameters, since there can be no guarantee
that it will be a reliable guide to behaviour modes under an altered policy
regime.

These caveats may appear to make the task of the econometrician asked
to infer from empirical evidence how alternative policies would affect an
open economy, a hopeless one. Such a conclusion has indeed been drawn by
some econometricians (e.g. Sims (1980)), who believe that we had best stick
to charting empirical regularities in and covariation between macroeconomic
variables. However, others are more optimistic. Sargent (1978a, 1978b) in
particular has been pursuing a research strategy of estimating the structural
parameters of the US economy, sector-by-sector, using the twin assumptions
of quadratic objective functions (for preferences and technology) and rational expectations market equilibrium. There are also attempts to estimate
full econometric models of economies where the parameters are held to be
structural in the sense that they are determined either by preferences and
technology or by institutional set-ups that would not change significantly
within a relevant time period under the impact of regime change; this work
includes Taylor (1979), Holly and Zarrop (1979), and our own at Liverpool
(Minford (1980) and Minford, Brech and Matthews (1980)). It is the latter
category that appears to hold out some hope for answering the questions
posed in this symposium since, while having a reasonable claim to the
necessary invariance, it also supplies the necessary integration in its treatment of markets.

We are emboldened in the attempt to apply our own work to the
questions posed, by the unattractiveness of the alternatives, which appear to

* This paper enlarges on themes I first developed at the City University Conference on
Exchange Rate Policy, Sept. 1980. I am grateful to the conference participants for their
comments, especially to Desmond Fitzgerald and Ivor Pierce; I have also received helpful
comments on the ideas embodied here in seminars at Bristol, Cambridge and Liverpool, in
particular from Christos Ioannidis and Satwant Marwaha, who carried out the simulations, and
from David Forrest, Roger Latham and David Peel.

be either ad hoc regression-mongering or armchair pontification. What follows therefore after a preliminary section describes a theoretical framework, the empirical successes and failures of this framework when used to predict inside and outside-sample experience for the UK, and its implications for the effects of changes in the policy and other environment. A concluding section reviews the arguments.

Preliminaries and conclusions

This paper focusses on the possible clash between monetary policy and the objective of maintaining competitiveness. As such, it presupposes that independent monetary policy is possible. This presupposition is only valid under floating exchange rates (whether 'clean' or not). Hence this paper will assume a floating exchange rate regime, with or without foreign exchange intervention. The behaviour of the economy under fixed rates (i.e. when monetary independence is surrendered) is discussed elsewhere at some length (Minford (1980)), for those who (in spite of our discussion here) despair of reasonable behaviour under the present system.

The exchange rate which is at the centre of our stage, can most conveniently be considered in two parts, the 'real' and the 'nominal' exchange rate. Let S be \$/£, P be the domestic price level, P_F the foreign ('US') one. Then

$$\frac{S \cdot P}{P_F} \equiv e$$

where e is the 'real' exchange rate (the ratio of prices in one currency or 'competitiveness'). Therefore:

$$\log S \equiv \log e + \log (P_F/P)$$

which reveals that the real exchange rate and foreign prices constant, a doubling for example of domestic prices will halve the nominal exchange rate.

Concerns about the exchange rate are similarly divided into a real part and a nominal part. Much popular economic commentary would like policies to deliver high competitiveness (low e) so as to 'encourage manufacturing' and zero inflation (stable P) implying a rising S if there is world inflation. At the same time, the same commentary fears that these two aims are incompatible. It is often said for example that monetary targets low enough to deliver stable prices necessarily will cause low competitiveness. The mechanism popularly cited runs: tight money works by raising the nominal exchange rate, some of this rise shows up in a P lower than would otherwise have been, but some shows up in a higher real exchange rate because money wages will not fully drop by the change in the nominal exchange rate. This thesis divides those who accept it into one camp which rates inflation control—so a 'high' nominal exchange rate—the highest priority and another camp which rates the health of manufacturing—and so a 'low' exchange rate—the highest one. The first accordingly favours 'tight' money, the second attacks it.

Another example of these concerns is provided by North Sea oil. This is widely perceived as raising both the nominal and the real exchange rate. The same camps regard this respectively as blessing or curse.

I shall argue that these perceptions are confused and in general wrong. Monetary growth provided it contains no 'surprises' will not show up in the real exchange rate at all. The determinants of the real exchange rate are real things—notably, the social security/taxation regime. North Sea oil probably implies some rise in the real exchange rate, but this rise has been highly exaggerated. Furthermore, the aggregate effect has been to benefit British industries, even though the distribution of these benefits could have caused actual contraction in some. Abrupt policy changes ('surprises') can cause jumps in the real exchange rate which subsequently are eliminated.

Policy conclusions will be that as much advance warning as possible should be given of monetary and fiscal changes; hence the desirability of medium term targets. Secondly, social security benefits should be reduced relative to productivity per man. Thirdly, that foreign exchange intervention as such is pointless in a regime of monetary targets since it will have to be exactly offset by changes in domestic credit. Fourthly, though one may conceive of money supply rules one of whose objectives is the minimisation of shocks to the real exchange rate, these are unlikely to be worthwhile; money supply targets should be reduced as rapidly as possible and should be adhered to as tightly as possible. The only worthwhile (real) exchange rate policy is therefore one for the labour market—reducing government inter-vention through benefits, reducing union intervention, and improving the workings of closely related markets (notably housing). But it should not be surprising that the only way to obtain lasting improvements in real perfor-mance is via the elimination of market distortions.

The model

Let us suppose, as in the 'Scandinavian' model (Aukrust (1970) and Edgren *et al.* (1969)), that there is a non-traded and traded goods sector. The price of traded goods is given in competitive world markets as $P_T = P_{T,F}/S$.[1] There is mobility of labour between these two sectors at a nominal wage rate, W.

The supply of labour in total to the two sectors depends upon the wage, W, relative to the social security rate, B; it is assumed that under the social security system it is possible for men and women to obtain benefit when not working, regardless of whether there is a job they could do or not. The reason is that the criteria of the 'distance' of an available job for a claimant's

---

[1] This assumption of 'purchasing power parity' in tradeables can be dropped without altering any of the conclusions; but it is a convenient simplification to assume that the price elasticities of demand for exports and imports are infinite.

'qualifications' are applied generously; the job has to be reasonably 'close' in area (e.g. not in Manchester for a Liverpool worker) and in description (e.g. not a streetcleaner for a welder). The system assumes, for better or worse, that society should compensate a man if a job rather like his previous one is not available. Therefore, in practice we argue men or women can choose relatively freely whether to take a job *unlike* their previous one or to take benefit. Such a choice implies that the ratio of the wage rate to the benefit will be a major determinant of labour supply. Notice in passing that this is quite different from the usual argument that the benefit/wage ratio affects *search* activity and so may raise the duration of unemployment; though it is not ruled out that a rise in benefits will raise the ratio and so also raise such search activity. Rather it predicts that *permanent* unemployment will be raised by higher benefits at any given level of wages. Evidence on this is provided by a variety of time-series work (e.g. Holden and Peel (1979), Benjamin and Kochin (1979)), as well as by our own model.

We therefore write the level of labour supply,

$$L = \left(\frac{W}{B}\right)^{\lambda}$$

and unemployment,

$$U = \bar{L} - L$$

where $\bar{L}$ is the 'registered' labour force; i.e. those working plus those registered for benefit.

For convenience, we assume that the non-traded sector (NT) provides services so that output, $Q_{NT} = L_{NT}$, labour employed there, and $P_{NT} = W$ and that technology in the traded goods sector is Cobb-Douglas with a specific factor, T (which we can regard as representing 'entrepreneurship' and 'land') or $Q_T = L_T^{\alpha} K_T^{\beta} T^{1-\alpha-\beta}$. If capital is freely available (internationally mobile) at a real cost of r, then we can write

$$Q_T = T\left(\frac{W}{\alpha P_T}\right)^{-\alpha/(1-\alpha-\beta)} \left(\frac{r}{\beta}\right)^{-\beta/(1-\alpha-\beta)} \equiv \left(\frac{W}{P_T}\right)^{-\alpha'} k \quad \text{and} \quad L_T = \alpha\left(\frac{W}{P_T}\right)^{-1} Q_T$$

Q_T is the supply of traded goods, all of which will be sold at P_T the international price. In so far as the domestic demand for traded goods, D_T, exceeds Q_T there will be a current account deficit and vice versa. Domestic demand for non-traded services D_{NT}, must be equal to the supply of these services, L_{NT}. This is achieved by driving up the wage, W, until the total supply of labour equals the total demand i.e.

$$L_{NT} + L_T = L$$

If we write the demand as depending on real spending ('absorption'), a, and relative prices of traded and nontraded goods, P_T/W, we have:

$$D_{NT} = \left(\frac{P_T}{W}\right)^{\sigma} a; \qquad D_T = a - \frac{W}{P_T} D_{NT};$$

$a = A/P_T$, where A is nominal spending and we deflate by tradeables' prices. So the market clearing wage is given by:

$$\left(\frac{W}{P_T}\right)^{-\sigma} a + \alpha k\left(\frac{W}{P_T}\right)^{-1-\alpha'} = \left(\frac{W}{B}\right)^{\lambda}.$$

The current account supply deficit (deflated by P_T) is:

$$xval = Q_T - D_T = \left(\frac{W}{P_T}\right)^{-\alpha'} k - a\left(1 + \left(\frac{W}{P_T}\right)^{1-\sigma}\right)$$

The particular functional forms are of little interest; they are supplied to illustrate the possibilities. The essence of the analysis can be captured in a simple diagram (Chart 1).

In the right hand quadrant are shown the demands for goods and the supply of traded goods (the supply of non-traded goods is identical to the demand; this is forced through the labour market clearing condition). At any given (market-clearing) wage relative to traded prices, there is defined a demand for non-traded services and traded goods which both shift to the right with rising absorption, a, and a supply of traded goods, which shifts to the right with increases in specific factors, T, and falls in the cost of capital, r, (summarised as k). Turning to the left hand quadrant we see the total demand for labour, L_D, which is the sum of L_T (depending on Q_T) and D_{NT} and so shifts to the left with rises in a and k. The supply of labour is illustrated as being asymptotic to the total labour force, $\bar{L}$, at one extreme and the real benefit rate, B/P_T, at the other; this assumes we could get zero work at wages equal to real benefits and that there is some physical maximum to labour supply at $\bar{L}$. Registered unemployment is shown as $\bar{L}$ minus equilibrium L.

To simplify matters, we have assumed that the unemployed man gets benefits only and does not work. But in practice he may choose to work part of the time in the 'shadow economy'—i.e. in undeclared activities. An overwhelming amount of (by definition) casual evidence suggests that this is

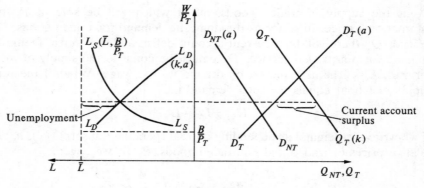

CHART 1

a flourishing part of most Western economies today; for the UK, the former chairman of the Inland Revenue (Pile (1979)) has estimated it at $7\frac{1}{2}\%$ of GNP.

Allowing for the shadow economy would complicate but not alter the essentials of our analysis. It means that we have two labour markets and that the official labour market, for any given benefit rate, obtains a lesser labour supply than it would without the shadow economy. This increases registered unemployment. It also means that the registered unemployed are to some extent usefully occupied, so that the figures overstate the wasted resources. Whether the emergence of the shadow economy improves resource allocation overall or not is a problem of second-best which cannot be settled without detailed analysis. But for our purposes we simply need to note that our supply curve would become an aggregation over both the official and the shadow economy, and that $\bar{L} - L$ would be, not registered unemployed, but that proportion of their time not devoted to the shadow economy. Raising the benefit rate would reduce total labour supply, as before.

Reading then from the left hand side the market-clearing real wage, we can derive the level of output, $y = Q_T + D_{NT}$, and the current account balance, $xval$. We can see that both $xval$ and y tend to fall as W/P_T rises. Notice that real wages W/P and the real exchange rate, $S \cdot P/P_F = e$ are a simple transform of W/P_T. If $P = W^\pi P_T^{1-\pi}$ (π is the weight on the non-traded services in the general price index, P), then

$$\frac{W}{P} = \left(\frac{W}{P_T}\right)^{1-\pi} \quad \text{and} \quad e = \left(\frac{W}{P_T}\right)^{\pi}.$$

So the diagram illustrates that real wages (the real exchange rate) determine output and the current balance, technology and absorption constant; and that real benefits are a major determinant of real wages. If we suppose finally that absorption is forced over time to equal output so that there is zero net borrowing from abroad ($xval = 0$), then we can argue as follows. A rise in real benefits (technology constant) raises real wages and the real exchange rate, which cuts output and via the resulting current deficit forces a cut in absorption.

What we have been discussing is the 'supply side' of the economy, and in doing so we have abstracted from any 'short run dynamics' such as would be provided by the assumption of adjustment costs, union labour contracts and information lags. These elements give rise to a wage equation of the form:

$$\Delta \log W = (\underset{-1}{E} \log P - \log P_{-1}) + \Delta \log w^* + \gamma(\log w^*_{-1} - \log w_{-1}) + \varepsilon$$

where $\underset{-i}{E} x_{+j} = $ expectation (formed at time $t - i$) of x at $t + j$, $w(w^*) = $ actual (equilibrium) real wage, and ε is an error term which may exhibit autocorrelation. The arguments of w^* are given by our 'supply side' analysis, as that level of real wages where there is current account balance, given the real benefit rate, technology and the labour force.

The derivation of this short run equation is in Minford (1980). Its properties are that real wages and the real exchange rate converge on full equilibrium at the rate γ; 'shocks' to prices unanticipated at the time of contracting will cause shocks to real wages and the real exchange rate; along the converging path back to full equilibrium the labour market is clearing continuously as labour shed (acquired) by the union sector alters the market-clearing real wage in the non-union sector. It is worth noting that this real wage will probably not drop even in the short run below the 'floor' set by the real social security rate, which makes the social security system implicitly the 'employer of last resort'. If one wishes to explain 'real wage rigidity', one need look no further than such government intervention in the labour market.

To complete the model, we require a 'demand side' in the short run (in the long run as we have seen demand has to be equal to supply as set out in our previous analysis). This is described at length in Minford (1980) and Minford, Brech and Matthews (1980). In this model, financial markets are 'efficient', which is taken to mean that given publicly available information expected returns are equated on domestic and foreign securities at all maturities; this implies perfect international capital mobility at any point in time. Expectations are rational in the now familiar sense of Muth (1961); in the simulations here this implies that expectations and the forecasts of the model are constrained to be one and the same. Demand for money and goods is overwhelmingly determined by the desire of consumers and firms to achieve equilibrium in their portfolios between goods and financial assets and, within financial assets, between money and bonds; this 'portfolio balance' motive implies inter alia that, when financial assets fall unexpectedly, private demand for goods suffers an unexpected cut as private agents attempt to save in order to increase their holdings of financial assets.

Another corollary of portfolio balance is that the government cannot in the long run finance a deficit by issuing bonds and money in proportions different from those that the private sector would wish for at constant interest rates. This argument therefore underlines the medium term link between the money supply growth rate and the public sector borrowing requirement or deficit.

The predictive performance

This model has been estimated over annual data from 1955 to 1976 by an iterative method described in Minford by which the expectations generated through the model are used to estimate the model itself; iterations continue until there is convergence. This method yields estimates that are consistent, as does the instrumental variables method originated by McCallum (1976); but it also yields a gain in efficiency over this alternative method, because it incorporates the restrictions imposed by the model on the expectations series.

The major interest for policy purposes however must lie in the predictive performance of the model over the floating rate period (1972–1980). To assess this, we supply the model with information, for example, for 1971 on the current and lagged values of exogenous and endogenous variables. It uses this information to project the exogenous variables (of which there are five: world trade, short and long run world real interest rates, the long run budget deficit, and the aggregate tax rate). It then uses these projections to solve the model for a rational expectations path from 1972 for all the endogenous variables. The outcomes for 1972 onwards compared with this path give us respectively the 1-year-ahead, and 2-year-ahead errors.

This process is repeated for each year to 1980, yielding us 9 1-year-ahead errors (5 within sample, 1972–76, and 4 outside sample, 1977–80) and 8 2-year-ahead errors (4 within, 4 outside sample). The root mean square of these errors is shown in the table for five major variables. As a test of forecasting efficiency we also show the error auto-correlations. Efficiency would require at least that available lagged errors are uncorrelated with current ones (a comprehensive test would check correlation between current errors and all relevant available information). As a sample we show the 1st-order autocorrelation coefficients for 1-year-ahead errors, and the 2nd order for 2-year-ahead; in the latter case the information available excludes the 2-year-ahead errors from 1 year previously. These correlations are only reported for the full sample.

It is fairly obvious that with such a restricted sample no very earth shaking conclusions can be delivered. However, if a framework of approach to policy with fairly radical implications is to be even reluctantly accepted, some assurance about its capacity to predict needs to be provided. The model errors are compared with some available 'public' forecasts (the NIESR's) as well as with the results of simple time series forecasts.

The comparison between the model and the NIESR needs careful interpretation. Within its sample, the model has the advantage over NIESR that the parameters of both the exogenous processes and the structural model were estimated over the data of the period forecast. However, this advantage disappears for the outside sample comparison. Also, both inside and outside sample, the NIESR has the advantage that in reaching its forecasts it supplements its model with extraneous information (e.g. surveys of investment or consumer intentions, reports on wage negotiations); this can be a considerable advantage, particularly for short-run (1-year) forecasts.

This comparison differs from those traditionally reported where a model 'forecasts', given the *actual* values of exogenous variables. For a rational expectations model this is an unsatisfactory test because agents' expectations are formed on the basis of expected not actual future exogenous variables. To test the forecasting capacity of our model, we are forced to test the models of the exogenous processes jointly with the structural model, as in the procedure described above. A completely 'like-with-like' comparison with other models, such as the NIESR's, would involve specifying exogenous processes from each starting date, and then running the model from this date with these forecasts. This is not feasible with any of these models at present, because their authors have not specified the processes for the many exogenous variables involved. The comparison with actual forecasts from other model-builders is thus the closest currently available.

The time-series models have a considerable advantage within the sample period, being fitted directly to the actual series they are forecasting. This advantage disappears outside the sample period, when they indicate the minimum forecasting performance desirable from the model or the NIESR.

The table shows that broadly the model holds its own in relation to the competition; this is true both within and outside sample, so that the model's 'advantage' over actual forecasters in being estimated over the sample period appears to be of little significance.

Taking therefore the errors over the whole sample as a guide, then on *inflation* the model outperforms time series, and beats NIESR 2-years-ahead. It is worse than NIESR 1-year-ahead, when the information of wage settlements already available in November of the previous year may be a useful leading indicator (not used by the model). The model also exhibits autocorrelation on 1-year-ahead, suggesting the short-run dynamics are faulty.

On *output*, the model is better than both time-series and NIESR, but only marginally. The NIESR shows severe autocorrelation on 2-year-ahead; this could indicate an insufficient tendency for NIESR output forecasts to regress towards the underlying trend of potential output.

The model and the market's *interest rate* errors are virtually the same, not surprisingly since the model assumes financial market efficiency. The time-series do somewhat better than both.

Current account errors are indistinguishable. The model's *real exchange rate* errors are rather worse than the time-series.

In fact *none* of the differences we have noted are statistically significant, given that there are only 9 observations. However, the general point is this: macroeconomists have typically paid serious attention to the policy utterances of the NIESR partly because of their respected ability to make reasoned predictions. The ability of the model to predict when put into a state of effective ignorance is at least no worse than the NIESR (or simple extrapolative, 'leading indicator', predictions). Therefore in this respect there seems to be no reason to refuse serious attention to policies based on this model.

Some implications of the model:

This model's simulation properties differ in quite a number of ways from those of the now-conventional 'neo-Keynesian' model. This can be illustrated by the affects of an unanticipated fall in the budget deficit (due to

TABLE 1
Model errors under floating rates compared with alternatives

Inflation (% p.a.)		Root mean square error[1]		Autocorrelation Coefficients[2] (standard error)	
		1	2	1	2
Model	1972–80	4.6	4.5	0.62	0.04
	1972–76	3.0	5.1	(0.32)	(0.47)
	1977–80	6.0	3.9		
NIESR	72–80	3.0	6.8	0.54	0.47
	72–76	3.3	7.5	(0.35)	(0.33)
	77–80	2.5	6.1		
Time Series	72–80	5.0	5.7	−0.35	0.15
	72–76	5.0	7.5	(0.36)	(0.46)
	77–80	5.0	3.0		
Level of Real GDP (%)					
Model	72–80	2.0	3.7	−0.00	0.07
	72–76	2.2	4.7	(0.39)	(0.51)
	77–80	1.7	2.3		
NIESR	72–80	2.4	4.2	0.02	0.81
	72–76	2.9	4.6	(0.38)	(0.21)
	77–80	1.7	3.8		
Time Series	72–80	3.1	3.8	0.38	0.15
	72–76	2.9	3.6	(0.50)	(0.57)
	77–80	3.4	4.0		
Interest rates, Long term (% p.a.)					
Model	72–80	1.6	2.6	0.04	−0.09
	72–76	1.7	3.5	(0.44)	(0.31)
	77–80	1.4	1.4		
Market[3]	72–80	1.6	2.8	0.28	−0.04
	72–76	2.0	3.6	(0.39)	(0.32)
	77–80	1.0	1.5		
Time Series	72–80	1.4	1.9	−0.08	0.31
	72–76	1.6	2.3	(0.41)	(0.58)
	77–80	1.0	1.3		
Current account surplus (% of GDP)					
Model	72–80	1.0	1.6	−0.14	−0.61
	72–76	1.2	1.4	(0.39)	(0.53)
	77–80	0.8	1.7		
NIESR	72–80	1.3	1.6	0.24	−0.45
	72–76	1.1	1.9	(0.78)	(0.44)
	77–80	1.6	1.2		
Time Series	72–80	1.6	1.6	0.06	0.31
	72–76	1.4	1.3	(0.49)	(0.55)
	77–80	1.8	1.8		

(continued overleaf)

TABLE (continued)

	Real exchange rate (%)	Root mean square error		Autocorrelation Coefficients	
		1	2	1	2
Model	72–80	10.3	10.1	0.52	0.22
	72–76	10.1	7.4	(0.30)	(0.73)
	77–80	10.5	12.2		
Time Series	72–80	5.9	7.8	0.24	−0.77
	72–76	4.1	4.2	(0.40)	(0.90)
	77–80	7.5	10.2		

(NIESR n.a.)

Notes: N.I.E.S.R.: 1-year-ahead forecast taken from November Review of previous year; 2-year-ahead forecast from February Review of previous year (except in the case of forecasts made in 1972–4, when the May Review is used because the February Review forecasts only the first half of next year).

Extrapolative forecasts calculated from best regression equation relating variable to its own past (annual data). Equations used here were:

$\dot{p}$, inflation, 1954–76
$$\dot{p} = -0.1605 + 0.00299t + 0.9526\dot{p}_{-1} - 0.5589\dot{p}_{-2}$$
$$(-1.79) \quad (1.98) \quad (3.05) \quad (-1.11)$$
$\bar{R}^2 = 0.72 \quad SE = 0.05 \quad BP_4 = 5.46$ (Box-Pierce statistic, 4 lags)

y, Real GDP, 1953–76
$$y = -14254.08 + 537.77t + 0.4108y_{-1}$$
$$(-2.69) \quad (2.94) \quad (2.06)$$
$\bar{R}^2 = 0.9877 \quad SE = 720.505 \quad BP_4 = 5.35$

R (long term interest rates), 1954–76
$$R = -0.1106 + 0.002467t + 0.9474R_{-1} - 0.6042R_{-2}$$
$$(-2.20) \quad (2.63) \quad (3.37) \quad (-1.93)$$
$\bar{R}^2 = 0.8809 \quad SE = 0.01145 \quad BP_4 = 6.61$

xval, current account surplus (£million, 1963 prices) 1955–76
$$xval = 2570.36 - 39.66t - 0.829xval_{-3}$$
$$(2.12) \quad (-2.20) \quad (-2.364)$$
$\bar{R}^2 = 0.3055 \quad SE = 428.4 \quad BP_4 = 4.58$

RXR, real exchange rate, 1954–76
$$RXR = 0.001417 + 0.5520RXR_{-1} - 0.2697RXR_{-2}$$
$$(0.168) \quad (2.28) \quad (-1.112)$$
$\bar{R}^2 = 0.1455 \quad SE = 0.0374 \quad BP_4 = 0.3716$

Further Notes:

[1] Units of the errors are bracketed beside each variable. Errors in column 1 are for 1-year-ahead, in column 2 for 2-year-ahead.

[2] The autocorrelation coefficients are: in column 1 for 1-year-ahead errors (1st order coefficient), in column 2 for 2-year-ahead errors (2nd order coefficients; i.e. error regressed on itself lagged twice). Standard errors of the coefficients are parenthesised.

[3] Consols 2½%. Market forecast of long term interest rates taken to be the latest actual value.

lower public spending) by 1% of GDP, assuming that the money supply grows at a consistent rate (about 2% p.a. lower) shown in Chart 2.

This decrease lowers expected inflation when it occurs and with it nominal interest rates. The latter fall raises the real value of financial assets and this in turn causes private demands to rise by roughly as much as (initially by more than) public demands have fallen; output consequently is little affected after initial 'bumpiness'. The fall in interest rates and the rise in the real value of financial assets both raise the demand for money; the supply of money having fallen, the incipient excess demand for money causes an incipient capital inflow which causes the (nominal) exchange rate to rise. As it rises, it lowers prices and this serves to equilibrate the money market. Thus inflation falls (the nominal exchange rises) immediately in response to this policy. A final twist is that since wages were fixed by contract before the policy change, real wages and so the real exchange rate also rise (so called 'overshooting') when inflation falls unexpectedly; this effect, the simulation suggests, could be substantial. As time passes real wages, real assets and real GDP are gradually adjusted back to an equilibrium in which all real variables are the same but inflation, interest rates and money supply growth are 2% lower, the budget deficit 1% (of GDP) lower.

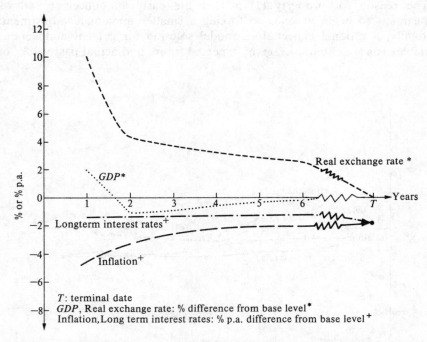

CHART 2. Budget deficit cut by 1 per cent of GDP (Money Supply Growth by 2 per cent p.a.). No pre-announcement.

This illustrates some general properties of the model worth remarking on:

(1) Any change in the expected future sequence of the exogenous variables causes plans to be revised (is a 'shock'); but the *further ahead* in the sequence the change is, the less the shock. It follows that *announcing* policy changes well in advance lessens the shock to the system; the economy moves more smoothly to the new equilibrium than if announcement and policy change coincide. (Chart 3). Notice in passing that there can be no such thing as a 'fully' anticipated change; however a change can be anticipated x periods before (at which point the shock would have occurred), and the implication of Chart 3 is that x should be made as large as possible—in fact as $x \rightarrow \infty$, the shock $\rightarrow 0$.

(2) Major shocks to real variables (such as consumption or investment, or relative prices) cause minor shocks to the important nominal variables, inflation and interest rates (though the price level may be substantially affected), major shocks to other real variables. Relevant real shocks are the discovery of North Sea oil (Chart 4) (equally relative oil prices) and changes in real social security benefits (Chart 6).

(3) Major shocks to nominal variables will however cause major shocks to both real and nominal variables. Such a shock is the fall in public borrowing and money supply growth shown in Chart 2.

The reason for property (1) is that the early announcement allows adjustment to begin at once so forcing a smaller immediate adjustment. Formally, a rational expectations model solution for current endogenous variables is a weighted average of expected future and actual past values of

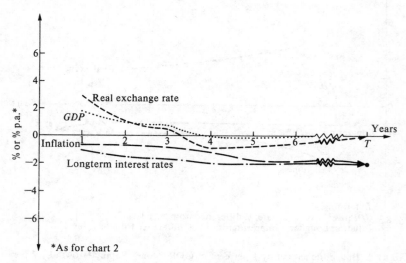

CHART 3. Budget deficit cut by 1 per cent of GDP (Money Supply Growth by 2 per cent p.a.) from Year 3, announced in Year 1.

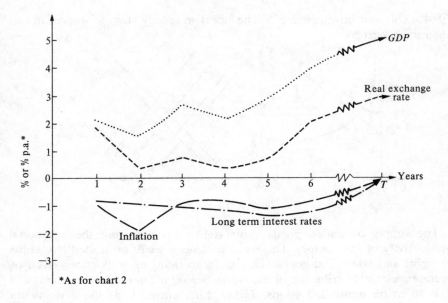

CHART 4. North Sea oil discovery.

the exogenous variables, where the weights decline both forwards and backwards; therefore an unexpected change in a distant future forecast event will have a smaller effect on current values than the same unexpected change in a current or nearby future forecast event.

Property (2) reflects the absence of money illusion that is an inherent feature of rational expectations models.

Property (3) is a characteristic of all rational expectations models in which information on general monetary conditions is available only with a lag or there are 'contracts'.[2] In this case the shock to nominal variables will respectively be misperceived (partly as a real shock) or be perceived too late for avoiding action to be taken.

We begin with the real shocks.

North Sea Oil (Chart 4)

We assume for illustration that North Sea oil was discovered in 1975 and that actual real revenues (net of foreign factor earnings) as a share of GDP were then (correctly) expected to be: 75:1%, 76:2%, 77:3%, 78:3%,

---

[2] It is possible for contracts to be 'contingent' on e.g. nominal shocks. Indexed contracts are an example. Such contracts avoid Property 3; but presumably there is some (transactions) cost attached to such indexing or contingent clauses which limits their adoption.

79:4%, 80 and onwards: 5.5% The effect in steady state is shown, in our diagram (Chart 5):

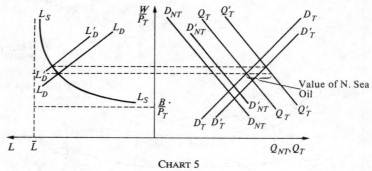

CHART 5

The supply of traded goods shifts rightwards reflecting the additional productivity of UK factors. This extra income is spent on traded (D_T shifts to right) and nontraded goods (D_{NT} shifts to right) in proportions given by preferences and distribution of the North Sea oil income.[3] To the extent that it is spent on nontraded goods, $L_D L_D$ shifts outwards as the demand for labour rises; this raises real wages and the real exchange rate. In the new

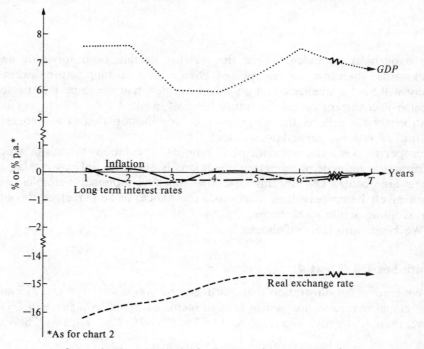

CHART 6. 10 per cent reduction in real social security benefits.

[3] I am grateful to Harold Rose for discussions on this point.

equilibrium total output and employment are higher, not just by the increase in oil output but also by the increased non-oil output induced by higher real wages. However, there is some reduction in non-oil traded goods production as a result of the real wage rise. In the more general model where there is imperfect competition between these and foreign traded goods, then there is not necessarily a net reduction in traded goods; for traded goods as for non-traded goods the income effects of the extra oil income may outweigh the substitution effects due to the higher real exchange rate.

Notice that in the two models the polar cases where the real exchange rate does not change are when all extra oil income is spent respectively on traded goods and on imported goods; in these cases output rises only by the extra oil income.

The path the economy takes when the North Sea oil discovery is announced is one of reasonably straightforward convergence to the steady state but some fluctuations in the early stages as the real exchange rate appreciation effects slightly outweigh the wealth effects. There are minimal effects on inflation and interest rates, as noted.

Social Security Benefit (Chart 6)

We assume a cut in real social security benefit by 10%. It is not assumed to be announced in advance. The steady state effect is shown in Chart 7:

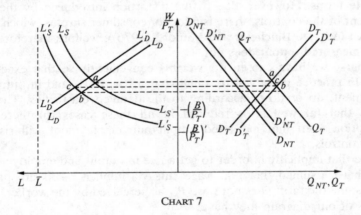

CHART 7

from initial equilibrium (a) the first effect is to shift $L_S L_S$ to the left as labour supply expands, thus lowering W/P_T. This causes a rise in traded and non-traded goods output. Demand for traded goods however falls. There is therefore a trade surplus with W/P_T at point b. This eventually causes absorption to rise so that trade balance is re-established; $D_T D_T$ and $D_{NT} D_{NT}$ shift rightwards moving $L_D L_D$ leftwards and raising W/P_T until a new equilibrium with trade balance is established at (c). We can see that employment is raised in two stages by the 'direct' effect on labour supply (a) to (b) and also by the 'indirect' effect as labour demand shifts ((b) to (c)).

By contrast with North Sea oil where the rise in non-oil output is caused by higher demand for UK goods, here it is caused by a lower supply price of UK goods. So there the real exchange rate rose, here it falls.

In response to this unexpected cut in benefit the economy moves rapidly to equilibrium as the change in real exchange rate is immediately discounted and acted upon.

Import Controls

Although our diagram considers traded goods in aggregate we can use it if we now think of P_T as a weighted average of import prices inclusive of tariffs, P_M and of export prices, P_X; let us for simplicity suppose that the exportables and the importables industries are of the same size and have the same supply/demand elasticities so that we can assign them equal weights. Now hold aggregate P_T and W constant and ask what alteration import controls would make in our equilibrium. P_T held constant implies that P_X goes down by as much as P_M goes up; so for example, a tariff of 10% would imply a rise in the exchange rate of 5%. Labour supply is unaltered; non-traded goods demand is unaltered. The supply of importables goes up, demand for importables goes down, and vice versa for exportables; by our assumption on elasticities the net effect on supply of traded goods and on demand for them is zero. The equilibrium is completely unchanged in aggregate terms. However, due to the distortion introduced by the tariff-equivalent of the controls, there is a loss of consumer surplus, which can be evaluated (e.g. see Batchelor and Minford (1976)); welfare therefore drops even if measured output does not.

Of course we have chosen the weights conveniently so that exactly this occurs. In practice there will be small changes in W/P_T and in output and employment, up or down according to the detailed elasticities. The point remains that (a) welfare is reduced in *all* these cases (b) there is no presumption even that measured output and employment will rise with import controls.

Notice that implicitly in order to get a rise in output and employment the CEPG have assumed that real wage cuts via implicit tariffs are possible. They assume the tariff does not raise P_M as perceived by the worker. Hence in terms of our diagram they have:

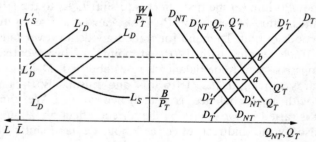

CHART 8

In the above assume P_T is a weighted average of import prices exclusive of tariff, and of export prices. Now, when the tariff is imposed, for a given W/P_T there will be (according to the CEPG) no shift in L_SL_S, but $D_{NT}D_{NT}$, Q_TQ_T shift to the right, D_TD_T to the left as importables rise in market price. Hence L_DL_D shifts to the left. The new equilibrium at (b) is one where output and 'real wages' (in terms of ex-tariff prices) are higher. Yet it is clear that this is fallacious owing to the CEPG's failure to assume that workers care about wages relative to tariff-*inclusive* import prices (i.e. L_SL_S would shift to the right). The CEPG assumption is inconsistent *even with their own wage equation*.

Nominal Shocks

We now turn to *nominal* shocks. The major ones that concern us are the two policy-induced shocks: (1) fiscal and monetary policy changes towards more or less 'expansion' (2) devaluation/revaluation which in the floating rate system is equivalent to a once-for-all unannounced money supply expansion/contraction.

We have already discussed the former in Chart 2. This showed that a shift to 'expansion' will in general lower the real exchange rate for a time since contracted wage earners are taken by surprise. However, it is unlikely to deliver a significant expansion in output even in the short term and in spite of this real depreciation. Inflation and interest rates rise immediately and the nominal exchange rate also depreciates immediately.

Can then the authorities engineer a real depreciation without worsening inflation? Chart 9 shows a once-for-all unanticipated rise in money supply

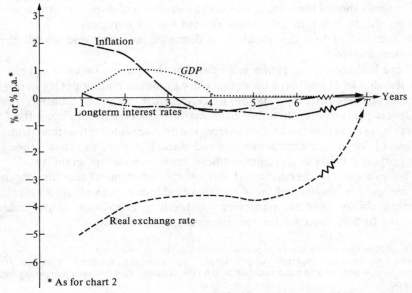

* As for chart 2

CHART 9. Rise in money supply by 2 per cent causing exchange rate depreciation.

by 2% (i.e. in year 2 money supply maintains the higher year 1 level). It shows that indeed the real exchange rate is lowered for a time; but the operation yields only small temporary gains in output as well as serious temporary inflation. In the steady state there is no change in any real variable, as revealed by our diagram. Devaluations cannot change real wages.

Stabilisation of the real exchange rate

An issue that worries many policy makers is the gyration of the real exchange rate in response to shocks of the sort we have discussed. Central Bankers frequently express the desire to stabilise these gyrations. Can this be done?

It is a by now familiar point (Fischer (1977), Phelps and Taylor (1977)) that if there are contracts extending over some period of time, the Central Bank can react to shocks within a *shorter* period and so stabilise. We can simulate this within our annual model (with annual wage contracts) by assuming that the Bank reacts 'contemporaneously' to shocks—Chart 10.[4] Chart 10 is very interesting. It reveals that, given the parameters of this model, attempts to stabilise the real exchange rate by raising money supply growth as it appreciates (or equivalently in this model, selling sterling and buying foreign exchange) will not always dampen fluctuations in the real exchange rate. If the shock is a nominal foreign shock, it will worsen them substantially. This is a serious qualification since presumably many of the shocks to the exchange rate *are* foreign in origin.

Furthermore, this policy may worsen inflation and output fluctuations. For real foreign shocks both these are worsened, for real domestic and nominal foreign shocks inflation gets worse though output improves.

In fact only when the shock is a domestic nominal one do all three variables improve.

There is therefore no prima facie case for this policy, unless one believes that the shocks of exclusive importance are domestic and monetary in origin. That belief has little foundation in general for an open economy; even though in recent years there has been major monetary instability in the UK, it is far from clear that this has arisen from the private sector rather than from the actions of the authorities themselves and if the latter are the cause, then the appropriate remedy is to remove official monetary unpredictability.

This exercise has been carried out on the assumption that the model's parameters are unchanged, as is necessarily the case with all such exercises. The possibility that in particular contracting behaviour could change weakens further the case for this monetary intervention.

---

[4] Fiscal reactions within this time period can presumably be ruled out.

Fiscal and monetary reactions with a longer time scale (i.e. feedback from *last* year's information) is able to affect the variance of the real exchange rate but only marginally within this model.

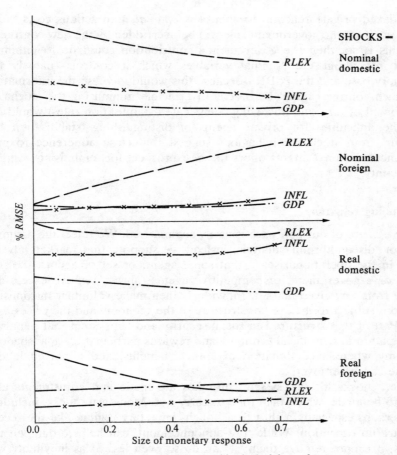

CHART 10. Effects of monetary 'stabilisation' of the exchange rate.

Notes on Chart 10

4 Separate shocks were applied to the 1980 model solution for 1 year: to inflation ('nominal domestic'). To foreign real interest rates ('nominal foreign'), to nondurable consumption ('real domestic'), and to exports ('real foreign'). The money supply growth rate was allowed to respond to the *unexpected* change in the real exchange rate, with progressively larger positive coefficients (e.g. '0.4' means that for every unexpected rise in the real exchange rate by 1% of its equilibrium value money supply rises 0.4% faster in the same year). The Chart plots for each shock the Root Mean Square effect of the shock for inflation (INFL, %p.a.), output (GDP, % of base level), and the real exchange (RLEX, % of equilibrium). Negative responses of the money supply to the exchange rate are not shown because they give uniformly much worse results than no response.

The real exchange rate could perfectly well be stabilised by the contracting parties themselves—e.g. by indexing nominal wages. Perhaps it is not because the transactions cost of indexation are too high. If this is so, and the government transactions costs are lower, then presumably private agents would happily accept government stabilisation. But it may also be that the nonindexed private reaction to shocks is *optimal*, transactions costs being very low; if so, the government rule will be overridden by the new contracts.

If this is so, then the government's contribution could be to minimise uncertainty about the nominal variables which it controls—namely the monetary base and the PSBR—because this would increase the information on which contracts could be based. In principle minimising the stochastic component of *any* rule (including complicated stabilisation rules) would do. But the difficulties for private agents of distinguishing 'stabilisation behaviour' from stochastic behaviour suggest that close adherence to pre-announced nominal targets offers the best prospect for minimising nominal uncertainty.

Concluding remarks

The essence of our approach is easily summarised. We reject the assumptions of 'disequilibrium' analysis; instead we suppose that markets always clear, in the operational sense that some agent, or set of agents, (be it a union or a government, or competitive agents) always remove excess demands from any given market. Individuals then make voluntary maximising decisions subject to the market structure of the economy and the prices they face. Part of that structure is a social security and tax system that penalises participation in the official economy and rewards participation in a 'shadow' economy where a combination of leisure, benefits, and nontaxed labour income can be enjoyed.

When shocks hit this system, mistakes are made and adjustments also need to be made, which take time to carry out. Monetary shocks, including and perhaps especially a shift to a 'tough' monetary regime like the recent one, are no exception. While 'pre-announcement' can help to dampen the effects, it cannot remove them; it can do so even less, if as inevitably will occur to some, perhaps considerable, extent, the announcements are not believed.

One consequence of monetary shocks is volatility in the real exchange rate in an institutional structure where wages are negotiated for longer periods than the home economy prices of traded goods. However, if monetary policy attempts to reduce this volatility, it will—so we find— typically cause increased volatility in other respects. More reconditely the institutional structure, and hence the pattern of volatility, may be optimal, in which case this sort of monetary intervention will cause this structure to alter, at needless cost, in order to frustrate the authorities' attempts to change the pattern.

The change in regime to lower monetary growth will itself cause a shock in the real exchange rate because wage contracts drawn up prior to it will have been 'mistaken'. However, since this mistake can be put right in subsequent contracts, it should be regarded as a purely transitional feature, part of the monetary 'transmission process'; there will be no alteration in the long run real exchange rate.

The determinants of this are, on the contrary, the 'supply-side' features of the economy, notably the tax and social security system. It is possibly kindness and social justice but it is certainly wasteful, to combine a generous social security system available 'on demand' for an unlimited period with a tax system that 'fairly' exacts the costs of that system from those employed in the official economy (through National Insurance and direct taxes). These actions raise true unemployment and the real exchange rate and they lower output.

North Sea oil may well have some upward impact on the real exchange rate because the extra trade income will partially be spent on non-traded goods; but the size of this effect is probably under 10%. Furthermore the overall effect is to raise output, even if particular sectors may contract. Some economists' notion of it as a malignant disease is therefore hard to understand.

Variously import controls or devaluation have been urged as a way of permitting 'fiscal expansion without balance of payments constraint'. We have seen that a devaluation could be engineered by a once for all shock increase in the money supply, but that the operation would impose a pointless transitional cost on the system without altering anything other than the price level and the nominal exchange rate in the long run. The scope for the real economy to expand through fiscal measures does not exist in any case; a fiscal expansion, accompanying the 'devaluation', would simply raise inflation permanently. As for import controls, these would have no effect on prices in the absence of accompanying monetary expansion; but they would raise the real exchange rate, in order that real wages could be restored to equilibrium, they would worsen resource allocation, and otherwise make no significant difference. In particular, the effects of fiscal expansion would be quite unaltered.

The ordinary man has rightly over the ages been suspicious of politicians and economists who proclaimed he could have something for nothing. Sometimes nevertheless he has given them his votes, perhaps out of sheer bewilderment. Occasionally he has bitten the hand that doled him out confetti welfare. The message of this paper is that the ordinary man is right; commonsense pays in economics. Balance the budget, be severe in monetary policy, do not give handouts, try no tricks on people. It may take time for the regime to register, but once it has, the rewards are great and people will get on with their business.

REFERENCES

AUKRUST, O. (1970), 'Prim I: A Model of the Price and Income Distribution of an Open Economy', *Review of Income and Wealth*, Vol. 16.

BATCHELOR, R. A. and MINFORD, A. P. L. (1976), 'Import Controls and Devaluation as Medium Term Policies' in *On How to Cope with Britain's Trade Position*, (H. Corbet et al).

BENJAMIN, D. and KOCHIN, L. (1979), 'Searching for an Explanation of Unemployment in inter-war Britain', *JPE*, 87, No. 3, 441–478.

Cambridge Economic Policy Group, *Economic Policy Review*, annually, 1975–80, Dept. of Applied Economics, Cambridge.

EDGREN, G., FAXEN K. O. and OHDNER, G. E. (1969), 'Wages Growth and the Distribution of Income', *Swedish Journal of Economics*, 71 (3). September, pp. 133–160.

FISCHER, S. (1977), 'Long term contracts, Rational Expectations and the Optimal Money Supply Rule', *JPE*, 85, 191–206.

HOLDEN, K. and PEEL, D. A. (1979), 'The Determinants of the Unemployment Rate: Some Empirical Evidence', *The Statistician*, Vol. 28, No. 2.

HOLLY, SEAN and ZARROP, MARTIN B. (1979), 'Calculating optimal economic policies when expectations are rational', PROPE Discussion Paper No. 30, Imperial College, London, June.

LUCAS, R. E. (1972), 'Econometric testing of the Natural Rate Hypothesis', in *The Econometrics of Price Determination-Conference*, (O. Eckstein, ed.) Board of Governors of Federal Reserve System, Washington D.C.

McCALLUM, BENNETT, T. (1976), 'Rational expectations and the Natural Rate Hypothesis: some consistent estimates', *Econometrica*, Vol. 44, 43–52.

MINFORD, A. P. L. (1980), 'A rational expectations model of the United Kingdom under fixed and floating exchange rates', in *The State of Macroeconomics*, Carnegie-Rochester Conference Series on Public Policy, 12, 293–355.

MINFORD, A. P. L., BRECH, M. J. and MATTHEWS, K. G. P. (1980), 'A Rational Expectations Model of the UK under floating exchange rates', *European Economic Review*, 14, 189–219.

MUTH, J. F. (1961), 'Rational expectations and the theory of price movements', *Econometrica* 29, 315–335.

PHELPS, E. and TAYLOR, J. (1977), 'Stabilising Powers of Monetary Policy under Rational Expectations', *JPE*, 85, 163–190.

PILE, SIR WALTER (1979), Evidence to House of Commons Public Accounts Committee, London, HMSO, 26.3.79.

SARGENT, THOMAS J. (1978a), 'Rational Expectations, Econometric Exogeneity, and Consumption', *JPE*, Vol. 86, No. 4, 673–700.

SARGENT, THOMAS J. (1978b), 'Estimation of Dynamic Labour Demand Schedules under Rational Expectations', *JPE*, Vol. 86, No. 6, 1009–1044.

SIMS, CHRISTOPHER A. (1980), 'Macroeconomics and Reality', *Econometrica*.

TAYLOR, J. B. (1979), 'Estimation and control of a macroeconometric model', *Econometrica*.

MONETARY POLICY AND INTERNATIONAL COMPETITIVENESS: THE PROBLEMS OF ADJUSTMENT

A story of smart speculators and sticky prices, set in a world of high-speed capital movements

By WILLEM H. BUITER and MARCUS MILLER*

I. Introduction

MOST advocates of controlling the money supply as a cure for inflation are willing to concede that there is a lag between changes in the money supply and their effects on the price level. Thus, in evidence to the Treasury and Civil Service Committee (1980, p. 59) Milton Friedman put this lag at roughly two years "for the U.S., U.K. and Japan".

Some recent contributions of authors belonging to the "New Classical Macroeconomics" school[1] deny the existence of such a lag for fully perceived or anticipated changes in the money supply. In the U.K. this position has been adopted by Patrick Minford (Minford (1980)). We reject the efficient markets hypothesis that generates this short-run monetary neutrality proposition as a valid characterization of the operation of labour and product markets in an economy like the U.K. Instead we postulate inertia (sluggishness or stickiness) of the domestic price level or, in a variant of our basic model, of both the price level and its rate of change.[2] While the domestic price *level* is therefore always treated as predetermined, its rate of change is endogenous to the model via an augmented Phillips curve. To capture what appears to us to be the spirit of optimistic monetarist analysis, we assume in most of what follows that the rate of inflation responds *ceteris paribus* one-for-one to changes in the rate of growth of the nominal money stock. The case in which there is more inertia in the underlying or "core" rate of inflation is also considered.

Throughout our analysis we assume that the inflation equation, and the degree of nominal inertia it incorporates, is invariant under the policy changes and the other parameter changes that we consider. Endogenous changes in the degree of price stickiness in response to perceived changes in monetary policy etc., (say because of induced changes in contracting behaviour in labour and product markets) may qualify our results. They will

* Our thanks are due to several participants in the Warwick Summer Workshop (particularly Stanley Black, Avinash Dixit, Paul Krugman and Nissan Liviatan) and to the N.B.E.R. Summer Institute for providing the opportunity to write an early draft of the paper. Buiter would like to acknowledge financial support from the N.S.F. Any opinions expressed are those of the authors and not those of the National Bureau of Economic Research.

[1] See e.g. Lucas (1972, 1975), Sargent and Wallace (1975, 1976) and Barro (1976).

[2] Nominal stickiness due to long-term contracts is also characteristic of the labour market. This is not explicitly considered in our model.

not negate them unless instantaneous transformations of contracting procedures implausibly turn long-term contracts into the equivalent of a sequence of efficient spot contracts.

In the paper we analyse the consequences of stickiness in domestic costs and prices for the behaviour of international competitiveness and real output when the government announces a (previously unexpected) programme of reductions in the rate of growth of the nominal money supply. For the purposes of this exercise, we assume both that there exists a stable, simple and well-behaved demand for money function and that the money supply can be controlled precisely by the authorities. Recent events in the U.K. and in the U.S. cast considerable doubt on both these assumptions, but an attempt at resolving these issues is beyond the scope of our paper.

Even when there is an instantaneous response of the rate of inflation to (previously unanticipated) monetary deceleration, there is likely to be an immediate adverse jump in international competitiveness as the exchange rate jumps towards its new equilibrium path and in the process changes the "real" exchange rate. The mechanism that causes this is the interaction of an efficient international financial market and a sticky domestic price level (or an "inefficient" domestic output market). After the reduction in monetary growth the sluggish domestic price level gradually approaches its new lower equilibrium path. This path is characterized by a lower rate of inflation, corresponding to the lower rate of growth of money; it also has to be sufficiently low relative to the new target path for the money supply to generate the larger long-run stock of real money balances that will be demanded at the lower steady state nominal interest rate. Initially financial capital is assumed to be perfectly mobile internationally, with speculative and arbitrage transactions conducted by economic agents endowed with rational expectations and perfect information about everything except for the policy and parameter changes discussed below. The exchange rate, unlike the domestic price level, is an asset price determined in an efficient market, and is free to jump in response to new information. After the announcement of the reduction in monetary growth, well-informed speculators cause the exchange rate to jump towards but not necessarily onto its new, lower equilibrium path. With the price level predetermined, this jump appreciation of the nominal exchange rate corresponds to a jump appreciation of the real exchange rate, a sudden loss of international competitiveness.

The combination of sticky prices, mobile capital and rational expectations in the foreign exchange market thus implies that even "gradualist" monetary policy actions can have significant transitional effects on the level of international competitiveness, and hence presumably on the sectors of the economy most exposed to international competition. While, as we shall see in Section III, mobile capital and rational exchange rate expectations are not necessary to produce large transitory swings in the real exchange rate, they are, when combined with sticky prices or wages, one empirically important source of such shocks to competitiveness.[3] Is the squeeze on the internationally competitive sector an inevitable consequence of the "gradualist" monetary cure? Is the observed sharp loss of competitiveness one of the "unpleasant side effects" of which Friedman and others have spoken, or has this come as an unanticipated shock? These are two of the questions to which this paper is addressed.

At least since Dornbusch's 1976 paper on rational exchange speculation and sticky prices, the idea that competitiveness may be prone to suffer from "jumps" of this sort has been widely canvassed (and we use his approach to discuss the consequences of monetary policy in this paper). Yet the behaviour of a floating exchange rate under monetary contractions gets rather cursory treatment in the evidence which Friedman supplied to the Committee on the Treasury and Civil Service earlier this year.

This may be seen from his answers to questions specifically addressed to the behaviour of the exchange rate under contractionary monetary policy. First in respect to an explicit question on whether the exchange rate is the principal "transmission mechanism" of monetary policy in the U.K. Friedman writes (Treasury and Civil Service Committee (1980, p. 61)):

> "I strongly disagree. Monetary policy actions affect asset portfolios in the first instance, spending decisions in the second, which translate into effects on output and then on prices. The changes in exchange rates are in turn mostly a response to these effects of home policy {on output and prices?} and of similar policy abroad. The question is topsy turvey."

> (parentheses added)

Second, on whether "the loss of price competitiveness on British exports and against foreign imports and/or the squeeze in profit margins because of the strong £ should be of concern to the authorities in their conduct of monetary policy", Friedman's answer is "No". Finally when asked whether the conduct of monetary policy would be assisted by limiting the opportunity or incentive for international financial capital movements, he says "No, hampered rather than assisted". (Treasury and Civil Service Committee (1980, p. 61)).

After spelling out the details of how monetary policy might affect the real exchange rate assuming perfect capital mobility in Section II below, we consider the opposite extreme of zero capital mobility in Section III. We call this "current account monetarism". If capital mobility is ignored and in addition the "augmentation" term in the Phillips curve is sluggish then there will be no discrete movements in the exchange rate or in competitiveness in response to changes in monetary growth. This model, which we refer to as "Manchester current account monetarism", seems to give results which are closest to what Friedman said in evidence (and corresponds closely to what

---

[3] Without sticky nominal prices, rational expectations and mobile capital are, of course, not even sufficient to produce real or nominal exchange rate overshooting.

Laidler himself has written on an earlier occasion, Laidler (1975)—whence the label).

In response to the question on taxes on capital movements, Dornbusch wrote to the Committee (Treasury and Civil Service Committee (1980, p. 72)):

> "It is quite apparent ... that both from the point of view of public finance and from the perspective of macroeconomic policy, a real interest equalisation tax is called for."

His emphasis on the need for such fiscal intervention can be appreciated from what he said earlier about the effects of an overvalued exchange rate (Treasury and Civil Service Committee (1980, pp. 71–72)):

> "If pursued over any period of time the {high real exchange rate} policy will lead to a disruption of industry; reduced investment, shutdowns, declining productivity, loss of established markets and a deterioration of the commercial position."
>
> (parentheses added)

In a recent paper Nissan Liviatan (1980) also recommends a tax on capital inflows (a subsidy to capital outflows) as a desirable accompaniment to monetary contraction, and Flood and Marion (1980) argue the virtues of a two-tier exchange rate in these circumstances.

In the last section of the paper therefore, we show what happens when such a tax is included in a model where capital is otherwise perfectly mobile. It is shown that a tax that equalizes after-tax real rates of interest is equivalent to a real exchange rate stabilization tax and that, at any rate in our model, this tax takes a rather simple form. Thus, perhaps not surprisingly, the highly open economy model, when insulated by such a tax, generates behaviour not very different from the current account monetarist model with sluggish "core" inflation.

If indeed the U.K. government and its advisers have been operating with an approach to monetary policy which ignores the role of international capital mobility then the analysis in this paper will explain how on this occasion the speculators have had the jump on the "gradualists". By way of conclusion, we indicate how monetary authorities who adopt fixed growth rate rules for the money stock can beat the speculators—by appropriate jumps in the *level* of the money stock.

II. Real balances, the real exchange rate and monetary policy

The model

In this section a simple macroeconomic model of a small economy in a world of freely floating exchange rates is specified in which the exchange rate is determined by the actions of risk-neutral speculators possessed of rational expectations and perfect information about the parameters of the model (including those describing government behaviour). The basic specification is derived from recent papers by Dornbusch (1979) and Liviatan (1980); it can be used as a convenient and tractable vehicle for discussing the effects of monetary policy in an open economy. (We also include some discussion of the effects of discovering oil on the exchange rate.)

The log-linear equations of the model are as follows:

$$m = k(y+\rho) - \lambda(r-r_d) + p + \theta; \quad k, \lambda > 0 \ (LM \text{ curve}) \tag{1}$$

$$y = -\gamma(r - Dp) + \delta(e-p) + \chi\rho_\infty; \quad \gamma, \delta > 0 \ (IS \text{ curve}) \tag{2}$$

$$Dp = \phi y + \Pi; \qquad\qquad \phi > 0 \ (\text{Phillips curve}) \tag{3}$$

$$\Pi = \mu \ (\text{Core inflation}) \tag{4}$$

$$De = r - r^* - \tau \ (\text{Covered interest parity}) \tag{5}$$

List of symbols

m logarithm of the nominal money stock   exogenous
p logarithm of the domestic price level "at factor cost"
   i.e. excluding indirect taxes
y logarithm of real non-oil domestic income (zero represents "high employment" real income)
ρ oil production expressed as a fraction of real non-oil income (assumed to be constant and lasting only a few years)   exogenous
ρ_∞ permanent income equivalent of $\rho(\rho_\infty < \rho)$ exogenous
r domestic nominal interest rate on non-money assets
r_d nominal rate of interest paid on domestic money
r^* foreign nominal interest rate on non-money assets   exogenous
θ rate of indirect tax   exogenous
e logarithm of the exchange rate (domestic currency price of foreign currency)
Π trend or "core" rate of inflation
μ rate of growth of the domestic nominal money supply;
   $\mu \equiv Dm^4$ exogenous
τ rate of tax on capital inflows (subsidy on outflows)   exogenous

D is the differential operator, so for example $Dm = \dfrac{dm}{dt}$.

The first equation describes the condition for equilibrium in the money

---

[4] $Dm(t)$ is to be interpreted as the right-hand side derivative of $m(t)$:

$$Dm(t) \equiv \lim_{h \to 0} \left(\frac{m(t+h) - m(t)}{h} \right), \quad h > 0.$$

Neither $p(t)$ nor $Dp(t)$ respond instantaneously to changes in the *level* of $m(t)$.

market: the demand for nominal money balances depends on real income (from non-oil production and from oil production, assumed to be a fixed percentage, ρ, of non-oil production), the opportunity cost of holding money $(r - r_d)$ and the price level net of taxes, p, plus the rate of indirect tax θ.[5] The condition for equilibrium in the market for non-oil production is given next: output is demand-determined and, after eliminating the effect of non-oil income, demand depends on the instantaneous real rate of interest $(r - Dp)$, the real exchange rate $(e - p)$ and permanent real income from oil production, ρ_∞.[6] Inflation is generated by an augmented Phillips curve, equation (3) and so depends on the level of (non-oil) production, and the trend or "core" inflation rate (Π). For simplicity the explicit dependence of the domestic price level on the exchange rate and the price of foreign goods is ignored in this paper.[7] By choice of units the "full employment" level of output, at which current demand adds no extra pressure to the trend rate of inflation, is set at unity, so its logarithm is zero. The coefficient ϕ relating inflation to the log of output is kept as a constant for simplicity.[8]

Trend or core inflation is assumed in equation (4) to equal the rate of monetary expansion, a constant denoted by the letter μ. Finally, we have the condition (5) for equilibrium in the foreign exchange market, which is characterized by risk-neutral speculators endowed with perfect information and infinitely-elastic covered interest arbitrageurs. As a result, the uncovered interest differential in favour of the domestic country, net of any tax on capital imports, must equal the forward discount on the currency; and the forward discount must, in the absence of unannounced exogenous changes, accurately forecast the change in the spot rate.

It will be convenient in what follows to define explicit variables for the level of real balances and for the real exchange rate as follows:

$$l \equiv m - p \\ c \equiv e - p$$ where p is the price level *net* of indirect taxes, and the foreign price level is assumed constant.

The first of these is a measure of the liquidity in the economy (though it does not, by construction, take account of indirect taxation); the second is a measure of international competitiveness—if the price of foreign currency, e, is high relative to the domestic price level, p, (excluding VAT) then, for given foreign prices, domestic producers will be in a favourable competitive position.

---

[5] Permanent income and the expected rate of inflation could be included as arguments in the money demand function without qualitatively altering our results.

[6] Permanent income from non-oil production is identified with its long-run equilibrium or steady-state value. This equals 0 in the model.

[7] The qualitative properties of the model are not affected by this simplification. See Buiter and Purvis (1980).

[8] If, instead, the coefficient were to increase with y itself then the stability condition appearing below $(\Delta < 0)$ would be more easily satisfied at low levels of output than for high levels.

The dynamics of adjustment

Using these definitions we may rewrite the structural equations in matrix form:

$$
\begin{bmatrix} D & 0 & \phi & 0 \\ 0 & D & \phi & -1 \\ 1 & 0 & -k & \lambda \\ 0 & -\delta & 1-\phi\gamma & \gamma \end{bmatrix}
\begin{bmatrix} l \\ c \\ y \\ r \end{bmatrix}
=
\begin{bmatrix} 0 \\ -\mu & - & r^* & - & \tau \\ \theta & + & \lambda r_d & + & k\rho \\ -\gamma\mu & + & \chi\rho_\infty \end{bmatrix}
\tag{6}
$$

The last two equations are simply the *LM* and *IS* curves (1) and (2) above. The other two describe the evolution of liquidity and competitiveness by combining the augmented Phillips curve with the money growth parameter and with the interest parity condition respectively. The income and interest rate variables can be eliminated to obtain a two equation reduced form in liquidity and competitiveness, as follows:

$$
\begin{bmatrix} Dl \\ Dc \end{bmatrix} = \frac{1}{\Delta}\begin{bmatrix} \phi\gamma & \phi\lambda\delta \\ 1 & \delta(\phi\lambda-k) \end{bmatrix}\begin{bmatrix} l \\ c \end{bmatrix}
$$

$$
+\frac{1}{\Delta}\begin{bmatrix} \phi\lambda\gamma & 0 & 0 & -\phi\gamma & -\phi\gamma\lambda & -\phi\gamma k & \phi\lambda\chi \\ \lambda & -\Delta & -\Delta & -1 & -\lambda & -k & -(k-\phi\lambda)\chi \end{bmatrix}
\begin{bmatrix} \mu \\ r^* \\ \tau \\ \theta \\ r_d \\ \rho \\ \rho_\infty \end{bmatrix}
\tag{7}
$$

where $\Delta = \gamma(\phi\lambda - k)-\lambda$ and is assumed to be negative throughout the paper. (The effects of the change in sign of $\phi\lambda - k$ as ϕ and λ vary is discussed in the text). This relationship may be written more compactly as:

$$
\begin{bmatrix} Dl \\ Dc \end{bmatrix} = A\begin{bmatrix} l \\ c \end{bmatrix} + Bx
$$

where x is the vector of exogenous variables shown in equation (7).

The corresponding equations defining the long-run equilibrium (to be discussed in the next section) are:

$$
\begin{bmatrix} \tilde{l} \\ \hat{c} \end{bmatrix} = \begin{bmatrix} -\lambda & -\lambda & -\lambda & 1 & \lambda & k & 0 \\ 0 & \gamma/\delta & \gamma/\delta & 0 & 0 & 0 & -\chi/\delta \end{bmatrix}
\begin{bmatrix} \mu \\ r^* \\ \tau \\ \theta \\ r_d \\ \rho \\ \rho_\infty \end{bmatrix}
= -A^{-1}Bx
\tag{8}
$$

The dynamic behaviour described by this system is illustrated in Fig. 1. For given values of the exogenous variables the paths followed by liquidity and competitiveness depend on the matrix A. From the values given for the

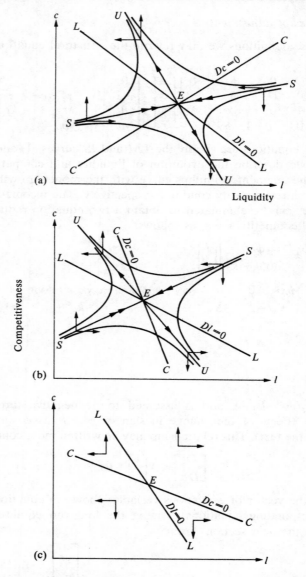

FIG. 1. The dynamic behaviour of real balances and competitiveness.

first row of the matrix in equation (7) we find that $Dl = 0$ implies $\left.\dfrac{dc}{dl}\right|_{Dl=0} = \dfrac{-\gamma}{\delta\lambda} < 0$. The locus of the stationary value of l is labelled LL in the figure. The arrows show liquidity declining to the north east of LL, where high levels of real balances and competitiveness (and so high demand pressure) lead to inflation which exceeds the fixed rate of growth of nominal money. From the values given for the second row of A we find that the locus of stationary values for the real exchange rate drawn as CC in Fig. 1 has the slope $\left.\dfrac{dc}{dl}\right|_{Dc=0} = \dfrac{1}{\delta(k-\phi\lambda)}$ whose sign depends on the size of ϕ, the coefficient in the Phillips curve. For low values of ϕ CC slopes positively. As ϕ increases CC rotates anti-clockwise so the slope becomes infinite then negative.

The exchange rate (and therefore competitiveness) is a forward-looking or "non-causal" variable. As it is a price that clears an efficient international financial market it is not a predetermined state variable. It is free to make discrete jumps at a point in response to "news". "News" includes all previously unanticipated current or future changes in exogenous variables and policy instruments. Since e and c can make discrete jumps, De and Dc are to be interpreted as *right-hand side* time derivatives of e and c. This agrees with economic intuition because the current value of the forward-looking variable e (and its rate of change) are found by solving forwards in time for the entire (expected) future path of e. This in contrast with the backward-looking or "causal" variables p and l that are predetermined at a point in time and are continually "updated" by dynamic equations for Dp and Dl. In a dynamic linear model with n_1 backward-looking and n_2 forward-looking variables, there exists a unique saddle-path converging to the long-run equilibrium provided there are n_1 stable characteristic roots (the ones "corresponding to" the n_1 predetermined variables) and n_2 unstable characteristic roots (the ones "corresponding to" the n_2 jump variables). In our two equation dynamic model with one causal and one non-causal variable, the existence of a unique convergent saddle path therefore requires the presence of one stable and one unstable root. The assumption of long-run and short-run perfect foresight and the transversality condition that rational agents will not choose an unstable solution mean that the jump variable (e or c) will always assume the value required to put the system on the unique convergent solution trajectory.

For there to be one stable and one unstable root it is necessary and sufficient that the determinant of A be negative, i.e. that $\phi\delta/\Delta<0$. We show below that $\Delta<0$ is necessary and sufficient for an increase in aggregate demand to raise output at a given level of competitiveness. As $\Delta = \gamma(\phi\lambda - k) - \lambda = \lambda(\gamma\phi - 1) - \gamma k$, a sufficient condition for the long-run equilibrium to be a saddlepoint is a sufficiently small value of ϕ, the slope of the short-run Phillips curve. The equilibrium will always be a saddlepoint if the $Dc = 0$ locus is upward sloping ($\phi\lambda - k < 0$). This case is illustrated in Figure 1A. Even if the $Dc = 0$ locus is downward-sloping, the equilibrium can be a saddlepoint provided the $Dc = 0$ locus is steeper than the $Dl = 0$ locus. This case is drawn in Figure 1(b). Note that the condition that the downward-sloping $Dc = 0$ locus be steeper than the downward-sloping $Dl = 0$ locus

$$\left(\left|-\frac{\gamma}{\delta\lambda}\right| < \left|\frac{1}{\delta(k-\phi\lambda)}\right| \quad \text{where} \quad k-\phi\lambda < 0\right)$$

is simply the condition that Δ be negative. If ϕ is very large and Δ becomes positive, the $Dc = 0$ locus is downward-sloping and less steep than the $Dl = 0$ locus. In this case the equilibrium ceases to be a saddlepoint and is completely unstable instead. Figure 1(c) illustrates this. A completely stable system is ruled out for our model, but this is just as well. Such a comforting configuration in a model comprising only backward-looking variables would be very disconcerting in a model including forward-looking variables. With two stable roots the transversality or terminal condition that the model converges to equilibrium can no longer determine a unique initial condition for e and c. There is a continuum of values of c for any given value of the predetermined variable l that converge to equilibrium. In what follows we rule out the case of Fig. 1C from further consideration and assume $\Delta < 0$ throughout. Both Figs. 1(a) and 1(b) show qualitatively similar behaviour for l and c. To the east of CC liquidity is high, so interest rates will be low, but low interest rates are associated with appreciating currencies in a world of high capital mobility, so the arrows show competitiveness declining to the east of CC. Both Figs. 1(a) and 1(b) show a unique upward-sloping saddlepath SS converging to the equilibrium.[9]

Our assumption that the economy is stable places it on SS. In terms of the figure, the stickiness of the price level (though not of its rate of change) together with the assumption that the money supply is exogenously determined means that real balances are, at any time, given by past history, and it is the real exchange rate which adjusts, by jumps in the nominal exchange rate, so as to put the economy on SS.

The long run and impact effects of monetary policy

The long and short run effects of various monetary policy actions can now be analysed. Formally, the long run equilibrium values of liquidity and competitiveness, denoted $\hat{l}$ and $\hat{c}$, can be found by setting Dl and $Dc = 0$ in equation (7) and solving for the coefficients shown in equation (8). The long run effects of three contractionary monetary policy actions can be seen very easily as in the lower panel of Fig. 2, which shows the demand curve for real balances as a function of the nominal rate of interest on non-money domestic assets, assuming "full employment" real income.

A reduction in μ, the rate of monetary expansion, will in the long run reduce the domestic nominal rate of interest by the same amount, and so will shift the system from an initial equilibrium at point A, for example, to a new equilibrium at point B. Real liquid balances will increase accordingly by an amount determined by the slope of the demand for money, so $dl = -\lambda \, d\mu$ i.e. the percentage increase in real balances will be the % fall in monetary growth multiplied by the "semi-elasticity" of demand.

An increase in the demand for real balances due to a reduction in τ or an increase in θ or r_d will shift the demand curve over to the right as shown in the

---

[9] The unstable root defines the locus UU.

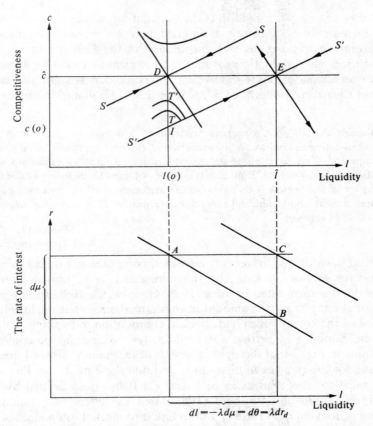

Fig. 2. The impact and long-run effects of contractionary monetary policy.

figure. If for example, the rate of indirect taxation were to be increased,[10] then the desired ratio of money balances to prices net of indirect tax would increase by the same percentage which would appear as a shift in the demand curve in Fig. 2. Since a change in the standard rate of VAT in the U.K. changes the average rate of indirect tax by half as much (as many goods escape VAT), a rise of VAT by 8% would increase market prices by about 4% (given factor costs) and so would shift the demand curve in the figure by 0.04. In the absence of monetary accommodation restoration of long-run equilibrium requires the path followed by factor costs to fall so that market prices return to the path they followed before the VAT increase. Since the trend rate of monetary growth has not increased, there will be no change in the equilibrium rate of interest, so the new equilibrium at C will be horizontally to the right of A.

[10] By assuming offsetting fiscal action by the authorities, we ignore the effects of changes in indirect tax on aggregate demand—cf. the 1979 budget.

Another change which will shift the demand for money schedule in Fig. 2 is an increase in r_d, the rate of interest paid on money. An increase in competition in banking (as was encouraged in the U.K. by the regime of Competition and Credit Control in 1971 for example) may be expected to lead to an increase in the rates paid on bank deposits. In the Bank of England Quarterly Bulletin of September 1974, Graham Hacche observed that:

"Although the MC {i.e. company holdings of M_3} and M_3 {i.e. broad money} equations estimated before the introduction of the new approach failed to forecast subsequent behaviour at all accurately, it has been found that equations which fit the data to the end of 1972 quite well may be obtained by inclusion of the CD rate over part of the period. This supports the argument that the own rate on money became a more significant and powerful determinant of demand for M_3 from the end of 1971 onward."

Hacche (1974) p. 296
(parentheses added)

On the basis of this argument, increased competition would increase the demand for money by $\lambda\, dr_d$, by the semi-elasticity of demand times the change in the own rate. In June 1980 Greenwell's Bulletin suggested a figure of about 5% for the amount of reintermediation that might follow the removal of the corset which had checked competition in banking. This effect could be captured by setting $\lambda\, dr_d = 0.05$. (For diagrammatic convenience we assume in Fig. 2 that the rightward shift of the money demand function is the same for the changes in θ and in r_d and that the equilibrium increase in l is the same for the changes in μ, θ and r_d.) It has been argued by others, notably by Tobin and Brainard (1963), that the effect of competition in banking is not simply to raise r_d, but to link it to market interest rates and so make it endogenous. If r_d is endogenous and moves with r, then the effect of r on the demand for money correspondingly falls and the LM curve becomes steeper. Many of the effects of an increase in MLR are also captured by an increase in r_d as the deposit rate is tightly linked to MLR.

We assume that all policy changes (and other shocks) are unanticipated until they are "announced". When we come to look at the impact effects of these policies it is necessary to specify whether they are implemented when they are announced or whether there is some delay in implementation. Assuming that announcement and implementation are simultaneous, then the impact effect on the exchange rate can be shown in the upper panel. (All the policies shown in the lower panel will simply shift the long-run *equilibrium* from D to E. As can be confirmed from Table 2, none of these policies change the equilibrium real exchange rate—although they would if a real balance effect were included in the aggregate demand equation).

The stable path leading to E is shown as $S'S'$. Since the level of real balances cannot change discretely, the level of competitiveness must fall from its initial level of $\hat{c}$ to $c(0)$ as shown by point I in the figure. It is the intersection of the stable path $S'S'$ and the initial condition $l = l(0)$ which determines the initial level of competitiveness and hence the jump it makes in response to exogeneous changes.

If the authorities announce a monetary policy action which they say will be implemented after a delay then, at the time of announcement, there will be a jump in the level of competitiveness, but by less than if the action were implemented immediately. Following Wilson (1979), we can show this in Fig. 2 by noting that there are an infinite number of paths leading from $l(0)$ to the line shown as $S'S'$. Two such paths are shown labelled as T and T', where the label indicates how long it takes to get from $l(0)$ to $S'S'$, and $T' > T$. For any given delay of length T between announcement and implementation, the exchange rate will jump *to that path which takes an interval of length T to reach $S'S'$*. Consequently when the policy is actually implemented, the exchange rate will be placed on the convergent path and will not have to "jump" onto it. The mathematical treatment of anticipated future changes in exogeneous variables is given in Appendix 4 of Buiter and Miller (1980).

The medium term financial strategy and the credibility of policy announcements

The centrepiece of the medium term financial strategy announced by the present Conservative administration is the *sequence* of annual one point reductions in (the target range for) monetary growth planned for the next four years. Following the same principles as described above, one can portray the response of the system to such a strategy as in Fig. 3. The (unanticipated) reduction of monetary growth in the first year would, if implemented immediately, lower competitiveness down to point A on S_1S_1; but allowance has also to be made for the present effects of the announced future policy. With rational expectations, the system should follow a path which will, without future jumps in competitiveness, end up on S_4S_4, the stable locus associated with the fourth (and subsequent) years of the

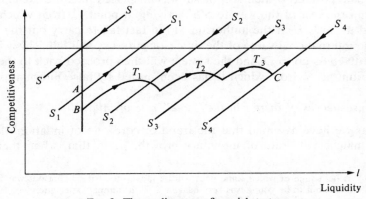

FIG. 3. The medium term financial strategy.

strategy. There is no way of getting from a point such a A on to the south west branch of paths such as S_2S_2, S_3S_3, S_4S_4 without a jump, so competitiveness must initially fall further than A. We have therefore chosen an initial value of B which leads to a sequence of connected, one-year-long paths, each "driven" by the level of monetary growth prevailing in the year in question, which will put the system at point C on S_4S_4 as the fourth and final year of the medium term strategy dawns.[11]

The absence of "jumps" in the path shown satisfies the requirement that there should be no unexploited profit opportunities. The presence of the "humps" or kinks reflects of course the discontinuous nature of a gradualist policy which lowers monetary growth in steps. If the reduction in monetary growth were smooth (as described by $D\mu = -a\mu$ for example) then the exchange rate path would be correspondingly smoothed, and in the numerical examples below we consider the consequences of such a policy (of "crawling gradualism") for the initial level of competitiveness.

So far we have assumed both that the Government carries out its announced policy and that the public firmly believes that it will. But what if policy announcements are *not wholly believed*? One simple way of analysing the case of a not-wholly-credible announcement of a change in monetary growth T periods in the future, is to assume that agents in the private sector attach probability weights $1-w$ and w, $0 < w < 1$, to two possibilities, first that the policy is implemented at time T as announced today and second that there is *no* change in policy at time T. This will lead to an "expected" rate of monetary growth for time T, $\mu^e(T) = w\mu(0) + (1-w)\mu^a(T)$, where $\mu^a(T)$ is the announced figure. In this case, the exchange rate would jump on to the path which will take the system to the point corresponding to the "expected" rate of monetary growth at the time T periods from the announcement. This is shown in Fig. 4 where the path towards which the speculators push the system is shown as $S''S''$ and competitiveness jumps to $c(0)$.

At time T, the truth will out, and agents will discover which of the two prospects is correct. If their scepticism was misplaced then the exchange rate will jump the rest of the way to $S'S'$ arriving at point C, from which it will proceed towards E. If the authorities do in fact fail to carry out the policy, then the international value of the domestic currency will fall. This will push competitiveness up to D, and the system will then proceed back to the initial equilibrium at A, from which it has been misled by false information.

The consequences of inertia in the "core" rate of inflation

So far we have assumed that the trend or core rate of inflation, denoted by Π, matches the rate of monetary growth, μ, so that, when there is a

[11] Will this be a time of which some poet will be moved to write: "Glorious was it in that dawn to be alive, but to be young was very heaven"? With rational expectations, of course, he will have penned his lines long before then!

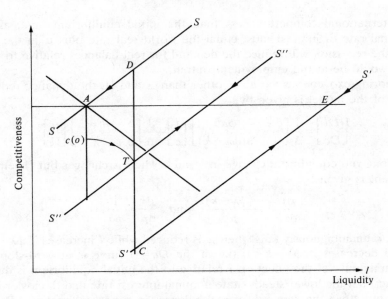

FIG. 4. The effect of not-wholly-credible policy announcements.

monetary slowdown, the rate of wage and price inflation falls immediately by the same amount, even without any recession; the latter will cut the rate of inflation even further.

Most monetarists would be willing to allow for some delay between the slowdown in monetary growth and its effect on core inflation. For example, both Friedman and Laidler in their evidence to the House of Commons Committee on the Treasury talked of a delay before monetary policy affected "expected inflation"—which is how they refer to the core rate of inflation. As we will see in more detail below, the assumption that core inflation does respond instantly implies a bigger fall in the nominal interest rate on the initiation of a monetary slowdown than seems plausible.

In this section, therefore, we examine how the existence of a lag of length T between the policy action and the effect on the trend rate of inflation affects the analysis. The way we proceed is first to see what would happen if there was a monetary slowdown and trend inflation *never* adjusted; and second to allow for expectations that full adjustment will come after a delay of T periods, (with no adjustment till then).

If there was never any change in Π, despite a fall in μ, then the system would not approach a full employment equilibrium with a lower rate of inflation, as has previously been the case. The equilibrium will exhibit the same, lower rate of inflation as before, but a permanent recession will be necessary to compensate for the unyielding inflationary psychology now postulated. As the real rate of interest must equal the world real rate of interest in equilibrium, this recession must be associated with a lower level of international competitiveness than the initial equilibrium; and, as the nominal rate of interest must equal the world real rate plus μ in the long run, the recession will reduce the demand for real balances relative to what they would be at full employment output.

Ignoring exogeneous variables other than μ and Π, the dynamic reduced form of the model is given by:

$$\begin{bmatrix} Dl \\ Dc \end{bmatrix} = \frac{1}{\Delta} \begin{bmatrix} \phi\gamma & \phi\lambda\delta \\ 1 & \delta(\phi\lambda - k) \end{bmatrix} \begin{bmatrix} l \\ c \end{bmatrix} + \frac{1}{\Delta} \begin{bmatrix} \Delta & \gamma k + \lambda \\ 0 & \lambda \end{bmatrix} \begin{bmatrix} \mu \\ \Pi \end{bmatrix}$$

The long run equilibrium change in l and c when μ changes but Π remains constant is given by:

$$\frac{d\hat{l}}{d\mu} = \frac{-(\phi\lambda - k)}{\phi} \quad \text{and} \quad \frac{d\hat{c}}{d\mu} = \frac{1}{\phi\delta} .$$

Thus, c unambiguously falls when μ is reduced while l increases if $\phi\lambda - k > 0$ and decreases if $\phi\lambda - k < 0$ (i.e. if the $Dc = 0$ curve is upward-sloping). The ambiguity of the effect on l relative to the initial equilibrium is due to the fact that the lower steady-state nominal interest rate and the lower level of output affect the demand for real balances in opposite directions. Rather than going through the entire catalogue of possible configurations, we shall present a single example. Figure 5 is drawn on the assumption that $\phi\lambda = k$, i.e. that there is no long-run change in money balances. The initial long-run equilibrium is at A. If Π changes by the same amount as μ, the new equilibrium would be E. If only μ changes, the long-run equilibrium is at E'. The saddlepath through E is SS, that through E' is $S'S'$. The effects of a delay of length T in the adjustment of Π to μ can now be described in Figs. 5(a) and 5(b). If core inflation never adjusts, an unanticipated monetary growth reduction from an initial equilibrium at A will immediately worsen the level of competitiveness to E' which is also the new long-run equilibrium.[12] The jump of c from A to E' can either exceed (as in Fig. 5a) or fall short of (as in Fig. 5b), the jump on to the saddlepath SS through E that would occur if core inflation were to adjust immediately. If speculators correctly anticipate a delay of length T before core inflation adjusts, the level of competitiveness will fall to a point between E' and I which we have labelled D. From there it will proceed along the unstable path shown as DT which arrives on the converging path SS through E after a period of length T. Hence when the rate of core inflation does adjust after an interval T, the exchange rate will not need to make any discrete adjustment in order to follow the new path SS thereafter.

If core inflation adjusts slowly towards the new rate of monetary growth, rather than moving quickly after a fixed delay, then of course the appropriate dynamic equation should be added to the model (e.g. $D\Pi = \zeta(\mu - \Pi)$).

---

[12] If steady state real money balances are not invariant under changes in μ, c will jump to the point on $S'S'$ given by the predetermined level of l. The system will then gradually move to E' along $S'S'$.

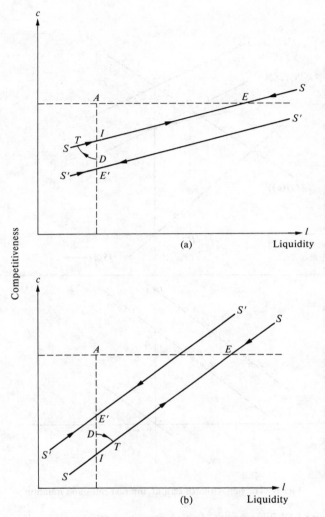

FIG. 5. The consequences of inertia in the 'core' rate of inflation.

Our analysis avoids adding another differential equation, but the size of the jump for the case of sluggish adjustment may be handled without difficulty by the methods described in Appendix 1 of Buiter and Miller (1980).

The behaviour of output, interest rates and inflation

Before moving on to variants of the basic model described in this section, we show what happens to output, interest rates and inflation in response to the three principal policy actions described above, both on impact and over time. This is most easily done with reference to Fig. 6. In the bottom panel is

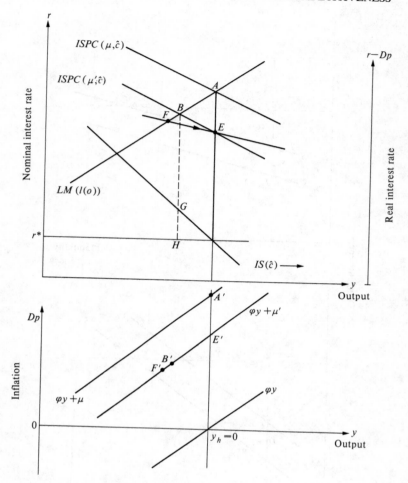

FIG. 6. The behaviour of output, interest rates and inflation.

the augmented Phillips curve. Initial equilibrium is at point A', with output at its "high employment" level, y_h (where units are chosen so $y_h = 0$), and inflation equal to the rate of monetary growth, μ. The same equilibrium is shown at point A in the upper panel. As the *IS* curve is drawn with reference to the *real* rate of interest $(r - Dp)$ on the right hand vertical axis while the *LM* curve is drawn with respect to the *nominal* rate on the left, equilibrium requires that the *IS* and *LM* schedules are vertically separated by the rate of inflation. This is achieved by "adding" the augmented Phillips curve vertically on top of the *IS* curve.[13] The resulting curve labelled *ISPC* is shown passing through point A. This schedule will slope down to the right

---

[13] Algebraically, this schedule is obtained by substituting the Phillips curve, equation (3) into the *IS* curve, equation (2); the coefficients are given in the bottom row of (6) above.

if $\phi = 0$, but becomes horizontal when $\phi = 1/\gamma$, and slopes up as ϕ increases further. We assume that the *ISPC* curve does not slope up so steeply as to cut the *LM* curve from below. This condition

$$\left(\frac{dr}{dy}\bigg|_{LM} = \frac{k}{\lambda} > \frac{dr}{dy}\bigg|_{ISPC} = \frac{\phi\gamma - 1}{\gamma}\right)$$

is equivalent to the condition that $\Delta = \lambda(\phi\gamma - 1) - \gamma k < 0$. If it holds, an increase in effective demand increases output at a given nominal interest rate and a given level of competitiveness. The equilibrium then is a saddlepoint.

When the rate of monetary growth is reduced, the augmented Phillips curve shifts down in the bottom panel and so the *ISPC* schedule shifts down in the top panel. The intersection of this *ISPC* schedule with the high employment level of output, y_h, indicates the new level of equilibrium, E, where neither the real exchange rate nor output differ from what they were at A, but nominal interest rates have fallen by the amount of the monetary slowdown. It might be thought that B would describe the *impact* effect but this cannot in general be so. In the case represented in Fig. 6, the distance from B to H must measure the change in the exchange rate (De) as it shows the excess of domestic interest rates above the world interest rate, and the distance from B to G on the *IS* curve measures the rate of domestic inflation (Dp), so the difference GH shows the change in competitiveness ($Dc \equiv De - Dp$). Hence at all points to the left of E competitiveness will be improving—which is why the economy cannot start at B and proceed along *ISPC* to E.[14] Instead what happens, as has been discussed above, is a sharp initial fall in competitiveness which lowers both the *IS* curve and the *ISPC* curve so that the latter intersects the *LM* curve at a point such as F. This will represent the initial equilibrium for nominal interest rate and output, with the inflation rate shown by F' in the lower panel. Since the model is linear and, if stable, is driven by only one root, the system must proceed in a straight line[15] from F to E with increasing real money balances shifting the *LM* curve to the right and improving competitiveness shifting the *IS* and *ISPC* curves to the right. The derivation of this convergent path in $r - y$ space is given in Appendix 2 of Buiter & Miller (1980). The initial equilibrium, given by the intersection of the *LM* curve and the *ISPC* curve corresponding to μ' and $c(0)$, shows the nominal interest rate *falling* in response to the monetary disinflation. The initial level of the rate of interest can indeed lie beneath its long run equilibrium value if ϕ is large enough, so that the *ISPC* curve is flat or upward sloping; in this case the rapid fall of inflation causes a more serious recession with interest rates beneath their long run level given by E. What this possibility brings out is the very strong assumptions built into the Dornbusch-Liviatan model, namely that core

---

[14] Unless there is a real interest equalisation tax in force, see IV below.
[15] This line is, of course, the stable locus corresponding to SS in the earlier figures.

inflation falls instantly in line with monetary growth and that output adjusts instantly to changes in interest rates and the real exchange rate.

The cases where the VAT rate is increased and where the own rate on money rises[16] (not shown) result in an initial contractionary shift in the *LM* curve, with no direct effect on the *ISPC*. Note that in this case the nominal interest rate will *rise* on impact if the *ISPC* curve is sufficiently downward-sloping. For reasons which have been discussed the currency appreciates and this lowers the *ISPC* to give the initial equilibrium at a lower level of income and higher nominal interest rates than in the initial equilibrium. In this case there is no immediate response of core inflation Π as there is no change in monetary growth. Only excess capacity lowers Dp.

The strong assumptions about the speed of clearing for the goods market and of the responsiveness of the "core" rate of inflation to monetary growth which characterise the Dornbusch-Liviatan model used here are by no means required to obtain the real exchange overshooting propositions of this paper. Relaxing them does however lead to a higher order differential equation system requiring numerical, rather than purely algebraic, analysis.

The impact of oil

While the preceding analysis has emphasised the impact of monetary policy actions on the level of competitiveness, there are some observers of the current scene who argue emphatically that, for the U.K., a major factor affecting international competitiveness is the discovery and extraction of North Sea oil, see Forsyth and Kay (1980) for example. Hence, although we are principally concerned with monetary policy, we do briefly discuss the effect of discovering and exploiting a previously unknown endowment of natural resources in the context of our simple model. (As the following exposition is greatly simplified, the reader is referred to Buiter and Purvis (1980) for a more adequate treatment).

We distinguish between the value of *current oil production* (which is taken to be a fixed percentage, ρ, of the value of non-oil production, and to last for only a limited period) and the *permanent income* equivalent of this stream ρ_∞ (i.e. that constant percentage of non-oil income which has the same present discounted value as the finite flow of oil). As can be seen from the structural equations (1) and (3) listed above, the value of current production ρ affects the demand for money (by $k\rho$ per cent), while the permanent income value of the oil is assumed to affect the demand for home-produced non-oil goods (whose high employment supply is taken to be unaffected). As is apparent from equation (2) the impact of this increase in demand for given r and y is to lead to an offsetting loss of competitiveness $dc = \dfrac{-\chi\rho_\infty}{\delta}$ which will reduce the demand for non-oil output to match the fixed supply. In Fig. 7 this loss

---

[16] Or where the *level* of the nominal money stock is reduced.

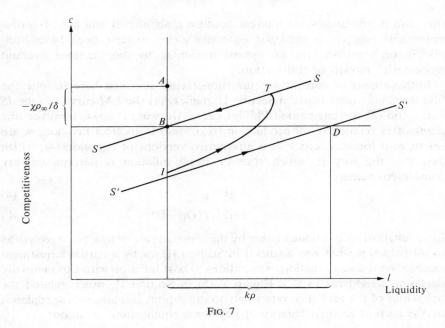

FIG. 7

of competitiveness is shown by the fall of c from A to B, and, in the absence of the effect of current oil production on the LM curve, this would be the end of the story.

The effect of the temporary element, ρ, is rather like the effect of a temporary contraction of the nominal money supply: it reduces the amount of real balances left to "turn over" non-oil production. While oil is being produced therefore, the level of real balances required to maintain full-employment of labour will rise by $k\rho$, and this is shown by point D in Fig. 7. The exchange rate will not move the system on to the path $S'S'$ associated with point D, however, as the flow of oil is assumed to end after T periods. Instead the level of competitiveness will fall to point I; from which, after T periods, the system would reach the stable path SS, which will take it ultimately to point B, the long run equilibrium.

III. Immobile capital or "current account monetarism" and the real exchange rate

Without any international mobility of financial capital, the mechanism through which a reduction in monetary growth affects real output and the real exchange rate changes significantly. The interest rate now clears a domestic bond market that is segmented from the rest of the world. The momentary equilibrium values of output, interest rate and exchange rate are determined by IS, LM and trade balance equilibrium. Financial autarchy may not be of great relevance to the U.K. economy, but consideration of this case is nonetheless of interest because a significant amount of earlier monetarist analysis of the open economy seems to have been based, implicitly or explicitly, on an approach similar to the "current account monetarist" models of this section.[17]

Both variants of current account monetarism specified here include the first three equations listed in Section II, namely (1) the *LM* curve, (2) the *IS* curve and (3) the augmented Phillips curve. (In what follows, however, the parameters relating to oil production (ρ, ρ_∞) and to indirect taxation, θ, are set to zero for simplicity.) Two alternative versions of equation (4), which describes the way in which core or trend inflation is determined, are considered, namely:

$$\Pi = \mu \tag{4}$$

$$D\Pi = \zeta(Dp - \Pi) \tag{4'}$$

Core inflation is determined *either* by the constant rate of monetary growth as in (4) (which is what was assumed in Section II), *or* by a partial adjustment mechanism relating inflation expectations to past inflation with exponentially declining weights as in (4'). Equation (5) in Section II, which related the behaviour of the exchange rate solely to the capital account, is now replaced by the current account balance of payments equilibrium condition:

$$\eta(e - p) - \nu y = 0 \qquad \eta, \nu > 0 \tag{5'}$$

where the current account surplus, $\eta(e - p) - \nu y$, is assumed to rise as competitiveness rises and fall as income rises. So the exchange rate is now determined by the need to balance the current account.

Thus equations (1), (2), (3), (4) and (5') define what we refer to as the Dornbusch–Liviatan[18] variety of current account monetarism, denoted *D–L*. Replacing (4) by (4') defines what we call "Manchester" current account monetarism. This latter specification imparts significantly more inertia to price behaviour: not only the price level but also the core rate of inflation take time to adjust to changes in monetary growth.

D–L current account monetarism

Using (4) the model can be represented as in equations (9)–(12).

$$Dl = -\phi\Omega\gamma\lambda^{-1}l - \phi\Omega\gamma\mu \tag{9}$$

$$y = \Omega\gamma\lambda^{-1}l + \Omega\gamma\mu \tag{10}$$

$$c = \nu\Omega\gamma\eta^{-1}\lambda^{-1}l + \nu\Omega\gamma\eta^{-1}\mu \tag{11}$$

$$\Omega = [1 + \gamma(k\lambda^{-1} - \phi) - \delta\nu\eta^{-1}]^{-1} \tag{12}$$

$$= [-\lambda^{-1}\Delta - \delta\nu\eta^{-1}]^{-1}$$

[17] See for example, Laidler (1975, Chapter 9), Friedman (Treasury and Civil Service Committee (1980, p. 61)).

[18] Neither Dornbusch nor Liviatan have to our knowledge applied their price equation to the study of "current account monetarism".

The steady-state equilibrium is given by

$$\begin{bmatrix} \hat{l} \\ \hat{c} \end{bmatrix} = \begin{bmatrix} -\lambda\mu \\ 0 \end{bmatrix} \tag{13}$$

The model will be stable if $\Omega > 0$. We shall assume this to be the case. The evolution of the real money stock and the real exchange rate is depicted in Fig. 8. As before there is no long-run effect of a reduction in μ on the real exchange rate, but the steady state stock of real money balances increases. The impact effect of an unanticipated reduction in μ is an immediate adjustment of the real exchange rate from E_1 to E_{12} in Fig. 8(b), unless $\gamma = 0$ in which case there is no effect. After this there is a gradual recovery towards the original value of c, at E_2. Output also first declines and then increases back to the fixed full employment level. With l given, the

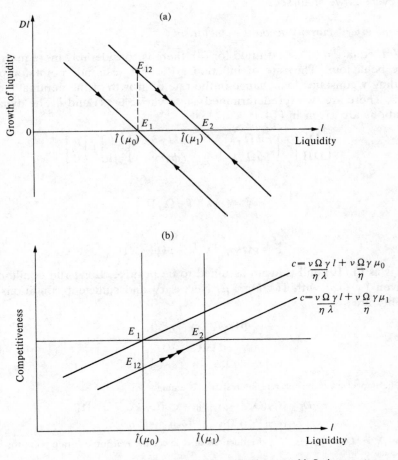

FIG. 8. Current account monetarism with jumps in the rate of inflation $\mu_1 < \mu_0$.

impact effect of a reduction in μ on r is to lower it: $r = k\Omega\gamma\lambda^{-1}\mu + \lambda^{-1}(k\Omega\gamma\lambda^{-1} - 1)l$. The steady state real interest rate remains unchanged.[19] To maintain current account balance as real output declines the real exchange rate appreciates. While the transmission mechanism is quite different here from what it is under perfect or limited international capital mobility,[20] the effects on y and c are qualitatively similar although in all probability quantitatively smaller. With the D–L specification of the "core" inflation rate, an unanticipated reduction in the rate of monetary growth initially leads to a decline in output and a "jump" fall in the real exchange rate followed by a gradual (monotonic) return to their original long-run equilibrium levels. Some exchange rate "overshooting" can occur even without capital mobility.

Jumps in the real exchange rate in response to monetary disinflation are ruled out in the Manchester version of current account monetarism (4), however, as we shall see.

"Manchester" current account monetarism

With equation (4') substituted for (4), there is considerably more inertia in price behaviour. The rate of inflation no longer responds point for point (holding y constant) to a change in the rate of growth of the nominal money stock. There are two (predetermined) state variables: Π and l. The dynamic equations are given in (14).

$$\begin{bmatrix} Dl \\ D\Pi \end{bmatrix} = \begin{bmatrix} -\phi\Omega\gamma\lambda^{-1} & -(\phi\Omega\gamma + 1) \\ \zeta\phi\Omega\gamma\lambda^{-1} & \zeta\phi\Omega\gamma \end{bmatrix} \begin{bmatrix} l \\ \Pi \end{bmatrix} + \begin{bmatrix} \mu \\ 0 \end{bmatrix} \tag{14}$$

Also:

$$y = \Omega\gamma\lambda^{-1}l + \Omega\gamma\Pi \tag{15}$$

and

$$c = \nu\Omega\gamma\eta^{-1}\lambda^{-1}l + \nu\Omega\gamma\eta^{-1}\Pi \tag{16}$$

Ω is as in (10) and is again assumed to be positive. Long-run equilibrium is given by (13) with $\Pi = Dp = \mu$. Necessary and sufficient conditions for stability are

$$\Phi\Omega\gamma(\zeta - \lambda^{-1}) < 0 \tag{17}$$

$$\zeta\phi\Omega\gamma\lambda^{-1} > 0 \tag{18}$$

---

[19] The impact effect on the real interest rate is ambigous:

$$r - Dp = [\Omega\gamma(k\lambda^{-1} - \phi) - 1]\mu + \lambda^{-1}[\Omega\gamma(k\lambda^{-1} - \phi) - 1]l$$
$$= [\delta\nu\eta^{-1} - 1]\Omega\mu + \lambda^{-1}[\delta\nu\eta^{-1} - 1]\Omega l.$$

If $\phi = k/\lambda$, $r - Dp = -\mu - \lambda^{-1}l$ and reductions in μ lower the *real* interest rate point-for-point on impact.

[20] The limited capital mobility case is analyzed in Buiter and Miller (1980).

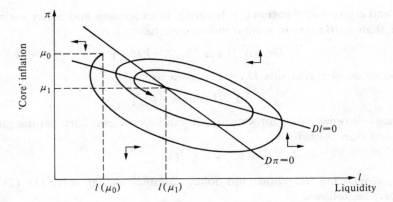

FIG. 9. Current account monetarism with sluggish inflation.

The behaviour of the model is necessarily cyclical if it is stable, as in that case the discriminant of the characteristic equation is negative $(\phi\Omega\gamma[\phi\Omega\gamma(\zeta-\lambda^{-1})-4\zeta\lambda^{-1}]<0)$.

A stable cyclical adjustment path is drawn in Fig. 9.

From (16) it is apparent that changes in the rate of monetary growth do not lead to jumps in the real (or nominal) exchange rate: c is a function of l and Π both of which are predetermined. The continuous adjustment path of c is given by:

$$Dc = v\Omega\gamma\eta^{-1}\phi\Omega\gamma\lambda^{-1}[\zeta-\lambda^{-1}]l + v\Omega\gamma\eta^{-1}[\phi\Omega\gamma(\zeta-\lambda^{-1})-\lambda^{-1}]\Pi \quad (19)$$

With both l and Π behaving cyclically, c is also likely to exhibit cyclical behaviour, even though in principle the cyclical trajectories of l and Π could neutralise each other as regards their influence on c. Explicit numerical solutions are required to obtain the exact trajectory of c in this case.

Omitting the capital account and attributing significant inertia to both p and Π—as is characteristic of Manchester monetarism—rules out the possibility of the dramatic appreciation of the real exchange rate in response to a reduction in monetary growth that has characterised recent U.K. experience. However, because of the cyclical nature of the dynamic adjustment path, the maximal extent of overshooting of the long-run equilibrium on the solution trajectory may well be significant if $\gamma\neq 0$ and could even exceed the jump overshooting of our earlier models.

IV. A real interest rate equalization tax

One proposal for eliminating jumps in the real exchange rate due to monetary disinflation or other internal or external disturbances involves a real interest equalization tax. Liviatan (1980) has suggested a tax on capital inflows (subsidy on outflows) that will exactly achieve the aim of keeping international competitiveness constant. Consider the dynamic reduced form for l and c given in equation (7). Ignoring all exogenous and policy variables other than τ, the tax on capital inflows, we have

$$Dc = \Delta^{-1}l + \Delta^{-1}\delta(\phi\lambda - k)c - \tau \tag{20}$$

The value of τ that sets $Dc = 0$ is given by:

$$\tau = \Delta^{-1}[l + \delta(\phi\lambda - k)c] \tag{21}$$

Since c is now a constant we can, without loss of generality, set it equal to zero and thus obtain

$$\tau = \Delta^{-1}l \tag{22}$$

Again ignoring exogenous and policy variables we can solve (1), (2) and (3) for y as follows:

$$y = -\Delta^{-1}[\gamma l + \delta\lambda c] \tag{23}$$

With $c = 0$ by choice of units we can rewrite (22) as

$$\tau = -\frac{1}{\gamma} y \tag{24}$$

This is Liviatan's result that to stabilise the real exchange rate, the capital import tax should be proportional to the deviation of actual output from high employment output. Note that since this tax achieves $De = Dp$, it follows that

$$r - Dp = r^* + \tau \tag{25}$$[21]

Referring back to Fig. 6 we observe that the tax τ is designed so as to fill the gap between the IS curve, which shows the domestic real interest rate at the equilibrium level of competitiveness, and the world real interest rate r^*. While it prevents any loss of competitiveness, the tax does not prevent a contraction of income after a monetary slowdown. Thus in Fig. 6 income contracts immediately to point B from which it proceeds gradually towards E along the ISPC schedule. (We show later that appropriate monetary action can offset both the income and real exchange rate consequences of a monetary slowdown).

A tax on capital inflows that perfectly stabilizes the real exchange rate also equalizes the real after tax rates of interest at home and abroad. It is this sort of tax which Dornbusch recommended for the U.K. in his evidence to the Treasury Committee cited above.

V. The size of the initial loss of competitiveness

To illustrate how large the jump in the exchange rate might be relative to the extent of the monetary slowdown, we include some calculations for the equations used in Section II.

[21] $r = r^* + De + \tau$ implies $r - Dp = r^* + De - Dp + \tau$.

The factors affecting the size of the jump are best explained with reference to Fig. 10. With time measured along the horizontal axis, the paths followed by the money stock, the price level and the exchange rate (the price of foreign currency) can, by appropriate choice of units, be represented by the single line AB until time t_0 when an unanticipated slowdown occurs (where for convenience $t_0 = 0$). The subsequent path of m is BC. In long run equilibrium the level of real balances must rise by $-\lambda\,d\mu$, as discussed in Section II, so the price level must approach the path labelled FE which lies the appropriate distance beneath BC. Under the assumptions that the *derivative* of prices responds instantly to the monetary slowdown, but the price *level* is slow to adjust, the price level will approach BC from above as shown by the path BG in the figure.

As the model is super neutral, the equilibrium real exchange rate will be unaffected by the change in the rate of monetary growth; so the exchange rate must also approach the path FE. Indeed, one can think of the line FE as defining a path for the "equilibrium" exchange rate, $\hat{e}$, as follows. The slope of FE (which is equal to μ) corresponds to the difference between the trend rate of inflation domestically (μ) and the trend rate of inflation overseas (assumed to be zero), and so measures the trend rate of change of

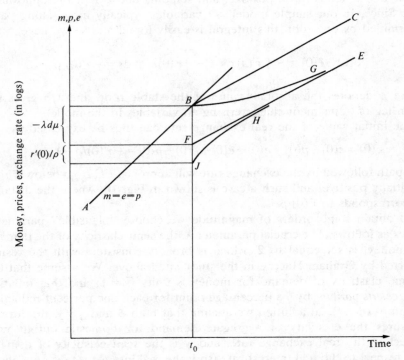

FIG. 10. The consequences of a monetary slowdown and the determinants of the initial loss of competitiveness.

the exchange rate; the level of FE is, as we have seen, such as to generate the correct real exchange rate in the long run.

Whether the actual exchange rate will, on the implementation of the slowdown, attain this path immediately or not is related to whether or not the domestic interest rate moves immediately to its new equilibrium level, as we shall show using the equation relating the rate of change in the price of foreign currency to the interest differential $(De = r - r^*)^{22}$ and the definition of $\hat{e}$ which implied $(D\hat{e} = \mu)$. We see that the price of foreign currency moves relative to its equilibrium path according to $De - D\hat{e} = r - r^* - \mu$. The assumption that the exchange rate is a forward looking variable can be expressed by showing the relationship between the initial disequilibrium and expecture *future* interest rate "disequilibria", as follows:

$$e(0) - \hat{e}(0) = - \int_0^\infty [r(s) - (r^* + \mu)] \, ds = - \int_0^\infty [r(s) - \hat{r}] \, ds \equiv - \int_0^\infty r'(s) \, ds$$

where $\hat{r}$ defines the equilibrium domestic interest rate, and r' is the discrepancy between the current value and this equilibrium value. So the initial level of the exchange rate, relative to the point F in the figure, depends on the integral of future values of r', with the price of foreign currency lying below F if r' tends to be positive, and standing above F if the opposite is true. Since, in our simple model, all variables typically move along paths determined by one root, this integral is easily found and so we have

$$e(0) - \hat{e}(0) = - \int_0^\infty r'(s) \, ds = - \int_0^\infty r'(0) e^{-\rho s} \, ds = - r'(0)/\rho$$

where ρ denotes the absolute value of the stable root, and $1/\rho$ gives the mean lag of adjustment characterising all variables in the model.

The initial value of the real exchange rate can thus be expressed as

$$c(0) = e(0) - p(0) = e(0) - \hat{e}(0) + \hat{e}(0) - p(0) = - r'(0)/\rho + \lambda \, d\mu.$$

The path followed by the exchange rate will approach FE from below if $r'(0)$ is initially positive, and such a case is shown in Fig. 10, where the distance FJ corresponds to $r'(0)/\rho$.

To obtain some orders of magnitude we choose "plausible" parameter values as follows. The crucial parameter λ, the semi-elasticity of the demand for money, is set equal to 2, which is broadly consistent with the results reported by Graham Hacche in the study cited above. We assume that the income elasticity of demand for money is unity ($k = 1$) and that inflation falls, *ceteris paribus*, by $\frac{1}{2}$ a percentage point for each one per cent reduction in output ($\phi = \frac{1}{2}$). In addition we assume that both δ and $\gamma = \frac{1}{2}$; the former measures the elasticity of aggregate demand for domestic output with respect to the real exchange rate, and γ is the *semi*-elasticity of demand with respect to the real interest rate (so if the real interest rate is only about

---

[22] Assuming $\tau = 0$ for convenience.

0.05, this means a real interest rate *elasticity* only $\frac{1}{20}$ as large as the real exchange rate elasticity).

From an initial position of equilibrium, a 1% slowdown in monetary growth leads to an initial loss of competitiveness of about $2\frac{1}{3}$% with these parameter values.[23] This can be broken down into the 2% loss due to the fall in the "equilibrium" exchange rate $(\lambda\,d\mu)$ and an additional 0.3% to 0.4% due to the fact interest rates do not immediately fall by 1% to their new long run level. (The stable root is -0.42 and the initial level of interest rates is calculated as about $\frac{1}{6}$ of a point above equilibrium, so the integral $-r'(0)/\rho$ is (approximately) 0.33%).

Not only is an initial loss of competitiveness of about $2\frac{1}{3}$% to be expected from an (unanticipated) 1% monetary slowdown but according to the analysis in Section II, the same $2\frac{1}{3}$ loss of competitiveness is to be expected from a 1 percentage point increase in the rate paid on money (r_d), and from a 2 point increase in the general rate of indirect taxation (θ). We can thus estimate, very roughly, the impact to be expected in our model from the sort of monetary actions planned and taken in the U.K. in the last year or so on the level of competitiveness. An (unanticipated) 1% point monetary slowdown, plus a 2% point rise in r_d, and a 4% rise in the general rate of indirect tax would give a total loss of competitiveness of $5\times2\frac{1}{3}=11\frac{2}{3}$%. The recent loss of competitiveness in Britain has been much greater than this, exceeding 30% for manufacturing; but the calculation we have performed is biased downwards in at least two ways , which we now discuss.

We have so far assumed that the trend rate of inflation (Π) responds immediately to the announcement of the monetary slowdown, which is undoubtedly over-optimistic. We can at least allow for some delay in the response of trend inflation to the monetary slowdown. If we assume an *infinite* delay, then for the above parameter there will be an immediate 4% loss of competitiveness as the economy moves into a recession with output falling by 2%. (This equilibrium corresponds to that shown by the point E' in Fig. 5 in Section II.) For a delay of 2 years between the reduction in monetary growth and the response in core inflation, the initial loss of competitiveness turns out to be 3.1%, and for a 1 year delay it falls to 2.8%. So a delay of a year or so could add half a point to the loss of competitiveness to be associated with 1% slower monetary growth.

In calculating the impact of the monetary slowdown above, we ignored the present impact of actions announced for future years as in the Medium Term Financial Strategy. Instead of calculating a precise figure corresponding to the effect of a (credible) policy of 4 successive 1 point reductions in

---

[23] Let ρ_s be the stable characteristic root of the system. In Buiter and Miller (1980) we show that the initial jump in competitiveness can be calculated as follows:

$$c'(0) \equiv c(0) - \hat{c} = \left(\frac{\rho_s - \phi\gamma\Delta^{-1}}{\phi\lambda\delta\Delta^{-1}}\right)(l(0) - \hat{l}) = -\left(\frac{\rho_s - \phi\gamma\Delta^{-1}}{\phi\lambda\delta\Delta^{-1}}\right)\lambda\,d\mu$$

$\rho_s = -0.4215$ and $d\mu = -1$. Therefore $c'(0) = -2.36$.

monetary growth spread over 4 years, we simply examine the effects of a policy of smooth monetary deceleration (as described by the formula $D\mu = -a\mu$). If the initial rate of monetary growth is 10% p.a. and a is equal to 0.173, then this implies cutting monetary growth to 5% in 4 years; if a is reduced to 0.139 then the half life of the monetary slowdown rises to 5 years. Either of these seems to be a reasonable description of the general policy adopted, one of initiating a monetary slowdown designed to eliminate inflation, with a half life of about 4 or 5 years. Using the same parameters as before we find that the implication of such a programme is to reduce competitiveness initially by around 8% points (7.5% for the 5 year half life, 8.7% for the 4 year case).

This calculation suggests that the current effect of policy announced for future years may be considerable. Of course such announcements may not be wholly credible, and so they may not get their full effects on impact (as we have discussed in Section II). If the authorities nevertheless pursue them vigorously, their credibility will doubtless increase over time, so the "impact effect" will get spread over time.

While it is not our present purpose to produce accurate point estimates of the impact of monetary policy actions on the real exchange rate, we believe that the illustrative calculations reported here lend support to the view that monetary policy actions have made a significant contribution to the alarming loss of international competitiveness recently experienced in the U.K. (Others have concluded likewise: in a recent paper Krugman (1980), for example, argued that a one point monetary slowdown alone might lead to a 5 point loss of competitiveness. This is on the basis of output being constant and prices continuing completely unaffected for two years, before jumping immediately to their long run equilibrium.) Further light may be shed on this by examining more adequate dynamic models[24] and by empirical investigations which explicitly recognise the forward-looking nature of the exchange rate.

VI. Conclusions

By attributing rational, forward-looking expectations to private agents one can analyse the current consequences of anticipated and unanticipated current and future policy changes and exogenous shocks. We have examined some aspects of the Medium Term Financial Strategy and of oil and V.A.T. shocks from this point of view. If foreign exchange speculators are forward-looking in a world with high capital mobility and a flexible exchange rate but a sticky domestic price level, then competitiveness is the first casualty in the fight against inflation.

Jumps in the real exchange rate would not occur if prices were perfectly flexible, however; because with an "efficient" market for goods comple-

---

[24] Allowing for lags of adjustment in the response of income to the real exchange rate and real interest rates, for example.

menting an efficient foreign exchange market, a "superneutral" real economy is unaffected by monetary actions, even in the short run. This postulate of perfect nominal wage and price flexibility, which we reject, is adopted by others both for theoretical analysis and for policy prescription; thus Patrick Minford, in a small econometric model fitted to annual data for the U.K., has money wages and prices responding immediately and fully to perceived monetary shocks (see his evidence to the Treasury and Civil Service Committee (1980, pp. 131–143) and the reference given there).

One way in which jumps in the real exchange rate can be avoided is by imposing a real interest-equalization tax. While precisely such a tax has not, to our knowledge, been implemented anywhere, it is interesting to note that two tight-money, market-oriented economies (W. Germany and Switzerland) have made use of taxes on capital inflows in attempts to check their overvaluation.

Real-exchange rate overshooting and departures of output from its full employment level are, in the model used in this paper, due to the inability of the *real* money stock to respond promptly to changes in demand for liquidity. This reflects stickiness of both the domestic price level and of the *level* of the nominal money stock. Even if the inertia in the wage-price mechanism is taken to be an unalterable institutional constraint, changes in the real stock of money balances can be implemented immediately and without need for departures from full employment, by making the level of the nominal money stock respond to changes in the demand for real money balances without further need for change in the *level* of the path of the sticky domestic price level. For any policy change or exogenous shock, the required equilibrium change in the real money supply can be calculated from the steady-state conditions (see equation (8)). If the level of the domestic price path is to remain unchanged, the required proportional change in the nominal money stock simply equals the required percentage change in real money balances. The paths of m, p and e when there is an unanticipated reduction in μ and time t_0 and an unanticipated increase in m (with $dm = -\lambda \, d\mu$) are shown in Fig. 11.

As a topical example of how the real exchange rate can be stabilized by an appropriate jump in the nominal money stock, consider the policy of reducing the rate of growth of money to reduce the rate of inflation. Since this increases the steady state demand for real money balances, transitory real exchange rate appreciation and loss of output can be avoided by immediately increasing the *level* of the nominal money stock (by $-\lambda \, d\mu$) at the same time that the *rate of monetary growth* planned for the future is reduced. If one has adopted monetary targets and does not wish to be forced into a U-turn because of the effects on the real exchange rate, the appropriate policy is an M-jump!

The obstacles to such an accommodating monetary policy include both uncertainty about the model and credibility of such a combination of policy actions. The calculation of the nominal money supply change required to

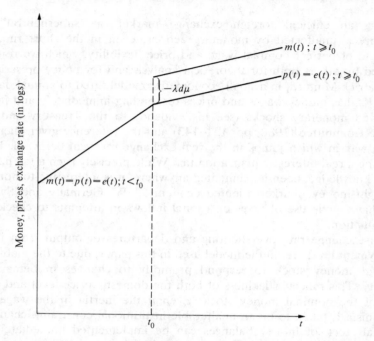

FIG. 11. The effect of an unanticipated reduction in monetary growth μ at t_0 accompanied by a real exchange rate and output stabilizing increase in the money supply m.

achieve the new long-run equilibrium corresponding to the new values of the policy instruments or exogenous variables immediately and without departures from full employment only appears simple because both policy makers and private agents in our model have full knowledge of the structure of the economy and the behaviour of the exogenous variables.

The policy credibility problem is obvious from our conclusion that in order to avoid exchange rate overshooting and excess capacity when the announced future rate of growth of the money supply is *cut* in order to reduce inflation, it is necessary to once-and-for all *increase* the level of the nominal money stock. The intentions of the government are likely to be in doubt when a policy of monetary disinflation is initiated with an expansion of the nominal money stock!

Not only do changes in the *monetary growth* rate require adjustments in the targeted path for the money stock if real exchange rate changes are to be avoided; so too do variations in the rate of indirect tax and changes in the demand for bank deposits arising from varying the regulations governing bank behaviour. Since there have been policy actions on all three fronts in 1979–1980 it will be interesting to see whether the authorities will choose to accommodate the resulting increased demand for real balances, or whether they will choose to stick to the path for the nominal money stock announced in the 1980 Budget. A policy of "rebasing" the monetary aggregates to grow as targeted before but from the higher level that has been reached after the rapid expansion over the year would be a convenient way of avoiding the costs of deflation which would be required to stay within the previously announced target range.[25]

REFERENCES

BARRO, ROBERT J. (1976) "Rational Expectations and the Role of Monetary Policy", *Journal of Monetary Economics*, 2, January, pp. 1095–1117.

BUITER, W. H. and MILLER, M. H. (1980) "Monetary Policy and International Competitiveness", University of Warwick Economic Research Paper No. 183, October.

BUITER, W. H. and PURVIS, D. D. (1980) "Oil, Disinflation and Export Competitiveness", University of Warwick Economic Research Paper No. 185, October.

DORNBUSCH, R. (1976) "Exchange Rate Dynamics", *Journal of Political Economy*, 84, December, pp. 1161–1176.

—— (1979) "Exchange Rate Rules and Macroeconomic Stability", mimeo.

FLOOD, R. P. and MARION, N. P. (1980) "The Transmission of Disturbances Under Alternative Exchange Rate Regimes with Optimal Indexing", National Bureau of Economic Research Working Paper No. 500, July.

FORSYTH, P. J. and KAY, J. A. (1980) "The Economic Implications of North Sea Oil Revenues", *Fiscal Studies*, 1, July pp. 1–28.

GREENWELL, W. & Co. (1980) *Monetary Bulletin*, No. 106, June, London. W. Greenwell & Co.

HACCHE, G. (1974) "The Demand for Money in the United Kingdom: Experience since 1971", *Bank of England Quarterly Bulletin*, 14, September, pp. 284–305.

KRUGMAN, P. (1980) "Anti-inflationary Policy and the Exchange Rate", mimeo.

LAIDLER, D. (1975) *Essays in Money and Inflation*, Manchester: Manchester University Press.

LIVIATAN, N. (1980) "Anti-inflationary Monetary Policy and the Capital Import Tax", Warwick Economic Research Paper, No. 171.

LUCAS, ROBERT, E. (1972) "Expectations and the Neutrality of Money", *Journal of Economic Theory*, 4, April, pp. 102–124.

—— (1975) "An Equilibrium Model of the Business Cycle", *Journal of Political Economy* 83, December, pp. 1113–44.

MINFORD, PATRICK (1980) "A Rational Expectations Model of the U.K. under Fixed and Floating Exchange Rates" in *The State of Macroeconomics*, K. Brunner and A. Meltzer eds, Carnegie-Rochester Conference Series on Public Policy.

SARGENT, THOMAS and WALLACE, NEIL (1975) "Rational Expectations, the Optimal Monetary Instrument and the Optimal Money Supply Rule", *Journal of Political Economy*, 83, April, pp. 241–254.

—— and —— (1976) "Rational Expectations and the Theory of Economic Policy", *Journal of Monetary Economics*, 2, April, pp. 1–44.

TOBIN, JAMES and BRAINARD, W. C. (1963) "Financial Intermediates and the Effectiveness of Monetary Controls", *American Economic Review*, 53, May, pp. 383–400.

Treasury and Civil Service Committee (1980) *Memoranda on Monetary Policy*, HC720, London, H.M.S.O.

WILSON, CHARLES A. (1979) "Anticipated Shocks and Exchange Rate Dynamics", *Journal of Political Economy*, 87, June, pp. 636–647.

[25] (added in proof) The monetary targets were substantially "rebased" in the 1981 budget.

MONETARY TARGETS AND THE EXCHANGE RATE: A CASE FOR CONDITIONAL TARGETS

By M. J. ARTIS *and* D. A. CURRIE

Introduction

SINCE the abandonment of fixed exchange rates and the widespread adoption of floating rates, a number of countries have adopted policy regimes of pre-announced monetary targets. The adoption of such open-loop policy rules has usually been advocated on the basis that it promises the control of inflation. Theoretical and empirical work bearing on the determination of the exchange rate has in recent years given prominence to the money supply and expectations of its growth as determinants, and consequently accounts of how monetary targets yield control of inflation indicate that in an open economy the exchange rate is a significant part of the transmission mechanism.

At the same time, however, the experience of practical monetarism has given rise to reservations about the costs of pursuing open-loop monetary growth rules; in particular, the perceived costs of following these rules seem to have been related to large and persistent real appreciations of the exchange rate. In Germany, these costs forced a modification of the monetary rule in 1978–79 and in the same year in Switzerland its complete, if temporary, abandonment; in the United Kingdom, whilst monetary targets have not been abandoned for this reason, a great deal of concern has nevertheless been expressed about the extent of appreciation of the real exchange rate experienced under monetary target regimes, both in 1977 and more recently in 1979–80.

These considerations lead to some obvious questions. If the exchange rate is an important part of the transmission mechanism of monetary policy, and if the link between monetary policy and the exchange rate is not precise, would not exchange rate targets promise at least as good a regime for inflation control as one of monetary targets? Alternatively, recognizing that monetary growth rules cannot be costlessly thrown away, what mechanisms exist for reducing the conflict between their continued pursuit and the maintenance of competitive exchange rates?

In this paper we seek to explore these questions by specifying a model in the deterministic form of which a monetary target has a dual in an exchange rate target, but in the stochastic form of which a real choice can arise between the two. The analysis suggests that as between the two, for a variety of shocks to the system, there is little to choose—indeed, if anything the exchange rate target fares rather better. One suggestion for removing the conflict between monetary targets and the exchange rate is to employ an interest equalization tax; the analysis is extended to allow for this, comparing a regime of monetary targets-cum-equalization taxes with one of exchange rate targets. Not surprisingly, this tilts the comparison away from exchange rate targets. However, the practicability of such taxes can be, and has been questioned, and in this light we go on to consider whether monetary targets would not be improved if made conditional on the behaviour of the exchange rate.

The paper as a whole is structured as follows: in Section I, we refer in more detail to the evidence on real exchange rate variability in monetary targeting regimes. In Section II we refer to the body of theory and empirical evidence bearing on the weight of monetary factors in exchange rate determination and to the evidence suggesting that nominal exchange rate changes have transitory real effects. In Section III we analyse alternative targetting regimes, and in Section IV consider conditional policy rules. Section V provides some conclusions, while the Appendix presents our analytical model and formal results.

I

Under a regime of floating exchange rates the adoption of pre-announced monetary targets is seen as providing a critical requirement in respect of promising an expectation of stable domestic financial policies. Without this, or some equivalent device, speculators would be forced to lay bets in a void of doubt, on nominal as well as real developments, resulting in an erratic and chaotic system of exchange rates with disruptive feedback effects. With the assurances provided by monetary targets or their equivalents, exchange rates will of course still change, but real rates, it is supposed, will reflect 'real things' and should not change erratically or persistently in response to purely nominal shocks, although, because speeds of adjustment in goods markets are slower than those in asset markets, real exchange rates will certainly undergo transitory deviations from their real 'trend' path as nominal shocks occur.

Against this, there is mounting evidence that the pursuit of pre-announced monetary targets has been associated with acute policy conflicts as real exchange rates in some instances have undergone very substantial and persistent appreciation. Vaubel (1980) has noted that each of the two countries who were first to adopt the policy of pre-announced monetary targets—Germany and Switzerland—have undergone such experiences. The United Kingdom is a third country for which a similar experience now seems to be in train. The German Bundesbank moved from a central rate target to a target band formulation between 1978 and 1979 and the Swiss National Bank exchanged its monetary target for a maximum (DM/SF) exchange rate target in October 1978. In both cases, the pressure for change was attributed to the appreciation of the exchange rate, and in both cases overruns of the monetary targets occurred. In the German case, influential opinion was led to announce that change in the real exchange rate could justify suspension of the monetary target,[1] whilst the Swiss National Bank was explicit in its exchange rate objective. The Swiss experience, on Schiltknecht's (1979) account, suggested that the target band reformulation adopted by Germany would not have been helpful in their case, since very substantial target overruns seemed incapable of stemming the troublesome appreciation there. In both cases, the real appreciation of the exchange rate has been widely diagnosed as due to currency substitution against the US dollar (a diagnosis with which Vaubel (1980) concurs) and the experience seems to have established an implicit 'emergency clause' in pre-announced monetary targets, foreshadowing their suspension in the face of disruptive real exchange rate changes.

It is of course clear that the establishment of credibility in monetary targets requires sparing use of such 'escape clauses', and also that some real exchange rate changes are inevitable and unavoidable. Perhaps it is on grounds of these two considerations that the experience of conflict between maintaining monetary targets and maintaining competitive exchange rates has not so far, in the case of the United Kingdom, yielded any instance in which the resolution of the conflict has favoured the exchange rate. Indeed, in 1977, the conflict issued in a resolution favouring the monetary target, although in this case excessive appreciation did not seem a long-lasting problem. Looking back on the mid-October (1977) decision to 'uncap' the exchange rate, the authors of the *Midland Bank Review*'s survey in its Summer 1978 issue, were able to comment that those among the authorities "who had argued against appreciation may well have comforted themselves with the reflection that they had succeeded in delaying the decision to permit it until it was too late to do much damage in their own estimation or much good in that of their opponents". In this respect, the problems of the 1979–80 period are of a different order of magnitude in that the appreciation has been much more substantial and persistent; but whilst there is evidence of official concern,[2] there has also been argument that the exchange rate has been required to appreciate in this period by real factors— 'North Sea oil effects'—which it is implied are unavoidable.

It is worth considering what the sources of concern about an appreciating exchange rate are. Despite the intensity of the policy conflicts referred to above, official sources actually give little explicit clue as to the nature of the problem, most plausibly because it is all too obvious that the burden of adjustment placed on the trading sector by an over-appreciating exchange rate is considered excessive. However, this bears further elucidation. A useful starting-point is to consider the nature of the problem of inflation control in a setting where expectations formation in the labour and goods

---

[1] Vaubel (1980) refers to the pronouncement of the Council of Economic Experts (Sachverstandigenrat) on the matter.

[2] See, for example, the Bank of England's Oral Evidence to the House of Commons Select Committee on the Treasury and Civil Service (Minutes of Evidence taken on 7th July 1980).

markets is adaptive. This provides the classic ground for 'gradualist' strategies of inflation control by gradual de-escalation of monetary growth. If such a programme is announced before-hand, the faster adjusting asset markets will tend to mark up the exchange rate in advance of the delivery of lower inflation and will assist in the process by enforcing a transitory appreciation of the real exchange rate. This has the effect of reducing inflation by reducing imported inflation and exerting deflationary demand pressures on the trading sector. The case for gradualism, however, rests on the point that in light of the adaptive processes characterizing expectations formation in goods and labour markets the present adjustment costs (by way of unemployment in excess of the natural rate) are likely to be high and—even if the integral of excess unemployment implied by a given inflation reduction target were constant—concern to reduce peak unemployment would favour a gradualist strategy.[3] In this perspective, an unexpected over-appreciation of the exchange rate may be viewed as speeding up the inflation control programme, thus increasing present unemployment and conflicting with gradualism. Such a consideration seems evident in the point made by Emminger (1979) that the target switch by the Swiss National Bank in 1978/79 did not compromise the achievement of its inflation targets.

Whilst the cause for concern about unexpected exchange rate developments which re-phase a gradualist inflation control strategy can be stated on a purely comparative static basis, in which the long run real development of the economy is assumed to be independent of short run adjustment paths, an additional concern is provided by the notion of 'cumulative causation'. Proponents of this view would stress that the trading sector is the source of technical progress for the economy as a whole and emphasize the irreversibility of the effects of exchange rate changes; accordingly, a greater premium is attached to the maintenance of a competitive exchange rate by appropriate policy.

II

In this section we consider first the role of the exchange rate in the transmission mechanism of monetary policy and, subsequently, the role of monetary policy in determining the exchange rate. The impact of changes in foreign prices for a given exchange rate or of the exchange rate for given foreign prices has long been understood to involve a cost-plus mechanism which transmits foreign price impulses via domestic costs of production to prices charged to final consumers. This traditional import cost mechanism has been supplemented in more recent writing on the subject by two further considerations: the responsiveness of wages to prices and the domain of validity of the "Law of One Price". Wage-price responses have themselves

---

[3] Whilst the current government's inflation control strategy clearly favours gradualism (see *Financial Statement and Budget Report* 1980/81), the precise underpinnings for this have not been made explicit.

of course a long history,[4] but the real wage resistance hypothesis and the augmented Phillips curve sharpen the predicted response. Both hypotheses indicate that at an unchanged level of activity foreign price impulses or equivalent exchange rate variations will produce exactly corresponding changes in wages and domestic value added prices so that domestic prices and wages display homogeneity in the foreign price level or exchange rate. Indeed, in so doing, these hypotheses go rather too far, for neither model of the wage process allows real exchange rate changes (real terms of trade changes) to take place; such changes have to be imposed on the models rather than explained by them.[5] Be that as it may, the assumption of homogeneity of wages and prices is widely made, differences arising empirically chiefly over the length of the adjustment period. Law of One Price considerations also receive more extended attention in contemporary modelling than was the fashion even a decade ago; whilst the argument that commodity arbitrage must ensure equality of prices in common denomination of goods of similar specification was always held to be of obvious application to a wide range of primary products, the newer extension is to entertain its application to a wide range of manufactured goods presumably in recognition of diminished location-specific rents and underlying changes in production techniques and specialization.[6] Empirically, where data flows are inevitably too coarse to permit identification of products of comparable specification, Law of One Price prejudices amount to supplying foreign prices with a non-negligible weight in domestic price formation, especially in export prices.

Assuming output and productivity given, all of the above may be simply expressed as follows:

$$P_d = \alpha_1 L + \alpha_2 e P'_w + \alpha_3 e P''_w \tag{1}$$

$$L = \beta P_d \tag{2}$$

where, with all variables in logarithms, equation (1) states that domestic prices depend on unit labour costs (L), the world price of complementary imports P'_w, and the world price of competing goods, P''_w, e being the exchange rate in domestic currency per unit of foreign currency. The second equation maintains that wages (or equivalently here unit labour costs) respond to prices according to the parameter β. This simple schema leads to

$$P_d = \frac{e}{1 - \alpha_1 \beta} [\alpha_2 P'_w + \alpha_3 P''_w] \tag{3}$$

and so, setting $P'_w = P''_w = 1$ for convenience, and assuming that $\alpha_1 + \alpha_2 +$

[4] Phillips, for example, looked to import price push to explain displacements of or loops around his wage inflation-unemployment relationship (Phillips, 1958).
[5] See Artis and Miller (1979).
[6] There remains a good deal of controversy as to whether the significance of Law of One Price considerations has in fact increased in the manner that seems to be implied by the shift in econometric specification of pricing functions. See Ormerod (1980) for a recent account.

$\alpha_3 = 1$ to

$$\frac{\partial P_d}{\partial e} = \frac{1 - \alpha_1}{1 - \alpha_1 \beta} \tag{4}$$

indicating homogeneity if, additionally, $\beta = 1$.

An important aspect of contemporary modelling of the relationships presented in simplified form above is that they are held to apply in a way which assumes a relatively short lag in the establishment of homogeneity, or something fairly close to it. A study by economists at the Bank of England (Brown, Enoch and Mortimer-Lee, 1980), provides up-to-date evidence drawn from a variety of models on the characteristics of the key wage and price equations in these models. For a subset of these (the models of the Treasury, National Institute and London Business School) we have shown elsewhere (Artis and Currie, 1981) that on the basis of just two key equations in each (for prices and for wages), the prediction of comparatively short run homogeneity (or near-homogeneity) of prices in the exchange rate is borne out. Such comparisons, whilst usefully standardized as between models in respect of such key assumptions as the level of activity, lags in the direct impact of exchange rate changes on prices, the pass-through from wholesale prices (typically what is determined in the model analogue to equations (1)) to retail prices and thence wages (it is retail prices which appear in model analogues to equation (2)), by making strong assumptions on all these and other associated points do tend somewhat to overstate the case by comparison with what full model simulations tend to show.

The table below, however (Table 1), brings together the results of simulations on two of these models and an *LBS* 'relative' (the model by Beenstock and Burns), of a five per cent appreciation. In each case the results shown are derived from a comparison between a control run and an alternative run in which the effective exchange rate was set five per cent higher than in the control. Whilst the simulations differ in the initial

TABLE 1
Effects of a 5% appreciation

Model:	Wholesale prices			Competitiveness[a]		
	HMT	BB	NIESR	HMT	BB	NIESR
Year 1	−0.9	−2.0	−1.1	−1.7	−3.0	−3.3
2	−1.7	−2.9	−2.0	−1.7	−1.9	−1.6
3	−2.6	−3.6	−3.2	−1.2	−1.2	−1.3
4	−3.1	−4.3	−3.5	−0.9	−0.4	−0.9
5	−3.6	−4.9	−3.8	−0.7	−0.2	−0.6

[a] Relative export prices

Sources: HMT model from simulations on the February 1979 public release (HM Treasury, 1979) conducted at UMRCC; BB from Beenstock and Burns (1980); NIESR from G. D. Worswick (1980).

conditions assumed in the control run, and the scope of the model employed,[7] the exercises seem sufficiently similar to warrant comparison. At face value, they suggest that it takes some five years for an appreciation to be reflected as to 72–98% in domestic wholesale prices, the process being completed most quickly in the BB model.[8]

The parameter values of all these models, though based on recent experience, inevitably reflect more or less strongly the prior beliefs (disciplined by experience) of the model constructors, both in the range of determining variables entertained, and the choice of estimation procedures. Clearly they cannot provide evidence independently of these inputs of economy responses, as opposed to model responses. But they are of obvious value in the reflection they give of the homogeneity postulate with respect to nominal exchange rate changes and support the view that if monetary policy can affect the exchange rate it will have an important bearing on the transmission of inflation, the more so in that none of these models gives space to rational expectations effects on wage behaviour, nor permits very significant interest rate-demand effects: these alternative avenues of transmission are simply not strongly represented. This brings us to the next question: how does monetary policy affect the exchange rate?

The simplest statement of the connection between money and the exchange rate is provided by the conjunction of the quantity theory, on the one hand, and the doctrine of purchasing power parity (PPP) on the other, a statement which is, however, capable of a considerable degree of refinement and sophistication;[9] indeed, with the additional inclusion of rational expectations, 'Fisher effects' and assumptions about capital mobility, the approach yields results sympathetic to the view that foreign exchange markets must be treated, to a high order of approximation, as efficient asset markets—though a similar position can of course be reached by alternative approaches which stress the role of wealth adjustment and entertain a somewhat broader view of events which account for exchange rate changes (e.g. Dornbusch, 1980). Whilst the efficient market view tends to inhibit exchange rate forecasting to the extent that a large part of exchange rate variation appears in fact to be due to unanticipated events, it does not prevent *ex post* explanation in principle, though the odds against success still seem quite high despite the superior vantage point afforded by working over past data, since the ability of econometric procedures to capture expectational processes is not high.

Nevertheless, some success has been claimed for what seem in some cases to be relatively rudimentary monetary explanations of the exchange rate. A starting point is provided by the following: let equations (1) and (2) below represent money demand functions for the home and foreign country

[7] The HMT model simulations were conducted on the NIF sector of that model, and thus exclude interactions with the monetary sector of the full model.

[8] The BB model overshoots after year five and gives full homogeneity after 10 years.

[9] A very useful recent review of the literature, encompassing alternative approaches to the monetary PPP approaches emphasized here is to be found in Hacche and Townend (1980).

respectively, expressed in logarithmic form, with the interest rate variables (denoted r, r^*) being understood for later convenience to stand for $\log(1+r)$ and $\log(1+r^*)$ respectively. Equation (3) is a statement of purchasing power parity (PPP) the exchange rate, e being expressed in units of domestic currency per unit of foreign currency; equation (4) is a testable reduced form.

$$M = \alpha_0 + \alpha_1 Y - \alpha_2 r + p \tag{1}$$

$$M^* = \beta_0 + \beta_1 Y^* - \beta_2 r^* + p^* \tag{2}$$

$$p = p^* + e \tag{3}$$

$$e = (\beta_0 - \alpha_0) + (M - M^*) + \beta_1 Y^* - \alpha_1 Y - \beta_2 r^* + \alpha_2 r \tag{4}$$

Actually, this system provides several possibilities for testing and for plausible amendment prior to testing. One obvious test is examine equation (3) directly. Does PPP hold directly over observed price indices or not? A number of investigators have concluded that it does not (for a recent test, see Dornbusch, 1980); however, proponents of equation (4) may argue that the relevant price indices are not directly observed, and so suggest that (4) should be tested directly despite the verdict on (3). In doing so, various plausible amendments can be entertained on the basic formulation; examples include allowance for lags in the money demand function, time trend-related shifts in the relationship between the prices for which PPP plausibly holds directly (traded goods prices) and the prices relevant to money demand (which include non-traded goods), and allowances for the simultaneity problem introduced by the presence of official intervention in foreign exchange markets, accompanied by successful sterilization. Collinearity between the explanatory variables additionally encourages the imposition of restrictions, most common being restriction of the two countries' money demand parameters to equality with one another. It is probably fair to say that the more successful estimates of (4) are those which impose restrictions of this kind, although their propriety is not always clear when money supply definitions often differ between countries and the implied money demand specification are quite often primitive in comparison with the specifications deployed at national level.

A rather different kind of modification consists in regarding the result of (4) as a value of the equilibrium exchange rate, towards which the actual exchange rate adjusts. A wide range of adjustment schemes can then be entertained. As one of its options, the scheme contained in the UK Treasury's macroeconomic model falls into this range: (see Denham and Lomax, 1978): a relative money supplies hypothesis (purged, however, of interest rate effects) provides a long run equilibrium exchange rate which the market combines in weighted fashion with the current exchange rate to form a 'short run' equilibrium or 'expected' rate. The current spot rate is then determined by the interaction of current account imbalance and rather imperfect capital-stock adjustment processes in the capital account so as to clear the overall balance, with the expectation of exchange gain or loss based on the short run expected rate, entering the calculus which, along with interest rates, determines capital flows. In this type of mechanism a 'magnification effect' is possible, since although the expected short run rate depreciates by less than the long run equilibrium rate following an increase in the current money supply, the spot rate is required to depreciate relative to the short period expected rate by enough to continue to clear the overall balance in the face of possible interest rate declines occurring in association with the money supply expansion.

Whilst the Treasury's modelling gives prominence to a detailed account of capital flows, adjustment schemes based on an underlying *PPP*-determined equilibrium rate need not do so. The London Business School modelling for example, seeks to apply a generalized adjustment scheme (Ball, Burns and Warburton, 1979) whilst the National Institute's reduced form exchange rate sector introduces *PPP* considerations as one among a set of factors bearing on exchange rate determination (NIESR, 1979).

An apparent oddity of the *PPP*-monetary approach to exchange rates, as exemplified in (4) is the sign given to relative interest rates, whereby a positive differential is associated with a depreciation of the exchange rate. The explanation of this leads directly to the 'asset market' formulation, wherein the role of expectations of the future can be clarified. The explanation proffered is that whereas in the long run the international capital market equalizes real rates of interest, nominal interest differentials may persist up to the point warranted by expected inflation differentials. In short, the 'interest rate' in the money demand functions (1) and (2) stands for the inflation rate, provided the real rate is constant.[10]

Assuming then that nominal rates are given by the Fisher relation as an expected inflation markup on real rates and that the latter are forced to equality across countries by capital market arbitrage, we may re-write (4), assuming for convenience that $\alpha_0 = \beta_0$, $\alpha_1 = \beta_1 = a$ and $\alpha_2 = \beta_2 = b$, as

$$e = (M - M^*) + a(Y^* - Y) - b(\Pi^* - \Pi) \tag{5}$$

where Π, Π^* is the expected inflation rate. On the same assumption, but further simplifying for convenience by assuming that $E(\dot{y}) = E(\dot{y}^*) = 0$, monetary 'super-neutrality' suggests that:

$$e = (M - M^*) + a(Y^* - Y) - b(\dot{m}^* - \dot{m}) \tag{6}$$

---

[10] The implication that, apart from this disguised inflation effect interest rates are of no significance for long run equilibrium, whilst plausible in light of the generally accepted view that the capital account is determined by stock adjustment processes and must therefore be zero in the long run, can be misleading, however. The more general portfolio approach, incorporating wealth adjustment effects, demonstrates that even though equilibrium requires a zero capital account, flows of interest derived from accumulated stocks of wealth change the composition of the current balance and thus the real exchange rate required to clear it. Thus the long run equilibrium real rate may be affected by short run adjustment paths: a hysterisis effect (see, e.g. Isard, 1979).

where $\dot{m}$, $\dot{m}^*$ are the expected monetary growth rates. The last term suggests that a credible announcement of a reduced growth rate will enforce an immediate appreciation of the exchange rate. Current money supply changes may also have 'magnification' or 'perverse' effects depending on the perceived connection between such changes and the expected monetary growth rate. On the one hand, a current increase in the money supply may excite anticipation of a rise in the growth rate of money, implying a reinforced depreciation; on the other, a current increase may (in the context of an existing pre-announced set of money supply targets) reduce the expected growth rate, leading to a dampening-out of the depreciation or conceivably to an appreciation. Equation (6) has been expressed in unduly restricted form for purposes of convenience.

A somewhat less restrictive formulation, due to Bilson (1978) runs as follows. Replacing r in equation (4) by $r = r^* + f - e$ where f is the forward exchange rate, and assuming that the forward rate is an unbiased predictor of the future expected spot rate ($f = E_t e_{t+1}$) and assuming as before the equality of the coefficients in the money demand function, we have that

$$e_t = \frac{1}{1+b}(Z_t) + \frac{b}{1+b}(E_t e_{t+1}) \tag{7}$$

where $Z_t = (M - M^*) + a(Y^* - Y)$, so that

$$e_t = \alpha \sum_{j=0}^{\infty} (1-\alpha)^j E_t(Z_{t+j}) \tag{8}$$

where $\alpha = 1/(1+b)$. This clearly states the dependence of the current spot rate on present information about the current and future values of exogenous variables and structure (the Z_{t+j}). However, this formulation is still restrictive in its starting point, even assuming that the particular restrictions on the parameters of the money demand functions are relaxed.

The assumption of interest parity, net of the expected rate of depreciation may, however, be usefully assumed as a starting point for an estimating equation for the exchange rate (as in Frankel, 1979) without imposing the assumption of instantaneous *PPP*; similarly, the assumption that the forward rate is an unbiased predictor of the future spot rate allows exchange rate determination to be viewed in "news" form, with unanticipated exchange rate changes being related to unanticipated events (as in Dornbusch, 1980). There seems to be strong evidence that forward rates are not in fact at all good predictors of future spot rates, suggesting that 'innovations' are of considerable significance.

The inherent difficulty of explaining exchange rate changes in such a context seems confirmed by the failure of a recent extensive study of the determinants of the UK effective exchange rate to produce a viable explanation (Hacche and Townend, 1981), and by the difficulty inherent in the simpler form of the monetary approach in accounting for real exchange rate changes which, as Dornbusch (1980) has observed, and as demonstrated in

Section I above, have been substantial and persistent in recent years.[11] None of this means that monetary forces are not of the greatest significance for exchange rate determination, but it is evident that econometric explanation is difficult when hard-to-quantify expectational influences are significant; accordingly, in policy applications it is appropriate to assume substantial stochastic shocks in any exchange rate determination sector.

III

The formal model, to be analysed below, is an *IS/LM* system extended to include a price-wage sector in which allowance is made for the exchange rate-price-wage pass-through mechanism discussed in Section II and for a capital flows sector. Rational expectations are assumed. The details of the model, and the results we derive from it, are given in the Appendix. We consider four distinct regimes:

(A) exchange rate targets, whereby the nominal money supply is altered so as to stabilize the nominal exchange rate ε.

(B) monetary targets, whereby the nominal money supply is given exogenously.

(C) monetary targets (as in (B)), together with an interest equalization tax manipulated so as to stabilize the real 'effective' exchange rate $(\pi_1 + \varepsilon - p)$.

(D) monetary targets (as in (B)), together with an interest equalization tax manipulated so as to stabilize the nominal exchange rate (ε).

In all cases, it is assumed that the conduct of policy is to maintain the longer run stance of policy identical under all four regimes. What is at issue, therefore, is the relative short run stabilization properties of the four regimes. In all cases, we measure the volatility of prices and output relative to their expected values.

We first make a comparison between an exchange rate target regime (A) and a pure monetary target regime (B). A convenient representation of the model in output/price space appears in Fig. 1. Here *DD* represents the aggregate demand schedule (derived from equation (1) of the Appendix). A rise in the domestic price level leads to a fall in aggregate demand via a decline in net exports; moreover, with a given longer run stance of policy, the expectation that the price level increase will be temporary increases the expected real interest rate, thereby also depressing demand via this channel. Thus the slope of the *DD* schedule is given by the sum of the elasticities of aggregate demand with respect to the real interest rate and the terms of trade $(\beta + \phi$ in the notation of the Appendix). *MM* depicts the money demand schedule (derived from equation (2) of the Appendix), which has a negative slope equal in absolute magnitude to the inverse of the income elasticity of money demand (k^{-1}). *SS* depicts the short run supply schedule,

---

[11] Hacche and Townend (1981) attempt to cope with some of these real changes by introducing OPEC and 'North Sea oil' effects, but to no avail.

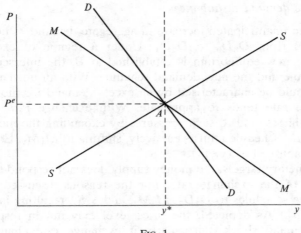

Fig. 1

whereby output depends positively on unforeseen price changes. In the absence of unanticipated disturbances, equilibrium is established at (y^*, p^e), corresponding to an equilibrium level of output. Unanticipated disturbances will cause the schedules to shift from their equilibrium levels, inducing corresponding adjustments in output and prices. Under a regime of exchange rate targets, the money stock is accommodating, so that the MM schedule adjusts passively to shifts in the DD and SS schedules. Under monetary targets, the exchange rate adjusts to equilibrate the system, shifting all three schedules. Thus an appreciation of the exchange rate (a fall in ε) causes a loss of competitiveness and a fall in net exports, shifting the DD schedule to the left; while by improving the terms of trade it shifts the SS schedule downwards. Finally, since an appreciation of the exchange rate induces the expectation of a future depreciation (at least with given longer run monetary targets), it permits a rise in domestic interest rates relative to world rates. To the extent that the demand for money is interest elastic, this lowers the demand for money, and the MM schedule shifts to the right.

The slope of the DD schedule may either be flatter than the MM schedule (as in Figs. 4 and 5) or steeper (as in Figs. 1, 2, 3 and 61). This proves to be critical in comparing the two regimes in the face of an aggregate supply shock. The condition for the DD schedule to be flatter may be seen from the above to be that $k(\phi + \beta) > 1$. In the short run, we would not expect this condition to be satisfied, since the short run income elasticity of money demand is likely to be less than unity; while the elasticities of aggregate demand with respect to the terms of trade and the expected real interest rate are likely to be low. But in the longer run, this condition can easily be satisfied, particularly for a small open economy.

We may now illustrate the impact of alternative shocks under the two regimes.

(a) *Aggregate demand disturbances*

Consider an unanticipated increase in aggregate demand, which shifts the DD schedule from D_0D_0 to D_1D_1. Under a regime of exchange rate targeting, the new equilibrium is established at B, the intersection of the supply schedule and the new demand schedule. With an unchanged money supply, B would be characterised by an excess demand for money, so that the exchange rate tends to appreciate. With exchange rate targets, the authorities will respond to such pressures by expanding the money supply, so that the MM schedule adjusts passively, shifting to M_1M_1. Equilibrium is therefore established at (y_1, p_1).

Under monetary targets, the money supply does not respond to check the appreciation of the exchange rate. For the reasons discussed above, this shifts all three schedules to D_2D_2, M_2M_2, and S_2S_2, resulting in an equilibrium at $(y_2, p_2.)$ As depicted, the price level may fall in response to an aggregate demand shock, particularly if exchange rate changes have a marked effect on domestic pricing so that the shift in the SS schedule is marked, and if the money demand schedule is interest inelastic, so that the MM schedule does not shift.

In terms of output stabilisation, the results given in Table 3 of the Appendix show that monetary targets are unambiguously superior, and this result is illustrated in Fig. 2. However, monetary targets may give greater

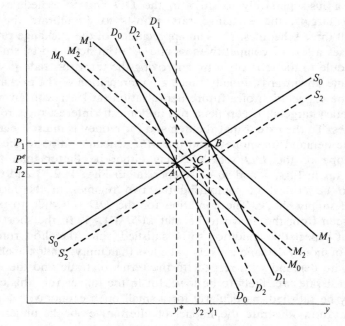

FIG. 2. Aggregate demand disturbance

variance in prices. This is more likely the greater the effect of exchange rate changes on domestic pricing behaviour, (i.e. the larger the shift of SS), the less responsive are domestic prices to aggregate demand (i.e. the flatter the slope of SS), and the more interest inelastic is the money demand schedule (i.e. the smaller the shift of MM). However, in this case, it will be noted that prices move in opposite directions under the two regimes, so that a compromise between the two regimes would be superior for price stabilisation. Indeed, such a compromise will be superior in all cases where a rise in demand depresses prices under monetary targets.

(b) *Money demand disturbance*

An unanticipated rise in money demand will shift the MM schedule to M_1M_1 (Fig. 3), so that an excess demand for money tends to appreciate the exchange rate. Under an exchange rate target regime, the money supply will expand, automatically accommodating the rise in money demand, so that the equilibrium remains at A with no disturbance to prices or output. Under monetary targets, the appreciation of the exchange rate shifts SS down to S_2S_2, DD leftwards to D_2D_2 and MM rightwards to M_2M_2. Equilibrium is established at C, with falls in both prices and output. The disturbance is larger the more sensitive is domestic pricing to the exchange rate, the smaller the influence of aggregate demand on pricing, and the more interest inelastic is the demand for money.

It is obvious from this that an exchange rate targeting regime is preferable for dealing with money demand shocks.

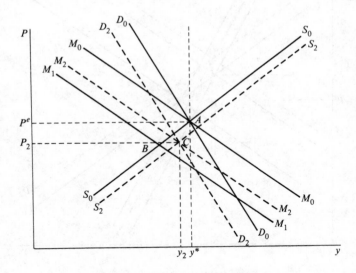

FIG. 3. Money demand disturbance

(c) *Aggregate supply disturbances*

An inflationary supply shock shifts the SS schedule upwards to S_1S_1 (see Fig. 4). If, as depicted, the DD schedule is more price elastic than the MM schedule (so that $k(\phi+\beta)>1$), then B corresponds to a position of excess supply of money. Under a regime of exchange rate targets, the tendency towards depreciation of the exchange rate will be stemmed by an induced reduction in the money supply, so that the MM schedule shifts to M_1M_1. If, on the other hand, the DD schedule is steeper than the MM schedule, B will correspond to a position of excess demand for money, so an expansion in the money supply will be induced. In any event, under a regime of exchange rate targets, the MM schedule is accommodating, so equilibrium is established at B at the intersection of the SS and DD schedules.

Under monetary targets, the exchange rate will adjust to equilibrate the system. In the case depicted in Fig. 4, the exchange rate depreciates, causing all three schedules to shift upwards, so that an equilibrium is established at C. The induced change in the price level is therefore greater than that under exchange rate targets. But in the case where the DD schedule is steeper than the MM schedule, the induced appreciation of the exchange rate dampens the rise in prices under monetary targets as compared with exchange rate targets.

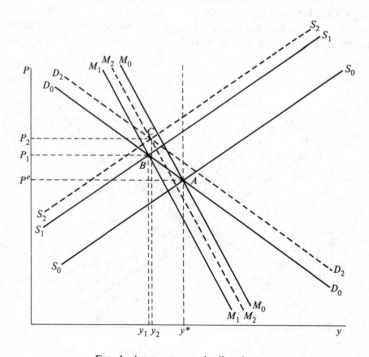

Fig. 4. Aggregate supply disturbance

(d) *Foreign capital shocks*

A rise in international interest rates shifts the *DD* schedule to the left and the *MM* schedule to the right, as depicted in Fig. 5. Under a regime of exchange rate targets, the resulting tendency of the exchange rate to depreciate induces a reduction in the money supply, establishing an equilibrium at *B*, with a lower level of both prices and output. With monetary targets, the fall in the exchange rate leads to a new equilibrium being established at point such as *C*. Unless the money demand schedule is relatively elastic, it is straightforward to establish that the price level rises under monetary targets.

If the objective of policy is to stabilise prices, a mixed regime will prove superior to either a monetary target or an exchange rate target regime.

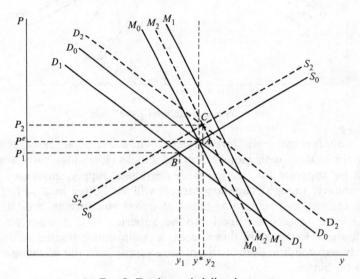

FIG. 5. Foreign capital disturbance

(e) *Foreign price level shock*

A rise in the foreign price level shifts both the *DD* schedule and the *SS* schedule upwards (Fig. 6). Under exchange rate targets, the resulting excess demand for money is offset by an accommodating shift of the *MM* schedule to M_1M_1, establishing an equilibrium at *B*. Under monetary targets, the appreciation of the exchange rate shifts the *DD* schedule to the left, *MM* and *SS* to the right, establishing an equilibrium at *C*. Clearly the volatility in both output and prices is less under monetary targets than under exchange rate targets.

The main implications of this analysis for price stabilisation may be summarized as follows. Monetary targets are unambiguously superior for

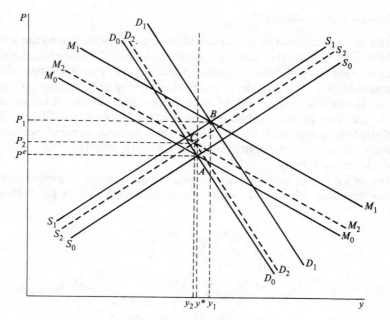

FIG. 6. Foreign price level disturbance

dealing with foreign price level shocks, while exchange rate targets are superior for dealing with money demand shocks. Exchange rate targets are likely to be superior for dealing with aggregate supply shocks in a fairly open economy, though monetary targets will be better in a rather closed economy. In the two remaining cases, demand and foreign capital shocks, exchange rate targets are likely to be superior if cost-mark-up pricing predominates. However, in these cases, a compromise regime, stabilising a suitable linear combination of the money supply and the exchange rate, is likely to be better.

These results are clearly somewhat ambiguous. Nonetheless there is a fairly strong suggestion that exchange rate targets will be superior to monetary targets in an open economy where cost-mark-up pricing predominates, unless the major source of disturbance to the economy is from shocks to the general foreign price level. There is also the possibility that a compromise betwen the two regimes may dominate either individually, particularly if the major sources of disturbances are from foreign capital flows and/or aggregate demand.

So far we have ignored the possibility of using an interest equalisation tax in conjunction with monetary targets (regimes (C) and (D)). Although there are some doubts about the feasibility of such a discretionary tax, it is nonetheless of interest to consider briefly the performance of such a regime.

A comparison of regimes (C) and (D) using the results presented in Table 3 of the Appendix leads to fairly intuitive conclusions. Thus (C) is superior to

TABLE 2
Preferable choice of regime to stabilise

Shock	Output	Price
Aggregate demand	D	D
Money demand	A	A
Aggregate supply	D[1]	A[1]
Foreign capital flows	D	D
Foreign price level	A[2]	D

[1] Reversed for a more closed economy.
[2] If cost-mark-up pricing prevalent.

(D) for stabilising real output in the face of aggregate supply, aggregate demand and money demand shocks if cost-mark-up pricing is significant, but clearly inferior in the face of foreign price level shocks. (Both regimes by design provide complete insulation from foreign capital disturbances.) For price stabilisation, (D) is superior to (C) unless foreign price shocks dominate.

Since our previous analysis suggests that exchange rate targets (A) may well dominate monetary targets (B) in terms of price stabilisation, and since (D) is superior to (C) for this purpose, it is clearly sensible to compare (A) and (D). The results of such a comparison, using the results of Table 3 of the Appendix, are reported in Table 2. Any assessment of the two regimes clearly depends on views concerning the relative probabilities and size of the different types of shock; but the results do suggest that an interest equalisation tax would perform at least as well, and possibly outstrip, a regime of exchange rate targets for purposes of price stabilisation. However, an alternative improvement on monetary targets consists in conditionalizing them upon the exchange rate. This suggestion is explored further in the next section.

IV

Conditional targets

In this section we broach the case for conditionalizing monetary targets on exchange rates. The argument depends on an assumption, which we hope to have justified in Section III of this paper, that either target affords a measure of inflation control and on an assumption that whilst there is a connection between current money supplies and monetary targets and the exchange rate, this connection is not at all firm over substantial 'short runs' of time. The commentary in the first two sections of this paper was designed to highlight this issue.

The case for unconditional, pre-announced, monetary targets is one which, except on extreme views of the matter, must be submitted to a cost-benefit analysis. However, the most significant elements in the cost-benefit calculus are implicit in these extreme views which are therefore worthwhile briefly recounting. The traditional case against the pursuit of open-loop ("no feedback") rules is that as a matter of logic, such rules can never be superior to closed loop ("feedback" rules), since the latter embrace as one among many possibilities the pursuit of an unvarying target for the intermediate variable in question; thus, by committing themselves to an unvarying target or open-loop policy, the authorities merely throw away degrees of freedom. This case is clear when private sector behaviour is hypothesized to be unaffected by the rule, whether announced or not, followed by the authorities, though it may still survive when private sector behaviour is allowed to be affected by the rule in operation provided that private sector response to knowledge of the rule pursued by the authorities does not inevitably result in completely off-setting behaviour. The alternative extreme view of the matter, however, 'extreme' rational expectations, maintains precisely this, so that in a world of clearing markets, with no contracts inhibiting the adjustment of nominal variables, and with no irreducible information advantage accruing to the authorities, there is no known systematic closed loop rule for the money supply which can impact on output. In this world the degrees of freedom attributed to closed loop rules by traditional optimal control analysis are illusory. Nothing is gained by following such a rule, and something may be lost to the extent that closed loop rules may be less clear to the market than open-loop rules, thus introducing random informational errors into the system.

Clearly, neither the primitive optimal control argument nor the extreme rational expectations approach is wholly convincing; rather, each provides elements in the cost-benefit calculus. In particular, the rational expectations approach reminds us that markets will try to second-guess unannounced discretionary (closed loop) policy rules and indicates a benefit of clarity in pre-announcement, whist the optimal control approach indicates that in a stochastic environment the continued pursuit of an unconditional rule in inappropriate circumstances will be costly. The case for considering contingent or conditional rules follows immediately from this. Unconditional rules which prove to be costly are liable to be abandoned; the market will lay bets on this contingency, but cannot do so efficiently in the absence of secure information on the likelihood of these costs arising and their penalty value. A contingent rule would improve the information content of an otherwise unconditional rule by pre-specifying conditions in which the rule would or might be abandoned or modified, and perhaps by pre-specifying in what way the rule would be amended in such circumstances. It may be argued that the potential gain of conditionalizing is small because the rule becomes too complicated, or because conditionalizing will encourage the market to suspect chicanery on the part of the authorities: these are empirical matters about which judgements will vary. However, it may be argued in mitigation of these potential criticisms, first that relatively sophisticated markets need have no difficulty in responding to more sophisticated rules; secondly, that existing practice already imports a degree of carte blanche flexibility into the operation of monetary targets, through the device of rolling targets, and the practice of announcing growth rate 'bands' rather than central rates. Adding explicit conditionality could be considered as an advance on such *ad hoc* devices for securing flexibility and might be regarded as a partial replacement for them. Finally, it can also be argued that the range of possible shocks is so broad that no amount (and *a fortiori* no *small* amount) of conditionalizing can completely remove the possibility of unanticipated suspensions of the rule; but this is part of the general case against pre-announced rules for intermediate targets and is not an argument against the improvement that might be sought from conditionalizing a primitive rule.

In view of the evidence both that exchange rates make a good alternative target to the money supply and that real exchange rate appreciation has led to the abandonment of monetary targets elsewhere and to evident strains on the maintenance of monetary targets in this country, we are led to the suggestion that conditionalizing the monetary target on the exchange rate might afford a worthwhile improvement in policy. Such a conditionalization could take one of the several forms: thus, one possibility is to set a pre-announced floor and ceiling to the effective exchange rate alongside the monetary target, the whole being subject to review at intervals; an alternative to this 'switching regimes' policy would be the adoption of a pre-announced combinatorial rule specifying a trade-off of monetary growth against exchange rate deviation from a pre-specified path. In either case, if review intervals were maintained at relatively short length, nominal exchange rate data should proxy the desired real rate data fairly closely.

Of course, neither system would be ideal, in that regime switches or monetary growth trade-off would be triggered by exchange rate deviations rather than (within the review interval) by an evaluation of the shocks impinging on the system. Thus the modification of the monetary rule might not always be appropriate.

To assess how important this qualification might be requires both some judgement as to the distribution of shocks across the system and an evaluation of the way in which the exchange rate would respond to them. Table 4 of the Appendix bears on the second part of this problem; it tabulates the exchange rate response, under a monetary target regime, for five types of disturbance in terms of the analytical model set out in Section III and analysed formally in the Appendix. The likelihood of a policy change can be read directly from the extent of the deviation of the exchange rate from its mean value indicated in the table (assuming for the moment a rectangular distribution of shocks). On the assumptions that the slope of the

Phillips curve is rather small in the short run, and that the slope of the *IS* curve and the interest rate elasticity of money demand are also rather low, whilst cost-mark-up pricing is prevalent, the results quoted in the table imply that switches are most strongly indicated for money demand and aggregate supply shocks, then for foreign price level shocks and finally for aggregate demand and capital flows disturbances. However, if—as seems a reasonable reading both of the Swiss and German experience and of the United Kingdom's—the distribution of shocks is skewed towards disturbances in capital flows and aggregate supply, and if foreign price level shocks are given a low probability, the implied ranking of the likelihood of regime switches is more favourable to the kind of conditionalizing proposed here.

That reliance should be placed on the comparatively low risk of foreign price level instability might seem at first sight unduly Quixotic. But since what is at stake here is simply the proposition that the domestic rate of inflation is likely to be less stable than the weighted average of relevant foreign rates of inflation, this does not seem unreasonable, particularly if the comparison is drawn for industrial countries, as seems appropriate.

There is, finally, the question of how a modification of monetary targets towards exchange rate targets, or their replacement by such targets would cope with such phenomena as North Sea oil. Our view on this particular question happens to be that the 'endowment' of North Sea oil requires, not an appreciation of the real exchange rate, but a reconsideration of absorption policy. Here, it seems clear, rigid monetary guidelines prevent the appropriate reconsideration of absorption policy, enforcing rather an unnecessary and harmful appreciation of the real exchange rate. By contrast a policy emphasizing the exchange rate would automatically induce a change in absorption and from this point of view would be superior. If, of course, the North Sea oil endowment—or any other such phenomenon—could be held to require a change in the real exchange rate, then matters are more complicated. The appropriate exchange rate target would need to be explicitly reconsidered.

V

Conclusions

Since this paper is already overlong, our concluding remarks will be rather brief. We have been concerned to argue that, for a small open economy in which cost-mark-up pricing dominates, stabilisation of the nominal exchange rate (by means of suitable changes in domestic monetary policy) offers rather better prospects for price stabilisation than do monetary targets. Only if disturbances to the economy arise primarily from changes in the general level of foreign prices are monetary targets likely to be clearly superior, and we would not regard this as the relevant case for the UK.

It would clearly be of interest to test the robustness of this conclusion in more complex and realistic model structures. But from our analysis, we may draw the following policy conclusion. In circumstances in which adherence to monetary targets requires large and unexpected movements in the exchange rate, it is likely to be sensible to modify the monetary target in the light of the exchange rate movement, either by switching to an exchange rate target or by modifying the monetary target by some proportion of the unexpected deviation of the exchange rate. Underlying this conclusion is the view that foreign prices may offer a better anchor for price stability than monetary targets, at least for a small open economy such as the UK.

APPENDIX

Our formal model may be set down as follows:

$$y = -\beta(r - p_{+1}^e + p) + \phi(\pi_1 + \varepsilon - p) + u_1 \tag{1}$$

$$m = ky - \eta r + p + u_2 \tag{2}$$

$$p = \theta_1(y - y^*) + \theta_2(\pi_1 + \varepsilon) + \theta_3(\pi_2 + \varepsilon)$$
$$+ \theta_4(\pi_1^e + \varepsilon^e) + \theta_5(\pi_2^e + \varepsilon^e) + \theta_6 p^e + u_3 \tag{3}$$

$$r = \rho + \varepsilon_{+1}^e - \varepsilon + \tau + u_4 \tag{4}$$

where all variables are expressed in logarithms except for the rate of interest which is a proportion and where:

y = real output
y^* = full employment real output
r = nominal interest rate
p = price level
m = nominal (high-powered) money stock
π_1 = price of imported competitive goods
π_2 = price of imported complementary goods
ρ = world nominal interest rate
ε = exchange rate (units of domestic currency per unit of foreign currency)
u_1 = random disturbance, $i = 1, \ldots, 4$
$+i$ = lead of i periods
e = subjective expectation
τ = interest equalisation tax.

Equation (1) is the aggregate demand schedule, where aggregate demand depends negatively on the expected real interest rate and the price of domestic goods relative to competitive world prices. Equation (2) is a standard money demand function where the demand for real money balances depends positively on real income and negatively on the nominal rate of interest. Equation (3) is the aggregate supply schedule. This is a reduced form equation derived from a complete wage-price model, the details of which are given in Artis and Currie (1981). Domestic prices are determined by a mark-up, varying with the state of demand, over costs, made up of wage costs and costs of complementary imports; while nominal wages are determined by the level of demand and the consumer price index, which is in turn a weighted average of domestic prices and prices of competitive imports. Long run homogeneity requires that $\sum_{i=2}^{6} \theta_i = 1$, but in

TABLE 3
Price and Output Fluctuations

Regime / Shock	Exchange rate target		Monetary targets					
			No interest equalisation tax		Interest equalisation tax, constant real exchange rate		Interest equalisation tax constant nominal exchange rate	
	price	output	price	output	price	output	price	output
Aggregate demand	$\theta_1 D_1^{-1}$	D_1^{-1}	$(\theta_1\eta - kc_1)D_2^{-1}$	$(\eta + c_1)D_2^{-1}$	$\eta\theta_1 D_3^{-1}$	$\eta(1-c_1)D_3^{-1}$	$\eta\theta_1 D_4^{-1}$	ηD_4^{-1}
Money demand	0	0	$-(c_2+\theta_1\beta)D_2^{-1}$	$-(\phi+\beta)(1-c_1)D_2^{-1}$	$-\beta\theta_1 D_3^{-1}$	$-\beta(1-c_1)D_3^{-1}$	$-\beta\theta_1 D_4^{-1}$	$-\beta D_4^{-1}$
Aggregate supply	D_1^{-1}	$-(\phi+\beta)D_1^{-1}$	$(c_5+k\phi)D_2^{-1}$	$-(c_4+\phi)D_2^{-1}$	$c_5 D_3^{-1}$	$-\beta(1+\eta)D_3^{-1}$	$c_5 D_4^{-1}$	$-c_4 D_4^{-1}$
Capital flows	$-\theta_1\beta D_1^{-1}$	$-\beta_1 D_1^{-1}$	$(c_2\eta + c_1 k\beta)D_2^{-1}$	$(\eta\phi - c_1 c_4)D_2^{-1}$	0	0	0	0
Foreign prices	$c_2 D_1^{-1}$	$(\phi - c_1(\phi+\beta))D_1^{-1}$	$(c_2\eta + c_1 k\beta)D_2^{-1}$	$(\eta\phi - c_1 c_4)D_2^{-1}$	0	0	$(c_2\eta + c_1 k\beta)D_4^{-1}$	$(\eta\phi - c_1 c_4)D_4^{-1}$

$D_1 = 1 + \theta_1(\phi+\beta)$, $D_2 = (\theta_2+\theta_3)(1-k(\phi+\beta)) + (\phi+\beta)(k+\theta_1) + \eta D_1$, $D_3 = (\eta+\beta k)(1-\theta_2-\theta_3) + \beta\theta_1(1+\eta)$, $D_4 = \beta(\theta_1+k)$, $c_1 = \theta_2+\theta_3$, $c_2 = \phi\theta_1 + c_1$,
$c_3 = \eta\phi + \beta$, $c_4 = c_3 + \beta\eta$, $c_5 = \eta + \beta k$.

general $\theta_6 \neq 1$, so that there may exist a short run trade-off between domestic prices and output even when prices are fully anticipated. (See Buiter (1979), Artis and Currie (1981)).

Equation (4) is based on the assumption of perfect capital mobility, so that expected returns (adjusted for exchange rate changes) on assets denominated in sterling and other currencies are equalised. We included in (4) a tax τ on foreign holders of sterling assets (and a corresponding subsidy on domestic holders of foreign assets), which we later consider as a possible instrument available for purposes of stabilisation.

All four equations include a random disturbance term u_i to capture the effect of unforeseen shocks to the system.

A variety of possible informational assumptions can be made in this model. The assumptions embodied in (1)–(4) are that agents have information on current prices (including the exchange rate) when determining their demands for money and goods;[1] but that wage settlements are negotiated prior to such information becoming available. This gives rise to a conventional upward sloping short run aggregate supply schedule.

To solve the system, we take expectations of the system, subtract the resulting equations from equations (1)–(4), and then solve for the endogenous variables. Thus for exchange rate targets (A), where ε is constant, we have that

$$\begin{bmatrix} 1 & (\phi+\beta) \\ -\theta_1 & 1 \end{bmatrix} \begin{bmatrix} y-y^* \\ p-p^e \end{bmatrix} = \begin{bmatrix} u_1 + \phi(\pi_1-\pi_1^e) - \beta(\rho-\rho^e) - \beta u_4 \\ \theta_2(\pi_1-\pi_1^e) + \theta_3(\pi_2-\pi_2^e) + u_3 \end{bmatrix} \tag{5}$$

while under monetary targets (B), we obtain

$$\begin{bmatrix} 1 & (\phi+\beta) & -(\phi+\beta) \\ -\theta_1 & 1 & -(\theta_2+\theta_3) \\ k & 1 & \eta \end{bmatrix} \begin{bmatrix} y-y^* \\ p-p^e \\ \varepsilon-\varepsilon^e \end{bmatrix} = \begin{bmatrix} u_1 + \phi(\pi_1-\pi_1^e) - \beta(\rho-\rho^e) - \beta u_4 \\ \theta_2(\pi_1-\pi_1^e) + \theta_3(\pi_2-\pi_2^e) + u_3 \\ \eta(\rho-\rho) + \eta u_4 - u_2 \end{bmatrix} \tag{6}$$

With an interest equalisation tax, the level of the tax, τ, becomes an endogenous variable. Thus under (C), we have that $(\pi_1+\varepsilon-\rho)$ is constant, so that

$$\begin{bmatrix} 1 & 0 & \beta \\ -\theta_1 & (1-\theta_2-\theta_3) & 0 \\ -k & -(1+\eta) & \eta \end{bmatrix} \begin{bmatrix} y-y^* \\ p-p^e \\ \tau-\tau^e \end{bmatrix} = \begin{bmatrix} -\beta(\rho-\rho^e) - \beta u_4 - \beta_1(\pi_1-\pi_1^e) + u_1 \\ \theta_3(\pi_2-\pi_2^e-\pi_1+\pi_1^e) + u_3 \\ -\eta(\rho-\rho^e) - \eta u_4 - \eta(\pi_1-\pi_1^e) + u_2 \end{bmatrix} \tag{7}$$

while under (D) we have that

$$\begin{bmatrix} 1 & (\phi+\beta) & \beta \\ -\theta_1 & 1 & 0 \\ -k & -1 & \eta \end{bmatrix} \begin{bmatrix} y-y^* \\ p-p^e \\ \tau-\tau^e \end{bmatrix} = \begin{bmatrix} -\beta(\rho-\rho^e) - \beta u_4 + \phi(\pi_1-\pi_1^e) + u_1 \\ \theta_2(\pi_1-\pi_1^e) + \theta_3(\pi_2-\pi_2^e) + u_3 \\ -\eta(\rho-\rho^e) - \eta u_4 + u_2 \end{bmatrix} \tag{8}$$

We may now solve (5)–(8) for the change in p and y resulting from exogenous disturbances. We consider five types of shock: an aggregate demand disturbance (u_1); a money demand disturbance (u_2); an aggregate supply disturbance $(u_3, \pi_2-\pi_1-\pi_2^e+\pi_1^e)$; a capital flow distur-

TABLE 4

Exchange Rate deviations under a monetary target

Shock	Deviation
Aggregate demand	$D_2^{-1}(\theta_1+k)$
Money demand	$D_2^{-1}(1+\theta_1(\phi+\beta))$
Aggregate supply	$D_2^{-1}(1-k(\phi+\beta))$
Foreign capital	$D_2^{-1}(c_5+\theta_1 c_4)$
Foreign price level	$D_2^{-1}(c_2(1-k(\phi+\beta))+k\phi)$

[1] The assumptions made by Artis and Currie (1981) differ slightly in that agents are not endowed with knowledge of the current aggregate price level when forming their inflation expectations. This modification gives rise to small differences in what follows.

bance $(\rho - \rho^e, u_4)$; and a foreign price level disturbance $(\pi_1 - \pi_1^e = \pi_2 - \pi_2^e)$.[2] The resulting variances are reported in Table 3.

Finally, for use in Section IV of the main paper, we present in Table 4 the size of response of the exchange rate, under a purely monetary target regime (B), to the five distinct exogenous disturbances considered above.

BIBLIOGRAPHY

ARTIS, M. J. and CURRIE, D. A. (1981) 'Monetary and exchange rate targets' in A. S. Courakis and R. L. Harrington (eds.). *Monetarism: Traditions, Debates and Policy*, Macmillan.

ARTIS, M. J. and MILLER, M. H. (1979) 'Inflation, real wages, and the terms of trade' in (ed.), J. Bowers: *Inflation, Development and Integration: essays in Honour of A. J. Brown*, Leeds University Press.

BALL, R. J., BURNS, T. and WARBURTON, P. J. (1979) 'The London Business School model of the UK economy: an exercise in international monetarism', in Ormerod, P. (ed.): *Economic Modelling*, Heinemann.

BEENSTOCK, M. and BURNS, T. (1980) 'Exchange rate objectives and macroeconomic adjustment in the UK in (ed.) Robin Major: *Britain's Trade and Exchange Rate Policy* (Heinemann: London).

BILSON, J. F. (1978) 'Rational expectations and the exchange rate', in (eds.) J. A. Frenkel and H. G. Johnson: *The Economics of Exchange Rates* (Addison-Wiley.)

BROWN, R. N., ENOCH, C. A. and MORTIMER-LEE, P. D. (1980) 'The inter-relationships between costs and prices in the United Kingdom', *Bank of England Discussion Paper No. 8*, March.

BUITER, W. (1979) 'Unemployment-inflation trade-offs with rational expectations in an open economy', *Journal of Economic Dynamics and Control*, Vol. I, pp. 117–141.

DENHAM, M. and LOMAX, R. (1978) 'The model of external capital flows', *Government Economic Service Working Paper No. 17*, (Treasury Working Paper No. 8).

DORNBUSCH, R. (1980) 'Exchange rate economics: where do we stand?', *Brookings Papers in Economic Activity*, I, pp. 143–205.

EMMINGER, O. (1979) 'The exchange rate as an instrument of policy', *Lloyds Bank Review*, July, pp. 1–22.

FRANKEL J. (1979) 'On the mark: a theory of floating exchange rates based on real interest differentials', *American Economic Review*, Vol. 69, No. 4, pp. 610–622.

HACCHE, G. and TOWNEND, J. (1981) 'Exchange rates and monetary policy: modelling sterling's effective exchange rate 1972–80', pp. 201–47 This volume.

ISARD, P. (1979) 'Exchange rate determination: a survey of popular views and recent models', *Princeton Studies in International Finance*, No. 42.

National Institute of Economic and Social Research (1979) *Listing of the Interim Model IV*, NIESR Discussion Paper No. 28.

ORMEROD, PAUL (1980) 'Manufactured export prices in the United Kingdom and the "Law of One Price" *Manchester School*, Vol. 48, September, pp. 265–283.

PHILLIPS, A. W. (1958) 'The relation between unemployment and the rate of change of wage rates in the United Kingdom', *Economica*, Vol. 25, November, pp. 283–99.

SCHILKNECHT, K. (1979) *Targeting the base—the Swiss experience*, paper presented to the Conference on Monetary Targets, City University, May.

H.M. Treasury (1979) *Treasury Macro-economic model. Public version.* February.

VAUBEL, R. (1980) 'International shifts in the demand for money, their effects on exchange rates and price levels and their implications for the pre-announcement of monetary expansion', *Weltwirtschaftliches Archiv*, pp. 1–44.

WORSWICK, G. D. N. (1980) 'Fixed and flexible exchange rates' in (ed.) Robin Major: *Britain's Trade and Exchange Rate Policy*. (Heinemann: London).

[2] Since a rise in the price of complementary imports relative to other import prices has an effect identical to a supply shock, it is convenient to take the foreign price level shock to be a general equiproportionate change in the price of all imports.

EXCHANGE RATES AND MONETARY POLICY: MODELLING STERLING'S EFFECTIVE EXCHANGE RATE, 1972–80

By GRAHAM HACCHE and JOHN TOWNEND*

I. Introduction

THIS paper describes our attempts to explain the behaviour of the effective exchange rate for sterling since the abandonment of a fixed parity against the dollar in 1972, and to investigate, in particular, the role played by monetary influences.

The object for explanation is shown in the upper half of Chart 1. From June 1972—when sterling was allowed to float having been withdrawn from the European "snake"—until November 1976, the nominal effective exchange rate fluctuated about a marked downward trend, declining between these dates by about 40%. After a brief recovery around the end of 1976 (following policy measures accompanied by arrangements to borrow from the IMF) the rate was stable until, in the latter part of 1977, a secular upward movement began which has since continued with few major interruptions. In February 1980—the end of the sample period for the econometric results reported below—the effective rate was 23% higher than in November 1976; and by the end of 1980 it was more than 30% above that nadir. The dominant impression gained from a cursory examination of the exchange rate data is thus one of a marked change in trend in 1976–77. This impression remains when, as in the lower half of the chart, the exchange rate is expressed in "real" terms using foreign and domestic price indices: indeed, in real terms the appreciation through 1977–80 is accentuated, since the nominal strength of sterling has coincided with relatively faster domestic inflation.

Determinants of the exchange rate movements exhibited in the chart—the trends and the fluctuations—are suggested by economic theory. Section II below outlines the main theoretical frameworks for the analysis of exchange rate determination, focusing on the role attributed to monetary influences in each model. Most attention is paid to the "monetary approach": simple single-equation models based on this approach provided the starting point for the econometric work reported in Section III, not least because a common feature of the recent empirical literature in this area is the claim that such models can explain the behaviour of exchange rates with a good degree of success. We argue, however, that these models ignore simultaneities entailed in the operation of monetary policy, and that the en-

* We are grateful to David Begg, Marcus Miller, Kerry Patterson, Peter Sinclair, and numerous colleagues in the Bank for helpful comments on an earlier draft. Views expressed are the authors' alone; in particular, they are not necessarily those of the Bank of England.

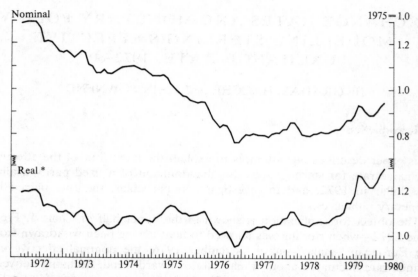

CHART 1. Effective exchange rate of sterling, January 1972–February 1980. *Nominal rate multiplied by ratio of domestic to main competitors' consumer price indices.

dogeneity of the authorities' operations in the foreign exchange and domestic money markets is reflected in their estimated parameters, which are consequently biased. Attempts to eliminate these biases by means of instrumental variables derived from estimated reaction functions for the authorities are then described. The results, though instructive in some respects, fail to provide a satisfactory explanation for the movements of sterling over the period of floating exchange rates. The fact that the recent course of the exchange rate is left largely unexplained seems to us to be partly a reflection of estimation difficulties which are inherent for a variable whose behaviour, at least in the short term, is strongly influenced and sometimes dominated by expectations, which are immeasurable and subject to instability.

II. Money and exchange rates in theory

The monetary approach to the balance of payments and exchange rates has added prominence to the proposition that the pressure on the value of a currency—materialising in exchange rate movements and official intervention— is closely linked to the relationship between domestic and external monetary conditions. Yet the proposition itself is a common thread running through most well-known models of open economies. The most distinctive feature of the monetary approach, it will be argued, is the way in which its special assumptions about price flexibility and competition in trade simplify analysis by allowing the exchange rate to be regarded, in effect, as the 'price' which clears the money market in a small open economy. Partly to clarify these points, this section reviews how monetary disturbances transmit their influence to the exchange rate in four well-known frameworks for the analysis of open economies with floating exchange rates: the Mundell–Fleming model; a portfolio balance model; various versions of the monetary model; and Dornbusch's model of exchange rate dynamics. It is the last two which form the basis of the estimates in the following section, and it is to these that we pay most attention. The main issues are summarised in II 5.

1. Mundell–Fleming model

It is interesting first to recall how Fleming (1962) viewed the influence of monetary policy on the exchange rate. The analysis, associated also with Mundell (1963), may be considered to remain "the backbone of macroeconomic models of the exchange rate" (Dornbusch, 1980, p. 152). It may be described in terms of a model obtained by opening the familiar IS–LM framework, with domestic price level fixed and output demand-determined, to foreign trade and capital flows. With prices and foreign real income exogenous, net exports are a decreasing function of domestic real income and the exchange rate (defined throughout this paper as the price of domestic in terms of foreign currency). On capital account, with the foreign rate of interest exogenous, net inflow is assumed to be an increasing function of the domestic interest rate and the expected rate of appreciation of the domestic currency. The model is then closed by the requirement of external balance. The assumption that capital flows depend on interest rate levels is characteristic of this model, contrasting with what is now generally recognised to be the more satisfactory hypothesis of stock adjustment to be explored in the following section.[1]

Now consider the implications for the exchange rate (on the assumption that it floats freely) of *an increase in the domestic money supply*. Starting from a position in which money and goods markets are in equilibrium and external payments balanced, an excess supply of money develops which puts downward pressure on interest rates. Interest-sensitive expenditure consequently increases, and output expands by the multiplier process until a new equilibrium is reached where the excess supply of money has been eliminated partly by a decline in interest rates and partly by a rise in income. But meanwhile, an incipient balance of payments deficit will have developed through both current and capital accounts; depreciation will have been needed to eliminate it. The extent of this depreciation is greater the less interest- and income-elastic is the demand for money, the more interest-elastic is domestic expenditure, the larger is the propensity to import, the smaller are price-elasticities in trade, and the less elastic are exchange rate expectations.[2]

---

[1] Mundell in fact assumed perfect capital mobility and neutral exchange rate expectations, so that in his version the condition for external balance collapses to the requirement that domestic and foreign interest rates be equal. This also represents a special case of stock adjustment.

[2] In the Mundell version, since the domestic interest rate is tethered to foreign rates, the restoration of monetary equilibrium occurs entirely through the increase in income generated by depreciation.

In sum, the Mundell–Fleming analysis predicted that domestic monetary expansion would lead to depreciation of the currency, to maintain, *mainly through the current account*, external balance with whatever mix of lower interest rates and higher output were required to restore equilibrium in money and goods markets.

A number of features of this analysis seem questionable, particularly in the light of more recent experience and theoretical developments—the absence of any price response, either to the monetary disturbance or to the consequent depreciation; the absence of dynamics (for example, lags in the response of output and trade, and *J*-curve effects); and the peripheral role of expectations. In addition, any interest rate effect on capital flows appears to be regarded as permanent, whereas if capital flows represent adjustments to inequalities between actual and desired stocks such effects will decay as the flows occur. A fuller analysis is needed to incorporate asset preferences and the requirements for portfolio balance, including the wealth effects of imbalances on current account.

2. Portfolio balance models

In portfolio balance models, the composition of wealth is in equilibrium dependent on relative interest rates, and it is changes in interest differentials which induce capital flows. This view moves the focus of analysis, at least for the short term, from the requirements for flow equilibrium in the goods market and the balance of payments to the requirements for stock equilibrium in the markets for domestic money, domestic securities, and foreign assets.

As an illustration, we take the model used by Branson (1979) and Branson and Halttunen (1979). Domestic residents hold domestic money and domestic bonds, both of which are public-sector liabilities, and foreign bonds, which form the only tradeable asset: domestic money and domestic bonds are not held by overseas residents, and any increase in liabilities to overseas shows up as a fall in domestic holdings of foreign bonds, which represent net foreign assets, assumed to be positive. The proportion of their wealth which domestic residents desire to hold in each asset depends upon relative expected common-currency yields, with gross substitutability assumed to apply.

In this framework, the exchange rate has three distinct influences. First, exchange rate changes entail revaluation, in terms of domestic currency, of foreign assets (denominated in foreign currency); and since domestic residents are assumed to be in a net credit position with overseas, total wealth in domestic currency will rise with depreciation and fall with appreciation. Secondly, exchange rate expectations, which we assume to be regressive, form a component of the relative expected yields of domestic and foreign assets. Thirdly, there is the influence which was predominant in the Mundell–Fleming analysis: the exchange rate affects the current account, the significance of which now is that it determines the net acquistion of foreign assets.

The exchange rate is then viewed as being determined, in the short run (with asset supplies given) by the equilibration of asset markets (or the maintenance of portfolio balance), with lagged feedbacks on to the current account and the accumulation of foreign assets, and in the long run by the requirement that the current balance be zero. In contrast with the Mundell–Fleming analysis, which drew no distinction between the flexibility of interest rates and exchange rates on the one hand and real variables on the other, and which emphasised the corrective mechanism provided by the exchange rate's influence on the current account, portfolio balance models thus distinguish between a long-run in which trade and other real variables are allowed to adjust, and a short run in which exchange rates, in helping to equilibrate asset markets, provide a quite different corrective mechanism for foreign exchange markets, operating through the capital account. This distinction, also present in the Dornbusch model below, has served to show that *the short-run and long-run responses of exchange rates to monetary shocks may be quite different.*

Consider, then, the implications in this framework of *an increase in the money supply* brought about by an open-market purchase by the authorities of domestic bonds. This will entail, at the initial equilibrium exchange rate and rate of interest, an excess supply of money and an equal excess demand for domestic bonds. Restoration of equilibrium in domestic asset markets requires a lower interest rate; but this will produce excess demand in the foreign bond market which can be eliminated only by depreciation. In the new asset equilibrium, therefore, both the interest rate and the exchange rate are unambiguously lower. But this is not the end of the story: the balance of payments has not been considered.

Assume that the initial equilibrium was a full equilibrium with asset supplies stationary. Then for net foreign assets to have been stationary the current account must have been in balance, with positive net investment income (since the country is a net creditor and the foreign interest rate is positive) offset by a trade deficit. The movement to the new equilibrium described above will not have entailed any impact on the current account, since the changes in the interest rate and the exchange rate have re-established portfolio balance with net foreign assets unchanged: within the capital account, purchases of foreign bonds induced by the fall in interest rates have been matched by sales induced by the effect of the fall in the exchange rate on expectations and the composition of wealth. But in the new equilibrium, with goods prices unchanged the terms of trade have deteriorated: this will affect net exports and hence net foreign assets. If the usual conditions on the price elasticities of trade are satisfied, the depreciation will cause the current account to move into surplus and the supply of net foreign assets to grow. This implies a further disturbance of portfolio balance, so that the new equilibrium is only a temporary one: there develops an excess supply of foreign bonds, with corresponding excess demands for domestic bonds and money. Appreciation is then required for portfolio balance to be maintained. Thus one consequence of the improvement in the current account is a rise in the exchange rate which, by reducing net exports, will tend to bring the growth to a halt. Meanwhile, however, the rise in net foreign assets will also have been increasing net investment income, thereby tending to push the current account further into surplus. For stability, it has to be assumed that trade elasticities are sufficiently large for the latter effect to be outweighed by the former, so that the current account surplus generated by the initial depreciation is eventually eliminated and full equilibrium restored.

What can be said about the value of the exchange rate in this final long-run equilibrium? *First,* it must be higher than in the temporary asset equilibrium: a case of *overshooting,* accounted for by the assumption that exchange rates respond quickly, with interest rates, to maintain portfolio balance in the wake of a monetary shock, before trade has time to adapt. The short-term corrective mechanism provided by the exchange rate, through the capital account, in this process is obviously crucially dependent on the assumption that expectations are not extrapolative. *Secondly,* in the final equilibrium the current account is in balance, but with higher net investment income because net foreign assets are higher. Hence net exports must be lower. If there has been no 'Keynesian' change in real income to affect the trade account, the real exchange rate must therefore be higher than initially: if the price level has risen in proportion to the money supply, the proportionate depreciation must have been smaller. If output has increased in response to the monetary expansion, however, the direction in which the real exchange rate will have changed is ambiguous.

This is of some interest in relation to the next section: although in the portfolio balance approach the exchange rate is in the long run dictated by current account influences, it cannot be inferred, even in the absence of international divergences in the relative prices of traded and non-traded goods (which might arise from international divergences in growth rates of productivity) that the real exchange rate will be constant in the long run. In fact, a monetary expansion, with a pure price response in the long run, will tend to have associated with it a rise in the real exchange rate. Isard (1978, p. 30) refers to this result of Branson's as the 'knockout punch' for the "Law" of Purchasing Power Parity.

3. The monetary approach

(a) *The basic model*

The monetary approach may be regarded as a special case of portfolio balance theory. It looks to asset-market equilibrium conditions for an explanation of exchange rates, but is characterised by its exclusive isolation of the money market: the equilibrium of other asset markets plays no explicit role.

The basic monetary model states that the exchange rate must be such that the domestic price level implied by purchasing power parity (PPP) and foreign prices is such that the demand for money, for given real output and interest rates, matches supply. In IS–LM terms, the IS curve is vertical at a given level of output (interpreted as full employment) and the equilibrium exchange rate is such as to ensure, via PPP, that the real money supply is such that LM intersects IS at the interest rate given by perfect international mobility of capital. The exchange rate, "the relative price of national moneys"—a phrase much used by international monetarists as if to validate their approach— is viewed as being determined in the money market, and the PPP condition then provides a theory of the domestic price level. This is to be distinguished from the "insular monetarist" doctrine (Brittan [1977]), associated particularly with Friedman, that the domestic price level is determined directly by the money supply. PPP appended to the latter model provides a theory of the exchange rate, whereas PPP in more recent "international monetarism" explains the domestic price level.

The basic monetary model is most conveniently set out as three specific structural equations.[3] Assuming a demand for money function of the usual form in the price level P, real income Y, and the rate of interest i, domestic monetary equilibrium implies:

$$M = kPY^{\alpha}e^{-\beta i} \tag{1}$$

where M represents the domestic money stock. Corresponding assumptions for the rest of the world give a similar equation for the foreign money stock, with f-subscripts indicating foreign variables and parameters.

Next, the exchange rate S (the price of domestic in terms of foreign currency) is tethered by competition in international goods markets to proportionality with the ratio between foreign and domestic price levels— PPP holds:

$$S = k'P_f/P \tag{2}$$

where k' is a constant, not necessarily unity. Substitution yields the following equation for the exchange rate:

$$\ln S = K - \ln M + \ln M_f + \alpha \ln Y - \alpha_f \ln Y_f - \beta i + \beta_f i_f \tag{3}$$

With each of the right-hand side variables assumed exogenous (an assumption whose meaning we shall consider below) this equation may be estimated as the reduced form of the system; and this has been the usual procedure in empirical application.

Equation (3) shows that an *increase in the domestic money supply* will lead to an equi-proportionate depreciation. The elasticities of S with respect to M

---

[3] See e.g. Frenkel (1976), Bilson (1978, 1979).

and M_f are -1 and $+1$ respectively, as a consequence of the assumptions of PPP and unit price elasticity in the demand for money. The possibility of over-shooting, for example, is excluded. (It will be shown below that these *a priori* constraints on the coefficients of the monetary variables may be weakened by assumptions of lagged adjustment.)

The mechanism by which this influence on the exchange rate is exerted by such a monetary disturbance is usually imagined to be as follows. Corresponding to the initial excess supply of money, there will be excess demands for goods and assets. Unlike the two previous models, domestic income and interest rates are here exogenously determined and unavailable to relieve the strain: real income is assumed to be at its full-employment level, while the assumption of perfect capital mobility means that the domestic interest rate is tethered to foreign rates and exchange-rate expectations by uncovered interest parity (the circumflex indicating a proportional rate of change)—

$$i - i_f = -E(\hat{S}) \qquad (4)$$

Furthermore, domestic prices cannot directly respond since they are tied by foreign competition. The disequilibrium therefore spills over entirely into an excess demand for foreign goods and assets which lowers the exchange rate; this permits a restoration of equilibrium by allowing a rise in domestic prices compatible with PPP. The price-elasticity of unity in the demand for money means that this rise in prices (and the associated depreciation of the currency) must be in the same proportion as the monetary expansion. The real money supply is then unchanged. The exchange rate, not the interest rate, is thus in effect the 'price' which clears the domestic money market, via the domestic price level; and essential to the equilibrating mechanism which it provides is the assumption that the price level is sufficiently flexible for PPP to be maintained.

The interpretation of the signs of the income and interest rate coefficients follows in a similar way from consideration of the implications of changes in these variables for conditions in domestic and foreign money markets. The interest rate coefficients, however, are of special interest and require further comment.

The monetary model predicts that a rise in domestic interest rates, by causing an excess supply of money, will lower the exchange rate. But how is it that a rise in i does not increase the demand for domestic assets in relation to foreign assets, and so have the effect (familiar from the two earlier models) of appreciation through the capital account? The answer lies in the way the interest rate is assumed to be determined. The domestic interest rate, exogenous to the domestic money market where equilibrium is maintained by the exchange rate and the domestic price level, must satisfy the parity condition (4); and given the exogenous foreign interest rate, i is a reflection of and is determined by exchange rate expectations. Hence any change in i, for given i_f, is implicitly the *consequence* of a change in expectations, being required to keep expected relative yields equalised. Thus a rise in i does not represent an increase in the expected relative yield of domestic assets: it is assumed to be the result of and an offset to a deterioration in exchange rate expectations which would otherwise represent a decline in that yield.

If equation (3) is estimated as the reduced form for the exchange rate, it must be assumed that $E(\hat{S})$, the expected rate of appreciation, is exogenous to the current exchange rate and its determinants.

(b) Rational expectations

This last assumption conflicts with the hypothesis of *rational expectations* (RE).[4] Exogeneity might be defended, if expected exchange rate movements were held to depend on market perceptions of "underlying" inflation rates and monetary conditions, which could be insensitive in the short term to variations in the determinants of the current exchange rate. But this would not make expectations consistent with the maintained model. When expectations are assumed to be rational,[5] the interest differential and domestic interest rate become endogenous. Rewriting (4) as:

$$i_t - i_{ft} = \ln S_t - E_t \ln S_{t+1} \tag{5}$$

[where $E_t x_{t+j}$ represents the expectation of x at time $(t+j)$ conditional on information at time t] substitution into (3) gives:

$$\ln S_t = \frac{1}{1+\beta} Z_t + \frac{\beta}{1+\beta} E_t \ln S_{t+1} \tag{6}$$

where

$$Z = K - \ln M + \ln M_f + \alpha \ln Y - \alpha_f \ln Y_f + (\beta_f - \beta) i_f$$

Now the rational expectation of the exchange rate in any future period $(t+j)$ may be expressed in terms of the expected value of the composite exogenous variable Z and the exchange rate expected in the succeeding period $(t+j+1)$.

This allows us to derive the new reduced form for the exchange rate:

$$\ln S_t = \frac{1}{1+\beta} \sum_{j=0}^{\infty} \left(\frac{\beta}{1+\beta}\right)^j E_t Z_{t+j} \tag{7}$$

This shows that on the RE hypothesis the current exchange rate depends upon the expected future, as well as the actual current, values of the exogenous variables of the model. The domestic interest rate is no longer one of these.

Some implications of the RE model are worth noting here. *First*, the

---

[4] So, of course, does the absence of any distinction between anticipated and unanticipated movements in the exogenous variables which follows from this assumption.

[5] Here we follow Mussa (1976).

solution (7) describes a foreign exchange market which is efficient in the sense that all information relevant to future market conditions is discounted into the current exchange rate. The discount factor, $\beta/(1+\beta)$, is directly related to the interest elasticity of the domestic demand for money. In the special case where $\beta = 0$—when the interest rate does not influence the demand for money—the current exchange rate is independent of the interest rate and exchange rate expectations: it is determined by the current values of the exogenous variables alone, and expectations are important only in helping to determine the interest rate.

Secondly, the change in the exchange rate between any two periods $(t-1)$ and t may be shown to comprise a component which was expected, having been anticipated in the interest differential of $(t-1)$, and an unanticipated component reflecting fresh information or 'news'.

As Dornbusch (1978, pp. 111–3) has shown, a convenient decomposition of the rate of appreciation may be derived directly from the interest parity condition. For two-period decisions at $(t-1)$, the analogue of (5) is:

$$(i_{t-1} - i_{f(t-1)}) + E_{t-1}(i_t - i_{ft}) = \ln S_{t-1} - E_{t-1} \ln S_{t+1} \tag{8}$$

Subtracting (8) from (5) and re-arranging,

$$\ln S_t - \ln S_{t-1} = -[(i_{t-1} - i_{f(t-1)}) + [(i_t - i_{ft}) - E_{t-1}(i_t - i_{ft})]$$
$$+ [E_t \ln S_{t+1} - E_{t-1} \ln S_{t+1}] \tag{9}$$

The first term in square brackets measures the rate of appreciation between $(t-1)$ and t which was expected at $(t-1)$. The second and third terms represent 'news': the unexpected component of the interest differential at t (which represents a revision of expectations about appreciation next period), and the revision of expectations about the level of the exchange rate at $(t+1)$. The expression is a general implication of uncovered interest parity, being independent of the monetary model. Its interpretation, however, does depend upon the context. Thus Dornbusch's inference that 'an unanticipated increase in interest rates with unchanged expectations about future exchange rates will lead to an appreciation of the spot rate' only makes sense outside the monetary model, since in the latter interest rates are endogenous to the relationship between expectations about future exchange rates and the current spot rate.

Thirdly, although rationality and efficiency imply that unanticipated changes are serially uncorrelated, with zero mean, and hence unpredictable, it does not follow that $\ln S$ will follow a random walk, since the exogenous variables [in (7)] and the interest differential [in (9)] may well be serially correlated.

Fourthly, RE implies that the effect of an exogenous shock will depend upon its impact on expectations of the future evolution of the exogenous variables. Thus, for example, whereas the basic monetary model implies that a once-for-all monetary expansion will have a proportionate effect on the exchange rate, with rational expectations the immediate effect may be greater if expectations of monetary growth are temporarily raised as a result.

Finally, therefore, the *RE* hypothesis implies that econometric models of the exchange rate need to incorporate a description of how expectations of the exogenous variables are formed, so that both anticipations of exogenous changes and the effects of exogenous changes on expectations can be taken into account. The difficulties with such a procedure are, however, obviously immense, and go some way towards explaining the comparative scarcity of such work to date.

(c) *Partial adjustment and 'Pressure'*

The basic model set out in 3(a) conveys the essence of the monetary approach, but it describes a particularly restrictive version of it. At least for short-run analysis the equilibrium relationships (1)–(2) would usually be regarded as unrealistic, even within the monetary framework: most empirical studies of the demand for money have shown lagged adjustment, and PPP is almost always considered to be a distinctly long-run "law". Suppose, then, that there is partial adjustment to the desired money stocks and equilibrium exchange rate described by the above equations: the short-run demand for money functions then become:

$$\Delta \ln M = \gamma' \ln \left[\frac{kPY^\alpha e^{-\beta i}}{M_{-1}} \right] \quad \text{and} \quad \Delta \ln M_f = \gamma'' \ln \left[\frac{k_f P_f Y_f^\alpha e^{-\beta_f i_f}}{M_{f_{-1}}} \right] \quad (10)$$

where Δ is the first difference operator, and $(1-\gamma')$ and $(1-\gamma'')$ are the coefficients of adjustment in the domestic and foreign functions respectively. Similarly, (2) is replaced by:

$$\Delta \ln S = \gamma \ln (k' P_f / P S_{-1}) \quad (11)$$

Substitution yields the following equation in S:

$$\Delta \ln S = \gamma K - \frac{\gamma}{\gamma'} \Delta \ln M - \gamma \ln \left[\frac{MS}{M_f} \right]_{-1} + \frac{\gamma}{\gamma''} \Delta \ln M_f$$

$$+ \gamma \alpha \ln Y - \gamma \alpha_f \ln Y_f - \gamma \beta i + \gamma \beta_f i_f \quad (12)$$

This may be compared with the stronger version presented in (3). In particular, the short-run elasticity of S with respect to M is no longer -1 *a priori*, but is dependent on the speeds of adjustment in the exchange rate and the demand for money. It is numerically higher the larger is γ (the absolute value of the short-run elasticity of S with respect to P) and the smaller is γ' (the short-run price-elasticity of the demand for money). If the former exceeds the latter—if the exchange rate responds faster than the demand for money—then the exchange rate will again *overshoot* a new equilibrium created by a monetary disturbance.

Equations of a form similar to (12) have been estimated by some writers.[6] It may be argued, however, that the role played by PPP in international monetary theory would be better described by the lagged adjustment of relative price levels to exchange rates than by the lagged adjustment of exchange rates to relative price levels. This transmission mechanism suggests an alternative model, obtained by replacing (11) with:

$$\ln (P_f/P) = \gamma \ln (SP_{-1}/k'P_{f-1})$$

On substitution of prices from the demand for money functions the reduced-form equation for S has the following form, with coefficients given their *a priori* signs:

$$\ln S = \ln (kk'/k_f) + a_1 \ln M_f + a_2 \ln M_{f-1} + a_3 \ln M_{f-2} - a_4 \ln M$$
$$- a_5 \ln M_{-1} - a_6 \ln M_{-2} - a_7 \ln Y_f + a_8 \ln Y_{f-1} + a_9 \ln Y$$
$$- a_{10} \ln Y_{-1} - a_{11}(i - i_f) + a_{12}(i - i_f)_{-1}$$

The signs show that although the dynamics of this equation are more complicated that in the case of equation (12), the impact effects all have the same direction as in the former model; and this is true too of the long-term effects.

A related version of the monetary approach is the model proposed by Girton and Roper (GR) (1977) and adopted more recently by Budd and Burns (1978), Connolly and da Silveira (1979) and Saville (1980). Its most noteworthy feature is that it provides an equation to explain exchange-market "*pressure*", a composite dependent variable defined for any currency such that its value in any period is a function of both the current change in its exchange rate and the current volume of official financing of the balance of payments (or intervention). The parameters of this function are determined *a priori*, and the equation describing the determinants of the composite variable is independent of intervention policy. The model thus suggests that the pressure on a currency—a concept which has intuitive appeal as being applicable in all exchange rate regimes—is measurable prior to estimation; that its determinants can be estimated from data that span both fixed and floating exchange rate periods; and that it can be forecast directly, leaving the authorities to choose that combination of exchange rate changes and intervention which optimises their objective function. Before the appearance of the paper by GR, Whitman (1975) (p. 519) observed: "In a world of managed floating, market pressures on a currency are reflected both in the net international flow of reserves and in movements in the

[6] E. G., Bilson (1978); but although he also refers to evidence of lagged adjustment in the demand for money, his equation estimated for the £:DM rate on monthly data (April 1970–May 1977) assumes partial adjustment in the exchange rate only. Dornbusch (1978), p. 109, derives an equation similar to (16) (but with equal speeds of adjustment assumed) and finds it more successful in explaining monthly variations in the $:DM rate (March 1974–May 1978) than an equation similar to our (4). [The equation estimated by Frenkel (1976) for the £:DM rate, February 1921–August 1923, assumes no lags and corresponds to our (4).]

effective exchange rate, although no one has yet developed a single compo-site unit to measure empirically the total pressure reflected through both these channels". GR claim to have discovered such a measure and to have derived a monetary model in which it is the dependent variable. Their model may be set out, in simplified form, as follows.

With the money supply M decomposed into its domestic and external counterparts, D (domestic credit) and R (foreign exchange reserves) respec-tively, the monetary equilibrium condition (1) may be rewritten as:[7]

$$\ln M \equiv \ln (D+R) = K + \ln P + \alpha \ln Y - \beta i$$

First differencing[8] and subtraction of the corresponding equation for the rest of the world[9] gives:

$$\frac{\Delta D}{M_{-1}} + \frac{\Delta R}{M_{-1}} - \Delta \ln M_f = \Delta \ln P - \Delta \ln P_f + \alpha \Delta \ln Y - \alpha_f \Delta \ln Y_f - \beta \Delta i + \beta_f \Delta i_f$$

(13)

The procedure of the standard monetary approach would be now to invoke PPP and thereby replace the terms in (13) which represent the difference in inflation rates, $(\Delta \ln P - \Delta \ln P_f)$, with the rate of depreciation of the domes-tic currency, $-\Delta \ln S$. Rearrangement would then give an equation in $\Delta \ln S$ which, apart from the decomposition of the growth rate of the domestic money stock, would be the same as the first difference of (3):

$$\Delta \ln S = -\frac{\Delta D}{M_{-1}} - \frac{\Delta R}{M_{-1}} + \Delta \ln M_f + \alpha \Delta \ln Y - \alpha_f \Delta \ln Y_f - \beta \Delta i + \beta_f \Delta i_f \quad (14)$$

GR, however, depart from the standard approach and claim more generality by assuming that the movement of the exchange rate deviates from the inflation differential by a linear combination of the normalised rates of domestic credit expansion and foreign monetary growth:

$$\Delta \ln S = \Delta \ln P_f - \Delta \ln P + \theta_1 \frac{\Delta D}{M_{-1}} - \theta_2 \Delta \ln M_f; \quad \theta_1, \theta_2 \geqslant 0 \quad (15)$$

---

[7] Following Connolly and da Silveira, we construct the model here in terms of an aggregate money stock, whereas GR's model is in terms of base money. For the UK, if M is £M3 and D is domestic credit, R defined as the level of foreign exchange reserves does not satisfy the money supply identity, which is best thought of as an approximation in this context. In our empirical work described in the following section, changes in £M3 are decomposed into domestic credit expansion, the balance for official financing, and a residual which comprises a deduction for external flows not directly affecting the money supply, and the change in banks' net non-deposit liabilities.

[8] GR developed their model using continuous analysis. We obtain equivalent results in terms of discrete time for conformity with the equations set out earlier; the decomposition of $\Delta \ln (D+R)$ is an approximation, which is closer the smaller are ΔD and ΔR.

[9] GR in fact constructed their model for the two-country case to explain the exchange rate between Canadian and US dollars.

Substitution into (18) gives:

$$\Delta \ln S = -(1-\theta_1)\frac{\Delta D}{M_{-1}} - \frac{\Delta R}{M_{-1}} + (1-\theta_2)\Delta \ln M_f$$

$$+ \alpha \Delta \ln Y - \alpha_f \Delta \ln Y_f - \beta \Delta i + \beta_f \Delta i_f \quad (16)$$

This differs from (14), the corresponding equation of the basic monetary model, only in that the coefficients of $\Delta D/M_{-1}$ and $\Delta \ln M_f$ are no longer -1 and $+1$ a priori. But since (15) does not include the external counterpart of the growth of M, the coefficient of $\Delta R/M_{-1}$ is still -1, so that (16) may be rewritten:

$$\Delta \ln S + \frac{\Delta R}{M_{-1}} = -(1-\theta_1)\frac{\Delta D}{M_{-1}} + (1-\theta_2)\Delta \ln M_f + \alpha \Delta \ln Y - \alpha_f \Delta \ln Y_f$$

$$- \beta \Delta i + \beta_f \Delta i_f \quad (17)$$

The exchange rate and balance of payments terms are now together on the left-hand side, with all other variables on the right; and in this way *exchange-market pressure* has emerged as an unambiguously defined variable which can be measured without estimation—by the simple sum of the rate of appreciation and normalised intervention—and as the dependent variable in an equation derived from monetary theory. This is the novelty of the GR model.

But an equation in pressure defined in the same way was always available from the basic monetary model since the coefficient of $\Delta R/M_{-1}$ in (14) is -1 a priori. GR's contribution may therefore be represented by the gain in generality obtained from the replacement of the PPP assumption by expression (15). We have questioned in an earlier paper[10] the validity and appropriateness of this function. Here we note simply that in the GR model not only does (15) exclude adjustment lags, but also money balances are assumed to adjust instantaneously to the determinants of demand. It has been shown above that with partial adjustment in the demand for money and PPP the exchange rate equation (12) has a coefficient on the domestic money term which depends on relative speeds of adjustment. If the money supply is there decomposed into its counterparts, the coefficient of each will also have this property: in particular, the coefficient of the external counterpart representing official financing will need to be determined empirically, so that 'pressure' cannot be measured prior to estimation. This is true also when PPP is replaced by (15) amended for adjustment lags. The GR measure of pressure is therefore invalid when there is partial adjustment, and only when there is perfect adjustment is there an a priori measure of pressure.

This is scarcely surprising. GR's pressure variable implicitly 'provides a

[10] 'Monetary Models of Exchange Rates and Exchange Market Pressure: Some General Limitations and an Application to Sterling's Effective Rate', mimeo, February 1980.

measure of the volume of intervention necessary to achieve any desired exchange rate target' (p. 537). It would be remarkable if the parameters of such a measure were not a matter for empirical investigation on other than very special assumptions about behaviour. To be able to claim on theoretical grounds that there will be a regular, linear trade-off such that any 1% movement in the exchange rate may be avoided by intervention equivalent to 1% of the money stock, assumptions are required about the responsiveness of the demand for money and the behaviour of the exchange rate which are special, and of particularly doubtful validity for the short-run. Section III, nevertheless, presents estimates of the GR equation (17) as well as of the basic monetary model (3) and what we call the 'general' monetary model (12).

4. Dornbusch's model of exchange rate dynamics

We finally describe a model proposed by Dornbusch (1976) which has in common with the basic monetary model the domestic demand for money function (1) and the assumption of perfect capital mobility (or uncovered interest parity) (4) but which nevertheless gives results which are in some respects quite different, and more akin to Branson's portfolio balance model. These results are obtained from assumptions that competition in trade is imperfect, so that PPP does not hold; that there are differences in speeds of adjustment between assets and goods markets, with interest and exchange rates responding faster to shocks than goods prices and output; and that exchange-rate expectations are endogenous, so that the interest rate is also endogenous, and free to clear the domestic money market.

The model reduces to two relationships between the domestic price level and the exchange rate, one describing the condition for equilibrium in financial markets, the other the condition for equilibrium in domestic goods and money markets. They are derived as follows.

Exchange rate expectations are assumed to be regressive: the expected rate of appreciation depends upon the discrepancy between the expected long-run exchange rate $\bar{S}$ and the actual current rate:

$$E(\hat{S}) = \epsilon(\ln \bar{S} - \ln S) \tag{18}$$

An expression for $\bar{S}$ will be derived below: it is determined within the model, so that the expectations hypothesis is consistent with rationality and perfect foresight. Substitution of (18) and (4) into (1) gives the following condition for money-market equilibrium with perfect capital mobility:

$$\ln M = K + \ln P + \alpha \ln Y - \beta i_f + \beta \epsilon (\ln \bar{S} - \ln S) \tag{19}$$

In long-run stationary state, $S = \bar{S}$ (uncovered interest rates are equalised) and (19) then gives an expression for the long-run price level $\bar{P}$ which clears the money market for given M, Y and i_f:

$$\ln \bar{P} = -K + \ln M - \alpha \ln Y + \beta i_f \tag{20}$$

Equation (19) may also be re-arranged to give an equation in S:

$$\ln S = \ln \bar{S} + \frac{1}{\beta\epsilon} (\ln P - \ln \bar{P}) = \ln \bar{S} + \frac{1}{\beta\epsilon} (\ln P + K - \ln M + \alpha \ln Y - \beta i_f)$$

(21)

These expressions already, without substitution for $\bar{S}$, show the positive relationship between P and S which is implied in the condition that financial markets be in equilibrium. The relationship is positive because the higher is P, for given M and Y, the higher i must be for equilibrium in the money market; but the higher is i, the lower must $E(\hat{S})$ be, given perfect capital mobility; and for lower $E(\hat{S})$, S must be higher owing to the regressiveness of expectations.

To obtain an expression for $\bar{S}$, we turn to the goods market. The demand D for domestic output is related positively to real income and competitiveness (now variable in the absence of PPP) and negatively to the rate of interest:

$$\ln D = u + \delta \ln (P_f/SP) + \phi \ln Y - \sigma i$$

(22)

The rate of inflation is then assumed to be proportional to excess demand: the price level now has the role of clearing the goods market, rather than the money market as was the case with the monetary approach

$$\Delta \ln P = \pi \ln (D/Y) = \pi[u + \delta \ln (P_f/SP) + (\phi - 1) \ln Y - \sigma i]$$

(23)

This expression will be zero when the goods market is in equilibrium and in particular in the stationary state where $P = \bar{P}$, $S = \bar{S}$, and $i = i_f$; (23) then delivers an expression for the long-term exchange rate:

$$\ln \bar{S} = \ln (P_f/\bar{P}) + \frac{1}{\delta} [u + (\phi - 1) \ln Y - \sigma i_f]$$

(24)

This is the exchange rate which, when not expected to change, and for given P_f, Y_f, and i_f, makes competitiveness such that the demand for domestic output is equal to domestic income. Substitution of (20) into (24) gives:

$$\ln \bar{S} = \left(K + \frac{u}{\delta}\right) + \ln P_f - \ln M + \left[\alpha + \left(\frac{\phi - 1}{\delta}\right)\right] \ln Y - \left[\beta + \frac{\sigma}{\delta}\right] i_f$$

(25)

Further substitution of this equation into (21) then gives the first of the two equations in P and S, all other variables being exogenous:

$$\ln S = \left[\frac{u}{\delta} + K\left(1 + \frac{1}{\beta\epsilon}\right)\right] + \frac{1}{\beta\epsilon} \ln P + \ln P_f + \left[\alpha\left(1 + \frac{1}{\beta\epsilon}\right) + \frac{(\phi - 1)}{\delta}\right] \ln Y$$

$$- \left[1 + \frac{1}{\beta\epsilon}\right] \ln M - \left[\beta + \frac{\sigma}{\delta} + \frac{1}{\epsilon}\right] i_f$$

(26)

This is represented in (P, S) space by the upward-sloping AA curve in Fig. 1.

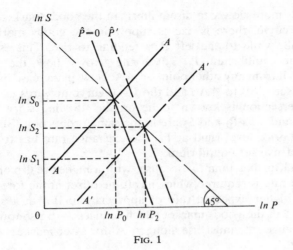

Fig. 1

To obtain the second equation, describing equilibrium in domestic goods and money markets, we return to (23), set $\Delta \ln P$ to zero, and substitute for i from the demand for money function:

$$\ln S = \left[\frac{u\beta - \sigma K}{\beta\delta}\right] - \left[1 + \frac{\sigma}{\beta\delta}\right]\ln P + \ln P_f + \left[\frac{\beta(\phi - 1) - \alpha\sigma}{\beta\delta}\right]\ln Y + \frac{\sigma}{\beta\delta}\ln M \tag{27}$$

The relationship between P and S entailed in this second equation is represented by the downward-sloping $\hat{P} = 0$ curve in the diagram. The downward slope shows that the higher is P, cet. par., the lower must S be for goods-market equilibrium, not only for competitiveness to be restored, but also for the effect of the higher i required for the maintenance of money market equilibrium to be offset. It is for the latter reason that the curve is steeper than a 45° line and the coefficient of $\ln P$ in (27) is numerically greater than unity. In the diagram ($\ln P_0$, $\ln S_0$) represents a full equilibrium; the value of S at this point is described in terms of the exogenous variables by a reduced-form equation (the solution of (26) and (27)) which is the same as (25).

Now consider the consequences of an increase in the *domestic money supply*. The reduced form (25) shows that in the new equilibrium the exchange rate will have fallen in the same proportion as the monetary expansion; and it may similarly be shown that there will also have been a proportionate rise in the domestic price level. But Dornbusch went beyond this comparative static result, which is similar to that obtained in the basic monetary model, by adopting the dynamic assumption that interest rates and exchange rates respond instantaneously to disequilibria in financial markets—so that the economy is always on the AA curve—while the price level responds more slowly to disequilibria in the goods market. To the right of the $\hat{P} = 0$ curve, there is excess supply in the goods market and P is tending to fall, while to the left P is tending to rise. This establishes the stability of the equilibrium (P_0, S_0): as the arrows show, the economy will move towards it from any other point on AA. Now an increase in M shifts AA downwards, (see (26)) to AA', and the $\hat{P} = 0$ curve upwards (see (27)) to $\hat{P}'$. The new intersection is known to lie on the 45° line since the eventual changes in P and S to P_2 and S_2 are in the same proportion. But in the short run, with the price level rigid at P_0, the exchange rate has to fall to S_1 to maintain asset-market equilibrium.

It has to fall further than S_2 because, with a higher real money supply, a lower interest rate is required which has to be offset in the foreign exchange market by a higher expected rate of appreciation. But at (P_0, S_1) there is excess demand in the goods market which induces P to rise towards P_2; and then the exchange rate must rise along $A'A'$ for asset-market equilibrium to be maintained.

Thus although in the Dornbusch model, as in the monetary model, monetary disturbances have no real effects in the long run, they do lead in the short run to changes in the real exchange rate. Following a monetary expansion, the exchange rate will *overshoot* its lower long-run equilibrium owing to the rigidity of the price level; but there will be a subsequent adjustment process, entailing appreciation together with rising prices (always assuming output to be given).

The assumption of differential speeds of adjustment between goods and asset markets is a particularly interesting feature of the Dornbusch model. The same idea underlies the portfolio balance analysis; and in both cases monetary disturbances are shown to lead to overshooting. Estimates of equations suggested by the Dornbusch model will be described below. They will represent a modified version of the above model, in that they allow for partial adjustment in the demand for money. It may be shown that when (1) is replaced by (10), the Dornbusch equation representing asset-market equilibrium (26) becomes:

$$\ln S = \left[\frac{u}{\delta} + K \left(1 + \frac{1}{\beta \epsilon} \right) \right] + \frac{1}{\beta \epsilon} \ln P + \ln P_f + \left[\alpha \left(1 + \frac{1}{\beta \epsilon} \right) + \frac{(\phi - 1)}{\delta} \right] \ln Y$$

$$- \left(1 + \frac{1}{\gamma' \beta \epsilon} \right) \ln M + \frac{(1 - \gamma')}{\gamma' \beta \epsilon} \ln M_{-1} - \left[\beta + \frac{\sigma}{\delta} + \frac{1}{\epsilon} \right] i_f \qquad (26a)$$

The only differences are the new term in lagged money and the appearance of γ' in the coefficient of $\ln M$. The former introduces the possibility of oscillatory responses to monetary shocks; the latter shows that slow responsiveness in the demand for money will accentuate any tendency to overshooting. Similar variants on (27) and (25) may be derived.

For example, (25) becomes

$$\ln S = \left(K + \frac{u}{\delta}\right) + \ln P_f - \frac{1}{\gamma'} \left[\frac{\delta + \gamma' \epsilon (\sigma + \beta \delta)}{\delta + \epsilon (\sigma + \beta \delta)}\right] \ln M + \frac{(1 - \gamma')}{\gamma'[\delta + \epsilon(\beta\delta + \sigma)]} \ln M_{-1}$$

$$+ \left[\frac{((\phi - 1)}{\delta} + \alpha\right] \ln Y - \left[\beta + \frac{\sigma}{\delta}\right] i_f \qquad (25a)$$

This reduces to (25) in the stationary state.

5. Summary: money, interest rates and the exchange rate

The asset-market view of exchange rates

In recent years, following the advent of the present system of managed floating by the main currencies, there has been an intensive re-appraisal of the theory of exchange rate determination. This section has attempted to survey the ensuing literature, focussing mainly on its monetary aspects, by examining four models—one taken to represent the previous orthodoxy, and three which may be regarded as representative of recent work.

Each of the models—not only the monetary approach—attributes to monetary developments and policy an influence on exchange rates, predicting that monetary expansion will lead to depreciation and conversely. But whereas the previously conventional approach emphasised the influence of the exchange rate on the current account, and the mechanism which this could provide for the correction of payments imbalances resulting from monetary (and other) disturbances, the more recent models all stress the role of the exchange rate in equilibrating asset markets.[11] This new view of exchange rates has clearly been motivated partly by empirical evidence, such as the long lags with which trade appears to respond to changes in prices and exchange rates, and the volatility of exchange rates (since the demise of Bretton Woods) in relation to movements in relative price levels and other real variables.

Prices, interest rates and expectations

Although the 'asset-market view' of exchange rates distinguishes all three of the recent models examined from the Mundell–Fleming analysis, there is another distinction of some significance which makes the monetary model stand on its own. This is its characteristically monetarist assumption that the domestic price level is sufficiently flexible (given flexibility in the exchange rate) to clear the money market, while the interest rate is determined elsewhere and not directly affected by monetary disturbances. In the

---

[11] The influence attributed to the current account has consequently generally diminished, although it has a role in the portfolio balance model of II 2, and in models which acknowledge wealth effects on the demand for money, real expenditures, and on risk premia in inter-currency portfolio management: see Dornsbusch (1980).

Mundell–Fleming analysis, the price level was taken as given, and a monetary expansion led to a decline in interest rates, an incipient capital account deficit, and a corrective depreciation. In the portfolio balance model, the price level is a datum in the short run; a monetary expansion requires a fall in interest rates to re-equilibrate domestic asset markets; and the fall in interest rates requires depreciation for the demand for foreign assets to be restored to its original level. In the Dornbusch model, the price level is again rigid in the short run; a monetary expansion requires a fall in interest rates to restore money-market equilibrium; and the fall in interest rates requires depreciation for relative expected yields to be held in equality, given the regressiveness of expectations:

$$i - i_f = -E(\hat{S}) = \epsilon \ (\ln S - \ln \bar{S}) \tag{28}$$

In all these cases, monetary expansion means real monetary expansion owing to the stickiness of the price level, and implies a fall in interest rates which is the mechanism that triggers depreciation. A fall in interest rates in each case reflects a loosening of domestic monetary conditions and results in a lower exchange rate. The rate of interest and the exchange rate are in each case positively associated.

In the monetary model, however, interest rates are determined (approximately) by expectations of inflation:

$$i - i_f = -E(\hat{S}) = E(\hat{P} - \hat{P}_f) \tag{29}$$

Perfect capital mobility ensures the first equality, while 'rational' expectations of PPP ensure the second. A monetary expansion will thus affect interest rates only if it affects (inflation) expectations, and if it does so (as would be the case with *RE*) it will tend to raise them. If, however, as has been assumed in most empirical applications, expectations of inflation depend upon underlying monetary growth and are insensitive to short-term disturbances, a monetary expansion will not affect the rate of interest: money-market equilibrium will be restored, with the real money supply at its initial value, by a rise in the price level permitted by a fall in the value of the currency. The rate of interest (and the expected rate of domestic inflation) is in this case negatively associated with the exchange rate.

It may therefore be argued that in the analysis of monetary influences on the exchange rate it is the monetary model rather than Mundell–Fleming which is distinctively different from the rest;[12] and it would seem that a good test of the monetary approach would be provided by an examination of the signs of estimated interest rate coefficients in exchange rate equations of the kind set out in II 3.

---

[12] It is particularly easy to see that something very much like the Dornbusch model begins to materialise when his assumption about dynamics is introduced into Mundell's perfect-capital-mobility version of the Mundell–Fleming IS-LM analysis.

A synthesis

An alternative test has been suggested by Frankel (1979). By combining the expectations hypotheses (28) and (29),

$$i - i_f = -E(\hat{S}) = \epsilon(\ln S - \ln \bar{S}) + E(\hat{P} - \hat{P}_f)$$

which gives

$$\ln S = \ln \bar{S} + \frac{1}{\epsilon}[(i - E(\hat{P})) - (i_f - E(\hat{P}_f))] \tag{30}$$

He assumes that the monetary hypothesis holds in the long run—when $S = \bar{S}$, the interest differential and expected inflation differentials are equal—but not necessarily in the short. Frankel then assumes that, with PPP also holding in the long run, $\bar{S}$ is determined according to the basic monetary model, but with the domestic and foreign interest semi-elasticities constrained to be equal and the interest rates taking their long-run values.

This implies that

$$\ln S = K - \ln M + \ln M_f + \alpha \ln Y - \alpha_f \ln Y_f$$

$$+ \frac{1}{\epsilon}(i - i_f) - \left(\frac{1}{\epsilon} + \beta\right)E(\hat{P} - \hat{P}_f) \tag{31}$$

In the 'monetary' case, $S = \bar{S}$, the interest and expected inflation differentials are equal, and $1/\epsilon = 0$. But if (in the short run) the interest differential deviates from the expected inflation differential, and if the latter can be proxied satisfactorily, then estimation of (31) should show the exchange rate to be related positively to the domestic interest rate. Estimation of (31) then offers an alternative test of the validity of the monetary model.[13]

Preview

The foregoing paragraphs have focussed on the theoretical implications for the relationship between interest rates and the exchange rate of different assumptions about price flexibility and expectations. The policy reactions of the authorities have not been mentioned, because they are outside the purview of the models. One of the main arguments of the following section, however, is that any empirical test of this relationship, or indeed any estimation of the determinants of the exchange rate, is unlikely to be valid unless account is taken of the simultaneous determination of monetary policy.

[13] In estimation, Frankel in fact used short-term interest rates for $i - i_f$, and the differential of long-term interest rates to proxy the expected inflation differential.

III. Sterling's effective exchange rate: 1972–80

1. Model selection and application

(a) Model selection

Despite the differences among the theoretical models discussed above, the choice of a model for econometric application is, for a number of reasons, both less problematical and less clear-cut than may at first appear. First, although there are structural differences, representing divergent views about the economic mechanisms and adjustment processes involved in exchange rate determination, the derived reduced-form equations are often similar in their arguments. They therefore often have similar data requirements. It also follows that, apart from when the predicted signs of the reduced-form coefficients differ, it may be difficult for econometric estimation to distinguish between the theories, and to validate one while rejecting the others. Secondly, there are structural similarities among the models which should temper any judgment about their relative economic plausibility. In particular, it might be thought that the assumption of a stable demand for money function causes the monetary model to stand out as particularly inappropriate to the context of the UK in recent years. In fact, however, the monetary approach is not distinguished by this assumption: there is a demand for money function (of similar form) in each of the four models reviewed, and in each case estimation would entail an assumption about its stability. Thirdly, although the theories may be set out as conflicting alternatives, they may be regarded to some extent as complementary interpretations of the real world, since the exchange rate is no doubt in practice determined in goods markets, money markets, and asset markets more generally. There is therefore something to be said for a pragmatic and open-minded approach to an examination of the data.

Nevertheless, the portfolio balance approach, since it allows for wealth effects and imperfect asset substitutability and is the most general asset market model, would perhaps attract the most widespread support. It has to date, however, received little attention in the empirical literature. This is largely due to difficulties in obtaining the requisite data, in particular for asset stocks; but it is also because the monetary approach, in particular, appears so much more tractable and yields straightforward implications for the relevant parameters. The monetary approach is often referred to as a special case of the portfolio balance model, but as was emphasised in II 5 its implications for the relationship between the exchange rate and the rate of interest, in particular, are different from those of the portfolio balance model and the other models reviewed. This distinctive feature of the monetary model is of some importance in the interpretation of the econometric results to be reported below: since it is derived from special assumptions about price flexibility and competition in trade whose plausibil-

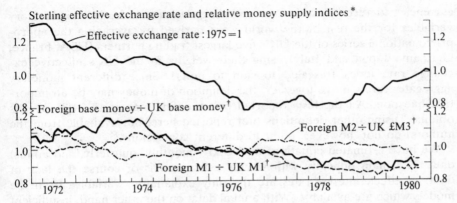

CHART 2. * UK 'base money' defined here as sum of notes and coin in circulation with the public, banks' till money and bankers' deposits at the Bank of England. Foreign monetary aggregates, weighted as described in footnote 17 from *International Financial Statistics*: base money = 'reserve money'; M1 = 'money'; M2 = 'money' + 'quasi-money'. All seasonally adjusted. † End 1975 = 1.

ity seems questionable,[14] apparent confirmation of the monetary prediction in this case (and for other explanatory variables as well) should obviously be treated with considerable caution.

Although the monetary approach is therefore not to be regarded simply as an empirically tractable representation of the portfolio balance model, we took the basic monetary model as our starting point because of the success with which it seemed, from the recent literature, to have been applied by others working in this area. These results, together with our own estimates of the basic monetary model and other variants of the single-equation monetary approach, are discussed in the following section. It is, however, worth noting at the outset that Chart 2, which plots sterling's effective rate against three ratios between foreign and domestic money stocks, reveals no immediately striking stable relationship.

(b) *Choice of exchange rate, monetary aggregates, and frequency of data*

Most previously published econometric work in this area has been concerned with bilateral exchange rates, and this approach was adopted in earlier work in the Bank which modelled the sterling-dollar rate (Saville 1980). We chose however to focus mainly on sterling's *effective* rate because of its greater relevance for the UK trade balance and for the determination of UK prices, especially given the instability of the dollar against other

[14] As Dornbusch (1980, p. 146) has remarked, "There is ample evidence accumulating that this assumption (of PPP) is not warranted". See, e.g., the papers in the symposium on PPP in the May 1978 issue of the *Journal of International Economics*, Frenkel (1980), and Chart 1 of this paper.

currencies in recent years. Corresponding data for 'effective' explanatory variables for the rest of the world were derived by averaging the appropriate national series of the UK's five largest trading partners (USA, France, Germany, Japan and Italy) using their weights in the UK's effective exchange rate index (rescaled to sum to unity). Since different monetary aggregates rarely move together, the definition of money may be an important question. All the tests reported below define money as £M3. Results obtained using other definitions (not reported here, but available from the authors) do not, however, point to different conclusions.[15]

We have estimated equations on weekly, monthly, quarterly, and annual data. The main difficulty with weekly estimation is of course the lack of data: in effect, interest rates are the only explanatory variables from the models which are available. With annual data, on the other hand, insufficient degrees of freedom are available for the estimation of any but the most simple models. Most of our own results reported below are based on monthly observations, since this frequency provides most degrees of freedom given the constraints of data availability.

(c) North Sea oil

In applying any of the models to the recent course of sterling, consideration needs to be given to the impact of the discovery and exploitation of North Sea oil, which allowed the UK towards the end of ths estimation period to become nearly self-sufficient in oil consumption. In principle the variables included in the reduced form equation of each of the models should capture at least some of the effects of the North Sea endowment. For example, in terms of the monetary model the route by which a natural resource discovery should have its impact is by raising domestic real income, and thus inducing an excess demand for money (on the assumption that the authorities' monetary policy does not accommodate the discovery); appreciation is then required to clear the money market. Anticipation of such an effect, for example on rational expectations grounds, implies, through the assumption of perfect capital mobility, a reduction in the domestic interest rate which would also increase the demand for money. Thus, depending on the precise nature of the expectations formation process, a more than proportionate rise in the exchange rate may be required to restore equilibrium in the short run.

In the monetary model the impact on the current account of the discovery of North Sea oil is immaterial. In contrast, in the Dornbusch model such a discovery is analogous to an increase in net exports, creating excess demand in the goods market but also raising exchange rate expectations. In the long run the restoration of equilibrium requires appreciation to equilibrate the goods market, but in the short run, if the additional expenditure induced by

---

[15] They are fully described in a Bank Discussion Paper (forthcoming).

the higher level of real income is slow to materialise, the exchange rate will nevertheless rise, leading to a contraction of demand and output.[16]

Whilst the effects of such a natural resource discovery may therefore appear relatively straightforward to capture within the models, the effect of North Sea oil on the exchange rate as an empirical issue is made considerably more complex by the massive step jumps in oil prices during the estimation period. It is unlikely that the direct and indirect effects of these changes can be easily captured empirically, in particular because their influence through exchange rate expectations is potentially crucial while measurement of this effect (in terms, for example, of interest rates) is problematical. (Although covered interest parity should be approximately maintained by riskless arbitrage, the identification of expectations with the uncovered differential requires the additional assumption of risk-neutrality which is clearly more contentious.)

In estimation we attempted to allow for those effects not directly captured in the income and interest rate variables already contained in the reduced forms by including additional variables which might be considered to measure the influence of oil-related developments. These ranged from the present discounted value of North Sea production to the direct effects of North Sea output on the current account and the impact of nominal and real oil prices. The results are described in the forthcoming Bank Discussion Paper referred to above. In our quarterly estimation, the only variable which consistently improved the fit of the equations was oil exporting countries' sterling balances, but this variable was clearly unlikely to be exogenous, and OLS parameter estimates were thus presumed to be biased. In the monthly estimates reported below, variations in oil exporters' (and other overseas countries') sterling balances are captured in the "Other External Flows" component of the change in £M3. The only other oil variable included in these equations is the world price, taken as the effective dollar price of Saudi marker crude oil.

2. Single equation estimates, 1972–1977

(a) The basic monetary model

A number of recent studies [for example, Putnam and Woodbury (1980), Shirakawa (1980)] have reported results for the most simple monetary model using monthly and quarterly data for the sterling:dollar rate over the floating rate period up to 1977. In their equations, parameter estimates are consistently right-signed and significant and Putnam and Woodbury, for example, are led to conclude that the monetary approach is "a powerful and simple explanatory device and that even for time periods as short as a quarter, purchasing power parity appears to be valid". Our own attempt to replicate these results revealed clear evidence of serial correlation: once

---

[16] An elegant treatment of the impact of a resource discovery in the Dornbusch model is provided by Eastwood and Venables (1980).

TABLE A

Estimation period: February 1972-October 1977

1	$\ln(\$:£) = 10.209 - 0.578 \ln M - 0.345 \ln M_{us} + 0.246 \ln Y$
	(12.7) (6.5) (1.5) (1.6)

$$-0.630 \ln Y_{us} - 0.019i + 0.007i_{us} + 0.626U_{t-1}$$
(5.0)   (8.0)   (1.4)   (5.6)

$\bar{R}^2 = 0.988 \qquad se = 0.017 \qquad DW = 1.775$

2	$\ln EER = 0.120 - 0.054 \ln M - 0.941 \ln M_f - 0.003 \ln Y$
	(0.060) (0.306) (4.214) (0.034)

$$+0.035 \ln Y_f - 0.008i + 0.003i_{us} + 0.942U_{t-1}$$
(0.182)   (4.747) (1.295)(22.546)

$\bar{R}^2 = 0.992 \qquad se = 0.014 \qquad DW = 1.805$

't' statistics in parentheses.

autoregressive rather than ordinary least squares techniques were used, the parameters on the monetary variables were substantially reduced in magnitude and significance, as shown in equation 1 of Table A. Nevertheless, the domestic money stock remains significant and the interest rate parameters apparently confirm the monetary, rather then the conventional or portfolio balance, model. We return to this feature below.

Nor is the claim that the basic monetary model is supported by the data limited to references to the sterling:dollar rate. Thus Bilson (1979, p. 220) cites a number of studies of various bilateral rates which 'support the general predictions of the monetary approach. In particular, most find that a monetary expansion results in a proportional depreciation of the exchange rate. In addition, ... higher levels of nominal interest rates ... tend to depreciate the exchange rate.' Mussa (1979, p. 45), in a slightly less sanguine judgment, considers that the 'body of evidence is sufficiently impressive to justify the conclusion that the monetary model ... does have empirical content'.

Our own results for a simple monetary model of sterling's *effective* rate over the period 1972–1977 are shown as equation 2 in Table A:[17] although the domestic money stock loses its significance entirely, there is again evidence of a negative relationship between domestic interest rates and the exchange rate.

(b) *The general monetary and Girton–Roper models*

Table B shows typical results derived from the estimation of both the general monetary model—equation (12)—and the Girton–Roper model

[17] Money, income and, where possible, interest rate variables were defined as weighted averages of the UK's major trading partners' data: consistent short-term interest rates are not published for all countries and a choice therefore had to be faced between using the three-month euro-dollar rate as representative of all short-term rates or using long-term bond rates where comparable data are available. The reported equation used short-term rates: similar results were obtained using long rates.

TABLE B

1. *General monetary model*

$$\Delta \ln EER = -0.409 + 0.575 \frac{\Delta R}{M_{-1}} - 0.153 \frac{DCE}{M_{-1}} - 0.220 \frac{OEF}{M_{-1}} - 0.393 \Delta \ln M_f$$

       (1.171) (2.049)   (0.761)   (0.632)   (0.609)

$$+0.026 \ln \left(S \frac{M}{M_f} \right)_{-1} - 0.053 \ln Y + 0.083 \ln Y_f - 0.001r$$

   (1.274)   (0.613)   (1.246)   (0.274)

$$+0.001 r_f$$

   (0.098)

$\bar{R}^2 = 0.193$ $se = 0.014$ $DW = 1.828$

2. *Unconstrained Girton–Roper*

$$\Delta \ln EER = -0.008 + 0.422 \frac{\Delta R}{M_{-1}} + 0.064 \frac{DCE}{M_{-1}} - 0.302 \frac{OEF}{M_{-1}}$$

       (1.227) (1.691)   (0.360)   (1.000)

$$-0.126 \Delta \ln M_f + 0.046 \Delta \ln Y + 0.222 \Delta \ln Y_f$$

   (0.226)   (0.543)   (1.151)

$$-0.007 \Delta r + 0.007 \Delta r_f + 0.268 U_{t-1}$$

   (1.829)   (0.563)   (1.932)

$\bar{R}^2 = 0.259$ $se = 0.014$ $DW = 1.890$

3. *Constrained Girton–Roper*

$$\Delta \ln EER + \frac{\Delta R}{M_{-1}} = -0.005 - 0.427 \frac{DCE}{M_{-1}} - 1.331 \frac{OEF}{M_{-1}} - 0.152 \Delta \ln M_f$$

           (0.676) (2.204)   (4.512)   (0.221)

$$+0.139 \Delta \ln Y + 0.314 \Delta \ln Y_f - 0.008 \Delta r - 0.003 \Delta r_f + 0.346 U_{t-1}$$

   (1.421)   (1.278)   (1.742)   (0.206)   (2.614)

$\bar{R}^2 = 0.486$ $se = 0.017$ $DW = 1.933$

(17), the latter with and without the imposition of the constraint entailed in their composite dependent variable. (The path of the composite pressure variable is shown in Chart 3). The similarity of the two models is apparent from a comparison of equations 1 and 2: they differ, however, in the inclusion in the first of the term in lagged relative money stocks and in the first-difference transformation of the income and interest rate variables in the second equation. It will be noted that in (1) all parameter estimates are insignificantly different from zero with the exception of intervention which is significantly positive. This result holds too for the Girton–Roper equation (2) in which the intervention parameter is allowed to be freely determined: the *a priori* prediction of their model that the coefficient be −1 is thus rejected by the data. The parameter estimates suggest, rather, that the authorities' purchases of sterling have tended to cause depreciation! This inference should not, however, be drawn: the sign clearly reflects the

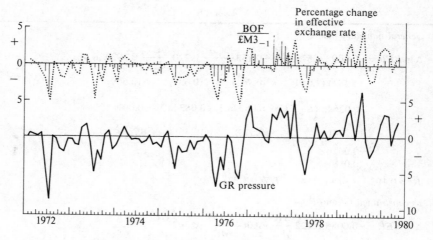

CHART 3. Exchange rates, intervention, and pressure

simultaneous determination of the exchange rate with intervention policy and in particular the authorities' operating tactics of "leaning into the wind", supporting sterling when it was weak and conversely.

Although in equation 3, where the parameter on intervention is constrained by adoption of the Girton–Roper dependent variable, the coefficients on DCE and domestic income are correctly signed and barely significant, this result hardly constitutes convincing support for the monetary model.[18] The domestic interest rate parameter, however, again retains its negative sign and it is to this consistent feature of the above results which we now turn, before returning to the problem of exchange-market intervention in Section 4.

3. Interest rate determination and the Dornbusch model

Charts 4 and 5 show the movements in the sterling dollar rate, the effective exchange rate and corresponding uncovered interest differentials between January 1972 and May 1980. Over the period up to October 1977—the period over which all the equations so far described were estimated—both charts show a negative relationship which is particularly clear in Chart 4.

Whilst this might be explained by the monetary model in terms of inflation and exchange-rate expectations, an alternative explanation is available which is supported by the post-1977 data. This lies in the determination of the authorities' interest rate policy, which was for most of the period up

---

[18] It is interesting to note that equations using quarterly data from 1973 Q1 to 1978 Q4 exhibited similar properties, including the rejection of the theoretical restriction on the intervention parameter, but the $\bar{R}^2s$ were considerably higher than those shown in Table B. This partly reflects the relative smoothness of the quarterly series but also the consistent significance of OPEC sterling balances which were included as an additional variable.

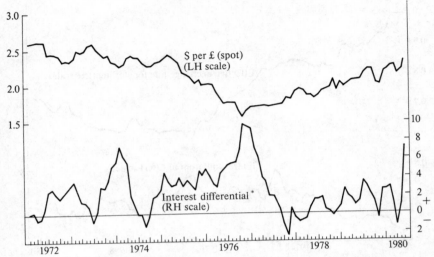

CHART 4. $:£ exchange rate and interest differential, January 1972–May 1980.
*3-month inter bank £ minus 3-month euro-$

to 1977 mainly determined by external pressure.[19] Typically weakness of
sterling provoked in response increases in interest rates either directly
through increases in MLR or through the authorities' money market operations; and conversely. Now from 1977 onwards the introduction of monetary targets and the clear indication given by the authorities in that year that
they were to be given prominence over any external objective,[20] should on
this hypothesis have resulted in a change in the relationship between interest

---

[19] This is clear from various issues of the *Bank of England Quarterly Bulletin*: see, for
example, September 1973 Bulletin, pages 276–7 "By the middle of July short-term interest
rates in London had become seriously out of line with those in foreign centres ..."; December
1973 Bulletin, page 414 "On wider grounds the Bank were at this period content to see a slight
easing of rates, in line with the movement in rates abroad"; March 1974 Bulletin, page 11.
"Monetary policy since the autumn has been dominated by two aims. The first, essential in view
of the balance of payments situation, was to maintain interest rates fully competitive with those
in other financial centres"; March 1975 Bulletin, page 15 "A sharp fall in US and other
overseas rates in early January permitted some general reduction in UK rates"; June 1975
Bulletin, page 135 "Short-term interest rates ... fell steadily during the early part of 1975. The
downturn ... followed reductions in rates abroad, particularly in the United States, and in the
euro-dollar market"; September 1975 Bulletin, page 219 "In the second half of June rates in
the US and in the euro-dollar market began to turn upwards, eroding the differential that had
been established in favour of sterling, and which it seemed desirable to maintain"; December
1975 Bulletin, page 334 "... the continued weakness of sterling, and further increases in rates
in the US and in the euro-dollar markets, suggested that another increase in UK short-term
rates would be appropriate"; September 1976 Bulletin, page 300 "... short-term interest rates
began to turn up—a development which was welcome to the authorities in view of the weakness
which sterling was displaying and the rise in US interest rates during the month"; December
1976 Bulletin, page 427 "With the exchange rate under heavy pressure, MLR rose by 1½%
to 13%".
[20] See, for example, the Governor's Mais Lecture, *Bank of England Quarterly Bulletin*,
March 1978.

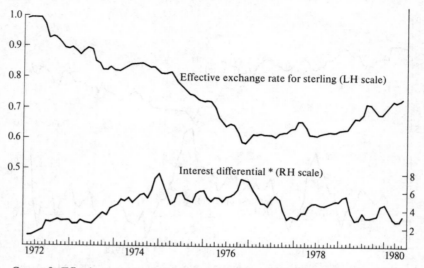

CHART 5. Effective exchange rates and interest differential, January 1972–May 1980.
*UK long term government bond rate minus weighted average of long term government bond rates in 5 countries

rates and the exchange rate; and this is what the charts show. In the last three years, causality has been reversed, with domestic considerations having a much more important influence on interest rate policy: external pressure over this period has largely been caused by, rather than the cause of, movements in domestic interest rates. The change in the relationship between interest rates and the exchange rate is well illustrated in Chart 6 which shows how the interest rate parameter estimated in the basic monetary model was found to change as the data set was gradually extended to include the post-1976 experience. Whilst the coefficient is relatively stable at about −0.010 to −0.015 until 1977, from then onwards it rises until, by the time the observation period extends from February 1972 to February 1980, it becomes positive. There are two important implications for the exchange rate: first, any equation which fails to take account of this simultaneity will yield a biased interest rate parameter; and secondly, since the introduction and implementation of monetary targets represents a significant structural break in interest rate determination, any predictions of exchange rate movements based on equations estimated over the floating rate period up to 1976/77 will be ill-founded.

Dornbusch

A way of avoiding this problem, however, is offered by the Dornbusch model, since its assumptions about expectations and perfect capital mobility cause the domestic interest rate to drop out of its exchange rate equations (25)–(27). It is at first sight surprising that since being published in 1976 this

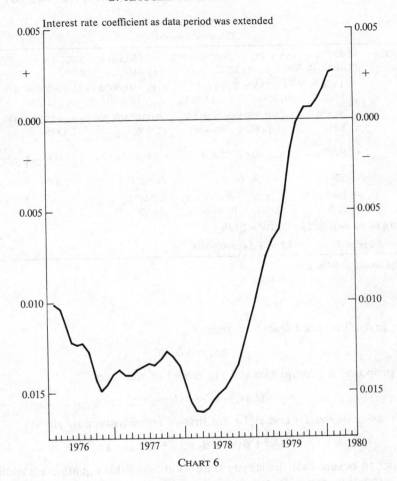

CHART 6

model has not to our knowledge been investigated empirically, despite its attractive theoretical properties. Some part of the explanation is perhaps revealed by the results shown in Table C.

Severe estimation difficulties were encountered. When equations (25) and (26) were estimated in levels, and even when lagged adjustment in the demand for money function was allowed for—as in (25a) and (26a)—significant autoregressive parameters of first and higher order were found. Estimation of the model in first-differenced form also proved unsatisfactory, not only because by such a transformation all long-run information in the data is lost but also because first-order serial correlation remained. This indicated that greater attention to the dynamics of the model was required; and the general specification proposed by Davidson *et al.* (1978) was therefore adopted. Rather than estimate a model such as:

$$x_t = k + w_t \tag{32}$$

TABLE C
Dornbusch model

$\Delta \ln EER = -0.472^* + 0.146\Delta \ln PC - 0.466^*\Delta \ln PC_{-1} - 0.858\Delta \ln P_f + 0.027\Delta \ln P_{f_{-1}}$
$\qquad\quad (2.462)\quad (0.708)\qquad\quad (2.213)\qquad\qquad (1.216)\qquad\quad (0.037)$

$\qquad + 0.148\Delta \ln Y - 0.023\Delta \ln Y_{-1} + 0.477^*\Delta \ln Y_f - 0.600^*\Delta \ln Y_{f-1} - 0.384^*\Delta \ln M$
$\qquad\quad (1.500)\qquad\quad (0.256)\qquad\quad (2.312)\qquad\quad (2.863)\qquad\qquad (2.200)$

$\qquad - 0.311^*\Delta \ln M_{-1} + 0.008\Delta r_f - 0.005\Delta r_{f-1} + 0.036^*\Delta \ln PFO + 0.041^*\Delta \ln PFO_{-1}$
$\qquad\quad (1.691)\qquad\qquad (0.772)\qquad (0.406)\qquad\quad (2.006)\qquad\qquad (2.137)$

$\qquad - 0.872^*\Delta \ln EER_{-1} - 0.677^*\Delta \ln EER_{-2} + 0.198\Delta \ln EER_{-3} - 0.004 \ln \left(\dfrac{S \cdot M}{P_f}\right)_{-1}$

$\qquad\quad (6.126)\qquad\qquad (4.300)\qquad\qquad (1.587)\qquad\qquad (0.252)$

$\qquad + 0.160^* \ln Y_{-1} - 0.000 r_{f-1} - 0.050 \ln Y_{f-1} - 0.541^* U_{t-1}$
$\qquad\quad (2.354)\qquad (0.084)\qquad (0.949)\qquad (3.819)$

$\bar{R}^2 = 0.444 \qquad se = 0.013 \qquad DW = 2.129$

Estimation period: May 1972 to February 1980

* Significant at 90% level

or its first-differenced transformation:

$$\Delta x_t = \Delta w_t$$

they proposed a general rational lag model of the form:

$$\alpha(L)x_t = k^* + \beta(L)w_t + v_t$$

which, assuming $\alpha(L)$ and $\beta(L)$ are first-order polynomials, gives:

$$x_t = k^* + \beta_1 w_t + \beta_2 w_{t-1} + \alpha_1 x_{t-1} + v_t \qquad (33)$$

In order to ensure that the steady state solution of this equation reproduces (32) estimation requires the imposition of the constraint that $\beta_1 + \beta_2 = 1 - \alpha_1$, yielding:

$$\Delta x_t = k^* + \beta_1 \Delta w_t + (1-\alpha_1)(w_{t-1} - x_{t-1}) + v_t \qquad (34)$$

The short-run dynamics of the model are revealed by β_1, and the long-run information in the data is identified by $(1-\alpha_1)$. In applying the general rational lag formulation to the Dornbusch model, the long-run properties of homogeneity with respect to domestic money and the foreign price level were imposed, and the model was left free to determine the long-run elasticities of the exchange rate with respect to income and the foreign interest rate.

The economic rationale for such a model may be thought of as being derived from the adoption of more complicated hypotheses about partial adjustment and the formation of expectations than those taken for simplicity in Part II. If for example adjustment to desired money balances takes the form not of

$$\Delta \ln M = \gamma' (\ln M^* - \ln M_{t-1})$$

which implies that (with $0 < \gamma' < 1$) following any shock money holdings fail to reach their desired level in finite time, but of

$$\Delta \ln M = \gamma'(\ln M^* - \ln M_{t-1}) + \delta(\Delta \ln M_{t-1}^{*e})$$

which allows expectations of changes in desired money balances to modify the adjustment process, and if this modification is applied consistently through the model, with the changes in the underlying expected variables assumed (for want of anything better) to depend on lagged actual data, these longer lags are carried through in all variables to the reduced form equation.[21]

Table C reveals a number of interesting features. First, a relationship is identified between current and lagged changes in the exchange rate. This result confirms the proposition that exchange rates are unlikely to follow a random walk. Secondly, the money stock (both current and lagged) is significant, and although the dynamics of the equation are complicated it appears that there is some evidence of overshooting. A sustained positive impulse to the money supply in time period 0 induces a more than proportionate fall in the exchange rate in the following period with further depreciation in period 2; subsequently the exchange rate recovers and in the long run the homogeneity property is satisfied (by imposition). Thirdly, without exception the other variables are either insignificant or wrong-signed. Foreign income which is omitted from the model but which we have included as an influence on domestic output through the foreign trade sector, is significant and positive as expected a priori, but is clearly highly collinear with lagged foreign income which appears with a significant negative coefficient of greater magnitude. Fourthly, oil prices exert a significant influence on the exchange rate in the short run, but interestingly their impact is offset in the following period. Finally, the long-run properties of the equation are poorly determined with only domestic income right-signed and significant. An F test on the overall equation reveals a barely significant relationship.

4. Reaction functions for intervention and interest rates

(a) Exchange market intervention

Difficulties in the econometric estimation of the authorities' intervention behaviour are obviously substantial: intervention is unlikely to be related in a stable way to a few identifiable variables, and we should not expect any such estimated relationship to have a high degree of explanatory power.

---

[21] We are grateful to J. S. Flemming for suggesting this modification to the partial adjustment mechanism.

Certainly one significant change in behaviour—already referred to above—stands out, although it involved a process of adjustment over a period of a year or so: whereas before late 1976 a clear external objective—of maintaining the exchange rate at a competitive level—was demonstrated by intervention policy, during 1977 the exchange rate "target" was first, because of the weakness of the dollar, changed (in June) from the $:£ rate to the effective rate, and then (in October) abandoned altogether because of what was seen as the expansionary effect of the sustained upward pressure and consequent inflows on the money supply. Over the period since then intervention has been confined to smoothing operations—aimed at ironing out fluctuations in the demand for sterling—although this has led in some months to substantial changes in net reserves.

These considerations are not inconsistent with the reaction functions shown in Table D estimated using both autoregressive least squares and instrumental variable techniques. The functional form chosen is best described diagrammatically, in Fig. 2. Part (a) shows the assumed form of smoothing operations: a tangent function was chosen, with the bounds at which intervention was assumed to become infinite defining the appropriate scaling of the data.

Figure 2(b) shows the assumed role of an exchange rate target defined in terms of competitiveness: the function chosen implies that the more uncompetitive is the exchange rate the greater will be the willingness of the authorities to increase the reserves in the face of upward pressure, and vice versa. The data were again scaled in relation to past experience. Figure 2(c) shows the impact of the growth in the money supply in relation to the monetary target.[22] The particular function employed (the reciprocal of the rate of monetary growth scaled to avoid discontinuities) implies that intervention is curtailed as the growth of the money supply increases, but never becomes negative on this account.

Finally because all the intervention data relate to banking months,[23] and since in some months these are affected by short-dated *EEA* swaps undertaken with a view to their money market consequences, a variable was incorporated to proxy money market pressure. This was defined as the differential between the London interbank rate and MLR.[24] Although money-market management suggests that the relationship of this proxy with total spot intervention should be positive (greater pressure in the domestic money market inducing greater offsetting swaps entailing a rise in the reserves) it is also true that downward external pressure has tended to be associated with both smoothing, negative intervention and higher domestic

[22] The originally published data for the growth in the money supply were used for this purpose, with no allowance for subsequent revisions, since this was clearly the data on which the authorities' policy decisions were based.

[23] To ensure correspondence with the only available (banking) monthly data for money and *DCE*.

[24] Over the period when banking monthly data on swaps are internally available in the Bank (from January 1978), there is a clear positive correlation between them and the chosen proxy.

TABLE D

1972 2–1977 10
Imposed scaling parameters: $\alpha = 34.9$; $\beta = 6.3$

1

$$\Delta R = -110.448 + 0.523 \tan \alpha \Delta EER - 402.588 \tan \beta \left(\frac{P_f}{P} - 1\right) + 14.109(i - MLR)$$

$\quad$ (1.544) (0.040) $\qquad\qquad$ (2.290) $\qquad\qquad$ (0.279)

$$+ 41.828 \frac{1}{\Delta \ln M \cdot 100} + 0.200 U_{t-1}$$

$\quad$ (3.463) $\qquad\qquad$ (1.542)

Estimation technique: autoregressive least squares (ALS)
$\bar{R}^2 = 0.28 \qquad se = 354.736 \qquad DW = 2.04$

2

$$\Delta R = -167.649 - 3.893 \tan \alpha \Delta EER - 487.974 \tan \beta \left(\frac{P_f}{P} - 1\right) + 94.294(i - MLR)$$

$\quad$ (2.073) (0.029) $\qquad\qquad$ (2.360) $\qquad\qquad$ (1.274)

$$+ 482.678 \frac{1}{\Delta \ln M \cdot 100} + 0.168 U_{t-1}$$

$\quad$ (3.795) $\qquad\qquad$ (1.397)

Estimation technique: autoregressive instrumental variables (AIV)
$\bar{R}^2 = 0.271 \qquad se = 360.301 \qquad DW = 2.015$

1977 11–1980 2

3

$$\Delta R = -91.883 + 109.085 \tan \alpha \Delta EER - 74.281 \tan \beta \left(\frac{P_f}{P} - 1\right) - 342.584(i - MLR)$$

$\quad$ (1.000) $\quad$ (2.837) $\qquad\qquad$ (2.776) $\qquad\qquad$ (3.994)

$$+ 214.173 \frac{1}{\Delta \ln M \cdot 100} - 0.327 U_{t-1}$$

$\quad$ (0.349) $\qquad\qquad$ (1.811)

Estimation technique: ALS
$\bar{R}^2 = 0.55 \qquad se = 253.9 \qquad DW = 1.95$

4

$$\Delta R = -67.953 + 311.954 \tan \alpha \Delta EER - 52.287 \tan \beta \left(\frac{P_f}{P} - 1\right) - 287.825(i - MLR)$$

$\quad$ (0.806) $\quad$ (2.795) $\qquad\qquad$ (1.803) $\qquad\qquad$ (1.863)

$$+ 67.244 \frac{1}{\Delta \ln M \cdot 100} - 0.379 U_{t-1}$$

$\quad$ (0.118) $\qquad\qquad$ (2.127)

Estimation technique: AIV
$\bar{R}^2 = 0.615 \qquad se = 236.991 \qquad DW = 2.034$

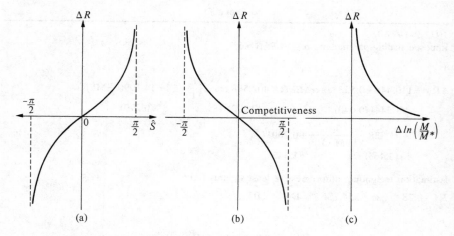

FIG. 2(a) Leaning into the wind (b) Competitiveness (c) Monetary targets

interest rates. The expected sign is therefore indeterminate *a priori*: it will depend on which influence is predominant.

The results demonstrate the importance during the early part of the decade of an exchange rate target defined in terms of competitiveness, and the considerably smaller weight this has had during the last three years. In contrast, 'leaning into the wind' has assumed a relatively greater, and significant, role in determining intervention since 1977; this is also suggested by the interest rate parameter which changes sign between the two periods as might be expected if smoothing intervention came to dominate money market considerations. Finally the influence of monetary growth is shown to be significant and positive over the pre-1977 period, but insignificant since then: although at first sight this might be thought odd, its significance during the first period is in fact due entirely to the observations from the autumn of 1976 after the announcement of the first monetary target,[25] and since then this variable may well have acted more as a constraint than as a direct influence on intervention. The results are thus generally in accord with our *a priori* expectations; they were in fact rather more successful than we had expected, given the inherent difficulties involved in estimating such a function.

(b) *Interest rates*

The above description of the determinants of exchange market intervention before and after 1977 would imply a corresponding and contemporaneous change in the determination of interest rate policy. A uniform

[25] Estimation excluding these observations rendered the monetary variable insignificant.

TABLE E

	CNST	Δ ln EER	ΔR	Δ ln PC	UNEM	Δ ln M	i_{t-1}	U_{t-1}	DW	$\bar{R}^2$	se	Estimation technique
1972 3–1977 10												
1 $i=$	3.015	−13.364	−0.002	−23.795	−0.428	0.129	0.860	−0.173	2.108	0.992	1.005	AIV
	(2.442)	(0.519)	(1.540)	(1.651)	(2.954)	(2.023)	(10.858)	(1.436)				
1977 11–1980 2												
2 $i=$	13.571	6.933	0.000	−10.046	−2.245	0.041	0.908	0.120	1.386	0.995	0.872	AIV
	(1.065)	(0.116)	(0.033)	(0.147)	(1.050)	(0.403)	(6.985)	(0.626)				

function was estimated over the two sub-periods used in the reaction functions for intervention. A simple linear relationship was chosen, with both intermediate objectives—the components of exchange market pressure,[26] and the growth of the money stock (again as described by the original data)—and the ultimate objectives of macro-economic policy—proxied by unemployment and the rate of consumer price inflation—as arguments. The results of estimation by auto-regressive instrumental variables are shown in Table E.

The results offer some very limited evidence of a relationship between pressure in the exchange market and interest rates, and they confirm the relatively greater importance of this external influence during the first part of the estimation period up to October 1977: subsequently, no significant relationship is identified. Monetary growth, which, because the mid-point of the monetary target range has been virtually constant since the first appearance of monetary targets may be thought of as representing deviations from target, is also right-signed and significant; but again, as in the reaction function for intervention, its importance derives solely from the transition period 1976–1977 when the priority attached by the authorities to the monetary objective was increasing. As for the ultimate policy goals, it is perhaps surprising that no clear relationship is identified with inflation— although the parameter is right-signed over the period since October 1977— while unemployment is correctly signed throughout, although significant only in the period before 1977.

Overall, these results, while confirming some of our prior expectations, were not as successful as those for intervention. The estimation of similar functions for MLR rather than the 3-month inter-bank rate met with no greater success. (The authorities' stance on interest rates is of course reflected not only in discrete changes in MLR but also in their money market operations both of which are encapsulated in movements in the inter-bank rate, which may therefore be argued to provide a superior indicator.)

---

[26] Taken to incorporate indirectly the effect of foreign interest rates.

5. Two-stage estimation of the exchange rate

Having estimated reaction functions for intervention and interest rates, we proceeded to estimate the implied reduced-form exchange rate equation, employing the auto-regressive instrumental variable technique to overcome the problems of simultaneity. Throughout, the instruments employed, in addition to those explicitly identified, included as many lagged endogenous and exogenous variables as was possible without inducing singularity in the variance-covariance matrix of regressors: this ensures consistency among the parameter estimates in the presence of serial correlation, as shown by Fair (1970).

As with the earlier Dornbusch model, when the general monetary model was estimated the Box–Pierce χ^2 test on the residual correlogram revealed significant first- and second-order serial correlation; the results in Table F are therefore for the general monetary model in a more general dynamic framework, using both autoregressive least squares and autoregressive instrumental variables. It will be recalled that when the general rational lag specification was applied to the Dornbusch model, a significant autoregressive process was identified, and this is also identified in both equations in Table F.

Other features referred to above are confirmed in the first equation, which does not allow for simultaneity: in particular intervention retains its significant positive coefficient although there is apparently some small, insignificant, lagged offset; and the coefficient on the contemporaneous domestic interest rate is negative, but again with a lagged offset, here larger in magnitude though less significant. For the rest, the monetary and income variables contribute nothing to the fit of the equation with the exception of lagged DCE which is barely significant.

Once allowance is made, in the second equation, for the simultaneous determination of intervention and interest rates, the estimates change in a manner consistent with the above arguments. The significance and magnitude of the parameter on intervention is considerably reduced, and it was found that by relatively minor adjustments either to the variables included or to the estimation period, negative but insignificant estimates were readily obtained. The interest rate coefficient similarly changes sign although again it is no longer significantly different from zero. Unfortunately the insignificance of almost all the other variables included in the general monetary model remains: the only exception is the nominal oil price which has a significant positive contemporaneous impact, which is, however, negated completely in the subsequent period, leaving no net effect.

6. Some further estimates

(a) The Frankel synthesis

Our estimates have shown that neither the Dornbusch exchange rate dynamics model nor the monetary model has any strong empirical basis in

TABLE F

General monetary model: general dynamic framework

1 $\Delta \ln EER = -0.001 + 0.434^*\Delta R/M_{-1} - 0.095DCE/M_{-1} - 0.158OEF/M_{-1} + 0.161\Delta \ln M_f + 0.009 \ln Y + 0.037 \ln Y_f$
   $\qquad\qquad\quad (0.006)(1.665) \qquad\quad (0.496) \qquad\qquad (0.502) \qquad\qquad (0.370) \qquad\quad (1.023) \quad (0.194)$

   $\qquad\qquad\quad -0.172(\Delta R/M_{-1})_{-1} - 0.294(DCE/M_{-1})_{-1} + 0.008(OEF/M_{-1})_{-1} - 0.129\Delta \ln M_{f-1} - 0.052 \ln Y_{-1} - 0.051 \ln Y_{f-1}$
   $\qquad\qquad\quad (0.648) \qquad\qquad (1.539) \qquad\qquad (0.270) \qquad\qquad (0.289) \qquad\qquad (0.053) \qquad (0.255)$

   $\qquad\qquad\quad -0.001^*r \qquad\qquad\qquad +0.043^* \ln PFO \qquad -0.017 \ln \left(\dfrac{S \cdot M}{M_f}\right)_{-1} +0.323^*\Delta \ln EER_{-1}$
   $\qquad\qquad\quad (2.137) \qquad\qquad\qquad (2.560) \qquad\qquad\qquad (1.292) \qquad\qquad (2.750)$

   $\qquad\qquad\quad +0.005r_{-1} \qquad\qquad\quad -0.045^* \ln PFO_{-1} \qquad\qquad\qquad\qquad\qquad\quad -0.343^*\Delta \ln EER_{-2}$
   $\qquad\qquad\quad (1.439) \qquad\qquad\qquad (2.788) \qquad\qquad\qquad\qquad\qquad\qquad\qquad (3.250)$

   $\qquad\qquad\quad +0.009r_f \qquad\qquad\qquad\qquad\qquad\qquad\qquad\qquad\qquad\qquad\qquad\qquad +0.035\Delta \ln EER_{-3}$
   $\qquad\qquad\quad (0.885) \qquad\qquad\qquad\qquad\qquad\qquad\qquad\qquad\qquad\qquad\qquad\qquad (0.327)$

   $\qquad\qquad\quad -0.001r_{f-1}$
   $\qquad\qquad\quad (0.094)$

$\bar{R}^2 = 0.440 \qquad se = 0.013 \qquad DW = 2.013 \qquad U_{t-1} = -0.005$
$\qquad\qquad\qquad\qquad\qquad\qquad\qquad\qquad\qquad\qquad\quad (0.051)$

Estimation technique: autoregressive least squares

2 $\Delta \ln EER = -0.000 + 0.082\Delta R/M_{-1} - 0.032DCE/M_{-1} - 0.521OEF/M_{-1} + 0.094\Delta \ln M_f + 0.095 \ln Y + 0.094 \ln Y_f$
   $\qquad\qquad\quad (0.037)(0.122) \qquad\quad (0.096) \qquad\qquad (0.851) \qquad\qquad (0.199) \qquad\quad (0.924) \quad (0.448)$

   $\qquad\qquad\quad -0.019(\Delta R/M_{-1})_{-1} - 0.030(DCE/M_{-1})_{-1} + 0.084(OEF/M_{-1})_{-1} - 0.258\Delta \ln M_{f-1} + 0.013 \ln Y_{-1} - 0.155 \ln Y_{f-1}$
   $\qquad\qquad\quad (0.069) \qquad\qquad (1.472) \qquad\qquad (0.247) \qquad\qquad (0.528) \qquad\qquad (0.111) \qquad (0.644)$

   $\qquad\qquad\quad +0.001r \qquad\qquad\qquad +0.042^* \ln PFO \qquad -0.022 \ln \left(\dfrac{S \cdot M}{M_f}\right)_{-1} +0.491^*\Delta \ln EER_{-1}$
   $\qquad\qquad\quad (0.064) \qquad\qquad\qquad (2.327) \qquad\qquad\qquad (1.596) \qquad\qquad (3.608)$

   $\qquad\qquad\quad -0.001r_{-1} \qquad\qquad\quad -0.044^* \ln PFO_{-1} \qquad\qquad\qquad\qquad\qquad\quad -0.401^*\Delta \ln EER_{-2}$
   $\qquad\qquad\quad (0.239) \qquad\qquad\qquad (2.529) \qquad\qquad\qquad\qquad\qquad\qquad\qquad (3.307)$

   $\qquad\qquad\quad +0.013r_f \qquad\qquad\qquad\qquad\qquad\qquad\qquad\qquad\qquad\qquad\qquad\qquad +0.061\Delta \ln EER_{-3}$
   $\qquad\qquad\quad (1.103) \qquad\qquad\qquad\qquad\qquad\qquad\qquad\qquad\qquad\qquad\qquad\qquad (0.536)$

   $\qquad\qquad\quad -0.010r_{f-1}$
   $\qquad\qquad\quad (0.627)$

$\bar{R}^2 = 0.382 \qquad se = 0.014 \qquad DW = 2.014 \qquad U_{t-1} = -0.114$
$\qquad\qquad\qquad\qquad\qquad\qquad\qquad\qquad\qquad\qquad\quad (1.121)$

Estimation technique: autoregressive instrumental variables (Fair)

* Significant at 90% level.

data for sterling during the floating rate period. For completeness we have also tested the equation proposed by Frankel as a synthesis of the two models, (31) above.

Because of highly significant positive serial correlation,[27] our results, reported in Table G, are in first-differenced form. Significant auto-correlation is still, however, apparent: the dynamics of the equation are by no means as simple as Frankel assumed.[28] We followed Frankel in using autoregressive least squares and instrumental variable techniques; but whereas he used instruments purely to overcome the errors-in-variables problem associated with the use of imperfect proxies—long-term government bond rates—for expected inflation differentials, we used them in addition to overcome the problem of simultaneity between interest rates and the exchange rate.

The results are unfortunately quite different from Frankel's and are inconclusive. Thus although the insignificance of the short differential in (1) and (2) might be taken, in conjunction with the significant, correctly signed, parameter on the expected inflation proxy, to be evidence in support of the monetary model, money itself, and income, are quite insignificant. Moreover once instrumental variables are used, the domestic short interest rate becomes significant with an incorrect sign.

(b) Dornsbusch: rational expectations

We report finally an attempt to take account of the rational expectations hypothesis, which some would use to argue that, in employing actual rather than unanticipated values of the regressors, all of the empirical results reported so far are deficient.

It was shown above, in equation (9), that the assumptions of perfect capital mobility and rational expectations allow a model to be derived in which changes in the exchange rate from period $t-1$ to t are related to the interest differential at time $t-1$ and 'news' which determines unanticipated changes in the rate: at any point in time, the interest differential fully discounts all information about the future.

In empirical application the validity of any estimates will depend crucially on a correct identification of 'news' or expected depreciation. Dornbusch (1980) tests the model by relating unanticipated depreciation, defined as

$$\ln S_t - \ln S_{t-1} + (i - i_f)_{t-1} \tag{35}$$

to 'news' measured by the deviations of such variables as income and the current account from OECD forecasts. The validity of his test clearly depends crucially on the assumption that OECD forecasts are representative of the mean expectations of market participants.

---

[27] Frankel appears to have experienced similar difficulty: in his Table for example the value of the autoregressive parameter is 0.98. (No significance level is indicated.)

[28] Even when he introduced the *lagged* short interest differential as an additional variable, $\hat{\rho}$ remained close to unity.

TABLE G
Frankel synthesis

Dependent variable	CNST	$\Delta(\ln M - \ln M_f)$	$\Delta(\ln Y - \ln Y_f)$	$\Delta(i - i_{us})$	$\Delta(r - r_f)$	$\Delta \ln PFO$	U_{t-1}	DW	$\bar{R}^2$	SE	Estimation technique
1 $\Delta \ln EER$	−0.003 (1.191)	0.016 (0.098)	−0.013 (0.194)	−0.000 (0.256)	−0.010 (2.914)		0.380 (3.734)	1.851	0.231	0.016	ALS
2 $\Delta \ln EER$	−0.004 (1.599)	0.029 (0.175)	0.015 (0.207)	−0.001 (0.779)	−0.010 (2.879)	0.028 (1.646)	0.352 (3.386)	1.846	0.244	0.015	ALS
		$\Delta \ln M$ $\Delta \ln M_f$	$\Delta \ln Y$ $\Delta \ln Y_f$	Δi Δi_{us}	Δr Δr_f	$\Delta \ln PFO$					
3 $\Delta \ln EER$	−0.005 (1.023)	0.052 (0.302) −0.015 (0.038)	0.026 (0.373) 0.253 (1.281)	−0.002 (0.964) −0.000 (0.086)	−0.008 (2.250) 0.012 (1.053)	0.024 (1.397)	0.392 (3.653)	1.824	0.232	0.016	ALS
4 $\Delta \ln EER$	−0.016 (2.046)	0.231 (1.036) 0.083 (0.167)	0.038 (0.363) 0.033 (0.144)	−0.009 (2.170) 0.002 (0.712)	−0.011 (1.486) 0.024 (1.868)	0.050 (2.298)	0.160 (1.213)			0.017	AIV (Fair)

TABLE H

	CNST	i_{-1}	$i_{us_{-1}}$	$\ln\left(\dfrac{SM}{Mf}\right)_{-1}$	$\ln Y_{-1}$	$\ln Y_{f_{-1}}$	$\Delta \ln Y_{-1}$	$\Delta \ln Y_{f_{-1}}$			
$\Delta \ln EER$	−1.320	−0.002		0.046	0.128	0.057	0.015	−0.360			
	(1.388)	(0.335)		(0.534)	(1.326)	(0.794)	(0.134)	(1.636)			

	$\left(\dfrac{DCE}{M_{-1}}\right)_{-1}$	$\left(\dfrac{\Delta R}{M_{-1}}\right)_{-1}$	$\left(\dfrac{OEF}{M_{-1}}\right)_{-1}$	$\ln M_{f_{-1}}$	$\Delta \ln PFO_{-1}$	$\Delta \ln EER_{-1}$	$\Delta \ln EER_{-2}$	$\Delta \ln EER_{-3}$	DW	$\bar{R}^2$	SE
	−0.549	0.049	0.179	0.181	0.016	0.156	−0.343	−0.146	2.015	0.350	0.014
	(2.643)	(0.168)	(0.505)	(0.404)	(0.814)	(0.638)	(2.462)	(1.129)			

Note: i_{-1} value −0.001 (0.279).

Estimation period: 1972 6–1980 2

But also, and perhaps more importantly, a prior condition for the appropriateness of his empirical test would seem to be the validity of the restriction imposed on the interest differential in his dependent variable: the freely estimated parameters on lagged domestic and foreign interest rates should not be significantly different from -1 and $+1$ respectively when regressed against the change in the exchange rate. In addition, because the assumption that asset markets are efficient implies that all available information is immediately incorporated in the rate, other lagged variables, data on which were already available to the market, if included in such a regression should not be statistically significant.

Our final equation in Table H, derived from the general dynamic monetary model reported above but with all *current* values of the variables removed, (thus incidentally eliminating the need for a simultaneous estimation technique) provides such a test. The first part of the test does not in fact reject the hypothesis, in that the coefficients of the interest rate variables are not significantly different from -0.0008 and $+0.0008$ which, on our data, correspond to the -1 and $+1$ priors of the above model.[29] The coefficients are, however, clearly poorly determined; and moreover, the second part of the test fails, since both *DCE* and the second lag of the dependent variable contribute significantly to the equation. Note however, that this is a *joint* test of perfect capital mobility and rational expectations, and nothing can be inferred about the validity of either assumption individually.[30]

7. Summary and conclusions

The predominant impression left by our results is one of failure: we have not succeeded in finding empirical regularities in the data to help explain in any satisfactory way the fundamental determinants of sterling's effective exchange rate during the floating rate period. Our research has failed, often dramatically, to yield empirical support for any of the theories tested (including most notably, the monetary model); and we are left without any stable empirical relationship which might be used for forecasting the exchange rate.

Looking positively at the results, it is true that we have identified an autoregressive process which provides some support for the proposition that the exchange rate will not follow a random walk. But apart from the significance of the lagged dependent variables, and the general significance of oil prices, few of the other variables in either the monetary or Dornbusch models even approach significance by the usual criteria. The only exceptions are the monetary variables in the Dornbusch model which together with the

---

[29] The dependent variable is the first-differenced log of monthly data, whereas the interest rate data are in per cent per annum.

[30] It may be argued that the results in Table H we distorted by non-conformity to the data in certain respects. To avoid this problem, we estimated a similar model for 3-monthly changes in the end-month £/$ rate. The results, not reported here, do not affect the conclusion that either rational expectations for uncovered interest parity (or both) does not hold.

general dynamic structure of the equation provide some confirmation that the exchange rate overadjusts in the short run to monetary disturbances: but it would obviously be wrong to make much of this in view of the overwhelmingly negative impression provided by the mass of results.

Taken at face value the overall results suggest, in particular, that monetary developments do not carry any strong or reliable implications for the behaviour of the exchange rate. Thus, if one were forced to argue on the basis of the equations alone, one would be tempted to conclude that the link between tight monetary conditions and an appreciating exchange rate is not as strong as many economists have argued: in particular, movements in £M3 (or its counterparts) cannot explain the current level of sterling's effective rate, nor its progress to that level. Nor can M1 or 'base money'. Similarly, after allowing for the simultaneities involved, we have found no significant relationship with interest rates—a result which many will find particularly surprising. Part of the explanation may lie in the inadequacies of our attempt to take these simultaneities into account; but the uncertain and unidentifiable impact of movements in exchange rate expectations may well have been more important. Although on conventional arguments higher nominal interest rates should lead to appreciation, whenever they are offset by more pessimistic exchange rate expectations the association will not be visible in the data unless the shift in expectations can be identified. The answer to this problem which the monetary approach provides—the assumption that expectations are measured by interest rates themselves—rests on special assumptions and is not supported by our results.

A further word of caution about apparent empirical regularities in this area hardly seems necessary but it is perhaps worthwhile to draw attention to the behaviour of the relationship between interest rates and the exchange rate beyond the end of our estimation period. Following $2\frac{1}{2}$ years in which there appeared to be a clear positive correlation between sterling and the uncovered differential—see, e.g., Charts 4 and 5 and, for weekly data over June 1979–May 1980, the chart on page 128 of the June 1980 *Bank of England Quarterly Bulletin*—between mid-June and end-October 1980 sterling appreciated by 4.3% against the dollar and by 7.3% in effective terms while the uncovered differential in sterling's favour vis-a-vis the dollar fell from 7.5% to 1.6%. (Subsequently, in November and December, a positive relationship re-appeared.)

What inferences might be drawn from our results regarding the conduct of policy? If we had found a close relationship between intervention and the exchange rate, with weak relationships both between money and the exchange rate and between interest rates and the exchange rate, we might infer that pursuit of a monetary target (through interest rates) had no systematic implications for the exchange rate or its management. And *vice versa* if the pattern of relationships were reversed: if we had found close relationships between the exchange rate on the one hand and money and interest rates on the other, with a weak relationship between the exchange rate and intervention, we might infer that an exchange rate target could be pursued through domestic monetary policy, with the attainment of the monetary objective ensured by intervention. If each of these relationships was close, the pursuit of independent monetary and exchange rate objectives might still be possible if sterilisation were feasible. Our results, however, conform to none of these patterns, and therefore carry no positive implications for policy.

In fact, however, our results may be much more a reflection of the technical difficulties involved in econometric estimation in this area—and in the econometric application of models of financial asset prices more generally—than of the weakness of monetary influences. It may be argued that because of the potentially dominant role played by non-systematic expectations, monthly data are unlikely to reveal any stable relationship between the exchange rate and its fundamental economic determinants, and further, that "it is impossible to forecast exchange rates successfully in a world dominated by the unexpected" (Whitman, 1980, page 200). On this view, it is unlikely that apparently more successful results which we might have obtained if we had adopted a less pragmatic approach to the data and imposed *a priori* parameter constraints based on theory (see, e.g., Bilson (1978)) would have been durable or reliable. This view about the dominance of expectations suggests that policy can nevertheless still play a powerful, if indirect role: in particular, by appropriate "smoothing" intervention in the foreign exchange market, and, more broadly, by pursuing stable and hence predictable monetary and fiscal policies, expectations may effectively be anchored and stabilised. As a result undue and damaging volatility in exchange rates may be avoided.

DATA APPENDIX

EER = Effective exchange rate for sterling, MERM weighted, as published by the Bank of England.

DCE = Domestic credit expansion, seasonally adjusted £mn.

ΔR = Change in reserves net of official foreign currency borrowing.

OEF = Change in money supply less DCE less ΔR.

M = Level of sterling M3, seasonally adjusted.

M_{US} = U.S. 'money' + 'quasi-money' (*International Financial Statistics*).

M_f = MERM weighted average 'money' + 'quasi-money', *IFS* seasonally adjusted.

Y = UK industrial production.

Y_f = MERM weighted industrial production.

Y_{US} = US industrial production.

i = 3-month sterling interbank interest rate.

i_{US} = 3 month Euro-dollar interest rate.

r = Long term UK government bond rate.

r_f = Long term MERM weighted average foreign bond rate.

P = UK export price index.

PC = UK consumer price deflator.

PC_f = MERM weighted foreign consumer price indices.

P_f = MERM weighted export price indices.

MLR = Minimum lending rate.

UNEM = Level of seasonally adjusted adult unemployed, excluding school leavers.
PFO = Effective $ price index of Saudi marker crude oil.

BIBLIOGRAPHY

BILSON, J. (1978) "The monetary approach to the exchange rate: some empirical evidence" *IMF Staff Papers*.

BILSON, J. (1979) "Recent developments in monetary models of exchange rate determination" *IMF Staff Papers*.

BRANSON, W. H. (1979) "Exchange rate dynamics and monetary policy" in *Inflation and employment in open economies* ed. A. Lindbeck, North-Holland.

BRANSON, W. H. and HALTTUNEN, H. (1979) "Asset-market determination of exchange rates: initial empirical and policy results" in *Trade and payments adjustment under flexible exchange rates* ed. J. P. Martin and A. Smith, Macmillan.

BRITTAN, S. (1977) "Sterling and the Dutch disease" *Financial Times* April 1978.

BUDD, A. and BURNS, T. (1978) "The relationship between fiscal and monetary policy in the LBS model" LBS Discussion Paper No 51.

CONNOLLY, M. and DA SILVEIRA, J. D. (1979) "Exchange market pressure in post-war Brazil: an application of the Girton-Roper monetary model" *American Economic Review*.

DAVIDSON, J. E. H., HENDRY, D. F., SRBA, F. and YEO, S. (1978) "Econometric modelling of the aggregate time-series relationship between consumers' expenditure and income in the United Kingdon" *Economic Journal*, 88, 661–92.

DORNBUSCH, R. (1976) "Expectations and exchange rate dynamics" *Journal of Political Economy*.

DORNBUSCH, R. (1978) "Monetary policy under exchange rate flexibility" in *Managed exchange rate flexibility: the recent experience*, Federal Reserve Bank of Boston, Conference Series No. 20.

DORNBUSCH, R. (1980) "Exchange rate economics: Where do we stand?", *Brookings Papers on Economic Activity*.

EASTWOOD, R. K. and VENABLES, A. J. (1980) "The macro-economic implications of a resource discovery", mimeo, University of Sussex.

FAIR, R. C. "The estimation of simultaneous equation models with lagged endogenous variables and first order serially correlated errors", *Econometrica*.

FASE, M. M. G. and HUIJSER, A. P. (1980) "A reaction function for foreign exchange intervention in the Netherlands" *Kredit und Kapital* 6 (1980) , Supplement.

FLEMING, J. M. (1962) "Domestic financial policies under fixed and floating exchange rates" *IMF Staff Papers*.

FRANKEL, J. (1979) "On the mark: a theory of floating exchange rates based on real interest differentials" *American Economic Review*.

FRENKEL, J. (1976) "A monetary approach to the exchange rate: doctrinal aspects and empirical evidence" *Scandinavian Journal of Economics*.

FRENKEL, J. (1980) "The collapse of purchasing power parities during the 1970s" *European Economic Review*, forthcoming.

GIRTON, L. and ROPER, D. (1977) "A monetary model of exchange market pressure applied to the post-war Canadian experience" *American Economic Review*.

ISARD, P. (1978) "*Exchange rate determination : a survey of popular views and recent models* Princeton Studies in International Finance No. 42.

MUNDELL, R. A. (1963) "Capital mobility and stabilisation policy under fixed and flexible exchange rates", *Canadian Journal of Economic and Political Science* reprinted in *International Economics* (Macmillan, 1968).

MUNNICH, F. "Comment" *Kredit und Kapital* 6 (1980), Supplement.

MUSSA, M. (1976) "The exchange rate, the balance of payments and monetary and fiscal policy under a regime of controlled floating", *Scandinavian Journal of Economics*.

Mussa, M. (1979) "Empirical regularities in the behaviour of exchange rates and theories of the foreign exchange market", in *Policies for Employment, Prices and Exchange Rates*, eds. K. Brunner and A. H. Meltzer, Carulgie-Rochester Conference Series on Public Policy.

Putnam, B. H. and Woodbury, J. R. (1980) "Exchange rate stability and monetary policy" University of Nebraska *Review of Business and Economic Research*.

Saville, I. D. (1980) *The sterling/dollar rate in the floating rate period: the role of money, prices and intervention* Bank of England Discussion Paper No. 9.

Shirakawa, M. (1980) *The monetary approach to the balance of payments and the exchange rate: an empirical study of Japan's case* Bank of Japan Discussion Paper No. 2.

Spencer, P. D. (1979) "Modelling the exchange rate" HMT Working Paper.

Whitman, M. (1975) "Global monetarism and the monetary approach to the balance of payments" *Brookings Papers on Economic Activity*.

Whitman, M. (1980) "Comments" *Brookings Papers on Economic Activity*.

THE STERLING RATE OF EXCHANGE
AND UK PROFITABILITY:
SHORT TERM EFFECTS[1]

By D. A. HAY and D. J. MORRIS

I. Introduction

THE impact of a change in the exchange rate of sterling on prices and costs in the UK has been investigated extensively in recent years. In contrast relatively few studies have attempted to extend the investigation into the overall consequences for profitability in the UK. This is not necessarily surprising. Profitability is itself difficult to explain adequately, being sensitive to interrelated changes in prices, costs, the level of output and the sectoral disposition of output.[2] The channels of influence from the exchange rate to aggregate profitability are similarly numerous and interrelated. In addition it is only in the 1970s that both the effects of exchange rate changes, and the determinants of UK profitability have become central areas of concern.

An era of fluctuating exchange rates, growing dependence on international trade and continuing weak trends in profitability and investment have served to heighten interest in the relationship. In particular between 1976 and 1980 the exchange rate moved from a level which in terms of usual indices was internationally very competitive to one which was very uncompetitive.[3] The possible implications of this for profitability and employment, especially in manufacturing, have been a cause for concern.

A number of existing models, which are reviewed briefly below, suggest a negligible long term impact of changes in the exchange rate. However there is no universal agreement on this proposition. Further there is still very considerable uncertainty about the shorter term impact on the UK economy, about the pattern and magnitude of responses and the time lags involved. All these are matters of interest in themselves. But if short term movements

[1] We should like to thank Vanessa Fry for her invaluable assistance in the preparation of this paper, Nick Pomiankowski and Clive Payne for help and advice on the computer work involved, and Chris Gilbert for comments.

[2] Recent work suggests a significant downward time trend after allowing for cost and demand effects. See T. A. Clark & N. P. Williams: Measures of Real Profitability, B.E. Q.B. Vol. 18 no. 4 Dec. 1978 pp. 513–522.

[3] It may be objected that this ignores the role of North Sea oil, the impact of which would be to generate a higher exchange rate. Indeed it has been argued that North Sea oil requires a relative contraction in other traded goods sectors and that the high exchange rate is part of the mechanism by which this comes about. See P. J. Forsyth and J. A. Kay, The Economic Implications of North Sea Oil Revenues. Institute of Fiscal Studies (1980), Working Paper No. 10. These structural changes are however in relation to the equilibrium one in 1976. Relative to both the actual and equilibrium structure in 1970, North Sea oil probably requires a shift the opposite way. See The Governor of the Bank of England: The North Sea and the U.K. Economy: Some Longer Term Perspectives & Implications B.E. Q.B. Vol. 20 (Dec. 1980) pp. 449–454 for elaboration of this point. In any event there is no compelling reason to believe that a particular high level of the exchange rate is either inevitable or 'correct' in terms of export competitiveness.

in profitability have more lasting effects via their consequences for invest-ment, rate of embodiment of technical progress and employment of best practice techniques, and hence influence future productivity and competitive-ness, then such effects became of greater significance.[4]

Our objectives in this paper are to identify the channels of influence, review previous empirical work, and present preliminary results of a small simultaneous equation model. The implications for profitability are then indicated.

The channels of influence from the exchange rate to profitability and back again are numerous. As a short term perspective is adopted in this paper, we shall only be concerned with the chain of causality from the exchange rate to profitability. The main effects may be listed as follows:

(1) Either or both the sterling or foreign currency price of exports will change, potentially affecting export competitiveness, volume and profit margin.
(2) Either or both the sterling or foreign currency price of final goods imports will change, potentially affecting the volume and profit margin on import-competing goods.
(3) The sterling price of imported inputs (commodities, semi-manufactured goods) may be affected, leading to a change in produc-tion costs and profit margins.
(4) These changes may directly or indirectly alter the extent of capacity utilisation via their effects on demand, again causing variations in profitability.
(5) The domestic price level will be affected by changes in input costs and unit labour costs. The latter will be affected by changes in earnings as they respond to realised and/or expected price changes, and by productivity as it changes with capacity utilisation. The price of import-competing products (and ultimately perhaps all products) may respond more directly, via competitive affects, to changes in the sterling price of traded goods sold on world markets. The Scandina-vian model, developed with small countries in mind, is clearly of interest in the UK case.

At the centre of this set of causal links lie three main issues: firms' pricing procedures, the extent and speed of response of demand and output to price changes, and the formation of price expectations in the determination of wages. Changes in profitability occur as a result of the working of these various processes.

Many of the components of the system have been examined in great detail. In addition to a useful collating of previous studies, Brown et al. have

---

[4] See for example B. Moore & J. Rhodes; The Relative Decline of the U.K. Manufacturing Sector, E.P.R. No. 2. (1976) Ch. 4, pp. 36–41. Also D. Morris, Industrial Policy, Ch. 19 in D. Morris (ed.): The Economic System in the UK (O.U.P.) 2nd ed. 1979.

provided their own estimates of price-cost relationships within a four-equation framework.[5]

$$PX = \alpha PF + (1 - \alpha)PD$$
$$PM = \beta PF + (1 - \beta)PD$$
$$PD = \gamma W + (1 - \gamma)PM$$
$$W = \delta PD$$

where

PX is the price of exports
PM is the price of imports
PD is the domestic price level
W is the nominal average earnings level.
PF is the world price level expressed in sterling.

Their summary of a number of models of the UK economy suggest approximate values for the parameters of 0.5 for α, 1.0 for β, and perhaps about 0.7 for γ but with some estimates as low as 0.28. δ is more problematic, being dependent on the way in which expectations are modelled, lag structures etc. Nevertheless it is widely thought to be equal to or near to unity in the long term. They also review a number of other related issues which are significant for profitability, in particular the effect of capacity utilisation on pricing, asymmetry of pricing behaviour when exchange rates change, and anticipated effects. On these matters the conclusions are ambiguous.

This price-cost system, and the wealth of evidence which now exists on each element of it, must represent a major component of any attempt to trace exchange rate effects to profitability. But the task also requires the consideration of output responses, for however the various price and cost elements are determined, there may be some short term demand responses which will affect capacity utilisation, employment and profits. The major divergence in the literature is between those who see a new equilibrium, after an initial disturbance, being established fairly quickly by price changes which restore the old level of relative prices without much effect on output, and those for whom new prices are validated as an equilibrium by some change in output. The former group may well ignore quantity adjustments as temporary and ultimately mistaken decisions by producers and consumers, which have no major implications for the long term. The rational expectations hypothesis can enable a new equilibrium to be established without any such 'mistakes'. The alternative view suggests that price responses are slower and that quantity adjustments are an important element in the overall response to an initial disturbance. Output changes may then have significant effects on profitability. A model needs to be constructed which can pick up any such effects by allowing for them explicitly.

[5] R. N. Brown, C. A. Enoch & P. D. Mortimer-Lee: The Interrelationships between costs and prices in the U.K., Bank of England discussion paper No. 8, 1980.

In the process of adjustment to a change in the exchange rate, three time-horizons may be defined. The *short term* is that in which changes in prices, and perhaps quantities and profitability occur, but capacity remains unchanged, i.e. there is no feed-through to investment. In the *medium term* capacity changes can occur but not all the repercussions of the initial change have occurred. In the *long term* all consequences have occurred.[6] Within this classification most previous work has focussed either on the path of response over the short term or on the ultimate long term effects, if any, that exist. But perhaps the most important question is what happens in the medium term. For changes in capacity, be they mistaken short term adjustments or part of the movement to a new real equilibrium, will have much more important and perhaps irreversible long term consequences than short term price or output adjustments.

Ultimately it is our intention to build up a complete picture of the repercussions from an exchange rate change over time. But in this paper we are concerned only with the short-term. We seek a clear understanding of the immediate reactions to exchange rate changes as an input to later analysis. This focus is reflected in the lag structures and specifications developed. In general we will restrict our enquiry to three quarters after a change in the exchange rate, in the belief that a longer period must start to introduce both capacity and monetary reactions.

There is however one difficulty in focussing on short term responses to exchange rate changes. If, starting from full equilibrium, the exchange rate changes then there is no problem in principle in examining the price, cost and output consequences. But the exchange rate is essentially an equilibrating relative price. Movements in it are responses to changes in underlying real or monetary variables such as natural resources, productivity, patterns of demand, money supply etc. If some or all of the effect of these on prices, assets and output have already occurred then a change in the exchange rate may itself represent a realignment to the new equilibrium, with consequently little or no subsequent short term effect on the variables in which we are interested.[7]

This does not mean however that the short term reaction is not of importance, particularly if there are grounds for thinking that the exchange rate diverges from time to time from its equilibrium value. Rather it means that the measured short run exchange-rate-elasticities of price and output are not necessarily constant or even particularly stable, given that they reflect the extent to which the exchange rate is itself moving towards or away from its equilibrium value. Indeed in principle we may be able to determine whether any given change in the exchange rate is equilibrating or not by observing the extent of short term price response to it.

[6] This cannot be defined purely in terms of long-run elasticities because of the monetary disequilibrium that will occur if the balance of payments is not then in balance.

[7] For elaboration of this point see M. Connolly & D. Taylor: Exchange Rate Changes and Neutralisation: A Test of the Monetary Approach to Developed and Developing Countries. Economica. Vol. 46. (1974) pp. 281–294.

II. Alternative macroeconomic frameworks

Views on the effect of exchange rate changes are grouped into three identifiable schools of thought, namely Keynesian, New Cambridge and Monetarist. All are familar, and therefore only briefly summarised with regard to their profitability implications.

Within a general Keynesian framework, devaluation can permit a long term improvement in profitability. The change in the ratio of world prices to domestic prices permits exporters either to expand exports at existing profit margin levels or to improve margins at existing foreign currency prices, or to achieve some combination of the two. The volume response depends on the price elasticities of demand and supply for exports, and the extent to which the devaluation is taken into the profit margin. The margin and volume of import-competing goods are similarly affected, depending on the pricing policy of imported goods. The relative importance of the margin and volume effects is regarded as an empirical question which affects the timing but not the nature of exchange rate adjustment. Input costs and earnings rise, in some models by less than the rise in domestic prices, bringing about a fall in real wages.[8] In other still essentially Keynesian models there is eventually a complete response of wages to price changes however, implying no change in real profits unless there are overall volume responses.[9]

The key features for the present study are as follows. First the Keynesian approach permits a very flexible approach to the pricing of exports and imports. Any type of pricing procedures may be presumed, considerable product differentiation may be encompassed, home and foreign markets may be totally or relatively little integrated, and either may be competitive or oligopolistic.[10] In general domestic prices are set by a mark-up on costs, with no separate demand effect, but this latter condition is not essential to the Keynesian scheme. Second, volume responses can occur which persist as long term consequences of the exchange rate change. Subsequent effects as a result of changes in competitiveness and the balance of payments need not offset these consequences. Third, it is not inevitable that real wages in the long term will remain unchanged in response to a change in the exchange rate. Incomes policy may play a role in constraining nominal or real incomes.

The New Cambridge framework is essentially a modification of the Keynesian one.[11] It is also more demanding in that it requires certain Keynesian effects to be fully offset eventually. The main elements are that domestic prices are fully cost determined, with no demand influence operat-

[8] See for example the National Institute of Economic & Social Research Model, summarised in K. Cuthbertson: Macroeconomic Policy (MacMillan) 1979 Ch. 2.

[9] See for example the Treasury Macroeconomic Model (HM. Treasury) 1979.

[10] See W. H. Branson: Keynesian & Monetarist Models of the Transmission of Inflation, A.E.R. Papers & Proceedings. Vol. 65. (1975). pp. 115–119.

[11] See for example W. Godley & R. M. May: The Macroeconomic Implications of Devaluation & Import Restriction C.E.P.R. No. 3 (1977) Ch. 2 pp. 32–42.

ing; that real wages grow at a 'target' rate over time and cannot, except very temporarily, be influenced by exchange rate changes or incomes policy; and that changes in the exchange rate are fully reflected in import prices. With regard to the domestic price of exports, two possibilities are admitted. In the first, they are entirely cost determined. But as all costs eventually rise by the full amount of a devaluation, so do export prices, and the foreign currency price is in the end unchanged. In the second, foreign currency prices are given. Devaluation creates profits by opening up a margin between the domestic price of exports and costs. Again however the effect is temporary, as cost changes induced by the devaluation erode higher profit margins. Indeed the initially increased margin will weaken resistance to wage claims of unions seeking to re-establish their target real wage after devaluation. Despite this however there are short term gains in profitability because there are volume effects on imports and exports. Full multiplier effects, including those of increased investment out of profits, leads ultimately to the offsetting of the balance of payments improvement, but augment the demand and output consequences of devaluation. In the long term however the pass through of prices into wages, and wages into prices, offsets the original price or profit margin advantage. Overall, as in the straightforward Keynesian model, various export pricing strategies can be embraced but domestic pricing is now only cost based, real wages cannot be reduced and long-term volume effects are probably negated.

Within a monetarist framework[12] the money supply determines domestic prices. Potentially the most rapid transmission mechanism operates via the exchange rate. Money supply growth in excess of that abroad will create a balance of payments deficit and a fall in the exchange rate. The "law of one price" holds, so that this change is rapidly reflected in the domestic price level for both traded and non-traded goods. These are taken account of in the labour market, so that wages rise to compensate completely for price rises. An 'exogenous' fall in the exchange rate, by raising prices reduces the real money supply and aggregate demand, and this is reflected in a balance of payments surplus. The money stock increases as a result, returning the ratio of money stock to the price level to its original level. In the long term, all prices and costs adjust. Aggregate demand returns to a level determined by the 'natural' unemployment rate and there are no profitability effects via either volume or margins. Full price responses to changes in the exchange rate are rapid, no long term volume responses occur and real wages cannot be changed.

Under the law of one price the prices of all goods, including non-tradables, are the same for all markets. Tradeable goods are sold in world

[12] See for example R. J. Ball, T. Burns & J. S. E. Laury: The Role of Exchange Rate Changes in Balance of Payments Adjustment: The U.K. Case EJ. Vol. 87 (1977) pp. 1–23. M. Beenstock & T. Burns: Exchange Rate Objectives and Macroeconomic Adjustment in the U.K. in R. Major (ed.). Britain's Trade & Exchange Rate Policy (Heinemann/N.I.E.S.R.) 1979. P. Robinson, T, Webb & M. Townsend: The Influence of Exchange Rate Changes or Prices: A Study of 18 Industrial Countries, Economica. Vol. 46 (1979) pp. 27–50.

markets at world prices. Non-tradeables are 'tied' to tradables both on the demand side and via the cost effects on imports and wages. Wages in the non-tradeable sector are determined in the same labour market as for the tradable sector. This hypothesis, more recently known as the 'Scandinavian' model, has always been implicit in the monetarist approach to the balance of payments. Tests of it however have not offered particular strong support. Kravis & Lipsey[13] found that substantial differences in absolute price levels persisted from 1950 to 1973. Price relationships between major industrial countries were not particularly stable, with up to 20% movement in this period. Consequently offsetting adjustments to exchange rate changes had not occurred even after 5 years. While the price of traded goods were more in line internationally than those of non-traded, substantial deviations were nevertheless apparent. Possible explanations were price discrimination by exporters, product differentiation, non-price competition and consumer ignorance. Such work is however beset by problems of change in product mix and product quality. The possibility remains that if these could be allowed for a 'homogeneous product' price series would reveal rather smaller deviations.

Using a somewhat different approach, Kreinin found generally a less than 100% 'pass-through' effect, at least over 3–4 years, with the more open economies (Japan and W. Germany) having stronger such effects than the U.S.[14] In another study Norman found quite weak responses to exchange rate changes.[15] Robinson, Webb and Townsend found total offset to operate in small countries within a year, 70–90% offset in medium sized countries including the U.K. and around 50% for large economies.[16] They also found that the rate of response had become faster in the 1970's perhaps because 'exchange-rate illusion' of the earlier period was breaking down.

Our conclusion is that there is less than full integration of world tradables markets. There is therefore scope for exchange rate changes to create price divergences which will generate short term output adjustments. However in all the approaches except one version of the Keynesian model, prices eventually adjust more-or-less completely to the exchange rate change. No long term output changes therefore occur. Irrespective of the framework adopted (though for very different reasons) there are few if any long-term implications for profitability. In the short-term however, the key issues which separate the models are firms' pricing procedures, the rapidity of such output repercussions as do occur, and the extent to which wage settlements embrace exchange-rate induced price increases.

[13] I. Kravis & R. Lipsey: Price Behaviour in the light of Balance of Payments Theories. J. Int. Econ. Vol. 8 (1978) pp. 193–246.

[14] N. E. Kreinin: The Effect of Exchange Rate Changes on the Price & Volume of Foreign Trade. IMFSP. Vol. 24 (1977) pp. 297–329.

[15] N. R. Norman: On the Relation between Prices of Home Products & Foreign Commodities. O.E.P. Vol. 27 (1975) pp. 426–439.

[16] P. Robinson, T. Webb & M. Townsend Op. Cit.

III. Firms' Pricing Decisions

The first of these issues concerning the role of pricing decisions in the overall transmission mechanism, has been the subject of very intensive study at a microeconomic level in the last 30 years. With regard to pricing generally the literature, both cases studies and econometric analysis, is vast and cannot be reviewed here.[17] A general conclusion would be that despite great diversity of products and of pricing rules, there is widespread adherence to relatively straightforward rules of thumb which reflect both cost and demand pressures. However the former influence is explicit and easily perceived; the latter is more diffuse, less systematically allowed for and frequently obscured by the behaviour of stocks, order books and non-price competition.

More limited in scope but central to the present purpose are a growing number of empirical studies of export pricing in general and reactions to devaluation in particular. In an early study Gribbin found that, in response to the 1967 devaluation of Sterling, the advantageous profit differential on home as opposed to export sales fell noticeably.[18]

	1966	1968[19]
Gross Margin on Turnover	+5.8%	+3.9%
Net Margin on Turnover	+7.7%	+4.0%
Net Return on Assets	+10%	0

Gribbin argued that while all production was affected immediately by higher costs, exports were more profitable because of a rise in sterling export prices in response to the devaluation. This would appear to contradict any purely cost-based view of the pricing of exports.

A subsequent study by Rosendale found that devaluation had helped export performance for from one to three years but suggested that eventually costs adjusted fully for the exchange rate change.[20] There were however marked differences in the extent to which different products experienced price competition and hence in the degree to which foreign currency prices were adjusted.

In a major study carried out by Hague, Oakshott and Strain,[21] of 19 manufacturing firms investigated 5 were 'passive' in the face of devaluation, leaving foreign currency prices unchanged. The rest cut their foreign currency prices either by the full amount of the devaluation or partially, using the improved margin to increase marketing and sales promotion. Domestic

---

[17] For a recent survey see D. A. Hay and D. J. Morris: Industrial Economics: Theory and Evidence Ch. 4 (O.U.P.) 1979.

[18] J. D. Gribbin: The Profitability of U.K. Exports. G.E.S. Occasional Paper No. 1. 1971.

[19] For 82 Firms providing profit figures out of initial sample of 152.

[20] P. B. Rosendale: The Short-Run Pricing Policies of some British Engineering Exporters. N.I.E.R. No. 65. Aug. 1973 pp. 44–51.

[21] D. Hague, E. Oakshott & A. Strain: Devaluation & Pricing Decisions (George Allen & Unwin) 1974.

prices tended to change with costs though a small number took the opportunity of the devaluation to improve domestic margins. As with the previous studies, the evidence strongly suggests that until cost pressures catch up, there is very much less than full adjustment of sterling prices of either exports or domestically offered tradables, with a substantial number of firms obtaining a competitive price advantage as a result. To this extent we would expect to find that changes in the volume of production were significant.

The two most recent studies have been carried out by Holmes and by the CBI.[22] The former undertook a study similar in nature to that of Hague *et al.* but on a larger scale. Only about one firm in 8 appeared to have changed the nature of its reactions as between the 1967 devaluation and the 1972 float. Of particular significance many firms felt that price cutting was becoming an unproductive response to devaluation partly because of supply constraints (with greater risk in export markets acting as a barrier to switching sales from home to export) and partly beause of the oligopolistic nature of international markets, with U.K. companies rarely being price leaders. While the former need be no more than a temporary and perhaps cyclical factor, the latter suggests a growing tendency for U.K. export prices to reflect world prices. In this case export volume would be determined by the supply side influences on profitability, and vary little in the short term in response to exchange rate changes.

In the CBI study, 3 of 23 companies felt devaluation would be harmful because of the effects on import costs and inflation generally. They were indifferent to the long run level of Sterling. Approximately half the companies saw some gain (one-third a significant gain). The rest were indifferent, mainly because the costs of imported inputs offset potential competitive price gains. A majority said they would lower export prices, but nearly all expected definite improvements in profit margins especially those selling to North America. Some feeling existed that domestic sales would gain as well, but through volume rather than margin changes. Potential supply constraints were a reason to favour only moderate devaluation. A quarter of the firms (mainly those heavily committed to exporting) thought investment would respond to a substantial devaluation via its effects on profits and cash flow.

In general these two studies fully support the earlier conclusions on export price behaviour. They suggest however a growing awareness in the 1970s of the importance of world prices in determining export prices and domestic costs. In other words there was a recognition of the growing significance of the "small open economy" assumption upon which the Scandinavian model is based. However the micro-economic evidence on pricing does suggest that there are still significant movements in export prices by some companies in response to a change in the exchange rate.

[22] P. M. Holmes: Industrial Pricing Behaviour & Devaluation (MacMillan) 1978. C.B.I.: Business Views on Exchange Rate Policy (CBI) 1978.

IV. Estimates of Response to Exchange Rate Changes

Having looked at the implications of micro-economic studies it would be appropriate to go on to review the much larger number of empirical estimates of price, output and cost responses in the aggregate. We prefer first to construct a model of the process, based on elementary principles and general enough in structure to pick up such effects if they exist. Subsequently we examine our results in the light of previous studies for consistency and plausibility.

Ideally we would wish to have a detailed and comprehensive model of the UK economy which embraces all the major relationships discussed previously and is sufficiently disaggregated to permit major sectoral shifts to be included. That is a far less utopian aim today than it once seemed as progress has been made with the development and manipulation of large and complex simulation models.

The current paper is however only an initial step towards investigating the full effects. A simple simultaneous equation system is developed which includes the main relations described above. We build a model from first principles, and modify it in the light of data availability and tractability. Then we derive results and compare them with other studies, before finally looking at the preliminary implications for profitability.

In this system, production occurs in the UK and in the rest of the world (ROW) and trade takes place between them. Four final markets exist: U.K. non-tradables, U.K. final domestic tradables (comprising UK production of final tradables and UK imports of final tradables), ROW nontradables, and ROW final domestic tradables (comprising ROW production of final tradables and U.K. exports of final tradables). In each market, price and output are determined by two demand-side variables, income and prices of other goods in that market; and by three supply-side variables; earnings and productivity to give unit labour costs, and the price of inputs. The system is completed by specifying the determinants of unit labour costs, the sterling price of imported commodities and aggregate demand. Appendix 1 contains the basic equation model which this approach generates, discusses some of the specification problems which arise and states the final results.

All equations were run in absolute values, log values, absolute changes and log changes, with log changes being the preferred formulation.[23] This permitted 62 quarterly observations between 1963 and 1978. Initially equations were tested separately, and polynomial distributed lag functions used in order to identify best fitting lag structures over the short-term horizon of 3 quarters.

In general the final set of price and cost equations were successful. When

[23] This however leads to a rather curious intepretation of the cost side of the equations, as it implies that costs are multiplicative rather than strictly additive, and that therefore there is some degree of substitutability between labour and materials. Against this, demand coefficients become conventional elasticities and heteroscedasticity is less likely.

run as a simultaneous set in log change form, all constants except that for non-tradables prices were insignificant and all significant variables had the anticipated sign. Domestic tradables prices are heavily dependent on unit labour costs and primary import prices, but the impact of competing final import prices is also significant. Both costs and the exchange rate are important in the setting of export prices over the three quarters considered but not world prices. Final import prices are heavily dependent on world prices and the exchange rate, with domestic demand changes irrelevant over 9 months. The feedback from prices to wages is quite strong, while domestic demand has either no effect on unit labour costs or a negative effect via increases in productivity depending on specification.

The quantity and demand side was much less infomative. Various specifications and short term lag structures were employed, and the equations estimated by two stage least squares, but results remained very weak. Domestic tradables, exports and domestic demand equations all generally had the right signs, sensible coefficient values and insignificant constants but virtually no significant variables. Data limitations are however more serious on this side of the model.

The implications of the significant coefficients in the best fitting equations are shown in Table 1. This shows the short term impact of a change in the exchange rate. For each dependent price and cost variable it gives the elasticity of response with respect to a change in the exchange rate, allowing for all interactions in the system.[24] The results may be compared briefly with estimates from other studies. With regard to domestic tradables prices, Artus' study of the 1967 devaluation found the intial effects on domestic prices to be very small within the first 2 years (though this may to some extent reflect restraints on inflation in the period immediately after devaluation.[26]) The full effect of 0.48 occurred only after 3 years.

Against this, investigation within a monetarist methodology by Robinson, Webb and Townsend[27] found the first quarter effect to be 0.49, with a total

TABLE 1
Elasticities with respect to the exchange rate (cumulative, negative)

	1st Quarter	2nd Quarter	3rd Quarter
Domestic tradable prices	0.03	0.12	0.17
Export prices	0.27	0.39	0.43
Final import prices	0.34	0.65	0.65
Primary import prices[25]	1.00	1.00	1.00
Non-tradables prices	0.00	0.02	0.05
Unit labour costs	0.00	0.03	0.09

[24] 'Full' effects could of course be calculated, but given the methodology employed would be meaningless.
[25] These figures are by assumption.
[26] J. R. Artus: The 1967 Devaluation. I.M.F. Staff Papers Vol. 22 (1975).
[27] P. Robinson, T. Webb and M. Townsend: op. cit.

effect of 0.71. Our rather low coefficient on final imports prices partly confirms Norman's finding that domestic prices were largely unresponsive to competing import prices. The same is true for the rather high unit labour cost coefficient relative to that of imported inputs.[28] Again a much higher figure is obtained from a monetarist approach, this time by Dewald and Marchon. While relatively closed economies such as the U.S. and Canada had coefficients of 0.16 and 0.10 respectively, Germany and the U.K. had values in the 0.3 to 0.4 range.[29] With regard to export prices, Artus and Sosa[30] estimated a coefficient of 0.67 on unit labour costs (against our figure of 0.57) and Goldstein[31] 0.63. Our coefficient of 0.22 on the world price level is also roughly in line with Artus' estimate of 0.24 over an equivalent time period.[32] The overall elasticity of 0.43 with respect to the exchange rate compares with his estimate of about 0.3 over three quarters. (The latter includes wage restraint effects which are separate in our specification). Again Robinson, Webb and Townsend find much higher figures; 0.47 for the first quarter and 0.79 overall.[33]

Interpreting export prices as a weighted average of domestic and world prices, our estimates suggest a weight of two-thirds (0.68) on domestic prices and one-third on world prices. As noted, this is higher than other estimates,[34] but this is to be expected given the short term horizon and the focus on manufacturing prices only. Winters also found domestic prices to be the main determinant though across countries the effect is weaker the greater the ratio of exports to domestic tradables output.[35]

On import prices, our formulation has separated out final and input goods prices. The effect on import prices overall depends on how semi-manufactures are then treated. If the price of these is regarded, like that of primary products, as completely determined in world markets then the overall import price response (i.e. weighted by shares in imports) is 0.88. At the other extreme, if semi-manufactures are priced on the same basis as final manufactures then the estimate is 0.76. These are very much in the range of previous estimates, with Ball, *et al.* Artus and Kreinin all finding a virtually

[28] N. Norman: On the Relation between Prices of Home Produced and Foreign Commodities. O.E.P. Vol. 27 (1975) pp. 426–439.

[29] W. Dewald and M. Marchon: A common specification of Price, Output and Unemployment Rate Responses to Demand Pressure and Import Prices in Industrial Countries. Weltwirtschaftliches Archiv Vol. 115 (1979) pp. 1–19.

[30] J. R. Artus and S. C. Sosa: Relative Price Effects on Export Performance. I.M.F. Staff Papers Vol. 25 (1978) pp. 25–47.

[31] M. Goldstein: The Effect of Exchange Rate Changes on Wages and Prices in the U.K.: An Empirical Study. I.M.F. Staff Papers Vol. 21 (1974) pp. 694–739.

[32] J. R. Artus: The Behaviour of Export Prices for Manufactures. I.M.F. Staff. Papers Vol. 21 (1974) pp. 583–604.

[33] P. Robinson, T. Webb and M. Townsend: op. cit.

[34] See page 250.

[35] L. A. Winters: Exports. Ch. 6 in T. S. Barker (ed): Economic Structure and Policy with Applications to the British Economy. 1976.

complete response,[36] Llewellyn estimating 0.61, and various simulation models generating figure in between.[37]

Turning to the effects of prices on wages there is considerable agreement as to the strength of the long term effect, but much disagreement on the short term. Of the many studies perhaps most pertinent is that of Goldstein. He found a weak effect (0.16) before 1968, but a very much stronger one (0.91) after that date. Averaged over the period with which we have been concerned this gives an estimated value of 0.65, which compares well with our estimate of 0.75. He also found static expectations to work better than other forms: (giving some explanation for the results on lag structure. See Appendix.[38]) Finally, comparing our results to the eclectic estimates of Brown, *et al.* we find our elasticities to indicate a generally somewhat lesser response,[39] as the short term perspective would suggest.

Our results suggest no significant short term response of output or demand. All that can be added is that if subsequent work were to confirm the estimated values, the elasticities with respect to the exchange rate over three quarters would be −0.17 on domestic tradables, −0.14 on exports and +0.10 on non-tradables. The fact that the elasticity is higher for domestic tradables than for exports, coupled with the evidence that final import prices rise less strongly (relative to domestic prices) in response to an exchange rate change (0.47) than export prices fall in foreign currency terms over the time period (0.55) suggest a slightly lower price elasticity on exports than domestic tradables. However the difference both in price response and exchange rate elasticities are very small.

VI. Implications for Profitability

We now translate the regression estimates into short term profitability effects. To do this we need to identify the appropriate cost/profit composition of output. We are concerned mainly with manufactured domestic tradables and exports. Census of Production figures provide a breakdown of expenditure and output of manufacturing industries. Adding expenditure on non-industrial services to purchases, and expenditure on industrial services to wages and salaries (5.2% and 2.6% respectively), and ignoring any net indirect tax payments and stock increases, gives the following breakdown of

---

[36] R. J. Ball *et al.* op. cit. J. R. Artus: op. cit. (1974), N. Kreinin: op. cit.

[37] G. Llewellyn: The Determinants of United Kingdom Export Prices E. J. Vol. 84 (1974) pp. 18–31.

[38] M. Goldstein: op. cit.

[39] The comparison is as follows:

Coeff.	Brown et. al.	Est. above.
α	0.5	0.68
β	1.0	0.76–0.88
γ	0.7	0.78
δ	up to 1	0.75

TABLE 2
Effects on profitability of a 10% sterling devaluation

	(a)	(b)	(c)	(d)
Domestic manufactured goods	−4.0%	−4.8%	−3.2%	+0.5%
Exports of manufactures	+20.5%	+18.4%	+20.1%	+23.4%
Services	−14.5%	−15.5%	−16.3%	−18.0%

output:−

Purchases	64.9% (64.3%)
Wages and Salaries	20.8% } (22.3%)
National Insurance	2.8% }

Beath provided figures for the composition of inputs in industrial output which are very similar and are shown in brackets.[40] These figures do not however subtract out figures of 2.8% for net indirect taxes and 0.2% for direct imports. The 1980 estimate for gross operating surplus is 10.4% against our residual of 11.3%.[41] Expenditure on imports is estimated by calculating the sum of all semi-finished manufactures, basic materials and fuel[42] and weighting by manufacturing's proportion of industrial output. This gives a net import weighting of 22.5%. Applying the figures in Table 1 to the above distribution gives the results shown in Table 2. For these estimates a 10% devaluation of Sterling is presumed to occur. Columns (a) and (b) give low and high estimates depending on the extent to which the price of non-imported purchases ultimately reflects earnings of manufacturing or of services.[43] (c) and (d) allow for quantity effects within 9 months should these prove to be significant. Both are based on (b) but whereas column (c) presumes marginal costs to be constant, (d) presumes no change in total labour costs as demand changes. Several points are of note in this table. First the gain in export profitability is quite substantial, mainly because of the rapid and quite large response of export prices to the exchange rate change. Second, there is generally a negative effect on domestically supplied manufactured goods despite the improvement in their competitiveness, because of the much more rapid response of input costs than of domestic prices. Third, allowing for the relative size of the two sectors, profits in manufacturing would overall be expected to rise only by

[40] J. A. Beath: Prices & Profits Ch. 9 in T. S. Barker: (ed). op. cit.
[41] Figures do not sum to unity due to rounding.
[42] A proportionate weighting on fuels was also allowed for but makes only marginal differences to final estimates.
[43] In column (a) the price of non-imported purchases are presumed to follow the price level of services. In column (b) we allow for the possibility that non-service non-tradables prices will reflect changes in earnings. This results in a larger increase in expenditure on non-imported inputs in response to devaluation than the services prices index indicates.

about 1% within the nine month period, as a result of a 10% devaluation. That is, a substantial improvement in export profitability is in the short term almost exactly offset by a deterioration in domestic profits as a result of the cost consequences of the exchange rate change. It is not clear how great an incentive to switch production this creates because the evidence on price behaviour suggests a relatively low degree of integration of home and foreign markets for manufactured goods. If this represents significant product differentiation, then switching in the short term may not be very easy. Fourth, the consequences for services appear quite large, but the results here are more suspect. Finally, if volume effects do operate they appear to be relatively small. However in the case of zero marginal unit labour costs they do reverse the direction of change for domestic manufactured goods.

These results must be regarded at this stage as provisional estimates. In particular it has not been possible to relate them to an equation system which includes data on profitability explicitly because of the absence of comparable quarterly profitability figures. Nevertheless, by focusing on the short term effects, it is possible to suggest two main conclusions. First, exchange rate changes can have rapid and substantial effects on the relative profitability of domestic and export operations. Second the overall effects are relatively small because of the offsetting import cost effects, which occur much more quickly than those associated with output prices, competitiveness and volume changes.

In general our results confirm those found at the micro-economic level. In the short term there is very much less than full adjustment of export or domestic tradables prices but none the less appreciable change in sterling export prices. A substantial change in relative export profitability occurs, and the harmful cost consequences of devaluation come through clearly.

With regard to the three alternative types of model described in section II, the results do not entirely support any one of them. Prices and costs do not appear to adjust rapidly, but quantities are barely responsive within the period. This at least raises the possibility of minimal 'real' response, as the monetarist framework predicts. But nonetheless there exists a considerably longer adjustment period than is generally postulated within that framework. It remains to be seen whether extension of the time period would reveal substantial volume changes or more complete price and cost reactions occurring first.

Finally, on the basis of these results, it is of interst to consider the likely consequences of the historically high exchange rate still obtaining in January 1981. At $2.40 to the pound, the exchange rate is of the order of 20% above the level necessary to restore the degree of competitiveness of manufacturing existing in the period up to the last quarter of 1979. Based on our estimates, this will have caused during 1980 a very serious short-term deterioration in export profits of probably about 40% of their previous level. However company earnings will have fallen very little overall over the three quarters because of the offsetting effects of lower import costs which operate across all sectors. Net of both effects earnings may well have deteriorated by only some 2%. There is little effect from a higher exchange rate on the level of output over three quarters. Clearly longer-term effects may differ substantially. As the adjustment in output prices follows that of input prices so the pattern of profitability will be modified. If export volume falls over a longer time period, as is likely given the short term fall in profitability of exports and higher export prices, then this will influence output levels in due course. This would further reduce profits, but overall long-term effects may or may not be significant. It is nonetheless important to stress that there is little evidence of a powerful effect in the deterioration in company earnings that occurred in 1980 from the rise in the exchange rate that occurred in 1979. In so far as the exchange rate mattered, it was the indirect effects of the rise that took place in 1977–9 that will have been important.

In addition some 3% may temporarily have been clipped from the rate of inflation as a result of exchange rate appreciation, and real wages improved about $1\frac{1}{2}$%. If, as our results suggest, world tradables markets are some way from being fully integrated, and if short-term switching of goods from export to home markets is not easy or feasible, the consequences of a high exchange rate for export manufacturers are likely to be severely adverse. But there are undoubtedly significant gains in terms of lower costs and lower inflation which need to be remembered when the overall short-term implications for industry are being assessed.

APPENDIX 1

In the derivation of a basic-equation model, the following notation is used.

P_{df}, Q_{df} = Sterling price and quantity of domestically produced tradable final goods supplied to the domestic market.

P_{xf}, Q_{xf} = Sterling price and quantity of UK exports (all final goods).

P_{mf}, Q_{mf} = Sterling price and quantity of imported final goods.

P_{wf} = Sterling equivalent of world price of foreign final tradables.

P_{mi}, Q_{mi} = Sterling price and quantity of imported input goods.

P_{dn}, Q_{dn} = Sterling price and quantity of domestic non-tradables.

Y_d = National Income in the UK.

Y_w = National Income in the ROW.

ULC_{df} = Sterling unit labour costs of all domestically produced tradable final goods supplies to domestic market.

ULC_{xf} = Sterling unit labour costs of UK exports.

ULC_{dn} = Sterling unit labour costs of UK non-tradables.

ULC_{mf} = Foreign currency unit labour costs of UK final imports.

P_{wf} = Foreign currency price of final foreign produced tradables.

P_{mi} = Foreign currency price of imported commodity goods

E = Exchange rate

D = Incomes Policy Dummy

T = Time trend

Following the supply and demand approach described on page 257 we obtain 8 basic reduced-form equations.[1]

$$P_{df}, Q_{df} = f(Y_d, P_{mf}, ULC_{df}, P_{mi})$$ (1) & (2)

$$P_{xf}, Q_{xf} = f(Y_w, P_{wf}, E, ULC_{xf}, P_{mi})$$ (3) & (4)

$$P_{mf}, Q_{mf} = f(Y_d, P_{df}, E, ULC_{mf}, P_{mi})$$ (5) & (6)

$$P_{dn}, Q_{dn} = f(Y_d, ULC_{dn}, P_{mi})$$ (7) & (8)

To provide a complete basic model it is necessary to add equations for unit labour costs, commodity prices and income. For the first ideally we need separate earnings and productivity equations for UK non-tradables, exports and domestically offered tradables. Here we assume that prices are based on trend unit labour costs and short term movements of earnings, rather than actual unit labour costs. This means that the effect of productivity on prices, via its influence on ULC, is an exogenous trend. We assume that the trend growth of productivity is the same for both tradables and non-tradables. This will introduce distortions, but it is not clear that they are any greater than those which arise in trying to measure productivity in the non-tradables sector. Hence we obtain one unit labour cost equation for the UK. The main determinants are taken to be demand, price expectations (themselves a function of prices), the operation of income policy and a time trend.

$$ULC = (Y_d, P_{df}, P_{mf}, P_{dn}, T, D)$$ (9)

Input prices are assumed to be determined in world markets, with domestic demand being too small to influence them. The U.K.'s contribution to world demand at less than 5% makes this a reasonable assumption. The sterling price of commodities is then the world price in foreign currency terms, mediated through the exchange rate:

$$P_{mi} = \frac{P_{mi}}{E}$$ (10)

To complete the model we need an aggregate demand equation. This is simply the identity

$$Y_d = Q_{dn} + Q_{df} + Q_{xf} - Q_{mi}.$$ (11)

Three modifications are now introduced:

(a) Rather than model explicitly the effect of the costs of production of final imports on their price and output in equations (5) and (6), we introduce the world final goods price level as a proxy for the two cost items. The equations therefore become:

$$P_{mf}, Q_{mf} = f(Y_d, P_{df}, E, P_{wf})$$ (5a) & (6a)

(b) Y_w is dropped from equations (3) and (4) as it is exogenous and likely to influence the simultaneous system through P_{wf} which is also exogenous,

$$P_{xf}, W_{xf} = f(P_{wf}, E, ULC, P_{mi}).$$ (3a) & (4a)

(c) Proxies have to be used for all four main output variables. This creates no problem in principle in the functional equations but clearly invalidates the identity in equation (11). To allow for this, and also presuming that Q_{mi} is a constant proportion of total national income we obtain

$$Y_d = f(Q_{dn}, Q_{df}, Q_{xf})$$ (11a)

[1] One implication is that tradables and non-tradables are not substitutes in demand. A comprehensive model would need to avoid this simplification. Here we are more concerned with the expenditure switching effects of exchange rate changes within the tradables sector over relatively short time horizons, and the extent to which tradables do or do not form a single market. The main effects on non-tradables profitability are therefore taken to be via changes in the supply conditions of non-tradables.

Data on tradables and non-tradables is difficult to obtain. We therefore use series for manufacturing as a proxy for final tradables, and series for services for non-tradables. The distortion introduced because of the existence of traded non-manufactures is likely to be less serious than that arising from the inclusion of manufactured input goods in final tradables, rather than assigning them to an intermediate products category. This could only be removed by constructing sectoral price series of a kind not currently available.

In the regression results recorded below the following data, sources and regression symbols are used.

Variable	Data Series	Source	Regression Symbol
Sterling Export Prices (P_{xf})	Manufacturing Export Unit Values	Monthly Digest of Statistics (MDS)	XU
Sterling Domestic Tradables Prices (P_{df})	Manufacturing Wholesale Prices	Economic Trends (ET)	PW
Unit Labour Costs (ULC)	Manufacturing Wages & Salaries per unit output	ET	UL
Sterling Final Import Prices (P_{mf})	Manufacturing Import Unit values	MDS	MU
Retail Prices (P)	Retail Price Index	ET	PR
Exchange Rate (E)	Effective Exchange Rate	Financial Stat.	ER
World Tradables Prices in Sterling (P_{mi})	World Manufacturing Prices	PFER/$_{ER}$	PF
Imported Input Prices (P_{mi})	World Commodity Prices	U.N. Monthly Bulletin of Stat.	(i) PM^2 (ii) PC
U.K. Demand (Y_d)	National Income	N.I.E.R.	DO
Sterling Non-Tradables Prices (P_{dn})	Service Prices	N.I.E.R.	PN
Autonomous Expenditure (A)	Government plus Inv. expenditure	N.I.E.R.	AU
World Tradables Prices (P'_{wf})	World Manufacturing Prices	N.I.E.R.	PFER
Incomes Policy (D)	Dummy Variable	N.I.E.R.	INCPOL
Time (T)			TIME
Domestically produced & offered tradables (Q_{xf})	Index constructed from manufacturing output & manufacturing exports	Blue Book & N.I.E.R.	QW
U.K. Exports (Q_{xf})	Manufacturing Exports	N.I.E.R.	QX
U.K. final goods imports (Q_{mf})	Manufacturing Imports	N.I.E.R	QM
U.K. Non-Tradables (Q_{dn})	Expenditure on Services.	N.I.E.R.	QN

Initially the basic equation model was tested directly as a set of single equations. Insignificant variables were dropped and the equations re-run. In addition specific tests were run, regressing

---

[2] *PM* is a non-ferrous base metals index, *PC* is a primary commodities index.

both export and final import prices on domestic & foreign prices in sterling with the coefficients constrained to unity. The final set of results are as follows:[3]

A Price & Cost Equations run as a simultaneous equation model.[4]

(1) $LDPW = 0.000015 + 0.65LDUL + 0.13LDUL1 + 0.071LDPC1 + 0.099LDMU$
    (0.0075)   (10.82)   (2.27)   (4.83)   (3.13)

(2) $LDXU = 0.0015 + 0.57LDUL + 0.11LDPC1 + 0.22LDPFER1 - 0.27LDER$
    (0.37)   (3.71)   (2.66)   (1.04)   (3.18)

(3) $LDMU = 0.0059 + 0.93LDPFER - 0.34LDER - 0.31LDER1 - 0.059LDDO$
    (1.42)   (5.45)   (3.37)   (3.10)   (0.27)

(4) $LDPN = 0.0080 + 0.59LDUL + 0.078LDUL1$
    (2.53)   (4.54)   (0.61)

(5) $LDUL = 0.0020 - 0.036LDDO + 0.75LDPW1 + 0.036LDMU1$
    (0.69)   (0.45)   (8.26)   (0.94)
        $+ 0.0002TIME - 0.00592INCPOL$
        (2.21)   (2.31)

B Quantity & Demand Equations tested by two-stage least squares.

(6) $LDQW = 0.003 - 0.51LDLU1 - 0.16LDPC1 + 0.47LDDO1 + 0.56LDMU$
    (0.27) (1.58)   (1.17)   (0.48)   (1.76)

(7) $LDQX = 0.012 - 0.75LDPW + 1.81LDPFER - 0.27LDER - 0.91LDDW$
    (0.38) (0.50)   (1.26)   (0.35)   (0.54)

(8) $LDQM = 0.041 + 0.41LDPFER - 0.41LDER - 1.36LDPW + 0.17LDDO1$
    (1.61) (0.33)   (0.70)   (1.24)   (0.10)

(9) $LDQN = 0.006 + 0.001LDUL1 - 0.12LDDO1 - 0.09LDPM1$
    (0.87) (0.004)   (0.23)   (1.3)

(10) $LDDO = 0.005 + 0.06LDQW + 0.01LDQX - 0.06LDQM + 0.35LDQN$
    (0.92) (0.18)   (0.07)   (0.33)   (0.99)

C Sterling Import & Export prices as a function of foreign & domestic prices, with coefficients constrained to unity.

(11) $DXU = 0.38DPW + 0.25DPW1 + 0.12DPW2 + 0.16DPF + 0.09DPF1$
    (2.0)   (2.8)   (2.6)   (2.5)   (2.0)

(12) $DMU = 0.18DPW - 0.11DPW1 + 0.38DPF + 0.33DPF1 + 0.29DPF2 + 0.25DPF3$
    (0.8)   (1.0)   (5.1)   (6.1)   (4.5)   (2.7)

---

[3] Prefix D indicates absolute changes, LD indicates log changes. The full set of tests, results and commentary are available in cyclostyled form from the authors.

[4] $\bar{R}^2$ for the single equations were as follows:
    LDPW 0.70
    LDXU 0.38
    LDMU 0.37
    LDPN 0.23
    LDUL 0.58

Serial correlation occurred in the single equations for domestic tradables prices ($DWS = 1.26$) and for unit labour costs ($DWS = 1.52$) but attempts to remove this using the Cochrane-Orcutt iterative technique did not alter the results significantly.

In the equation for domestic tradables prices, cost effects come through quite strongly, but the impact of competing import prices is also significant. However the coefficient on imported input goods is lower than the share of the latter in manufacturing output, and so in calculating profitability effects we have also allowed for semi-manufactures being priced similarly to final manufactures. For export prices only unlagged unit labour costs are important (single equations find lagged values significant) and while the exchange rate is significant, world prices are not. This suggests that the short term response of export prices to exchange rates changes is stronger than the response to changes in world prices, perhaps because the former is more immediately identifiable by price setters, especially in differentiated product markets. The elasticity of 0.27 with respect to the exchange rate is consistent with the test of the relative weighting of domestic and foreign prices in the determination of export prices.

The final import price equation is also consistent with this test. The domestic demand and price variables are insignificant, but world final tradables prices and unlagged exchange rate, are of the expected signs and significant. The estimated elasticity of U.K. final import prices with respect to world prices (0.93) is not statistically different from unity. However, in view of the fact that the estimate is for final goods only our estimated elasticity is more plausible, reflecting the fact that the U.K. domestic tradables market may constrain final import prices. The combined two-quarter effect of a change in the exchange rate is somewhat lower and significantly different from unity. The estimates reflect that to a limited extent final import prices will diverge from world prices, although as yet we are unable to identify quantitatively the domestic constraints which would cause this to be the case.

The analysis of non-tradables prices must be regarded as a failure, with only unit labour costs coming through as significant and the constant remaining significant. The unit labour cost equation is much more successful, although a negative and significant effect of demand found in the single equation analysis failed to emerge in simultaneous testing.

On the quantity and demand side the best regressions found still revealed no significant effects. Separate attempts to allow for changes in autonomous components of expenditure fared no better, and there are clear signs therefore that short term volume responses are negligible. However the data problems are severe on this side, and these results must therefore be treated with caution.

THE RATE OF EXCHANGE AND NON-PRICE COMPETITIVENESS: A PROVISIONAL STUDY WITHIN UK MANUFACTURED EXPORTS*

By M. J. BRECH and D. K. STOUT

I. Introduction

IN 1977, the National Economic Development Office wrote a paper for Council on the importance of non-price factors, like growing product quality, reliability and complexity in explaining the success of the UK's overseas manufacturing competitors. In that paper (Stout, *et al.*, 1977), we contended that changes in market shares within individual sectors of manufacturing where product differentiation was important owed a good deal more to competition in non-price terms, especially product improvement, than was recognized in the literature on devaluation and the usual estimates of trade elasticities.

The work on intra-industry trade flows between industrialized countries by Wells (1972) and Grubel and Lloyd (1975), building on the classical study by Brems (1951), and the OECD Trade Data Bank which we had recently acquired provided the main inspiration for that 1977 study of the long-term association between falling relative price per tonne and falling export share in sections of manufacturing.

The possible importance of effects of exchange-rate changes upon non-price competitiveness has since been referred to by Posner and Steer (1978) and by Thirlwall (1980). As far as we are aware, the effects, if any, of changes in the nominal and/or real rate of exchange upon measures of non-price competitiveness remain to be tested. It looks intuitively obvious that, in a market where the form of competition that is hardest to copy quickly is a design advantage, a devaluation benefit ought to appear through the effects on the profits available for investment in product improvement, observable in a higher long-run elasticity of exports to devaluation. In practice, we can see some reasons why devaluation in the UK might not have been having this effect, and in this paper we present some evidence to support this view.

II. Links between the exchange rate and non-price competitiveness

What we had found in 1977, and tried to explain, was a trend decline over the previous decade (and indeed longer) in the relative value per tonne of UK mechanical engineering products, alongside a *real* exchange rate (as

* Acknowledgements are due to past and present members of the Economics Division of NEDO who have contributed to the development of this work over the years. In particular, thanks are due to Adrian Boucher and John Whiteman for checking and commenting on earlier drafts. Responsibility for remaining errors rests with us.

variously measured) that had fallen a little, and a nominal rate that had fallen heavily; while at the same time the UK's share of the world market had continued to shrink fairly steadily, as it had done since 1950. The evidence was later developed and explored in a NEDO Discussion Paper (Connell, 1980). This work reinforced the impression that a large part of the relative cheapening of UK exports in most sectors had not represented the provision of better 'value for money' and that apparent price elasticities of demand for UK exports probably underestimated true price elasticities because of the relative product degradation which had been accompanying a series of devaluation episodes.

The question remained: to what extent were falls in the relative unit values of UK exports, within particular branches of manufacturing, genuine increases in price competitiveness, and to what extent did they represent 'trading down' on the part of British exporters or 'trading up' by their foreign competitors? In many manufacturing industries, changes in product design and specification are so pervasive and so frequent that the question is impossible to answer exactly. One of us suggested that, as a rough approximation, short-term deviations from the trend decline of relative unit values could be regarded as effects of devaluation (and of other sources of changes in *price* competitiveness), based on the crude assumption that changes in non-price competitiveness (hereafter NPC) take place steadily and continuously. Empirical work based on this approach (Connell 1980, Appendix B) suggested that declining non-price competitiveness was an important factor. The main characteristic of NPC appears to be improvements in product design, usually reflected in higher unit values; and it is here that British manufacturers as a whole have been losing out. In some recent work for the Council, NEDO reported on variations in the growth of value of UK export sales in manufactured products between 1975 and 1977, a period of rapid devaluation. Broadly speaking, the most buoyant were 'commodity' products like chemicals (+75%), plastic materials (+57%), and leather, rubber, wood, paper and non-metallic minerals (+60%). The most stagnant were those at the technology-intensive end of engineering, like professional and scientific instruments (−9%).

Over a longer period, the relation between increases in value per tonne (in $000s) and change in world maket share is revealing. Table 1 shows what happened in the non-elecrical machinery sector as a whole between 1962 and 1975. The UK had the second smallest increase in unit value and was the only country to register a significant fall in world share of exports by value.

The main divergence in UK growth of value per tonne of these products dated from the later 1960s to the later 1970s. Excluding aero engines, in 1967 unit values were equal for France and the UK and 14% higher for Germany. By 1976 French unit values were 29% and German 60% higher than UK (Connell, 1980, Appendix B). This covered a period of both nominal and real sterling devaluation: although much of the relative cost

TABLE 1

Exports of non-electrical machinery (SITC 71)

	$000 *per tonne*			*Change in world export share (%)*
	1962	1975	$\frac{1975}{1962}$	1962–1975
Japan	1.40	4.11	2.93	+5.3
France	2.00	5.11	2.56	+2.9
Italy	2.30	4.74	2.06	+1.6
Netherlands	2.08	5.77	2.77	+0.5
W. Germany	1.99	5.94	3.98	+0.3
Sweden	2.20	5.99	2.72	−0.3
UK	1.75	4.24	2.42	−6.3

(*Source*: UN Statistical Papers, Series D and Connell (1980) p. 17. No tonnage figures are available for US.)

benefit created in November 1967 had been eroded by inflation by late 1971, the nominal devaluation of nearly 40% between December 1971 and mid-1976 resulted in a 'real' depreciation of about 16%[1] between those years.

There are three alternatives to the product design argument that provide superficially plausible explanations of the unit value data. First, it might be that the relative unit value decline over the 1960s and 1970s simply mirrored the decline in sterling. However, the fact that Germany maintained its share of exports while the UK steadily lost out appears to us to rule this out. It does not do to argue that Germany merely compensated for the rise in the Deutschmark by "using increases in productivity to hold prices down" (Connell 1980) since, in that event the increase in German relative unit values would not have appeared. In any case, successful individual UK machinery manufacturers have emphasised the dependence of this success upon deliberate decisions to raise product quality.[2]

Second, it might be argued that on the basis of the structure of productive resources available in the economy, UK comparative advantage lies in broad classes of product which have relatively low unit values. In this case, the average unit value of manufactured exports might rise less fast than that of our competitors, without there being a design or technology gap within narrow categories of product.

Third, it is possible that the structural and institutional factors so often appealed to—industrial relations difficulties, X-inefficiency, failures of industrial policy to channel finance into R and D, and so on—by themselves

[1] The 'real' exchange rate that we use throughout this paper is the nominal exchange rate deflated by an index of relative (domestic to foreign) wholesale prices of manufactures, as published by Morgan Guaranty. This is similar to the relative wholesale prices measure of UK trade competitiveness published in Table 46 of Economic Trends (CSO).

[2] Examples from a BOTB study of successful UK exporters are given by Connell (1980) p. 23.

account for the trend decline in NPC, occasioning, until recently, sporadic sterling depreciation without feedback.

In an attempt to clarify some of these issues, we have sought to separate the non-price elements from the unit value data by deriving a product mix index which reflects the changing composition of exports as between high and low unit value products. In Section III we construct, for the UK alone, within one specific sector—Machine Tools—this index using quarterly data over the 10 years 1970 to 1980, and try to see whether any significant part of the change in this index is accounted for by changes in either the nominal or the real exchange rate. This index attempts to measure the movements between 40 types of UK machine-tool export, abstracting from broader structural changes in the composition of exports between wider categories of manufactures. As an index of 'trading up' or 'down', it comes closer to representing NPC change than an index of, say, changes in the value per tonne of mechanical engineering taken as a whole.

This index may not, however, cover the full extent of changes in NPC, because some of them may not be reflected in changes in product composition at this level of disaggregation. It is even conceivable, though implausible, that UK producers have been increasing their market share at the more expensive and elaborate *end* of each of the forty categories of machine tool, while still reducing relatively their share in the more expensive and elaborate of the forty categories themselves. In that event, our index could actually be overstating the revealed decline in NPC. However, from an examination of more detailed data that we have for certain sub-periods, we are fairly sure that such biases as there are understate this decline.

It has to be remembered that there are other aspects of changing NPC which will not be caught by any index of changing product-mix in highly product-differentiated markets, no matter how disaggregated. For example, such features as marketing effort, width of distribution, availability of spares and speedy delivery may change independently of changes in product mix; nor would they be fully revealed in international comparisons of value per tonne since economies of scale attach to them.

A plausible account of the relationship between nominal devaluation, NPC and export performance—though by no means the only explanation which would fit the facts so far described—might run along the following lines. For deep-seated structural and institutional reasons, economic agents in the UK adapt slowly and hesitantly to either market or technology changes. There is, therefore, a trend decline in UK NPC. This decline is reflected in a relatively low income elasticity of demand for UK manufactures. There are usually strong social and political pressures to try to maintain growth at a rate relative to the rest of the world which is inconsistent with this trend towards product obsolescence. The trend decline is therefore partially compensated for, in its effect on the balance of payments, by episodes of nominal and (temporarily *real*) devaluation. However, the remedy is inappropriate, not just because, after a lag of a few quarters, domestic inflation liquidates most of the relative price advantage, but because recourse to devaluation has two effects. The greater ease with which older products, which tend also to be more price elastic, can be sold, provides some exporters with a soft short-run option to the painful, expensive and risky process of developing superior products. On top of this, those firms who have launched products early in their life-cycle alongside older products, find, following devaluation, that the demand for the older products has risen more strongly. Those of them who behave passively, retain labour and expand investment for the production of the older products instead of moving more resources into the new. This type of outcome is consistent with the pricing behaviour to be expected at least in the less concentrated UK industries where some temporary rigidity in sterling prices can be expected following devaluation.[3] On balance, given some short-sightedness among UK entrepreneurs, the devaluation that was a result, in part, of failures of NPC in the past may therefore feed back and further reduce it, leading UK manufacturing even further downmarket.

This is principally what we set out to test in Section III, with respect to changes in both the *nominal* exchange rate, and in the *real* rate (in the sense defined earlier). As Section III shows, we found that changes in the exchange rate are significantly positively related to changes in the product mix index, with a distributed lag.

In Section IV, we attempt a broader cross-section test across the 5-digit SITC products contained in the whole of the Machinery and Transport Equipment sector (SITC 7), dividing the sub-sectors into equal numerical quartiles by value per tonne, and comparing the growth of exports (by value) for each quartile in two sub-periods: a complete cycle dominated by devaluation (1971 to 1976) and the two available recent years dominated by sterling *appreciation* (1978 to August 1980). Within the limits of its coarser definition of product structure, this study does appear to confirm the results of Section III. It turns out that the annual growth rate of the value of exports in the highest unit value quartile is dramatically greater than in the other three (20% p.a., compared with 4 to 5%) during the two years of sterling appreciation.

III. Machine tools: a time series study

In this section, we try to test the hypothesis that the product composition of UK exports of machine tools varies systematically over time with movements in the sterling exchange rate. Product composition is defined in terms of the mix of goods with different value to weight ratios as a rough proxy for the degree to which such NPC characteristics as technology and product differentiation are incorporated in individual products. Since there may also be an association between income-elasticities of demand and value to weight

---

[3] The effects on the foreign price of exports is discussed in Stout (1977, especially Appendix A) and Thirlwall (1980).

atios, various measures of world and home demand have been included in he analysis.

To represent changes in the value to weight composition of machine tools exports, we have constructed a product mix index from detailed trade statistics. This index is based on the discrepancy between the change in the overall value per tonne for the sector and the weighted average of the individual changes in value per tonne at the product level. The overall change can only exceed the weighted average of individual changes if there is a shift in the composition of exports towards higher value per tonne products, and vice versa.[4]

This product mix index is clearly sensitive to the degree of disaggregation in the product data. The more highly aggregated are the basic commodity classifications, the greater will be the proportion of the change in mix that will occur *within*, rather than between, commodity classifications, and hence be lost. We have constructed a product mix index for machine tools for the period 1970Q1 to 1980Q2 from the detailed 8-digit tariff code data within SITC(R) 715.10 as published by Customs and Excise. However, there have been two major revisions in the tariff codes over this period (in 1974 and 1978) and therefore a lot of re-aggregation has had to be done to generate a continuous series. Our final index is calculated on the basis of a 40-product breakdown of machine tools exports, although during one sub-period (1974 to end 1977) 124 categories are available in the original trade statistics. Two sets of regression analysis were performed on this product mix index, using different proxies for the relative price term. We use the sterling effective exchange rate as our first proxy. (A mechanism whereby nominal rate changes might affect product mix was described in Section II.) As a second proxy, we have taken the 'real' effective exchange rate, which combines the effects of relative cost trends with exchange rate movements to represent the change in international price competitiveness. However, the price indices used to reflect cost pressures in the construction of the 'real' exchange rate refer to wholesale prices of manufactured output supplied by domestic producers to the home market. It is therefore an imperfect proxy to the extent that (i) cost pressures and pricing policies of the machine tools sector differ from those of manufacturing as a whole, and (ii) differential pricing policies may lead to divergences between export and home market prices of similar products. Besides the price terms, a world income term was included to reflect cyclical elements and to pick up the expected 'up-market' bias in the structure of incremental demand. The results of regression analyses performed on the product mix index over the period 1972Q3 to 1980Q2 are given in Tables 2a and 2b. *A priori* we would expect the relationship between product mix and the exchange rate to be subject to a distributed lag, reflecting the different reaction times of individual firms and product types. We also expect a minimum lag of some quarters to represent the

---

[4] For more details on the construction and characteristics of this index, see Appendix 1.

TABLE 2a

Regression analysis of product mix of exports of machine tools; nominal exchange rate

$$\text{Model: } Log(MPTM) = C + \alpha t + \sum_{i=m}^{n} \beta_i \, Log(ERUK_{-i}) + \varepsilon$$

Eq.	Lag con- straints	c	α	$\sum \beta_i$	m	n	Mean lag (QTRS)	$\bar{R}^2$	DW	RSS
(1)	None	−3.5 (1.29)	−0.0145 (0.005)	1.79 (0.26)	3	9		0.9898	1.802	0.0534
(2)	None	−3.13 (1.61)	−0.0161 (0.006)	1.72 (0.32)	2	10		0.9895	1.803	0.0506
(3)		5.44	−0.050 (0.002)					0.9726	0.756	0.1881
(4)	Polynomial 2nd Degree*	−3.79 (1.42)	−0.0135 (0.006)	1.85 (0.41)	2	10	5.9	0.9900	2.076	0.0619

where

MTPM = Product mix index of exports of machine tools
ERUK = Sterling effective exchange rate
   t = trend
   m = minimum lag
   n = maximum lag
—standard errors in parentheses
—sample period 1972.3 to 1980.2, giving 32 observations
—β_i in equation (4) are: 0.188, 0.206, 0.218, 0.225, 0.225, 0.219, 0.208, 0.190, 0.167

* No end constraints.

TABLE 2b

Regression analysis of product mix of exports of machine tools; real exchange rate

$$\text{Model: } log(MPTM) = C + \alpha t + \sum_{i=m_1}^{m_2} \beta_i(RERUK_{-i}) + \sum_{i=n_1}^{n_2} \gamma_i(WIP_{-i}) + \varepsilon$$

Eq.	Lag con- straints	C	α	$\sum \beta_i$	m_1, m_2	$\sum \gamma_i$	n_1, n_2	$\bar{R}^2$	DW	RSS
(1)	None	−8.73 (2.43)	−0.0546 (0.004)	1.574 (0.45)	4,10	1.503 (0.40)	4,8	0.9876	1.876	0.0510
(2)	None	2.87 (2.14)	−0.0493 (0.002)	0.541 (0.45)	4,10			0.9715	0.725	0.1497
(3)	None	−0.856 (2.09)	−0.0598 (0.003)			1.405 (0.46)	4,8	0.9775	1.134	0.1284
(4)	None	−9.99 (2.06)	−0.0564 (0.002)	1.599 (0.262)	5,9	1.743 (0.33)	5,9	0.9906	2.013	0.0431
(5)	Polynomial 2nd degree	−10.68 (2.56)	−0.0565 (0.003)	1.698	4,11	1.810	5,11	0.9899	2.281	0.0514

where

RERUK = 'real' sterling effective exchange rate; i.e. the nominal effective rate deflated by relative wholesale prices of manufactured output.
   WIP = world (i.e. OECD area) industrial production
      — the β_i in equation 5 are: −0.008, 0.136, 0.240, 0.303, 0.325, 0.307, 0.247, 0.148
      — the γ_i in equation 5 are: −0.372, 0.113, 0.433, 0.589, 0.578, 0.405, 0.066

delay between orders and deliveries. Estimation was carried out in two stages. First, the appropriate lag lengths were ascertained by the successive inclusion and exclusion of terms at either end of the lag distributions in models in which no restrictions were imposed on the coefficients of the lagged price and income terms. The most satisfactory results suggested minimum lags of 2 to 5 quarters, and maximum lags of 8 to 10 quarters. Plausible lag distributions were then generated over these predetermined lag lengths by restricting the coefficients to lie on polynomials of second degree.

Both sets of results indicate that, in addition to a structural shift down market shown by the negative time trend, there is a negative association between movements in price competitiveness, as represented (inversely) by the exchange rate measures, and the value to weight mix of machine tools exports. These results therefore confirm that, although an improvement in price competitiveness may result in higher volume of exports of machine tools, it also entails some loss of earnings due to the substitution of low for high unit value goods. In equations based on the real exchange rate, the level of world demand, represented by total industrial production of the OECD area, was also found to exert a significant positive influence, as we had expected. In the Tables, we report and test only the *sum* of coefficients on the lagged price and demand terms, as our major concern is to establish the existence of the lag distributions.[5] We could not find any evidence of interaction between the pressure of home demand, represented by a measure of UK GDP, and the product mix of machine tools exports.

The two sets of results have been compared by considering the statistical relationship between the nominal exchange rate and the other variables in the model. The nominal and real exchange rates were found to be related by a coefficient that is close to (but significantly different from) unity, and the difference between the nominal and real exchange rates turned out to be positively and significantly related to the level of world activity (see Table 3). This can easily be justified: since the definition of the real exchange rate implies

$$\log (ERUK) = \log (RERUK) + \log (P_f/P_d)$$

where P_f, P_d are the foreign and domestic price levels of manufactured output, we can infer from the estimated results that world activity is associated with the relative price component: i.e., that the ratio of foreign to domestic prices of manufactures rises in line with increases in world activity. There is a sharp discrepancy between the estimated values of the time trend of the two sets of results (-1.5% per quarter in the case of the nominal rate equations and -5% in the case of the real rate).

This is part of a more general problem of collinearity between trended

---

[5] The joint tests on the lagged variables indicated by considering the standard errors on the sum of the coefficients can be confirmed by performing F-tests on the changes in the residual sums of squares (RSS) between the full models and the models excluding these variables; the presence of first order serial correlation in these truncated equations which is not present in the full equations also demonstrates their mis-specification.

TABLE 3

Estimated relationship between nominal and real exchange rates

Model: $\Delta \log(ERUK) = C + \beta \Delta \log(RERUK) + \gamma \Delta \log(WIP)_{-i} + \varepsilon$

$\varepsilon_t = \rho \varepsilon_{t-1} + u_t$

Eq.	c	β	γ	i	$\bar{R}^2$	DW	ρ
1	−0.016	0.895	0.208	0	0.933	1.82	0.615
	(0.0036)	(0.035)	(0.104)				
2	−0.012	constrained	0.224	0	0.404	1.94	0.514
	(0.0072)	= 1	(0.114)				
3	−0.018	constrained	0.354	1	0.478	2.01	0.519
	(0.0032)	= 1	(0.120)				

Note: standard errors in parentheses

TABLE 4

Correlation matrix of main variables

	1. MTPM	2. ERUK	3. RERUK	4. WIP	5. TIME
1.	1.00				
2.	0.91	1.00			
3.	−0.21	0.19	1.00		
4.	−0.89	−0.83	0.09	1.00	
5.	−0.98	−0.92	0.16	0.93	1.00

Notes: for definition of variables, see Tables 2a, 2b; all variables except time in logs; sample period: 1970.1 to 1980.2

variables, such as the nominal exchange rate and the world demand series (see Table 4). Whilst this does not invalidate our tests for the presence of the proposed effects, it does mean that less weight should be attached to the precise values of individual parameter estimates. An important exception is the estimated coefficient on the real exchange rate in the second set of results which is uncorrelated with other independent variables in the model.

IV. Machinery and transport equipment: a cross-section study

We have attempted to confirm the results of the previous section and to widen their applicability by analysing the value to weight composition of exports within the Machinery and Transport Equipment sector (SITC 7). This is a very large heterogeneous sector which comprises about 40 per cent of UK visible exports and includes the majority of both mechanical and electrical engineering. Our methodology has been to consider the change in commodity composition over 2 sub periods: the first, 1971–76, represents a period of depreciation and compares two years which are approximately at the same phase of the business cycle; the second, 1978–1980 (cumulative figures to August of each year) represents a period of sterling appreciation;

since the international trade classification (SITC) changed in 1978, it has not been possible to select comparable years in terms of the cycle in this case.

We have attempted to compare the change in product composition over the two sub periods in two ways. Firstly we have ordered the data in terms of value to weight ratios and considered the change in export value for each quartile. Secondly we have applied the methodology of the previous section to separate the overall change in value per tonne for the whole sector into components due to changes within products (defined here in terms of 5 digit SITC categories) and changes between products, i.e. changes in product mix.

The results for the first approach are shown in Table 5. For the period 1971–76, the data set consists of 113 products for which volume and value data exist in both years. After ordering the products by their average value per tonne levels for the two years, the change in export value per annum was calculated within each quartile group. Although the results are broadly similar, it is the lowest quartile which has the highest change in export value. For the period 1978–80, the data set consists of 208 products (after discarding products with zero or negligible flows). In this case whilst the changes in value for the three quartiles at the lower end of the scale were similar at around +5 percent per annum the growth in value of the top quartile was dramatically greater at +21 percent p.a.

To check whether this was due to erratic items, this quartile was sub-divided into two octiles: the change in value for the higher octile was +24%, and +16% for the lower octile, confirming that at the higher end of the value to weight spectrum at least, there was a positive association between export growth and value per tonne between 1978 and 1980, the period of currency appreciation.

In the second approach, we have calculated the weighted average of the change in values per tonne of the individual products within SITC 7 across each sub-period, using value shares in the base years as weights. We term this loosely the 'price' change by analogy with the construction of a price index, although it should be more correctly described as the 'within-products' changes in values per tonne. We then compare this with the

TABLE 5
Changes in UK export values within SITC 7 by quartiles by value to weight ratios

		Quartiles			
			% change per annum		
		lowest			highest
Sub-period		1	2	3	4
1971–76	(1)	+21.8	+19.2	+18.9	+20.0
	(2)	0.8	1.4	2.2	7.7
1978–80	(1)	+4.7	+5.2	+4.5	+21.1
(cumulative	(2)	1.5	2.9	4.3	15.8
to August)					

(1): % p.a. change in value
(2): (simple) average value per tonne (£'000)

TABLE 6

Product mix changes within SITC 7: machinery and transport equipment

Changes (% p.a.) in:	'price'	value per tonne	product mix
1971–76	+17.8	+17.3	−0.4
1978–80 (cumulative to August)	+11.0	+15.6	+4.1

change in value per tonne at the aggregate sectoral level.[6] As before, the difference is a measure of product mix change, a positive value being associated with a change in mix towards higher value per tonne commodities.

The results of this approach, given in Table 6, confirm those of the analysis of quartiles, namely that there has been a sizeable shift in product mix 'up-market' over the period 1978 to 1980 when sterling has been appreciating, whereas in the previous period of depreciation there had been a very small decline in the value per tonne composition of exports. The fact that the decline in product mix is not larger over the first period given the severe fall in the value of sterling may be accounted for by the fact that the long-term trend for all exporters is positive, reflecting the underlying rate of technical progress and relative demand growth. The inappropriate choice of years for the second period does not seem to have presented a problem. One might have expected that deepening home and world recession would have retarded product mix. Hence, when normalized, improvement between 1978 and 1980 may exceed 45%.

On its own, this cross section analysis does not establish any more than a casual association between change in the value per tonne composition of exports and the exchange rate. Taken together with the results of the previous section these observations provide some support for the view that the more disaggregated results found there may hold more generally across a wider spectrum of manufacturing exports.

V. Conclusions

This paper has reported what is really a pilot study of the possible inter-relationship between the trend rate of decline in NPC in UK manufacturing, and exchange rate changes which, until recently, followed from this trend decline, relative UK inflation and low relative growth in physical productivity.

The tentative conclusion we have reached is that there is, within engineering in general and machine tools in particular, a positive feedback from

---

[6] The ratio of the aggregate unit value change to the 'price' change is equivalent to the product mix index described in Appendix 1.

growing product inferiority, through devaluation, to increased product inferiority.

We intend to develop this work in several directions. The steps include: to carry out the machine tools work on changing unit value, product mix and market share for two or three competing economies; to replicate the study for other sectors where product differentiation is less important; to apply the analysis to the explanation of penetration of the *domestic* market; to gather more systematic information on UK exporters' pricing decisions, following changes in nominal and real exchange rates; to investigate the effects of alternative measures of the real exchange rate; and to attempt, within at least one sector, to fit a hedonic regression as an independent estimator of relative quality change. With its trade data bank, its software development and its contacts with industry through the Sector Working Parties, NEDO is well placed to pursue some of these lines of enquiry.

If there is a feedback from devaluation to further down-market movement, what is the moral to be drawn? We cannot stress strongly enough that no topsy-turvey recommendation follows for exchange rate policy from these results. We have not taken any account whatever in this study of the direct effects upon export earnings of changes in price competitiveness. There is still the question as to whether these changes in product mix occur largely as enforced reactions to market developments or as part of the planned strategies of exporting firms. This will also be covered by our future work programme. Furthermore, there may well be UK exporters who have used temporary devaluation profits to invest in higher value or newer products, with success. In any case, if the real exchange rate moves so high that normal profits can only be earned by those few exporters who are already producing the least price-sensitive goods, then it may become practically impossible for other producers, however strongly motivated, to join that small club.

REFERENCES

1. BREMS, H., Product Equilibrium under Monopolistic Competition (H.U.P., Cambridge, Mass.) 1951.
2. CONNELL, D., *The U.K.'s Performance in Export Markets—Some Evidence from International Trade Data*, Discussion Paper 6, (NEDO, London) 1980.
3. GRUBEL, H. G. and LLOYD, D. J. *Intra-Industry Trade*, (Macmillan, London) 1975
4. POSNER, M. and STEER, A., 'Price Competitiveness and Performance of Manufacturing Industry', in BLACKABY, F. (ed.), *De-industrialisation*, (Heinemann, NIESR, London) 1978.
5. STOUT, D. K. *et al.*, International Price Competitiveness, Non-price Factors and Export Performance, (NEDO, London) 1977.
6. THIRLWALL, A., *Balance of Payments Theory and the UK Experience*, (Macmillan, London). 1980.
7. WELLS, LOUIS, T. (ed) *The Product Life Cycle and International Trade*, (H.U.P., Boston) 1972.

APPENDIX 1: CONSTRUCTION AND PROPERTIES OF THE PRODUCT MIX INDEX

The product mix index used in this paper reflects shifts in the unit value composition of a group of traded products. It moves up in response to a shift in mix towards a higher proportion of the high value goods (trading-up) and down for a shift towards a higher proportion of the low unit value goods (trading-down).

We define the product mix index: M

$$M_1 = \sum q_{1i} U_{1i} \left(\sum q_{0i} U_{1i} \right)^{-1}$$

where $U_{1i} \left(\equiv \dfrac{V_{1i}}{Q_{1i}} \right)$ is the unit value (value per tonne) of the ith product in period 1,

V_{1i}, Q_{1i} being the value and volume (in tonnes) respectively of the same.

$q_{0i} \left(\equiv \dfrac{Q_{0i}}{Q_{0.}} \right)$ is the share of the ith product in total volume in period 0.

and $Q_{0.} \equiv \sum Q_{0i}$

$n \equiv$ number of products in the group.

It is evident that

$$M_1 = 1 \quad \text{if} \quad q_{1i} = 1_{0i} \quad \text{for all } i$$

Furthermore

$M_1 > 1$ implies

$$\sum q_{1i} U_{1i} > \sum q_{0i} U_{1i}$$

i.e. $\sum (q_{1i} - q_{0i}) U_{1i} > 0$

i.e. that there is a positive correlation between the changes in volume shares and the individual unit values.

Therefore M is an indicator of the change in composition of high and low unit value goods in terms of shares of total volume. It is free of any direct effect of the changes in the individual unit values, and hence the index is unaffected by exchange rate changes or export pricing policies other than to the extent that these factors influence the relative volumes exported. A linked product mix index can be calculated by chaining together the quarterly indices, selecting a convenient period (1974 1st quarter in this case), as a base. In practice, the set of products for which the index is calculated may differ from period to period, since no unit value can be calculated in a period for a product in which no trade occurred in that period.

APPENDIX 2: PRODUCTS DEFINED WITHIN MACHINE TOOLS AND 1979 EXPORT UNIT VALUES

	1979 Value per Tonne (£'000)
1. Designed for recycling of nuclear fuels—ACI*	NT**
2. —non ACI	
3. Physico-chemical—ACI	8.33
4. —non-ACI	6.73

* Automated by coded information
** NT: No Trade in this category in 1979

5.	Lathes—ACI	8.70
6.	—non ACI—automatic—bar	5.81
7.	—chucking	7.20
8.	—capstan and turret	5.54
9.	—centre	3.07
10.	—copying	5.04
11.	—vertical boring and turning mills	5.77
12.	—other	3.70
13.	—non ACI, used	0.68
14.	Boring Machines—ACI	4.34
15.	—non-ACI	3.68
16.	Planing Machines—ACI	NT
17.	—non-ACI	0.99
18.	Shaping Machines—ACI	†
19.	—non-ACI	4.11
20.	Milling Machines—ACI	7.13
21.	—non ACI—Milling	4.54
22.	—Drilling and Boring	4.58
23.	—non ACI, used	0.65
24.	Grinding machines—micrometric adjustment—ACI	6.51
25.	—non ACI	6.21
26.	—other ACI	NT
27.	—non traded ACI	4.81
28.	Jig-boring machines—ACI	9.02
29.	—non ACI	7.55
30.	Gear-cutting machines—cylindrical gears—ACI	NT
31.	—non ACI	7.11
32.	—other gears—ACI	14.81
33.	—non ACI	2.96
34.	Presses—ACI	1.95
35.	—non ACI	2.83
36.	Forming machines—ACI	5.11
37.	—non ACI	3.14
38.	Foreign and stamping machines—ACI	NT
39.	—non ACI	2.02
40.	Other Machine tools	5.81

† The recorded trade statistics, which imply a value of 150.44 for this item, are clearly wrong.

BRITAIN'S INTER-WAR EXPERIENCE

By J. F. WRIGHT

It is very widely accepted by economists that the return to gold in 1925 produced an overvaluation of the pound that caused Britain to be depressed in the late 1920s when the rest of the world was enjoying a boom and that the abandonment of the Gold Standard in 1931 contributed to Britain's relative prosperity in the 1930s. How far is this a correct characterization of interwar events?[1]

The appreciation of sterling that constituted the Return to Gold took place over several months in late 1924 and early 1925 and its effects cannot always be easily distinguished from those of a longer period of appreciation that had begun in 1920. The whole period of appreciation coincided with the disclosure, as the abnormal postwar period ended, of the operation of other factors adversely affecting Britain's position in some important export industries. The abandonment of the Gold Standard occurred at a time of rapidly deepening world depression and also at almost the same time as the extension of tariffs to nearly all imports. It should be said at once that this paper does not provide the sort of thorough quantitative analysis needed to determine with any precision the relative importance of the principal factors operating.

The diagnosis of overvaluation in the 1920s is attractive because of its direct relevance to the unprofitability and unemployment that existed in the sectors of the economy which produced tradeable goods. Amongst exporters these were principally textiles and coal, metals and engineering; amongst import-competing sectors, iron and steel and agriculture, though many other industries would also be affected less acutely. Most of these industries had products that were close substitutes for foreign products and so the adverse effect of overvaluation would show itself as much in low profitability as in visibly uncompetitive prices. To the extent that low profits caused suspension of production, the high valuation of the pound resulted in unemployment.

These adverse effects on sectors producing tradeable goods are natural effects of revaluation. But, in theory, there ought to be offsetting effects causing expansion in other nontraded sectors unless the appreciation produced weakness in the balance of payments position. Was there a deflationary effect brought about by policies of monetary tightness needed to maintain the convertibility of the pound?

I. Monetary tightness and the exchanges

In the operation of monetary policy the attention of both the Bank of England and the public focussed on interest rates, particularly short-term

[1] I have received valuable comments on an earlier draft from Alec Ford. Peter Andrews, of Balliol College, has been of particular help in allowing me sight of an unpublished paper of his own. This acknowledgment is not in any way to claim their agreement with my conclusions.

rates. Interest rates in 1925–26 were higher than they had been in 1923–24 though not as high as in 1920–21; or as high as they were to be in 1929, when external factors were certainly dominant. Bank Rate was five or four and a half percent while the yield on Consols was fairly stable at about 4.5%. By the standards of today these rates do not look high. But it was a period when prices were falling: so rates were very much higher than today in real terms. The rates were also high as compared with the last quarter of the nineteenth century, another period of falling prices.[2] On the other hand it is difficult to maintain that, by international standards, rates of interest in the U.K. were particularly high. Perhaps it would be truer to say in that respect that domestic borrowers had ceased to enjoy the relatively low rates with which their proximity to the centre of the international capital market had previously provided them.

It has sometimes been argued that changes of half or one percent at this level could not really make much difference. Whether or not this view is accepted, it is reasonable to see interest rates as also being important in providing indications of changes in the state of credit; changes that would manifest themselves to many lenders in the availability of credit as well as in its price. The Macmillan Committee[3] did not think that there had been quantitative restrictions of overdrafts by the banks; the banks themselves denied that there had been. But bank lending always involves some quantitative restrictions in individual cases on prudential grounds; and so it is very difficult to decide from simple verbal evidence on banks' procedures whether or not some abnormal restraint was being exercised in aggregate. This difficulty is particularly acute in looking at a period when falling asset prices were making prudential criteria more widely applicable. Moreover for the Committee this may have been seen as a "charge" against the banks on which it would be necessary to have overwhelming positive evidence. Taking a more detached view at a distance, we may note two fairly conclusive facts. By 1927 banks' loans and advances had crept up to, and levelled out at, about 55% of their deposits; and all the banking witnesses accepted that they were at about the conventional prudential limits. One bank (the Midland) said that it sought overseas deposits in order to be able to maintain its volume of loans to its domestic customers. How many borrowers in those days had a size and status that gave them independent access to a competitive market where they could borrow freely at something related to market rates—as distinct from sponsored access to the market by acceptances obtained from or through their own bank?[4]

---

[2] In that period the return on Consols had been below 3%—though a relatively narrow market made the Consol Rate less representative of overall conditions.

[3] Committee on Finance and Industry (Chairman H. P. Macmillan), Report, Cmd 3897 of 1931.

[4] We may also speculate whether the "fully lent" position reduced pressure on the banks to adapt their pattern and forms of lending to changing industrial needs; i.e. whether the persistent general tightness of credit was one cause of the famous gap in the provision of credit identified by the Macmillan Committee.

TABLE 1.
Money and interest rates 1920–38

Year	Money supply (£ millions)			Interest rates (%)					Percentage
	Net money	Quasi money	Encash-able	Bank rate	T. bill	Market	S-date	Consol	Advances
1920	2817	3256	4224	6.72	6.21	6.41	6.23	5.32	0.0
1921	2779	3225	4275	6.12	4.58	5.17	5.70	5.21	47.2
1922	2597	3066	4167	3.69	2.57	2.64	4.78	4.43	43.4
1923	2536	3031	4181	3.49	2.62	2.72	4.39	4.31	46.7
1924	2512	3039	4215	4.00	3.39	3.46	4.36	4.39	50.2
1925	2495	3053	4283	4.55	4.09	4.14	4.51	4.43	53.2
1926	2528	3108	4395	5.00	4.51	4.48	4.35	4.55	55.2
1927	2572	3185	4500	4.65	4.25	4.26	3.98	4.56	55.9
1928	2639	3307	4655	4.50	4.15	4.16	4.73	4.48	55.5
1929	2598	3308	4686	5.50	5.26	5.26	5.08	4.60	56.9
1930	2679	3462	4885	3.42	2.48	2.57	4.31	4.48	55.1
1931	2521	3358	4783	3.93	3.59	3.61	4.54	4.40	53.7
1932	2808	3726	5180	3.00	1.49	1.87	3.64	3.75	48.3
1933	2792	3778	5275	2.00	0.59	0.69	2.09	3.39	43.4
1934	2833	3911	5449	2.00	0.73	0.82	1.78	3.10	41.1
1935	2986	4157	5733	2.00	0.55	0.58	2.46	2.89	39.4
1936	3192	4470	6093	2.00	0.58	0.60	2.45	2.93	40.3
1937	3260	4643	6346	2.00	0.56	0.58	2.90	3.28	42.9
1938	3189	4671	6419	2.00	0.61	0.63	2.72	3.38	44.1

Columns 1–3, D. K. Sheppard, *The Growth and Role of UK Financial Institutions* 1880–1962, London 1971, Appendix Table 3.3.

Columns 4–8, Sheppard, Appendix Table 3.7.

Column 9, London and Cambridge Economic Service, *The British Economy Key Statistics* 1900–1970, London 1971, Table K.

Note

Column 9 is derived from Key Statistics by dividing Advances by Net Deposits. This produces a series for the whole period nearly comparable to that given by the Macmillan Committee for the 1920's. The series shown here is fairly consistently about 1.5% higher than that of the Macmillan Committee.

Although the policy makers did not pay much, if any, attention to the size of the monetary base the statistics of money supply do provide a simple indicator of the net effect of the combination of the direct effect of the balance of payments, the effect of government finance (particularly its management of the national debt), and the effects of central bank policy. The simplest indicator of monetary tightness would be a fall in the ratio of money stock to income i.e. a rise in the velocity of circulation. All three of Sheppard's estimates of income velocities do show a small absolute rise in 1924–5 and a constancy until 1929 that stands out as a temporary halt in a longer-term fall from 1920 to 1945.[5] The rise is most pronounced in the income velocity of money narrowly defined. Thus, if this movement over the longer period is regarded as a trend, there was an increase in velocity as compared with its trend value. But it is not clear whether it is legitimate to regard the overall change from 1920 to 1945 as a trend, other than in a mechanical arithmetical sense, since it was almost entirely the product of the 1930's, which would generally be accepted as a period of abnormal monetary ease, and the Second War; and it was subsequently sharply reversed.

The situation of monetary tightness vanished soon after Britain abandoned the Gold Standard. The Government and the Bank succeeded in bringing down interest rates to an abnormally low level which the economy enjoyed for the rest of the 1930's. And banks operated far below the proportion of advances that they would have liked.

The tight monetary conditions of 1925–31 were a consequence of pressure on the exchanges that showed itself by an exchange rate that was frequently below par. To what extent was the pressure on the exchanges the consequence of unfavourable changes on income account brought about by the high valuation of the pound?

Calculations given in the Appendix (page 304) suggest that the adverse effect on current account could have been as much as £80 million but it was very unlikely to have been much more. £80 million is quite large. But it is not so very large as to imply that the adverse effect on the current balance was the only significant, or necessarily the main, factor creating pressure on the exchange position.

It needs to be emphasized that, for policy makers in the UK, the operational objective lay in the exchanges and therefore, in the short and perhaps the medium run, the opinions of the investing financial institutions at home and abroad (who at that time were the main potential currency-switchers) were what mattered. The true extent of the effects of parity on current account was difficult for current observers to see clearly. It also would only be relevant to those taking a view on currency parities if, for the short period for which the view was taken, the reduced surplus on current account was significant in relation to the resources available to the authorities seeking to maintain the parity. This raises the question of the financial strength of London.

Before 1914 London was the leading financial centre of the world. For many parts of the world both inside and outside the Empire it was the only centre; their banks, including their central banks, held most of their reserves in Sterling in London. For every other country London was a convenient place to hold some assets, partly because of the large proportion of world trade in which the UK was a partner, and partly because the institutions of London offered ways of holding short term balances that were safe, convenient and income-earning. London was also an important source of longer

[5] Sheppard, op. cit. Fig. (3) page 50.

TABLE 2
Volume, prices, and terms of trade 1920–38
1963 = 100

| Year | Volumes | | Prices | | Terms of trade |
	Imports	Exports	Imports	Exports	
1920	56	53	69	60	86
1921	47	37	46	45	97
1922	54	51	37	34	90
1923	59	56	37	33	89
1924	66	57	39	33	86
1925	69	56	38	33	85
1926	70	50	36	31	87
1927	72	58	34	29	86
1928	69	60	35	29	82
1929	73	61	34	28	85
1930	71	50	29	27	92
1931	72	38	24	24	102
1932	63	38	22	23	102
1933	63	39	21	22	104
1934	66	41	22	23	103
1935	67	45	23	22	100
1936	72	45	24	23	99
1937	76	49	27	25	93
1938	72	43	26	26	102

Source
London and Cambridge Economic Service, *The British Economy Key Statistics* 1900–1970, London 1971, Table M.

term finance for the rest of the world—mainly because British savers were very willing to hold overseas securities. This in turn provided some reinforcement of the supremacy of London in the shorter-term market. London institutions were able to offer a comprehensive service to their overseas clients. Conversely the existence of the shorter-term market made the floating of quite large loans easier than it would otherwise have been.[6]

In individual cases or in changes between one year and another there were certainly instances where the export of long-term capital was being financed by short-term funds from overseas, and it has been maintained that the period of heavy capital export before 1914 saw an increase in London's

[6] Buttressing the short-term position were substantial holdings of longer-term securities for which there were ready markets abroad, and some of which would be sold abroad by their owners in the event of changes in relative interest rates making the switch worthwhile. Similarly a large proportion of goods in store or in transit was in the ownership of British merchants but the extent which these holdings bore to the ultimate volume of consumption could be varied in the short-run and would vary with interest costs.

short-term liabilities relative to her short-term assets.[7] Nevertheless it would be wrong to characterize London's pre-1914 international position as being that of a banker borrowing short to lend long; or as being like that of the USA after 1945—a banker with large short-term obligations against which large cash reserves had to be held. In 1914 the substantial amount of overseas-owned London deposits and bills was roughly matched by the total of short-term debts (particularly acceptance debts) of foreigners to London. That this was so is demonstrated by the events of mid-1914 when the winding-down of normal peacetime operations led to the exchanges being very strongly in favour of London. A corollary of the fact that Britain was not in the position of borrowing short to lend long was the ability of the Bank of England to defend the position of London with a relatively low gold reserve. The strength of London also enabled the Bank of England, though almost always varying the pressure it exerted on internal credit in accordance with the needs of the exchanges, usually to meet those needs by very small variations in interest rates with negligible domestic effects. It may be the case that before 1914 Britain suffered severe fluctuations that were mainly imported from the external world. But the fluctuations were not aggravated in their transmission by the institutions of the gold standard, and the now widespread view that they were was probably derived from the experience of the 1920s.[8]

By the twenties the position was very considerably changed. London was no longer the natural habitat of the balances associated with such a large proportion of trade. More important, its balance sheet position had deteriorated so that the short-term debts of foreigners to London were of the order of only half of the short-term assets of overseas holders in London. Initially the very visible counterpart of this was the large amount of British Government debt in the form of Treasury Bills held by overseas institutions in London. The amount of these was reduced as time passed. But the continued export of capital tended to exceed the positive surplus that there still was on the balance of payments current account, and had to be financed by the attraction of short-term funds. From 1928 there seems to have been some reduction in the net short-term indebtedness of London (Macmillan Report para 260). But, since these were short funds that had continually to be reborrowed it remained true that there was an important sense in which London was borrowing short to lend long. Thus, since 1913, the strength of London had visibly been greatly reduced and was no longer sufficient to stop holders of sterling feeling a need to take a view about how current changes in debts and credits might further weaken the position.

In looking for the sources of weakness of the foreign exchanges we need to consider flows on capital as well as on income account. On average in the 1920's there was a surplus on income account which would have permitted

[7] A. I. Bloomfield, *Short-term Capital Movements under the International Gold Standard 1880–1914*. Princeton 1963.
[8] C. A. E. Goodhart, *The Business of Banking 1981–1914*, London 1972, especially section III.

TABLE 3
Balance of trade and payments
(*in millions of pounds*)

Year	All trade		Balances			
	Import	Export	Trade	Divint	Other	All current
1920	1977	2064	87	246	4	337
1921	1148	1133	−15	178	30	193
1922	1074	1103	29	177	−5	201
1923	1140	1149	9	176	−2	183
1924	1309	1190	−119	196	1	78
1925	1343	1148	−195	232	15	52
1926	1277	1007	−270	237	15	−18
1927	1243	1080	−163	239	22	98
1928	1222	1083	−139	240	23	124
1929	1256	1088	−168	243	21	96
1930	1088	878	−210	215	31	36
1931	914	626	−288	163	22	−103
1932	754	572	−182	127	4	−51
1933	729	567	−162	154	0	−8
1934	789	603	−186	167	−3	−22
1935	835	684	−151	181	−7	23
1936	906	690	−216	195	−6	−27
1937	1080	835	−245	205	−7	−47
1938	982	750	−232	192	−15	−55

Source: C. H. Feinstein, *National Expenditure and Output of the United Kingdom* 1855–1965, Cambridge 1972, Tables 37 and 38.

Note: Imports, Exports, and Balance of Trade include trade in all goods and services and are derived by adding figures for visible trade to those for shipping, financial services, and travel.

The Balance of Dividends and Interest is segregated as being a large item primarily determined by the cumulative effect of past investment decisions.

Other items are conventionally included in current account but are not a consequence of economic activity. The main components are government receipts and payments; reparation receipts were quite important in this period.

some capital export. It was much smaller than the average of £192 million in 1909–1913; but that figure included the peak of the pre-war export boom. The crucial factor was not the actual or comparative size of the surplus in the 1920s but whether it was sufficient to match the contemporary desire to export capital. The fact that the Bank of England exercised fairly severe controls limiting new issues in London is clear evidence that it was not. What remains unknown is whether the demand by overseas borrowers in the new issue market was supplemented by an adverse or favourable balance in the movement of old securities.

The discussion above has not considered how far the pressures on capital account might themselves be due to revaluation. The consequences of lack of complete confidence in the pound may not have been entirely confined to movements of short term balances. It should also have detracted from the relative attractiveness to holders of securities denominated in Sterling. Similarly the attractiveness of borrowing in Sterling was increased if subsequent devaluation was expected. However probably as important in increasing the length of the queue to make new Sterling issues was the very fact that there was a queue and a very real possibility that the access to the London market (in which Empire borrowers enjoyed very favourable terms) might subsequently become even more restricted. The prospect of Sterling devaluation was not particularly attractive to most of those countries whose currencies could be expected to move with Sterling. In the event it proved a disadvantage for some whose currencies were devalued against Sterling.

The change in parity may also have generated an incipient export of capital even without speculative effects because of the increase in the prices of domestic relative to overseas capital assets and because of the consequences of this change in relative prices for portfolio composition. This incipient disequilibrium should then have caused some fall in the sterling prices of British capital assets to remove it; and this in turn would have reduced the incentive to create new assets in the U.K. There is no evidence that the portfolio-composition effect was important; and it may be doubted whether there were important investors in those days, other than banks, who were concerned with the distribution of their portfolio by currency. On the other hand although there is no relevant data of the size of the capital movements generated the effect via prices on the relative attractiveness of real assets in Britain and overseas cannot be ignored particularly in relation to U.S. shares.

In the longer run, the adverse consequences of revaluation for the balance of payments should have disappeared. On current account, insofar as there was a deflationary factor operating exceptionally in the U.K., the overvaluation should have been slowly removed; if not by actual wage reductions, then by a reduction in relative costs caused by wage increases in competing economies and by productivity gains. And in fact, though it did not occur as quickly as some had supposed it could, there was eventually a noticeable fall in British costs relative to those of some of her trading rivals. The net result was that by 1929 wage costs relative to France and Germany were slightly lower than they had been in 1924 before the Return to Gold; though they were higher in relation to the USA.[9]

By the end of the twenties the remaining pressure on the exchanges and any consequent monetary tightness came not from any remaining trading consequences of the actual level of the parity adopted in 1925 but from the continuing weak balance sheet position of the U.K. in a world economy that

---

[9] These remarks are based on E. H. Phelps Brown and M. H. Browne, *A Century of Pay*, London 1968, Figure 38 with its enlargement for 1925–29. But it should be said that the authors were primarily interested in constructing a series to show long rather than short term changes.

was experiencing increasing strain. The actual surplus on current account in 1928 and 1929 was still positive and quite large; and in those years there was no visible increase in the short-term indebtedness of London. In the same period the rise in short-term market rates in London followed closely the rise in short-term rates in New York.

The world recession brought a collapse of British exports. It is likely that the decline would have been less precipitate if the exchange rate had been able to move downwards before 1931. On the other hand the recovery in British export volumes, which rose by 30% between 1931 and 1937 would probably have been much less; i.e. there would have been some mitigation of the depths of the depression.

After the initial crisis of 1931 had passed, the 1930s were a period of very easy money. The degree of ease was the consequence of deliberate government action and until 1935 was the only significant form of anti-deflationary policy. It can be argued that, through the stimulation of the housing boom, it had significant expansionary effects.

Britain's relative prosperity in the 1930's was not accompanied by pressure on the foreign exchanges. The change to a regime of floating rates would, of course, have precluded a repetition of pressures like those felt in and before 1931 or in the quarter-century before 1971. But, after an initial period in which the dollar exchange rate fell very quickly, the pound recovered. Indeed, despite the attempts of ths Exchange Equalization Fund to hold down the pound the effective exchange rate continued to rise fairly continuously for the rest of the 1930s until it exceeded its 1931 level. Thus there never was any period in which a falling exchange rate posed the sort of problem that it did in 1976.[10]

1930 and 1931 had seen a drastic worsening of the balance of payments on current account as exports collapsed; a collapse that had its direct (and multiplier) effects on domestic demand. 1932 and 1933 saw a considerable improvement in the trading balance. Exports fell by only 10% in value and not at all in volume; and the import bill was reduced by a third. How much of this turnaround was due to the introduction of tariffs and how much to devaluation is not easy to determine; the more so since anticipation of each must have induced speculative trade flows. But clearly some, possibly much, credit must be given to the abandonment of gold. The improvement of the balance of trade had its direct counterpart in the increase of domestic demand: some increase in demand for exports; but more important a release of domestic income for the purchase of home products.

Thus, relative to the calamitous year of 1931, devaluation played a part, perhaps an important part in the British recovery that began to show itself in increased production and falling unemployment from some time in late 1932. However, the relative importance of different factors in contributing

---

[10] J. Redmond, An Indicator of the Effective Exchange Rate in the Nineteen-Thirties, *Ec. Hist. Rev. 2nd series*, Vol xxxiii No. 1, (February 1980), pp. 83–91.

to the beginning of recovery is not necessarily the same as the importance of factors in contributing to the strength of the subsequent upswing and boom. Here we must note that the balance on current account was, despite very favourable terms of trade, distinctly worse than in the 1920s! The average deficit in 1932–38 was £27 millions compared with a surplus of £67 millions in 1924–30. It seems likely that, whatever may have been the net expansionary effect of the 1931 devaluation taken by itself, it was not large enough to offset other autonomous factors reducing the net contribution to G.D.P. of the overseas trading account between the late twenties and the middle thirties.

The favourable effects of devaluation on current items in the balance of payments were not sufficient to explain the absence of a balance of payments constraint in the 1930s. The sources of balance of payments improvement were on capital account and caused by the end of the net outflow of long-term capital. This was produced by a combination of: tighter control on new issues for overseas borrowers in London; the effect of depression on prospects in the traditional destinations of British lending; and, later in the decade, the effect of political fears in Europe. These fundamental factors were not reinforced by the most obvious tool of exchange management—for interest rates in the short-term market were almost negligible: but how far they were reinforced by the cumulative effect of speculation in a currency whose managers were always under the suspicion of holding the rate down is an interesting question. So substantial was the improvement in the capital account position that there was an increase in reserves of £620 millions between 1932 and 1937 despite a deficit on current account of £133 millions.

II. Employment production and profits

There was not a deep absolute depression in the late twenties. The growth of GDP between 1924 and 1929, 12.2%, was not low by comparison with previous British experience; and its relation to growth in other countries was certainly no worse than before 1914. Industrial Production increased by 15.6% between 1924 and 1929. This average conceals very considerable disparities with some industries showing no growth or even a decline. It is normal for there to be some difference between the rates of growth of individual sectors; what was special about the 1920s was the coincidence of the abrupt reversal of the fortunes of several very important industries, coal-mining, textiles, and shipbuilding which had been prosperous in the pre-1914 period. If these industries had been excluded, the increase would have been more than 20%.

It might be said that what was really disappointing about the later twenties was the failure to recover further from the very deep depression of 1921. But to argue in this way is implicitly to accept that 1921 was no more than a deep cyclical recession from which full recovery might be expected in

TABLE 4
Indices of GDP and production 1920–38
(1913 = 100)

Year	G.D.P.	Agriculture	Ind. prod	Mining	Manufacture
1920	93.7	71.5	97.9	80.9	99.7
1921	82.3	72.8	79.7	57.9	77.6
1922	88.5	73.7	92.2	86.2	90.3
1923	91.4	74.9	97.6	95.9	96.7
1924	96.0	72.6	108.4	94.0	106.5
1925	98.9	78.2	112.7	86.6	109.8
1926	96.6	80.5	106.6	48.1	106.3
1927	105.0	80.7	122.8	90.1	117.5
1928	105.0	85.4	119.5	85.7	117.2
1929	107.7	85.6	125.5	93.1	122.0
1930	106.0	87.7	120.1	88.5	116.8
1931	102.3	79.9	112.3	79.8	108.8
1932	102.5	83.7	111.9	75.7	109.4
1933	106.8	89.7	119.3	85.8	117.5
1934	112.6	90.8	131.2	81.4	128.2
1935	117.6	88.5	141.2	82.2	139.8
1936	124.0	87.1	153.9	85.0	152.8
1937	128.7	86.7	163.1	89.6	162.1
1938	127.1	85.7	158.7	85.2	157.4

Source: Feinstein tables 8 & 51.
1913 Base includes Southern Ireland which is excluded in years tabulated.

due course—simply from the expansion of demand. It ignores the fact that the depression was a coincidence of cyclical depression and the onset for important staple industries of an era of intensive international competition. Almost all industries showed some recovery from the very low output of 1921 (shipbuilding being the prominent exception) but the output of textiles and chemicals was no more in 1924 than it had been in 1920. Coal was another exception: the beginning of intensive competition in the European market had to await the unimpeded working of German mines from 1924 onwards.

A feature that marked the late twenties as a period of depression was the high level of recorded unemployment. There was a noticeable rise between 1924 and 1925; a further rise in 1926 reflecting the miners' strike; and then a distinct fall in 1927. The overall picture was not of an absolute rise in aggregate unemployment—that did not happen until 1930—so much as a failure to achieve further recovery. Recorded unemployment was almost always more than 10%, a figure recorded only in years of deep crisis before 1914—though we should note that it was no worse than that achieved at the peak of the next cycle in 1937 after a substantial growth in output.

The unemployment rates for individual trades show very considerable

TABLE 5
Unemployment and profits 1921-38

Year	Insured unemployment (thousands)			Gross profits (millions)	
	Overall percentage	Selected areas	Other	Selected industries	Other
1921	16.9	N.A.	N.A.	117	214
1922	14.3	N.A.	N.A.	169	279
1923	11.7	753	481	168	286
1924	10.3	657	395	168	301
1925	11.3	889	373	151	310
1926	12.5	1184	480	133	291
1927	9.7	742	312	133	317
1928	10.8	948	406	132	318
1929	10.4	825	363	141	317
1930	16.0	1473	599	111	299
1931	21.3	1903	880	81	276
1932	22.1	1921	891	91	261
1933	19.9	1699	808	105	282
1934	16.7	1519	666	132	310
1935	15.5	1471	574	148	343
1936	13.1	1243	474	178	389
1937	10.8	1027	418	220	414
1938	13.5	1282	593	214	404

Column 1: Department of Employment, *British Labour Statistics Historical Abstract* 1886-1968, HMSO 1971, Table 160.

Columns 2-3: i.d., Table 162.

Columns 4-5: Feinstein Table 27.

Notes Col. 1: annual averages of percentages of insured employees unemployed in each month.

Cols. 2 & 3: thousands of insured employees unemployed in July of each year. Col. 2 is total for North-East, North-West, Scotland, Wales, and Northern Ireland for 1923-1936. For 1937-38 total includes North which was separated from North-East and North-West after 1936.

Col. 3 is total for remaining regions viz, London, South-East, South-West, Midlands.

Col. 4 & 5 are gross profits in Millions of Pounds.

Col. 4, "Selected" is total for Chemicals, Metal Manufacture, Engineering (except vehicles), Cotton, Other Textiles, and Coal Mining.

Col. 5, "Other" is total for "manufacturing and other industries" not included in Col. 4: Vehicles; Other Metal Goods; Leather and Clothing; Building; Building Materials; Paper and Other; Other mining; Gas, Electricity and Water.

differences.[11] The same difference of fortunes is brought out more concisely by considering the regions in which the depressed industries tended to be concentrated. The North-West, the North-East, Scotland, Wales and Northern Ireland, which between them had 52% of insured workers in 1930, had more than 60% of the country's unemployment in 1923 and 1924 and seldom less than 70% thereafter. The change between 1924 and 1925 is very abrupt—so abrupt that the increase in unemployment in those regions was greater than for the country as a whole. (Some, perhaps a large part, of this change is accounted for by the inclusion, from September 1924, of some workers on short-time.)

Because of the deficiencies of pre-1914 unemployment statistics we simply do not know the extent to which unemployment, in an economic as opposed to an administrative sense, was higher in the twenties than it had been before 1914. The extension of rights to unemployment pay between 1911 and the twenties (and more specifically in the immediate post-war period) vitiate any simple conclusions from the statistics available. Put simply the change was from a situation in which, apart from a few workers enjoying union organized unemployment insurance, financial relief was available only to those willing to incur the stigma and submit to the harsh tests of Poor Law relief (at worst evidence of complete destitution and a willingness to enter the workhouse, at best a willingness to accept a labour test) to a situation in which a very large proportion of the adult male labour force was effectively eligible for unemployment pay as of right. In the former case the pressure to seek any kind of work that was available (including part-time work), to fall back on the help of the extended family, to make very drastic economies in consumption (for example by sharing accommodation), to realize assets and to borrow to tide over short-term employment, was very much higher than in the post-war period. Beveridge did make some estimates of the extent to which changes in the actual coverage of the statistics may have led to an understatement of the relative scale of pre-1914 unemployment.[12] He came to the conclusion that perhaps the prewar statistics should be multiplied by 1.5 to make them comparable with those of the 1920s; but it should be emphasized that this sort of adjustment is designed to remedy lack of comparability in the statistics, not lack of comparability in the phenomenon itself.

This argument from ignorance should not be pushed too far. The particular regions and industries that were hard-hit in the twenties had been

---

[11] Apart from the large number of different employments, differing considerably in relative importance, which make it difficult to formulate a short summary of the distribution of unemployment, statistics of unemployment by trade have the disadvantage of classifying individuals by their most recent employment. Thus, for example, redundant miners who find temporary employment as unskilled workers in building or local government become classified by those occupations if they subsequently become unemployed. Thus at time goes by unemployment may appear to become more diffused among occupations and the importance of its origin become concealed.

[12] W. H. Beveridge, *Full Employment in a Free Society*, London 1944, pp. 72–73, 328–337.

prosperous before the War and there is nothing at all to suggest that they or other industries were experiencing anything like the level of underemployment of the later twenties. Where there must be real uncertainty is whether the apparently relatively high level of "background" unemployment, of 5% or so that existed in virtually all areas and all industries in the later twenties, was in any way abnormal by pre-1914 standards.

There is currently a debate whether unemployment was affected by changes in the benefit/wage ratio during the interwar period.[13] This is a much less important question than that discussed above and the contention that there was a positive relationship has been subjected to severe criticism. However, there were administrative changes[14] that increased the amount of recorded unemployment by 100,000 or more between 1922 and 1925.[15] Moreover it seems likely that reactions to changes as profound as that in the adminstration of unemployment relief would be unlikely to work themselves out very quickly. These points need to be borne in mind in looking at the changes as recorded between 1921 and the later twenties; together with the likelihood that the insured unemployed were not representative of the whole working population.

The mechanism by which overvaluation reduced employment and reduced the balance of payments on income account should have led to a noticeable reduction of profits. Long run estimates of the share of profits in the income of industry and commerce do suggest that profit-rates in the 1920s were low in comparison with the later 1930s and the 1950s. But they were much the same as in the 1960s and very distinctly higher than in the 1970s.[16] Thus it may be that it is the profit-rates of the 1930s, not those of the 1920s, that are remarkable. Perhaps they should be seen as indicators of the potentialities for exceptional growth that lay ahead after 1945.

Feinstein's estimates of profits, taken year by year, show a fall from 1924 to 1926 and thereafter a rise to 1929 after which there was a fairly steep plunge. It is difficult to know whether to attach much weight to these figures which are uncorrected for stock appreciation. When corrections for stock appreciation (negative in years of falling prices) are made the picture for the

---

[13] D. K. Benjamin and L. A. Kochin, Searching for an Explanation of Unemployment in Inter-War Britain, *J. P. E.* Vol. 87, (June 1979), p. 441 T. J. Hatton, Unemployment in Britain between the Wars: A Role for the Dole, (University of Essex Discussion Paper No. 139, June 1980).

[14] S. Glynn and J. Oxborrow, *Interwar Britain; a Social and Economic History*, London 1976, pp. 145–148.

A. Booth and S. Glynn. Unemployment in the Interwar Period, *J. Cont. Hist.* October 1975.

[15] Footnotes (Table 162) in the *Historical Abstract of Labour Statistics* identify specific changes in practice that if cumulated would have added a net total of 123,000 to the register by September 1924 and 153,000 by July 1928. Simple cumulation may somewhat exaggerate the resultant total effect but is unlikely to affect the magnitude of it.

[16] Bank of England, Measures of Real Profitability, *Bank of England Quart. Bull* Vol. 18 (December 1978) p. 513. The chart in this article is in turn derived from C. H. Feinstein, op. cit.

For estimates that attempt specific corrections to obtain a rate of return on capital see P. E. Hart (ed), *Studies in Profit, Business Saving and Investment in the United Kingdom 1920–62*, Vols. I and II, London 1965 and 1968.

mid-twenties is reversed and actually shows a distinct peak in 1925—which seems improbable. Estimates for individual industries show very low gross profits and even losses in coal; a decline for all textiles between 1924 and 1925 but thereafter a relative decline in cotton; and chemicals and metals and engineering (excluding vehicles) on a rough plateau.

The picture that has emerged, of considerable divergences between the older staples and the rest of industry, justifies a few comments on some individual industries.

In Lancashire Cotton it would be hard to argue that the revaluation of the pound did not aggravate the short term position of the industry in the 1920s. But would greater prosperity in the 1920s have helped the industry in the longer-run? The industry was to suffer very severe further decline. The fact that the steepest decline took place in 1930 and 1931 may suggest that the fixity of the parity was at fault. But, even after the pound floated freely, exports in 1937, at the top of the next cycle, were less than half their 1927 volume. With a longer view of comparative industrial development (which now includes the decline of the textile industry in Japan itself) it would surely now be accepted that in the case of textiles, particularly cotton, the relatively easy transplantability of techniques to countries in the early stages of industrialization made inevitable some, almost certainly very considerable, absolute decline in the British industry from its 1913 position when about 70% of its output had been exported (perhaps more than 80% in the case of Lancashire cotton). Moreover, possibly because of the way in which it evolved over the previous century, there seems to have been an inability to adapt to the opportunities there were: it is notable that for half a century after depression struck Lancashire other sectors, particularly Midland knit-wear, enjoyed expansion and prosperity.

Because of strongly growing bunker and export demand British coal output had continued to expand more rapidly than the rest of the economy right up to 1913 despite falling productivity and rising labour costs. Given the relative size of reserves abroad the British industry was destined to experience some setback. The setback when it came was aggravated by large increases in miners' productivity abroad, steady improvement at home and abroad in efficiency of coal use, and a loss to oil of the premium market for ships bunkers. British labour productivity had declined considerably between 1913 and 1923 (the best post-war year): production was 5% lower, the labour force 6% higher. Postwar disruption in Europe and temporary subsidies postponed and obscured competitive pressures until after 1923. The severity of the subsequent pressure showed itself in a fall in the price of coal of a third (so the final appreciation of the pound contributed at most a third to the pressure on the industry). The fall in prices forced widespread adjustment at the expense of employment. Between 1924 and 1930 the labour force was reduced by 22% while production fell by only 10%. Productivity continued to increase in the 1930s: in 1937 the same output as in 1930 was produced by 15% fewer miners. In the interval there had been a deeper slump with output and employment falling by 15% into the trough of 1933 but it may reasonably be asked whether this might not have been much steeper if there had not been the contraction of the later 1920s.

By the mid-twenties shipbuilding had an unemployment rate of 40%. Its main problem was the extent of its success in the last quarter of the nineteenth century when, quite quickly, it had expanded rapidly to produce more than 70% of the worlds ocean-going ships—a proportion that had only declined a little by 1914. Some considerable decline, in the relative share at least, was to be expected. There are no economies of scale in shipbuilding so considerable that they overcome the forces of technological dissemination especially when reinforced by national sentiment (underpinned by strategic considerations). It was the misfortune of the U.K. industry that the emergence of foreign competition that would have inevitably reduced its share of output occurred at a time when there was a slackening in the total world demand for ships. In view of the successful development of shipbuilding in other developed industrial countries in the next forty years it is difficult to say that shipbuilding in a country like the UK was then or subsequently at any inherent disadvantage other than the demoralization produced by its own decline.

With steel the situation was somewhat different. Though the industry had long been subject to foreign competition in the home market its actual weakness in the 1920s was due primarily to wartime expansion of relatively inefficient capacity; and secondly to the effects of disarmament on those sectors that had enjoyed prosperity before the First World War. As with coal there was also unprofitability internationally. In the longer run there was, however, scope for an even larger industry. The question then is whether if the industry had not been financially prostrated in the 1920s it would have achieved more for itself and been less in need of the specially high tariff and the associated quasi-public intervention of the Steel Board in the 1930s.

Agriculture was also financially prostrated in the 1920s by import competition. Despite this it had a growth in output much the same as that of Industrial Production. From the 1930s protection and other assistance was to produce a spectacular revival. Some part of this was due to the adoption of new ideas available in the 1920s. Would greater prosperity then have encouraged their adoption or were the twenties an essential final phase of a purging process?

It is being contended that the problems of several of the most prominent industries in the 1920s were long-term in the sense that for those industries there had been fundamental shifts in comparative advantage that would require contraction or very profound adaptation. It follows by implication that even success in achieving the "correct" purchasing-parity of the pound relative to that of other countries, as defined by 1913 levels, would not have been sufficient to avoid the need for other types of adjustment. To what extent, in such circumstances it would have been desirable to have a parity that was low by historical standards in order to provide mitigation of the position of the depressed industries is not easy to say. It would have eased the position of the capital and labour in the industries in the short run and the social value of that relief cannot be ignored but in doing so it would have removed some of the pressures to adapt. Is it possible to have cushioning without featherbedding?

Final adjustment for some industries would require a movement of labour from them. On the other hand it is difficult to see that in the twenties the growth of other sectors was being significantly impeded by lack of labour. A crucial question is therefore whether the other relatively prosperous sectors would have grown more quickly and absorbed more labour had there been a lower parity. Many of these industries already enjoyed protection in the home market and benefitted to some extent from the lower prices for their imports of materials that came from overvaluation. For them the possible adverse effects of overvaluation depended on the extent to which they failed to obtain as much growth in export volume as they might have done. In the twenties as well as in the sixties and eighties ICI complained about the overvaluation of the pound. But ICI's main interests in those days were as a producer of standard chemicals in which there was keen international price competition and should not be regarded as representative of "new" industries.

III. Wage flexibility

The discussion so far has been entirely concerned with the adverse effects of exhange rate appreciation. Some may say, as was said at the time, that, if wages had been more flexible downwards, the problems brought by the Return to Gold would have been less.

In the later twenties the fact that wages were imperfectly flexible (plastic was the word used at the time) seemed to be a new phenomenon; for earlier in the twenties a very considerable reduction in money wages had been achieved. The index of manual wages (January 1956 = 100) had fallen from 56.8 in December 1920 to 38.8 in June 1922 and 35.9 in June 1923. Explanations for the change was readily available: the increase in Union membership and power that had occurred during the First World War; and the extension of Unemployment Insurance after the War. Attempts by employers to reduce wages, under the threat that the alternative was short-time or dismissals, could be resisted by Union officials more readily because they knew that even if the threat was carried out their members could fall back on unemployment benefit; and that in the case of short-time working it was possible to schedule that work so that earnings were supplemented by benefit. Hicks, in *The Theory of Wages* (1932, p. 177), pointed to a significant detail in the conditions of eligibility for unemployment benefit: "willingness to accept work" was not deemed to require recipients to accept employment "at wages lower, or on conditions less favourable, than those generally observed in the district by agreement between associations of employers and employees." This condition did not prevent wages falling in all circumstances. In severe slump employers in concert might press for a reduction, but, by enabling Unions to resist the attempts of individual employers to use their particular position of financial weakness or lack of orders to press wage-reductions on their own employees, it did delay wage reductions until employers were ready for concerted action; and therefore in some cases altogether. Indeed the administrative provision would seem to give the Unions a strong incentive not to allow a precedent for lower wages to be established.

Pigou in *Employment and Equilibrium* (1941) expressed the firm opinion that while money wages showed quite significant falls between 1924 and 1934, "their stickiness is more marked than it used to be". In this he was referring not just to the immediate post-1918 period but also to the fifty years before 1914 on which he cited Bowley's *Wages and Income since 1860* (1937). He argued further about that period that "The general stability of the average percentage of employment through a long succession of cycles is striking evidence of an effective price mechanism at work balancing the supply and demand for labour more effectively than in the inter-war period".

However, an inspection of *Wages and Incomes since 1860* does not reveal very many instances of falls in average money wages before 1914;[17] and almost all the falls that did occur were either in industries where systems of sliding-scales operated (coal mining and iron making) or in the highly-cyclical trade of shipbuilding.[18] Other instances seem relatively rare even in industries subject to fairly sharp variations in the volume and profitability of trade, like cotton textiles. Looking back after 1918, Henry Clay attributed the long pre-war period of relative industrial peace in the U.K. to the absence of need for major adjustments. Thus the extent of the wage reductions in the early twenties was unprecedented.

It is consistent with this that Phillips, in fitting his curve derived from pre-1914 data to inter-war experience found no difficulty except for the changes in 1921 and 1922.[19] It might be said that if account had been taken of the price-level, which is not an explanatory variable in his equation, a break would have been found after 1922. But, even if this result were econometrically substantiated, it would tell us no more than we already know, i.e. that there was a difference in experience between the early and

---

[17] Bowley's series are a summary of a much larger collection of data particularly that reported by himself and Wood in the *Journal of the Royal Statistical Society*. But much of this is fragmentary and discontinuous and its bearing on wage flexibility cannot be derived by cursory inspection.

[18] S. Pollard and P. Robertson, *The British Shipbuilding Industry, 1870–1914*, Harvard, 1979, Chapter 9.

[19] A. W. Phillips, The Relationship Between Unemployment and the Rate of Change of Money Wage Rates in the United Kingdom 1861–1957, *Economica New series* Vol. XXV (1958), p. 283.

middle twenties. Any fitting of a new equation with a price term, would be dominated by 1921 and 1922, the points that are by far the most distant from the Phillips Curve.

It could be argued that, before 1914, the published statistics are sparse and unrepresentative because individual employers, say in building, might have cut actual rates below the published rates which stayed the same for years on end. But the argument from statistical deficiency works both ways. Pigou's contention that the labour market mechanism worked more efficiently depends entirely on taking the pre-1914 unemployment statistics at face-value although in fact they have much too insubstantial a basis to be used for long-term comparisions even within the pre-1914 period. Being based on returns by some trade unions of the number of their members unemployed they provide an unrepresentative sample and, more important, no measure at all of the extent to which in the longer term, the increase in employment was matching the growth of the available labour supply.

Thus, while is is undeniable that in the pre-1914 period several trades showed wage-flexibility upwards and downwards over the cycle, sometimes institutionalized in sliding scales, we should be cautious about generalizing to less cyclical trades or to longer-run adjustments. In the period before 1900 money wages fell very little despite the growth of foreign competition and despite a fall in prices that had caused a very considerable rise in real wages.

It should not be a forgotten that, in the pre-1914 period, the economy and its labour-force were growing and it was only in the few years of acute depression that GDP fell absolutely. Because of technical change there may have been a few more years in which the demand for labour fell absolutely but a distinction still needs to be drawn between situations of acute depression and the surrounding years of positive but sluggish growth. In the former, absolute falls in demand confronted the established workforces of individual plants with a choice between accepting a wage reduction and the unemployment of its own members. In situations of longer term slack any adverse effects of wages being above equilibrium level would usually manifest themselves in reducing the rate at which the labour force expanded and, at worst, in non-replacement of natural wastage. There would be much less pressure on those already in employment to accept reductions.

The distinction being drawn in the last paragraph does depend on the assumption that employers, even in Victorian England, were not completely free to substitute unemployed labour from outside the business for the labour of their employees. Quite apart from the sentiment of loyalty that would make many employers reluctant to do this, it would be a policy that had considerable costs and risks. The obtaining of a balanced, trained and integrated workforce would often have required a considerable investment in time and was an asset that could not be reduplicated at will. Moreover even when not unionized the labour force of a factory always had a latent unity (because they had worked together) and had to hand many means of coercive action that it would have been rash of employers not to recognize. This is not to deny that on occasion blackleg labour was used; but it should be recognized that for many employers it was a costly alternative only to be resorted to in desperation. This would not be the case where businesses were very small and labourers lacked any organization. Here threats to replace labour would be very effective—but it would be wrong to assume that this was typical of all industry.

Except for their unprecedented size the wage reductions of 1920–23 fit into the pre-war pattern of the removal or reduction in deep depression of increases conceded in the preceding boom. It is significant that many of the reductions took the form of the reduction of general bonuses which had not formally been incorporated in new basic scales. Many reductions too occurred automatically as the result of the operation of sliding scales. Even where this was not so prices, and everybody else's wages, were visibly plunging.

Thus while it does seem likely that some of the cyclical flexibility in wages that existed before 1914 may have vanished by 1925, it is also possible that in the 1920s there may have been some exaggeration of the extent to which wages had been flexible. 1920–23 seems to be a wholly exceptional period in which so intense and immediate were the pressures that wages showed a plasticity that in their normal state they do not possess.

Would wage flexibility in the 1920s have been an important factor in economic adjustment? On this matter the argument must be very similar to that about the effects of the exchange rate on the fortunes of the staple industries (except of course for differences in income distribution and the effects of this on demand). For the individual industries, lower wage costs would have brought some relief but would have reduced the pressure for adaptation to structural change.

It is possible, however, that we see the concern with wage-flexibility in the 1920s too narrowly by regarding it simply as concern with the diminished effectiveness of particular instrument of macro-economic adjustment. It was also concerned about Britain's capacity for longer-term adaptation to growing international competition. Economists frequently coupled concern with wage-rigidity with concern about rigidity in working practices and immobility. There was a profound caution about Britain's long-term prospects in the world economy and the possibility that new lines for suitable international specialization would not emerge fast enough to absorb all those who would be displaced from the old staples if existing levels of real wages were maintained in those industries. It is of interest how, despite what was already visible in the USA, observers in the twenties saw so little of the growth and prosperity that was in store for the UK in the postwar period.

As we know know the long-run adjustment that did occur and eventually brought with it unprecedentedly high levels of employment for two decades after 1945 was not obviously produced by a willingness of labour to accept lower real or money wages. "Not obviously" because it remains to be explored how far the location of new investment was affected by the existence of pools of relatively cheap labour (particularly female) and by supplies of labour which because of its adaptability (and therefore productivity) resulted in low labour costs. In the particular case of American investment in the UK how important was the level of labour costs.?

IV. Concluding reflections

This contribution has been produced primarily in response to the Editors' comments about "conventional wisdom". The intellectual triumph of Keynes may have led to an uncritical acceptance of all his opinions including his opposition to the Return to Gold. Moreover acceptance was easy as until recently the interwar period, particularly the twenties, seemed, against the long post-1945 experience of full employment and sustained growth in incomes and full employment, to be an aberration which must have been the consequence of economic mismanagement.

The appreciation of the Pound in 1924–25 must have had some adverse direct effects on employment and profitability in the tradables sector. In addition money was certainly tight in the later twenties because of the weakness of the Pound. This weakness was a consequence of a change in the balance-sheet of London and of capital outflow. How far it was aggravated by the effects of appreciation on current account is less clear. But taking the Balance of payments as a whole the pressure on the Pound would have been less at a lower exchange rate. The direct effects of the Return to Gold had probably spent themselves by 1928, but the commitment to a fixed exchange rate aggravated the effect on the U.K. of the first phase of the World recession.

Thus there are no grounds for reversing the views that the final stage of currency appreciation in 1924–25 did the economy no good and that depreciation in 1931 brought relief. Possibly, however, the effects of both have been exaggerated.

It should be pointed out that despite the apparently high level of unemployment there was a growth in the number of persons employed of 1.25 million between 1924 and 1929. Growth of GNP in the same period, 12.5%, was not negligible by previous British standards. It was distinctly lower than in the USA and several other countries which grew by 20% or more. Industrial Production showed a similar contrast. In 1939 or 1945, it is understandable that this relative performance should have been contrasted with that of the 1930s, in isolation from longer-term trends. But perhaps, in 1980, looking back on a hundred years during which other industrial economies have been catching-up and eventually overtaking the British, the events of the twenties may not seem so obviously to be the result of one ingredient in the economic policy of that period.

It seems fairly certain that there must have been some scope for higher employment and probably more output in the middle twenties and that a lower parity would have contributed to that. Nevertheless two questions must be asked. Might not the maintaining of greater "competitiveness" by a lower exchange rate have made some industries even more vulnerable to the world recession when it came? How far would it have contributed to the longer run structural adjustment required of the British economy? By this is meant not merely adjustments that would find jobs for the unemployed but adjustments that would enable full employment to be achieved without chronic balance of payments problems.

Britain achieved relative prosperity in the early thirties. That is easily demonstrable. But it is very unclear how far the weaknesses in Britain's current account position that had been exposed in the 1920s had been solved even by the end of the 1930s. The balance-of-payments problem that faced the British Economy after the Second War was not entirely the product of the disruptions of that war. There had been a sizeable balance of payments deficit in 1938 and some further deterioration of the very favourable terms of trade of the 1930s might have been reasonably expected. Some of the most important elements in Britain's prosperity in the quarter century after 1950 were external (the persistent growth in world demand for engineering products and the relatively slow dissemination of the relevant techniques and skills), or were legacies of the War (the expansion of capacity and trained labour force in engineering, vehicles and aircraft and the disruption of important potential rivals).

This is to be too sceptical. It must be accepted that the successes of very many firms in Britain after 1945 had their roots in earlier periods especially the 1930s. But how much of their success is attributable to the exchange rate which was only very favourable for a part of that decade? Other factors were at work: the expansion of industry, particularly the engineering industries, under the stimulus of rearmament and the demands from domestic consumers with rising incomes. The important feature of both is that they stimulated the expansion of capacity for products for which world demand would expand most rapidly in the post-war world. It cannot be disputed that with a higher parity in the 1930s some of the consumption demand would have been met by imports—but the level of tariffs was a more obvious factor in protecting the position of home suppliers.

A central theme implicit in this paper is the importance in the long-term development of the UK of the "chances" of history. The structural problems of the 1920s were due to what seem to be the chance coincidence of factors adverse to several previously great industries. Subsequent achievement of prosperity after 1945 was largely due to the pattern of development of world demand. In both cases the role of economic mechanisms, particularly those susceptible to influence by conscious macroeconomic policy were of subsidiary importance. For all our disappointments and dissatisfaction the British recovery of the second third of the twentieth century had in it substantial elements of good fortune that we cannot count on being repeated.

The present situation, in which the exchange rate is raised above the level at which it would otherwise be by the use of a tight money policy, is unprecedented. There never has before in the U.K. been a persistent rapid inflation to be halted: and never, therefore, has there been an objective for monetary policy other than the equilibrium of the exchanges. But the present resembles the 1920s in that then too a policy was pursued in furtherance of a long-term objective: the "Return to Gold" was made in the hope that it would lead to greater international stability and a resumed growth of international trade from which Britain would benefit—an objective that led to a higher exchange rate and tighter money than other objectives would have warranted. In two further respects there may be close parallels: first, the overvaluation of the currency in the 1920s was being imposed on an economy that already had structural problems and there must be a question how far it aggravated them; second, it may be asked whether there is not a danger that now, as then, concern with the more visible and easily reversible instrument of policy may distract attention from more fundamental and less tractable problems.

APPENDIX: THE EFFECTS OF REVALUATION ON CURRENT ACCOUNT

D. E. Moggridge (*British Monetary Policy 1924–31*, Cambridge 1975, Appendix 1) has calculated that, if the elasticities of demand for British exports and imports were 1.5 and 0.5 and making allowances for effects on invisibles, the adverse effect on current account would have been 80 millions. But in a footnote he implies that insofar as the demand elasticities "lie to the lower end of the range suggested in the literature . . ." the calculation may understate the adverse effect.

Although his calculation does implicitly make an assumption abut the values of the elasticity of supply it focusses on the two elasticities of demand, a simplification that has been common in the past forty years. Concentration on the two demand elasticities may produce a case that is simple to analyse but it has nothing to be said for it except its pedagogic simplicity. It has sometimes been said that unemployment in the interwar economies justifies the assumption that domestic supply would be infinitely elastic. This is not true. Even if the situation of underemployment could be portrayed as one in which the supply of labour was infinitely elastic it remains a fact that the mines and factories in which labour was employed differed greatly in efficiency because of age and natural endowments. Consequently they had very different levels of price at which they would suspend production. Another factor reducing the elasticity of supply in the important case of textiles was the very high import content of exports. The case that is being considered here, of contraction consequent on revaluation (rather than the more common analysis of the expansionary effects of devaluation), makes manifest the absurdity of assuming that the elasticity of supply was infinite or anything like it.

If we are to have a simplification at all the small country case, in which the overseas elasticities of demand and supply are infinite, is the most natural point to start from. For simplicity we shall reckon changes in old pounds (effectively in terms of gold).

In this case the gold prices of exports would not rise and revenue would fall to the extent that supply was elastic. Between 1924 and 1927 export prices fell by 13% and export volume rose slightly. Even if we make the assumption that prosperity elsewhere would have tended to increase exports by 5% per annum (an assumption that is optimistic given the commodity composition of British exports) the implied elasticity of supply would only be 1.0. In the shorter run it could be much less. If it were 0.5 an appreciation of 10% would reduce revenue by 5% (£40 million).

A simple assumption about invisible services is that, in terms of gold, their earnings would be unchanged. (This may be optimistic in the case of shipping where supply would not be perfectly inelastic. But, given the high capital element and the fact that many costs would be incurred at overseas prices, the elasticity was probably very low.) Earnings from dividends would also be unchanged except for interest payments on debt denominated in sterling which would be increased—giving a positive improvement of 10 millions. (This favourable effect would be much greater if we included the effect on repayment of debt—but that is an item on capital account.)

Among visible imports, there may have been a few sectors where demand was quite elastic but overall elasticity must have been very low for materials not produced in the U.K. and quite low for temperate foodstuffs (the domestic elasticity of demand here reflecting some elasticity of supply by competing British agriculture). Taking Moggridge's 0.5 as the overall average elasticity the adverse change would have been £57 million. The total adverse effect would therefore be of the order of 87 million 1924-pounds i.e. 79 million 1925-pounds. Thus an assumption of infinite elasticity of demand for exports leaves Moggridge's estimate of £80 millions unchanged.

Because of the relative importance of the U.K. in international trade the small country case is clearly inapplicable. Some 50% of world cotton textile exports still originated in the U.K.; and the U.K. was the largest importer of several foodstuffs. (In this connection it should be remembered that the revaluation of the pound pulled the currencies of several important trading partners with it.) To allow for the effects of the size of the British economy, let us suppose the elasticity of demand for visible exports to have been 3 rather than infinity; in which case gold prices would have risen by 1.4% and volume fallen by 4.2% giving a fall in revenue of 2.8% (£22 million). For imports an assumption of an elasticity of supply of 2 rather than infinity would have caused gold price to rise by 2% and quantity to increase by 4%—an increase in gold cost of 6% (£68 million). Allowing for the unchanged £10 million gain on interest the adverse effect is reduced to 80 million 1924-pounds or 72 million 1925-pounds.

(This discussion of the effects of size may take inadequate account of the very great importance of the UK in particular markets. The situation may have been somewhat like that of an oligopoly with Britain occupying the position of price-leader, not through competitive strength but simply because at that time it had the largest share of the market—a situation that would apply for both cotton and coal. It is fair to make this point in considering how far it is reasonable to suppose that the UK might have pursued a policy of a lower exchange rate. On the other hand the commitment to a fixed exchange rate, the variation of which was bound to be seen by the rival oligopolists as a deliberate move, did tie the hands of the "price-leader".)

A pure demand elasticity approach would imply a favourable shift in the terms of trade of the extent of the revaluation, 10%. Moggridge implies a favourable movement of 4%. The calculations here imply a negligible adverse movement of 0.5%. In fact as reported there was virtually no change in the terms of trade at all.

BRITISH MONETARY POLICY AND THE EXCHANGE RATE 1920–1938

By N. H. DIMSDALE

Introduction

IN '*The Economic Consequences of Mr. Churchill*' Keynes (1931) argued that sterling was overvalued by 10% on Britain's return to the gold standard in April 1925. He predicted that an attempt by the authorities to reduce domestic costs and wages to restore British competitiveness would give rise to stagnation and persistent unemployment. In the event Keynes' prediction proved to be correct and his conclusion that the overvaluation of the pound was a major factor contributing to the problems of the British economy in the 1920s has been accepted by the majority of later writers, both economists and economic historians. Keynes' view has been endorsed by Ashworth (1960) Pollard (1962) Johnson (1975) Moggridge (1969) and Friedman and Schwartz (1963).[1] Other writers, such as Morgan (1952) Sayers (1970) and Alford (1972),[2] have doubted whether the return to gold made much difference, and have not regarded it as the principal explanation of Britain's difficulties in the 1920s.

Before considering the return to gold and its consequences, a brief outline will be given of the postwar boom and slump. The behaviour of wages and prices in the depression of the early 1920s is of interest in itself and it also helps to explain why the problems of adjustment to the gold standard in 1925 may have been underestimated in the official discussions which preceded the decision to return. The steps towards gold are then discussed, followed by an account of the working of the restored gold standard and its effects on the economy. Britain's experience with a managed floating exchange rate in the 1930s is then outlined with an assessment of the effects of monetary and exchange rate policy on economic recovery from the depression of 1931–2. The causes of unemployment in interwar Britain are then discussed and the question of possible parallels between the present high value for sterling and British experience in the interwar years is briefly considered.

The postwar boom and slump 1919–1922

The Armistice in November 1918 was followed by several months in which demobilization proceeded and businessmen prepared to take advantage of the opportunities of the postwar world. The boom came in April 1919 and was extremely vigorous. There was a strong demand to rebuild

---

[1] Ashworth (1960) p. 387, Pollard (1962) pp. 220–221, Johnson (1975) p. 110, Moggridge (1972) pp. 1–2, Friedman and Schwartz (1963) p. 41. The last mentioned state that this is the conventional view but do not dissent from it.

[2] Morgan (1952) p. 367, Sayers (1970) p. 93, Alford (1972) p. 37.

stocks at home and abroad. The premature abolition of wartime controls led to sharp price increases in conditions of general scarcity. Fiscal and monetary policy were both lax as a result of wartime financial policies. There was a massive budget deficit in 1918/19 followed by a reduced deficit in 1919/20, as government spending was cut back after the war.[3] The finance of the deficit through heavy reliance on Treasury Bills and Ways and Means Advances from the Bank of England ensured that there was a high degree of liquidity in the banking system.

The cost of maintaining the sterling/dollar exchange, pegged at $4.76 since 1916, became prohibitive. The peg was withdrawn in March 1919 to check the loss of reserves and the unsupported exchange rate fell sharply, reaching a low point of $3.20 in February 1920.[4]

The immediate aims of the Bank of England and the Treasury were to check inflation, currently running at about 20% per annum, and to restore control over the domestic money market. The Cunliffe Committee in its Interim Report of August 1918 had recommended that the budget deficit be reduced, Ways and Means Advances be cut back and the floating debt be reduced by funding.[5] These recommendations were fully endorsed by the Bank of England and the Treasury, as also were the Committee's proposals for the restriction of the note issue.[6] In calling for a progressive reduction in a major component of high-powered money, the Committee was in effect recommending a form of monetary base control (Bank of England 1979).

At this time the most important rate in the money market was the tap rate for Treasury Bills, since the banking system could obtain cash at the tap rate by reducing its holdings of Treasury Bills without having recourse to the Bank of England.[7] As pressures built upon the Bank of England's reserve, the Bank urged the Treasury to raise the tap rate for Treasury Bills. Bank Rate could then be raised in line with the Treasury Bill rate. Bank Rate went up from 5% at which it had been held since April 1917 to 6% in November 1919 and then to 7% in April 1920. The Chancellor of the Exchequer (Austen Chamberlain) initially resisted pressures for higher interest rates because of the conflict with the Coalition government's plans for the finance of postwar housing. In March and April 1920 the banks ran down their holdings of Treasury Bills to increase loans and advances to the private sector. Montagu Norman, now Governor of the Bank of England, convinced the Chancellor that a rise in Bank Rate was essential, if the Treasury Bill issue was to be taken up by the market.[8] This episode was important in substantiating the official fears that the money market might refuse to take up the required volume of Treasury Bills, leaving the residual

[3] Morgan (1952) p. 98 and p. 104.
[4] Howson (1975) p. 11.
[5] Cunliffe Report (1918) and Sayers (1976) Appendixes. Appendix 7.
[6] Sayers (1976) pp. 62–64 and Morgan (1952) pp. 201–2.
[7] Howson (1975) p. 10 for relationship between tap rate for Treasury Bills and Bank Rate, also Morgan (1952) pp. 203–204, Sayers (1976) p. 112.
[8] Ibid p. 113, Howson pp. 18–23, Morgan (1952) pp. 206–206.

requirements for government finance to be met by direct borrowing from Bank of England on Ways and Means Advances. These were objectionable as leading to the creation of additional base money. It served to confirm the Bank's view that a flexible Bank Rate should be restored as the ruling rate of interest in the money market and that the volume of the floating debt should be reduced by funding.

The rise in Bank Rate to 7% in April 1920 came just as the economy reached its cyclical peak. A fall in home demand was followed by a decline in exports. The downturn was attributed by Pigou (1947) to real factors and later writers have accepted his view.[9] Tightening fiscal policy may have acted to retard the upswing but the rise in interest rates came too late to check the boom. The maintenance of Bank Rate at a crisis level for nearly a year must have aggravated the slump. As businessmen revised their price expectations downwards, the real burden of a historically high nominal interest rates increased sharply. As Howson (1973) has shown, Keynes strongly supported the deflating of inflationary expectations and recommended keeping interest rates at a high level for a considerable period.

Despite the severe recession the authorities persisted with a restrictive monetary policy because of their desire to eradicate inflation and to ensure that the Treasury Bill issue was taken up by the money market.[10] Under a flexible exchange rate the Bank Rate was assigned a domestic role in contrast to its traditional function of influencing short term capital movements as under the pre-1914 gold standard. Severe deflation in Britain led to a greater decline in UK than US wholesale prices, which was associated with a recovery of the sterling/dollar exchange rate from its low point of $3.20 in February 1920.

The main features of the contraction from 1920 to 1922 are summarized in Table 1. The fall in prices was steeper than the decline in output, the GDP deflator falling by nearly 25%, compared with a decline of 3.4% in real GDP, although output did decline sharply to 1921 and then recovered. The decline in UK prices reflected the collapse of world commodity prices, which followed the breaking of the postwar boom.[11] Prices in gold linked currencies, such as the US dollar, fell steeply. In Britain the restrictive monetary policy strengthened the exchange rate and ensured that lower prices measured in gold or dollars would be reflected in reduced sterling prices of imports. Import prices fell by 46% between 1920 and 1922 and retail prices by nearly 27%.

While unemployment rose from 2.0% in 1920 to 9.8% in 1922, according to Feinstein's figures, the associated decline in weekly wage rates of 23% was greater than could be explained by the rise in unemployment. Phillips (1958) attributed the difference to the fall in the cost of living. The unusual downward flexibility of money wages may be explained by the practice,

[9] Pigou (1947) p. 188 e.g. Howson (1975) pp. 23–24.
[10] Morgan (1952) p. 209, Howson (1975) pp. 25–27, Sayers (1976) p. 120.
[11] Friedman and Schwartz (1963) pp. 236–7.

TABLE 1
General developments in the British economy 1920–25

Constant prices	Percentage change	
	1920–22	1922–25
1. Gross domestic product	−3.4	+12.7
2. Gross fixed investment	+5.6	+36.7
3. Consumers' Expenditure	−2.7	+7.8
4. Exports of goods and services	+0.4	+12.6
5. Public current expenditure on goods and services	−4.9	−1.7
6. Imports of goods and services	+1.2	+20.8
7. G.D.P. deflator	−24.9	−9.0
8. Weekly wage rates	−23.0	−8.6
9. Real earnings	+2.5	−2.0
10. Unemployment %*	2.0–9.8	10.8–8.6
11. Money stock	−2.6	−6.6
12. Sterling/dollar exchange rate	+20.8	+9.1
13. Terms of trade	+4.8	−9.8
14. Average balance on current account £ million	+223	+108

* Percentage unemployment in beginning and end years: 1920–22 figures are for the working population, 1922–25 figures are for employees.

Sources: 1–10 Feinstein (1972) Tables 6, 5, 61, 65, 57, 58.
       11 Sheppard (1971) Table 3.3.
       12 L.C.E.S. The British Economy: Key Statistics 1900–1970 (nd) Table L.
       13 Feinstein (1972) Table 64.
       14 Sayers (1976) Appendix 32.

started in wartime, of linking wages to the cost of living.[12] When retail prices fell after the boom, the rise in wages in due course went into reverse. There was in addition, as Bevin explained to the Macmillan Committee,[13] a willingness on the part of labour to reconsider wartime methods of working and payment. This attitude may have helped to ease the downward adjustment of wages during the postwar slump but it was the product of exceptional circumstances, which were unlikely to recur in future.

The money supply was reduced by 2.6% between 1920 and 1922, according to Sheppard's (1971) estimates. The decline took place in the public's holdings of currency, that is notes and coin, which fell by 17.5%,[14] compared with a rise in bank deposits of 0.7%. The pressure on currency resulted from the enforcement of the Cunliffe Committee's recommendations on the restriction of the note issue.

Bank Rate was held at 7% until April 1921, when it was reduced to $6\frac{1}{2}$% and then by further downward steps of $\frac{1}{2}$% to 3% in July 1922. These reductions took place as market rates fell away against a background of severe recession.[15] 3% was not by historical standards a low Bank Rate for

[12] Routh (1960) p. 115.
[13] Macmillan Report (1931) Qu 3347 quoted by Sayers (1976) p. 212.
[14] Monthly figures in London Clearing Banks are analyzed in Howson (1975).
[15] Sayers (1976) pp. 124–5.

the lower turning point of the business cycle. It seems likely that the Bank of England did not wish to see further reductions in short-term interest rates in London because of the emergence of an unfavourable interest differential with New York in 1922. The Bank was already considering the conditions required for an appreciation of sterling, which would enable the Cunliffe Committee's recommendation for a return to the pre-1914 parity of $4.86 to be effected.[16] During the recession the Bank of England's control over the money market was increased by the gradual replacement of the tap issue of Treasury Bills by the issue of bills by tender, which started in April 1921. The Bank Rate now became the dominant short-term rate of interest and the Bank of England could vary it to influence short-term capital movements. The Bank regarded this as an essential pre-condition for the restoration of the gold standard. Treasury Bills were a convenient asset in which to carry out open market operations. The Bank of England began to use open market operations in Treasury Bills regularly in this period. Initially it carried out open market purchases of securities to facilitate domestic recovery, while keeping Bank Rate unchanged at 3%.[17]

A major factor weakening the position of the Bank of England compared with 1913 was the deterioration of Britain's short-term capital account, due to the sale of assets during the First World War.[18] This meant that interest rates in London had to be kept at an appropriate level to attract sterling deposits to London. The level of interest rates was now dominated by the rates prevailing in the New York market, which primarily reflected the state of the American economy. Any attempt to raise the sterling/dollar exchange rate to its old parity would, therefore, require close co-operation between British and American central bankers on interest rate policy.[19]

Towards the restoration of the gold standard 1922–1925

The strengthening of the sterling/dollar exchange rate in late 1922 may well have been due to speculation upon an early return to gold.[20] When these expectations were not fulfilled, the exchange fell back from $4.70 in March 1923 to $4.58 in July. In December 1923 the pound averaged $4.36 compared with $4.62 during December of the previous year. At a time when sterling stood within 5 per cent of the old parity, the narrowness of the gap prompted a proposal to ship gold worth £100 million to the United States under the Anglo-American War Debt Agreement.[21] It was intended that the influx of gold into the United States should raise American prices and so strengthen sterling against the dollar. The plan was finally rejected by the

---

[16] Sayers emphasizes the concern of the Bank of England about the exchange rate ibid. pp. 123–4, and see Moggridge (1969) p. 16.

[17] Howson (1976) p. 25 and Morgan (1952) p. 211.

[18] Moggridge (1969) pp. 19–20 and Oppenheimer (1966).

[19] Sayers (1976) pp. 120–22.

[20] Ibid p. 126.

[21] Ibid pp. 126–29 and Moggridge (1969) p. 17.

British authorities as being impractical, since it would have required either an increase in the Fiduciary issue or a breach of the Cunliffe Limit on the issue of Currency Notes to make up for the loss of gold backing for the currency. This was not the last to be heard of this proposal, since in 1925 Keynes was to recommend a release of £60–70 million of gold held against the internal note issue, which he argued, would tend to raise the American price level and so facilitate adjustment of the overvalued pound after the return to gold.[22]

The weakening of sterling in the summer of 1923 was associated with a persistent interest differential in favour of New York. The Bank of England responded by raising Bank Rate from 3% to 4% in July 1923. There was nothing in the state of the domestic economy to justify a rise in interest rates, which was motivated by the Bank's desire to strengthen sterling against the dollar. This increase in Bank Rate is seen by Morgan (1952) as the first step in the Bank's campaign to restore sterling to its pre-war parity.[23] The Treasury opposed the increase because of its adverse effect on the domestic economy, then slowly emerging from the severe recession.[24] Concern about the level of interest rates did not, however, prevent the Treasury from proceeding with its funding policy, which may well have tended to keep up the yield on long-dated securities.

1924 proved to be a more favourable year for the Bank of England than 1923. The Federal Reserve Bank of New York reduced its discount rate from $4\frac{1}{2}$% by stages to $3\frac{1}{2}$% in June, followed by a further reduction to 3% in August.[25] The Bank of England held Bank Rate at 4%, creating an interest differential in favour of London. The reduction in American interest rates was intended to promote domestic expansion and to encourage investment abroad. The volume of U.S. overseas investment expanded, following the acceptance of the Dawes Plan for the settlement of reparations. Borrowers, both long and short-term, were encouraged to switch from London to New York by interest differentials, reinforced by the Bank of England's informal restrictions on British overseas capital issues. The Bank also took steps to hitch up market rates close to Bank Rate to increase the demand for sterling. Thus a variety of factors contributed to the rise in the sterling/dollar exchange rate from $4.27 at the end of January 1924. The return of a Conservative government in the general election at the end of October heightened speculation on an early return to gold and pushed up the exchange rate still further.[26] The restoration of the gold standard was announced by Churchill in his budget speech in April 1925. The announcement was preceded by a rise in Bank Rate to 5% and the negotiation of a

[22] Keynes (1931) p. 266.
[23] Morgan (1952) p. 3.
[24] Howson (1976) p. 28.
[25] Sayers (1976) p. 139, Howson (1976) p. 33.
[26] Ibid p. 56, Clarke (1967) pp. 92–95, Sayers (1976) pp. 139–150 on stages in the return to gold.

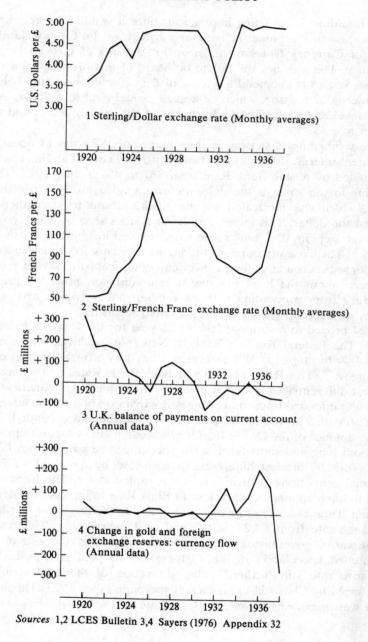

CHART 1. Exchange rates and the UK balance of payments 1920–38

credit from the Federal Reserve Bank of New York to be drawn on only in the event of severe pressure on sterling.[27] [See Chart 1]

Morgan has noted that from 1920 to 1923 the sterling/dollar exchange rate was principally influenced by relative wholesale prices in Britain and the United States.[28] After 1923 relative interest rates and speculative factors were more important. Stolper (1948) came to a similar conclusion on the basis of a comparison of relative retail prices and noted the importance of speculative factors in 1924.

Econometric studies of the behaviour of exchange rates after the First World War by Hodgson (1972) and Thomas (1973) suggest that the movement in relative wholesale prices was the main factor explaining the sterling/dollar exchange rate during this period, although interest differentials were also important. A difficulty with these results is that, while relative prices affected the exchange rate, causation running from the exchange rate to relative UK/US prices cannot be ruled out. This is likely to be so when wholesale prices are being used, since the indices are largely composed of commodities extensively traded on international markets the prices of which in a particular currency vary closely with the exchange rate.[29]

The discussions leading up to the decision to return

The discussions which took place in the Bank of England and the Treasury in 1923 on the proposed shipment of gold to the United States led to further consideration of the strategy to be adopted in returning to gold. The Cunliffe Committee had recommended the amalgamation of Currency Notes and the Fiduciary Issue into a single note issue. In April 1924 the Chamberlain-Bradbury Committee was appointed ostensibly to look into this rather technical monetary question but its real purpose was to consider the timing of the return to gold.[30] This question had to be examined, if only, because of the expiry in 1925 of the embargo imposed in 1920 on gold exports.

The discussions of the Chamberlain-Bradbury Committee have been recounted in detail by Moggridge, largely on the basis of Treasury papers.[31] Sayers has had in addition full access to the Bank of England's records and he has confirmed his substantial agreement with Moggridge's account.[32]

The Committee did not give serious consideration to returning to gold at a lower parity. The questions of the standard and of the parity were virtually inseparable. Devaluation or any form of managed money, as advocated by Keynes in 'A Tract on Monetary Reform' (1923), were regarded as dangerous expedients, discredited by the recent European experience of postwar

---

[27] Ibid p. 143.
[28] Morgan (1952) p. 364.
[29] Keynes (1923) p. 75.
[30] Sayers (1976) p. 137.
[31] Moggridge (1969) pp. 25–68.
[32] Sayers (1976) p. 134.

monetary mismanagement.[33] Not only was the gold standard traditional, it was also, in Bradbury's words, 'Knaveproof'.[34] The most extensively discussed question was not the form of the monetary regime, which was taken for granted, but rather the timing of the return to gold.[35] The behaviour of the exchange rate had an important bearing on this question. As Sayers explains, Norman did not wish to consider restoring the gold standard until the sterling/dollar rate had been held above $4.50 for several months.[36]

The strengthening of sterling against the dollar in the second half of 1924 reflected interest differentials and speculative factors, rather than improved British trade performance.[37] In the official discussions there was a tendency to accept the current level of the exchange rate and to consider only the additional adjustment necessary to raise sterling to $4.86. As the exchange rate appreciated, the amount of additional adjustment in UK prices relative to those in the US appeared to be reduced. A decision for a prompt return to the gold standard became virtually inevitable with the election of a Conservative goernment and the associated speculative appreciation of the sterling/dollar exchange rate. It could then be argued that the task of holding the exchange rate at $4.80, should market expectations be disappointed, would be as great as fixing the parity at $4.86.[38]

The report of the Chamberlain-Bradbury Committee in February 1925 recognised that some further adjustment in British prices relative to those in America would be necessary and put the additional change required for effective restoration of the gold standard at $1\frac{1}{2}\%$. Adjustment might come about either through a decline in British wages and prices or a rise in the American price level. In the final analysis less emphasis was placed on the prospect of a rise in US prices and so adjustment rested on British costs. In view of the flexibility of wages shown in the postwar recession, the relatively small reduction[39] in British costs did not appear to be excessively burdensome.

Churchill was convinced of the case for returning to gold largely on the advice of Sir Otto Niemeyer of the Treasury. Norman's role was subsidiary but he was equally emphatic on the need for a prompt return to gold. His views reflected a belief in gold as a matter of faith and his statements lacked the cogency of Niemeyer's lucid reasoning.[40]

During the discussions which preceded the return to gold considerable attention was given to comparisons of relative prices in Britain and America with the sterling/dollar exchange rate. These showed that in 1924 sterling

---

[33] See Niemeyer's comments on managed money, Moggridge (1969) p. 54, and summary p. 61.

[34] Quoted in Moggridge (1969) p. 61.

[35] Ibid p. 61.

[36] Sayers (1976) p. 136.

[37] Morgan (1952) p. 365, Stolper (1948).

[38] Moggridge (1969) p. 62.

[39] Ibid quotes Lord Brand's views on wage flexibility p. 65.

[40] Sayers (1976) p. 134. Their advice to Churchill is given in Moggridge (1969) pp. 47–50.

TABLE 2

Indices of purchasing power parity for the sterling/dollar exchange rate 1923–25

	1923	1924	1925
1. Sterling exchange as percentage of $4.86	94.0	90.8	99.2
2. Wholesale prices $\frac{US}{UK}$ 1913 = 100	97.0	90.3	99.1
3. Retail prices $\frac{US}{UK}$ July 1914 = 100	93.6	93.7	95.5
4. Implicit G.N.P. deflator $\frac{US}{UK}$ 1913 = 100	87.1	87.3	88.6
5. Implicit deflator consumers' expenditure $\frac{US}{UK}$ 1913 = 100	84.8	83.5	86.0

Sources: 1–3 Moggridge (1972) Table 4.
      2 U.S. Bureau of Labour, U.K. Board of Trade.
      3 U.S. League of Nations, U.K. Ministry of Labour.
4 & 5 U.S. Kendrick (1961) Appendix A.
      U.K. Feinstein (1972) Table 61.

had depreciated by 9.2% since 1913, compared with a rise in British wholesale prices of 10.7% relative to those in the United States.[41] By 1925 both sterling and relative wholesale prices had returned to their 1913 base values, indicating that sterling was not overvalued at its gold standard parity. In 'The Economic Consequences of Mr. Churchill' Keynes argued that a comparison of relative prices should be made using a retail price index, as a more appropriate measure of domestic costs.[42] Wholesale prices indices tend to move together for reasons which have already been noted, although differences in weighting may cause differences between index numbers composed of the same traded goods. In estimating that the return to gold overvalued sterling by 10%, Keynes compared the Ministry of Labour cost of living index with the Massachusetts index of retail prices. Professor Gregory (1926) showed that use of a broader measure of American retail prices, the Bureau of Labour index, did not support Keynes' conclusion.[43] Several indices are compared in Table 2, which is based on Moggridge's measures of purchasing parity for the sterling/dollar exchange rate.[44] Comparisons based on wholesale or export prices suggest that sterling was not overvalued in 1925. The result of comparing retail prices is ambiguous as Professor Gregory pointed out. But broader measures of domestic costs, such as the implicit deflators for GNP and consumers' expenditure suggest that sterling overvaluation was about 11–14% in 1925.

These comparisons do not, however, take account of the changes in economic structure which took place in Britain and the United States

[41] See Table 2.
[42] Keynes (1931) p. 250.
[43] Clay (1929) pp. 69–73.
[44] Moggridge (1969) p. 74.

between 1913 and 1925. The change in costs, technology and tastes was overwhelmingly in favour of the United States. Sterling would have to be considerably undervalued on a purchasing parity basis, if Britain were to be as competitive as in 1913. What was required to maintain British competitiveness was a marked decline in the real exchange rate, defined as the parity adjusted for the movement of relative prices. Purchasing power parity calculations confirm that this change did not take place.

Discussions prior to the return to gold concentrated on Anglo-American comparisons and failed to take account of important European economies, such as France and Germany. An indication of the appreciation of sterling against a basket of competitive currencies after 1920 is given in Table 3. The average exchange rate, defined as the price of sterling in dollars relative to the price of a weighted basket of competitive currencies, rose by 35% from 1921 to 1924, compared with the appreciation of the sterling/dollar rate of 15%.[45] The real exchange rate defined as the average rate adjusted for the movement in relative prices is shown in the same table. It increased by 8% over the same period, rising less than the average exchange rate because of the relative decline in British prices.

Some general indication of the deterioration in Britain's trading position between 1913 and 1924 may be obtained by looking at the contemporary balance of payments statistics, which are admittedly rather rough and ready.[46] Surprisingly little use was made of these data in the discussions which led up to the decision to return to gold.[47] The visible trade balance deteriorated in both nominal and real terms. There was a slight improvement in the balance of invisibles in nominal terms, which was less than the deterioration on visible trade, so that the balance on current account was less favourable in both real and nominal terms. The worsening in the visible balance reflected the decline in world demand for the products on which Britain had specialized before 1913, such as coal, textiles, iron and steel and ships.[48] In 1924 the volume of exports of goods was 24% down on 1913, which was partly offset by a favourable shift in the terms of trade. The balance of invisible earnings was reduced by the loss of ships during the war, while investment income suffered from the sale of private assets in wartime, which also weakened the balance between short-term assets and liabilities.

An important consequence of the change in Britain's balance of payments was that it was no longer able to lend abroad on the same scale as before 1914. The Bank of England was concerned about the tendency for new

[45] The French and Belgian francs, the lira and the yen depreciated against the U.S. dollar, so that the sterling average rate appreciated more than the sterling/dollar rate. The German mark is excluded from the bundle of currencies before 1925. For exchange rates see Svennilson (1954) pp. 318–19 and Morgan (1952) pp. 350–55.

[46] Contemporary and revised estimates of the balance of payments from Sayers (1976) Appendices Appendix 32 and BEQB (1972), (1974). For the change in Britain's balance of payments position, see, Moggridge (1969) pp. 18–23.

[47] Moggridge (1969) p. 65.

[48] Clay (1929) pp. 81–102.

TABLE 3
Sterling exchange rates 1920–31

	Indices 1929 = 100 annual averages				
	1	2	3	4	5
				Sterling average	*Sterling real*
	Sterling/ dollar	*Sterling/ French franc*	*Sterling/ mark*	*exchange rate*	*exchange rate*
1920	75.4	42.3		*66.9*	
1921	79.2	41.8		62.8	94.7
1922	91.1	44.0		68.5	90.8
1923	94.2	61.0		82.1	101.4
1924	90.9	68.7	99.4	84.6	*102.4*
1925	99.4	82.7	100.0	93.5	108.2
1926	100.0	122.9	100.3	102.3	111.1
1927	100.1	99.9	100.0	100.0	104.0
1928	100.2	100.1	100.0	100.0	102.6
1929	100.0	100.0	100.0	100.0	100.0
1930	100.1	99.9	99.9	99.6	98.5
1931	93.3	93.2	93.8	93.7	93.8

Sources and Methods:

1–3 L.C.E.S. Key Statistics 1900–1970 Table L and L.C.E.S. Monthly Bulletin.

4 I. Svennilson (1954) pp. 318–9 and L.C.E.S. Monthly Bulletin. Countries included in average exchange rate are U.S., Germany (from 1925), France, Belgium, Japan, Italy, Canada, Switzerland, Netherlands, India (from 1921) and Sweden. The exchange rates of 11 countries are weighted by shares of world trade in manufactures in 1929 from Maizels (1963) Table 8.1.

5 Data on retail prices from League of Nations Statistical Year-Book (various issues) used to adjust 4.

overseas issues to exceed the positive balance on current account. The excess of long-term lending over the current account surplus implied running down of reserves or increased short term borrowing, either of which would cause a deterioration in the balance of short term assets and liabilities. The Bank responded by keeping short-term interest rates in London at a relatively high level and by applying informal restrictions on the outflow of long-term capital.[49]

The general development of the economy between 1922 and 1925 is shown in Table 1. There was a recovery of GDP from the depths of the depression, associated with a sharp rise in investment and to a lesser extent a recovery of exports. The contribution of exports to recovery was checked from 1924 by the appreciation of the sterling/dollar exchange rate. The limited extent of the recovery is indicated by the slight decline in the unemployment rate from 10.8% in 1922 to 8.6% in 1925. The price level

[49] Sayers (1976) p. 148, Moggridge (1971).

continued to fall and this was associated with a decline in the money stock. Since nominal GDP rose by 3% there was an increase in the income velocity of money. The decline in bank deposits was 7.3% and currency outside the banks fell by 2.7%. The ratio of deposits to reserves remained steady as both bank reserves and deposits declined. The change in the gold and foreign exchange reserves was slight during this period,[50] indicating that there was something approaching a free float of the pound and the money supply was affected mainly by domestic influences.

The restored gold standard and the economy 1925–1931

After Britain's return to gold the US price level did not rise to ease the problem of adjustment as some had expected. In addition British wages showed less flexibility than in the early 1920s, despite the depressed conditions of the economy as indicated by the persistence of historically high levels of unemployment. Even at the cyclical peak of 1929 unemployment stood at 8.0% of total employees, according to Feinstein's estimates, which may be too low, while the unemployment rate among insured employees was 10.4%.

Wage rates, which had declined steeply from 1920 to 1924, became more resistant in the later 1920s.[51] Reductions in wages had been greater in the depressed staple export industries than in the sheltered trades serving the home market. This contrast between the two sectors of the economy is revealed by the breakdown of weekly wage rates by industry in Table 4. The restoration of competitiveness required further wage cuts in the unsheltered industries, which workers were unwilling to accept because of previous concessions. The attempt to reduce labour costs in the coal industry led to the bitter industrial disputes of 1926, as miners sought to prevent further reductions in their real earnings.[52] Those employed in the sheltered trades had fairly constant money wages, which implied an increase in real wages, as the cost of living declined due to the revaluation of sterling and the decline of world commodity prices. Between 1925 and 1929 real earnings rose by 5.8%, while retail prices fell by 7%.

Before 1914 wages had not shown great flexibility apart from those in industries, such as coal and iron, where sliding scales linking wages to product prices were prevalent. Phillips (1958) points out that the average change in wages between 1925 and 1929 could have been closely predicted from his equation estimated from pre-1913 data, and Lipsey (1960) confirms this result. It was the wage flexibility of 1919–23 that was exceptional and not the relative rigidity of 1925–29. A major factor making for greater stability of wages after 1925 was the fixed exchange rate, which was associated with smaller changes in sterling import prices and retail prices

[50] Sayers (1976) Appendix 32.
[51] Routh (1960) p. 120.
[52] Hicks (1932) pp. 174–77.

TABLE 4
Index of weekly wage rates by industry

	1920	1924 = 100 1925	1931
Coal mining	187	98.5	84
Iron and steel	202.5	99	91
Engineering	152	101	103
Shipbuilding	175	106	110
Cotton	162	100	94
Woollen and worsted	147.5	100	89.5
Printing	117	101	101
Furniture	134.5	101	99
Building	145.5	103	97
Gas	140	103	104
Railways	127.5	100.5	95

Source: Mitchell and Dean (1962) p. 351

than the preceding period of the floating pound. A close connection between changes in wages and changes in prices is suggested by Lipsey's wage equation, estimated for the periods 1923–29 and 1948–57. Thus it does not appear that wages were abnormally inflexible under the restored gold standard, although it may be argued that the general availability of unemployment benefits during the interwar period was a factor operating against wage flexibility as also was the greater membership of trade unions.[53]

Developments in other countries did not make the adjustment of the British economy to the gold standard any easier. Unit labour costs continued to decline faster in the United States than in Britain [Table 6]. France and Belgium returned to the gold standard at parities which undervalued their currencies and so aggravated the overvaluation of sterling. The strong revival of the German economy, following closely upon the stabilization of the mark in 1924, meant that Britain had to face increased competition in world markets. The average exchange rate rose from 93.5 in 1925 to 100.0 in 1929, reaching 102.3 in 1926, owing to the sharp depreciation of the French franc prior to stabilization [Table 3].

According to Maddison's indices of export unit values in current dollars there was little change in Britain's export prices relative to those of competing economies between 1925 and 1931 [Table 6]. Maizels' estimates of unit values of world exports of manufactures show that between 1913 and 1929 Britain's export prices of manufactures rose by 13.5% relative to other exporters of manufactured goods [Table 5]. It is not, therefore, surprising that Britain's share of world trade in manufactures declined from 30.2% in 1913 to 23.0% in 1929. Maizels suggests that lack of competitiveness was a

[53] Clay (1929) p. 155.

TABLE 5
*Unit values of world exports of manufactures in 1929 and 1937 and U.K.
shares of world trade in manufactures*

	1913 = 100 1929	1929 = 100 1937	
U.K.	151	90	
Belgium	122	96	U.K. share of
France	128	96	world trade in
Germany	136	116	Manufactures
Italy	111	66	1913 30.2*
Netherlands		93	1929 23.0*
Sweden	147	81	1929 22.4
Switzerland	148	102	1937 20.9
Canada	136	84	
U.S.	120	93	* excluding the
Japan	144	55	Netherlands
India	141	63	
Total manufactures	133	94	

Source: Maizels (1963) Appendix B and Table 8.1.

major factor contributing to Britain's loss of market share.[54] Little progress seems to have been made in remedying this problem under the restored gold standard.

A comparison based on the average exchange rate of competing economies adjusted for the movement of relative retail prices suggests that there may have been a decline in the British real exchange rate between 1925 and 1931. This indicates that there was some relative improvement in domestic costs in this period, due to the faster rate of decline of retail prices in the UK than in competing economies [Table 3]. But it may have led to higher real incomes in Britain rather than greater competitiveness in world markets.

Keynes' argument that the overvaluation of sterling on the return to gold would result in economic stagnation was forcefully restated by H. G. Johnson (1975):

"Had the exchange value of the pound been fixed realistically in the 1920's a prescription fully in accord with orthodox economic theory—there would have been no need for mass unemployment. With reasonably full employment in the 1920s, moreover, the economic adjustment to industrial obsolescence would probably have been easier and more effective".[55] Friedman and Schwartz expressed a similar view, emphasizing the deflationary effects of policies intended to bring about adjustment rather than the

[54] Maizels (1963) Table 8.14.
[55] Johnson (1975) p. 110.

TABLE 6
Measures of competitiveness and the terms of trade 1920–1931
1929 = 100

	1 UK relative export unit values	2 UK	3 US	4 Germany	5 Terms of trade
		Unit labour costs in current dollars			
1920					105
1921	127				118
1922	115				110
1923	104				107
1924	98	97	117		102
1925	102	105	111	89	99
1926	103	105	108	91	103
1927	101	102	106	90	101
1928	100	102	103	95	100
1929	100	100	100	100	100
1930	104	97	97	101	109
1931	106	89	87	96	120

Sources:

1 Export unit values in current dollars from Maddison (1962) for UK, France, Germany, Italy, Netherlands, Sweden, Switzerland, US, and Canada, and Belgium from 1925. Weighted by shares of world trade in manufactures in 1929 from Maizels (1963) Table 8.1.

2–4 Unit Labour costs for UK, US and Germany from Phelps Brown (1968) Appendix 3, converted to current dollars for UK and Germany using exchange rates from Svennilson (1954).

5 Feinstein (1972) Table 64 UK export prices/import prices as percentage.

contractionary effect of the overvaluation on the volume of exports and import substitutes (1963):

"The prewar parity overvalued the pound by some 10% or so at the price level that prevailed in 1925 at the time of resumption ... hence the successful return to gold at the prewar parity required a further 10% deflation of domestic prices; the attempt to achieve such further deflation produced instead stagnation and unemployment, from which Britain was unable to recover until it finally devalued the pound in 1931".[56]

Youngson (1960) has argued that "Keynes greatly exaggerated the ill-effect upon industry of those measures of credit restriction which a return to gold would probably require—the difficulties of British industry in the later 1920s were not caused by the gold standard".[57] Sayers (1970) has doubted "whether a choice of 4.40 as the 1925 parity would have made much

---

[56] Friedman and Schwartz (1963) p. 41.
[57] Youngson (1960) p. 234.

difference in any but the very short run".[58] Morgan (1952) has emphasized the deterioration of London's international position as the main source of weakness of the restored gold standard rather than the minor difference between British and American prices in 1925.[59]

An attempt has been made by Moggridge (1969) to quantify the effects of an exchange rate 10% lower than $4.86 in a typical year of the restored gold standard, which he takes to be 1928.[60] He assumes a foreign price elasticity of demand for British exports of goods of −1.5 and a sterling price elasticity of demand for imports of goods of −0.5. Export prices in foreign currency are assumed to fall by only 6% to allow for the import content of exports and for an increase in profit margins. Similarly the rise in the sterling price of imports is only 9% to allow for a decrease in profit margins. The outcome is that the balance of visible trade improves by £52 million, while the invisible balance for which separate assumptions are made rises by £15m. The current balance improves by £70 million with unchanged income. Assuming a marginal propensity to import of 0.3, Moggridge argues that the authorities could have used the strengthened current balance to reduce unemployment from 8.2% to 4.7%, which is the putative full employment level.

It may be that the elasticity of demand for exports assumed by Moggridge is too large. Thomas (1975) estimates the price elasticity of demand for exports of goods and services to have been −0.5, which is similar to the price elasticity of demand he obtains for imports of goods and services. On these assumptions for the elasticities and assuming that a 10% change in the exchange rate would alter export and import prices by 6% and 9% respectively, the net effect is a rise in exports and reduction in imports of £70 million at 1938 prices. Thomas obtains an estimate for the multiplier of 1.4. This would imply that GDP might have risen by £100 million or 2.4% after several years. In 1928 average GDP per employee at 1938 factor cost was £220.6, so that employment would have risen by 450 thousand reducing unemployment from 8.2% to 5.8% after 4 to 5 years.[61] These effects are not very impressive, particularly when due allowance is made for the questionable steps in the argument, including the assumption of infinite supply elasticities and no reaction of wages to the increased price level following devaluation. Nevertheless there seems little reason to dispute Moggridge's view that, while the choice of a lower exchange rate in 1925 would not have solved all the problems of British industry, it would have eased the transition to a more modern industrial structure.[62] The fact that such changes took place more easily in the 1930s, when sterling had depreciated, suggests that overvaluation may have been a significant handicap in the 1920s.

[58] Sayers (1970) p. 93.
[59] Morgan (1952) p. 367.
[60] Moggridge (1969) pp. 94–96.
[61] Feinstein (1972) Tables 5 and 58.
[62] Moggridge (1969) p. 79.

TABLE 7
General developments in the British economy 1925–31

Constant prices	Percentage change 1925–29	Percentage change 1929–31
1. Gross domestic product	+8.5	−5.8
2. Gross fixed investment	+12.4	−1.5
3. Consumers' expenditure	+7.3	+2.6
4. Exports of goods and services	+7.3	−30.6
5. Public current expenditure on goods and services	+6.5	+5.0
6. Imports of goods and services	+7.6	+2.4
7. G.D.P. Deflator	−5.1	−2.8
8. Weekly wage rates	−2.8	−1.7
9. Real earnings	+5.8	+7.6
10. Unemployment %*	8.6–8.0	8.0–16.4
11. Money stock	+4.7	−0.4
12. Sterling/dollar exchange rate	+0.6	−6.7
13. Terms of trade	+0.8	+20.0
14. Average balance on current account £ million	+50	−8

* Percentage unemployment among employees in first and last years.
Sources: As for Table 1.

The general developments in the economy from 1925 to 1931 are summarized in Table 7. There was moderate growth from 1925 to 1929, followed by a sharp contraction from 1929 to 1931, as the world recession struck the economy. The growth of output was constrained by the expansion of exports, which was limited by both inappropriate composition and lack of competitiveness. In 1929 exports were still only 81% of their volume in 1913 and by 1931 they had slumped to 51% of the immediate prewar level. Consumers' expenditure was maintained by the rise in real earnings of those still in employment. Real wages continued to rise in the recession because of the favourable shift in the terms of trade, as the price of primary products declined. Since 40% of British exports went to primary producing countries, the decline in their incomes was an important factor limiting the volume of UK exports.[63] The unemployment rate followed the course of GDP, declining slightly from 1925 to 1929 and then shooting up from 1929 to 1931 as the recession deepened.

Bank of England policy and the gold standard 1925–31

The response of the Bank of England to the problem of the overvaluation of sterling was not to pursue a policy of thorough-going deflation to bring about an adjustment in domestic costs. The Bank sought rather to use the instruments available to it to maintain the exchange rate on a day-to-day basis.[64] The gold standard in practice proved to be much more difficult to

[63] Maizels (1963) p. 231.
[64] Sayers (1976) p. 213.

manage than the simple automatic mechanism postulated by the Cunliffe Committee.

The Bank of England's policy of clinging to gold entailed keeping short-term interest rates at a high level by historical standards. The burden of nominal interest rates was increased by the downward movement of prices throughout the 1920s. The Bank's behaviour combined with the Treasury's policy of funding the National Debt made the overall impact of monetary policy and debt management more deflationary than the authorities may have intended.[65]

Following the return to gold in April 1925 there was an inflow of funds and the Bank of England reduced Bank Rate in two steps to 4% in October. As pressures on the reserves developed towards the end of the year, the Rate went up to 5% in December. The Treasury protested vigorously about the rise in short-term interest rates and the Bank of England responded by abandoning its flexible interest rate policy. Bank Rate was unchanged from December 1925 to April 1927, when there was a reduction of $\frac{1}{2}$%. It remained at this level until February 1929, when the rise in U.S. interest rates forced the Bank to make an increase to $5\frac{1}{2}$%.

The Bank needed to develop new techniques for dealing with a situation in which its freedom to vary Bank Rate was restricted. In 1926 it started to accumulate a private reserve of US dollars which were included under 'Other Securities' held by the Banking Department and did not appear as part of the reserves.[66] By accumulating foreign exchange the published figures of the reserves could be cushioned against the movement of short-term funds.[67] Stability in the Bank Rate could be underpinned by smoothing of the published figures. During the approach to gold in 1924 the Bank had kept up pressure on the money market to maintain a narrow margin between market rates and the Bank Rate. This technique proved useful under the restored gold standard, since market rates had a direct influence on the movement of international short-term funds. By tightening market rates capital inflows could be encouraged, while Bank Rate and associated bank lending rates remained unchanged.[68] In this way the Bank sought to protect British industry against fluctuations in short-term interest rates. In addition the Bank revived the pre-1914 practice of influencing gold movements through small variations in the price of gold as an alternative to changes in Bank Rate. It made extensive use of gold devices as its reserve position weakened after 1928.[69]

The real weakness of the restored gold standard was exposed by the rise in US interest rates in the second half of 1928. Speculation in New York led to an upsurge in the rates for call loans which the Federal Reserve was

[65] Howson (1979) p. 33.
[66] Sayers (1976) pp. 216–7.
[67] Moggridge (1971) p. 161 and pp. 171–193.
[68] Sayers (1976) p. 219.
[69] Ibid p. 221 and 225. Moggridge (1971) pp. 171–76.

powerless to prevent. In due course discount rates were raised in New York, putting pressure on the Bank of England, which raised Bank Rate to $5\frac{1}{2}\%$ in February 1929 because of the continuing loss of reserves. A further increase to $6\frac{1}{2}\%$ took place in September, following the Hatry failure. The Bank of England used this event as a domestic pretext to justify a rise in Bank Rate, which was motivated by external factors.[70] The Wall Street crash in October 1929 enabled Bank Rate to be reduced as short-term interest rates came tumbling down in America. Bank Rate was reduced from $6\frac{1}{2}\%$ by steps to 3% in May 1930, following the decline in New York interest rates. The reductions were part of a concerted move by European central bankers to ease monetary conditions, but the need to remain on gold limited the scope for further cuts in UK short-term interest rates.[71] As the forces making for world depression gathered strength, Bank Rate was reduced to $2\frac{1}{2}\%$ in May 1931. This was the same month as the failure of the Credit Anstalt, which set off the international financial crisis, culminating in the run on the pound and the suspension of the gold standard in September 1931.

A major factor contributing to the pressure on sterling was the growing recognition that British costs had not adjusted in the way that the proponents of the return to gold had expected.[72] The world depression reduced the demand for British exports and caused a deterioration in the current account of the balance of payments despite the favourable shift in the terms of trade. Outside observers might call for a reduction in British labour costs but experience since 1925 indicated that there would be considerable difficulty in bringing about a general reduction in money wages. The impact of the decline in economic activity on tax receipts in addition to increased expenditure on unemployment benefits created the prospect of a Budget deficit. In addition the Macmillan Committee revealed the precarious state of London's short-term capital account.[73] These influences contributed to the final speculative attack on sterling which forced the Bank of England to suspend the gold standard.[74]

The money supply and the domestic effects of monetary policy 1925–1931

Under the gold standard international movements of gold and foreign exchange affect the balances held by the commercial banks at the Bank of England. The Bank tended in practice to offset the expansionary effect of an inflow of funds by open market sales of securities. When the gold reserves declined, the Bank undertook open market purchases to cushion the reserves of the commercial banks. The offsetting of the effects of gold flows on the banks' reserves at the Bank of England was less complete for outflows

[70] Sayers (1976) pp. 223–229.
[71] Ibid pp. 231–34.
[72] e.g. Macmillan Report (1931) paras 242–257 and Addendum 1.
[73] Macmillan Report paras 347–352 and Appendix 1.
[74] For an account of the crisis see Sayers (1976) pp. 389–415 and for the factors underlying it, Oppenheimer (1966).

than for inflows.[75] After 1928 the stance of the Bank became more deflationary, so that gold losses were reinforced by sales of securities.[76]

The Bank of England regulated the volume of bankers' balances mainly by open market operations in Treasury Bills. The amount of open market sales which the Bank could undertake depended upon the availability of suitable securities in the portfolio of the Banking Department. Holdings of Treasury Bills were restricted by the need to maintain a sufficient quantity of long-dated securities to provide for the Bank's income requirements. This limit on the size of the holding of Treasury Bills restricted the Bank of England's ability to carry out open market operations. The situation was improved by the amalgamation of the Fiduciary and Currency Note issues in 1928 as recommended by the Cunliffe Committee. The Issue Department took over securities formerly held by the Treasury's Currency Note Redemption Account and so increased the size of the portfolio with which the Bank could operate in the market.[77]

While the Bank of England acted on the volume of bankers' balances, which with the addition of till money made up their reserves, the commercial banks adjusted their deposits in accordance with their desired ratio of deposits to reserves. This ratio was not uniform among banks and was not constant over time. For the London Clearing Banks the quarterly average deposit/reserve ratio rose from 8.4 in 1925 to 9.7 in 1931,[78] which was largely the result of a reduction in the reserve ratio of the Midland Bank and to a lesser extent of Barclay's.[79] In addition banks could conceal their true reserve position by 'window dressing' their balance sheets.[80] They made use of this freedom to reduce their true reserves in relation to their deposits. The result of the banks' behaviour was greater economy in the use of reserves which enabled the volume of deposits and the money supply to rise by 6.3% and 4.2% respectively between 1925 and 1931, according to Sheppard's estimates. During the same period published reserves for all UK banks fell by 11% and the increase in deposits was made possible by a rise in the deposit/reserve ratio from 10.1 in 1925 to 12.1 in 1931.[81]

The money supply grew broadly in line with nominal GDP and there was, if anything, a slight decline in the income velocity of money during the gold standard period, if 1931 is compared with 1925 [see Table 8]. There was, therefore, no marked downward pressure on the money stock after 1925 in contrast to the decline of 9.7% between 1921 and 1925.

The behaviour of the commercial banks could be interpreted as a deliberate thwarting of the Bank of England's intentions in view of the decline of bankers' balances at the central bank. It must, however, be remembered

[75] Sayers (1976) p. 312 Howson (1975) p. 36, Moggridge (1972) p. 151.
[76] Moggridge (1972) p. 153 and pp. 151–185 see also Sayers (1976) p. 313.
[77] Sayers (1976) pp. 306–8.
[78] Howson (1975) Appendix 1.
[79] Moggridge (1971) p. 154 and Balogh (1947) p. 47.
[80] Balogh pp. 45–56, Goodwin (1941), Howson (1975) 45–7.
[81] Sheppard (1971) Table 3.3.

TABLE 8
Money supply, velocity and interest rates 1920–1931

	£ million		$3 = \frac{2}{1}$	Yield % annual averages			
	1	2	3	4	5	6	7
			Income			Yield	Fed. Reserve
	Net	GDP at	velocity		Treasury	on	Bank of N.Y.
	money	current	of	Bank	Bill	$2\frac{1}{2}\%$	discount
	supply	prices	circulation	Rate	rate	Consols	rate
1920	2,748	5,982	2.18	6.72	6.21	5.32	6.50
1921	2,768	5.134	1.85	6.12	4.58	5.21	5.75
1922	2,676	4,579	1.71	3.69	2.57	4.43	4.25
1923	2,562	4,385	1.71	3.49	2.62	4.31	4.25
1924	2,520	4,419	1.75	4.00	3.39	4.39	3.75
1925	2,500	4,644	1.86	4.55	4.09	4.43	3.25
1926	2,509	4,396	1.75	5.00	4.51	4.55	3.75
1927	2,546	4,613	1.81	4.65	4.25	4.56	3.75
1928	2,601	4,659	1.79	4.50	4.15	4.48	4.25
1929	2,617	4,727	1.81	5.50	5.26	4.60	5.25
1930	2,639	4,685	1.78	3.42	2.48	4.48	3.25
1931	2,606	4,359	1.67	3.93	3.59	4.40	2.25

Sources:
1 Sheppard (1971) Table 3.3.
2 Feinstein (1972) Table 3.
4–6 Sheppard (1971) Table A (3–7).
7 L.C.E.S. The British economy key statistics Table O.

that the Bank of England did not accept a crude multiplier theory of the determination of bank deposits.[82] It did not expect to observe a simple relationship between the reserves of the commercial banks and their deposits, if only because of differing reserve practices among banks. In his evidence to the Macmillan Committee Harvey, the Deputy Governor, disagreed with the view advanced by Keynes and McKenna that the deposit/reserve ratio could be taken as fixed and used as a fulcrum for monetary control by the central bank.[83]

The Bank of England used Bank Rate as a means of remaining on gold by keeping short-term rates in London in line with those in other financial centres, in particular New York. When its freedom to vary Bank Rate was restricted because of Treasury objections, the Bank resorted to other devices to attract funds to London. It did not attempt to bring about an adjustment of domestic costs by deflation. In so far as its policy towards the reserves of the commercial banks was deflationary, the effect on the money supply was offset by the actions of the banks in raising the overall deposit/reserve ratio.

When questioned by the Macmillan Committee, Norman was unwilling to

[82] Sayers (1976) pp. 310–11.
[83] Macmillan Report (1931) paras 420–29.

admit that a rise in Bank Rate would cause unemployment. He was eventually driven to accept the connection by Keynes' persistent questioning.[84] The Treasury recognized that the level of short-term interest rates could affect the domestic economy, as shown by their repeated objections to increases in Bank Rate from 1923 onwards. The Treasury were, however, less concerned about the effect of their funding policy in keeping long-term interest rates high. This aspect of policy has been emphasized by Howson (1975).[85]

The maintenance of historically high short-term interest rates throughout the period 1925 to 1931 combined with the Treasury's funding policy kept interest rates at a level which may well have discouraged domestic investment.[86] Private housing is the sector which is most likely to have been sensitive to interest rates.[87] Industrial borrowing may also have been discouraged by the cost of raising debentures, but it seems likely that excess capacity was a greater deterrent to industrial investment than the cost of finance. One factor which may have discouraged investment was the burdening of industry with the high cost of debentures issued during the postwar boom. These could not be refinanced at a lower cost so long as interest remained at a high level. The attractive yields available on gilt-edged encouraged firms with funds to spare to avoid the risks of fixed investment by holding government securities. Industry also suffered from an institutional characteristic of the London capital market to favour overseas investment at the expense of home industrial issues and, in particular, the finance of small companies.[88] The tendency for overseas lending to exceed the current account surplus was, of course, a major influence keeping up short-term rates and limiting the Bank of England's scope for manoeuvre. There was a boom in home issues in the late 1920s but it was cut short following the increases in Bank Rate in 1929.[89] To conclude, the level of interest rates combined with the downward trend in prices seems likely to have discouraged investment in the 1920s.

The main depressing influence on the economy was the low level of demand for Britain's staple export industries. Their problems were not created by the restoration of the gold standard but they were aggravated by it. A devaluation of 10% would have reduced unemployment slightly and might have improved the balance of payments, but it is doubtful if it would have led to a general economic recovery. The monetary policy followed by the Bank of England after the return to gold was not sufficiently vigorous to bring about the internal adjustment required to correct the overvaluation. Had such an adjustment been attempted by more severe deflation, it is

[84] Macmillan Committee (1931) Evidence Q.3577–3402 and Q.3490–3.
[85] Howson (1975) pp. 36–43.
[86] For domestic impact of interest rates ibid pp. 50–54.
[87] Grant (1937) concedes this possibility p. 96–97.
[88] Macmillan Report paras 383–404.
[89] Sayers (1976) p. 224, Howson (1976) p. 52.

doubtful whether it would have been successful, because of the limited flexibility of money wages. The British economy was, therefore, stuck with unemployed resources and was partly bypassed by the boom of 1925–29, enjoyed by the United States and other industrial economies.

The floating pound and exchange management 1932–38[90]

When Britain left the gold standard in September 1931, the pound floated downwards. The Bank of England's reserves had been so depleted in the defence of sterling that pegging of the exchange rate could not be contemplated. When the pound showed signs of strengthening because of foreign expectations of a possible return to the old parity, the Bank of England intervened to push the exchange rate down and to build up its reserves.[91] Sterling remained weak during November and December because trade volumes had not yet adjusted to the depreciation and there was abnormal purchasing of imports in anticipation of the introduction of a general tariff by the National Government. The sterling/dollar exchange reached a low point of $3.24 in December and remained at $3.40–3.45 during January and February 1932. The Bank took advantage of any strength in the market to add to its reserves and to accumulate funds to repay the French and American credits used up in the defence of the pound during September.[92]

In February and March 1932 there was a major swing of opinion in favour of sterling. Confidence revived with the repayment of the credits and foreign funds flowed in on a large scale, partly because of the level of UK interest rates. Bank Rate had been raised to 6% on the departure from gold and was reduced to 5% in February, followed by a further reduction to $3\frac{1}{2}$% in March. These reductions in short-term interest rates did not discourage the inward movement of funds and in April the Bank of England let the sterling/dollar exchange rate rise to $3.75.[93]

The Bank of England and the Treasury gave much thought to exchange rate policy following the suspension of the gold standard.[94] The Treasury considered the advantages of a high rate of $3.90 against those of a low rate of $3.40. The case for a low rate was accepted because of the need to give British exporters a strong competitive position. In addition a low exchange rate was a way of promoting economic recovery from the depression through raising wholesale prices. It was recognised that too low an exchange rate might be offset by increases in money wages as workers sought compensation for higher import prices. The Bank of England emphasized that intervention in the foreign exchange market could only smooth out day-to-day fluctuations in the exchange rate without influencing the underlying trend. The Bank was less concerned than the Treasury to keep the exchange

[90] See BEQB (1968) Drayson (1976) Howson (1976) and Howson (1980).
[91] Sayers (1976) pp. 419–20.
[92] ibid pp. 422–3.
[93] ibid pp. 424–5 Howson (1975) pp. 86–88.
[94] Sayers (1976) pp. 418–9 and 426, Howson (1975) pp. 82–86 and Drayson (1976).

rate down and was prepared to let the rate rise when the demand for sterling was strong, as in March 1932.

The Exchange Equalisation Account (EEA) was devised by the Treasury as a means of overcoming the problem of the inability of the Bank of England to prevent the exchange rate from rising as foreigners bought sterling. The account was to purchase foreign exchange with sterling obtained from the release of Treasury Bills, when funds were flowing inwards and to sell foreign exchange for sterling, investing the proceeds in Treasury Bills when funds were flowing out.[95] The Treasury saw the former situation as being more likely than the latter and regarded the EEA as a way of keeping sterling down.[96] The day-to-day management of the account was to be conducted by the Bank of England with the direction of policy being determined by the Treasury. The EEA did not come into operation officially until July 1932. Until then the inflow of funds had to be handled mainly by the Bank of England.

The Bank did not attempt to offset fully the expansionary effect on the domestic money supply of its purchases of foreign exchange in the first half of 1932. There was a sharp rise in bankers' balances, which led to a reduction of interest rates in the money market. The volume of bank deposits rose and Bank Rate was brought down to 2% at the end of June. In this manner the way was prepared for the massive conversion of 5% War Loan to a $3\frac{1}{2}$% basis. The decline in British interest rates led to a weakening in sterling, so that the EEA came into operation at a time when the pound needed support on the foreign exchange market. The account initially intervened in support of sterling but then withdrew as selling pressures increased, intervening again at a lower level. Sterling fell to a low point of $3.14 at the end of November and then recovered, while the EEA intervened to stop the rate rising too sharply.[97] This episode served to convince the authorities that stabilization of the exchange rate was not a practical policy because of the massive intervention which would be required to offset movements of private short-term capital. The decline in sterling in November did not lead to suggestions from the Bank of England that Bank Rate should be increased, such was the importance attached to cheap money in the Treasury's economic strategy. The ability of the EEA to intervene in the foreign exchange market was increased by transferring some of its gold holdings to the Issue Department of the Bank of England and by increasing its powers of borrowing in May 1933.[98]

So far the account had been operating on the sterling/dollar exchange to cushion fluctuations in the rate. Following the American decision to prohibit gold exports in March 1933, the account switched its operations to the

---

[95] BEQB (1968), L. Waight (1938) Chapters 5–7 Sayers (1976) pp. 427–30 Howson (1975) p. 87.
[96] Howson (1980) Part I.
[97] Sayers (1976) pp. 452–3 Howson (1980) Part II.
[98] Sayers (1976) p. 456, Howson (1980) Part II.

sterling/franc exchange and at times to the London gold market. Sterling was loosely pegged to the French franc at Fr 88, equivalent to a pre-devaluation rate for the dollar of $3.50. Since President Roosevelt had been empowered by Congress to issue paper money and to devalue the dollar by up to 50%, the dollar weakened on the foreign exchange market and the sterling/dollar exchange rate rose towards $4.86.[99] The British authorities did not wish to follow the dollar downwards, since such action might have provoked competitive depreciation by the United States. They also wanted to support the franc which was overvalued in terms of both sterling and the dollar. Sterling was, therefore, poised uneasily between an undervalued dollar and the overvalued exchange rates of France and other European currencies linked to gold. The EEA lacked the foreign exchange resources to peg the sterling/franc rate, which drifted under the influence of market forces. It sought merely to smooth exchange fluctuations by adding to its reserves when sterling was strong and selling foreign exchange when sterling was weak.[100]

In January 1934 the price of gold was fixed in the US at $35 per oz. implying stabilization of the dollar against the gold based currencies. At a sterling/franc rate of 77 the equivalent sterling/dollar rate was $5.10. The uneasy relationship between the leading currencies continued until the Tripartite Agreement of September 1936, which provided for the orderly devaluation of the franc. The Agreement did not provide for currency stabilization on British insistence. The Treasury feared that a pegged exchange rate would lead to a more restrictive stance being adopted by the Bank of England, which would be inconsistent with maintaining Bank Rate at 2%.

The weakness of the franc persisted after its devaluation in 1936 and was associated with a continuing outflow of gold to Britain and the United States. World gold production was responding to the rise in the price of gold and there were fears of a gold glut. The inflow of gold into the EEA reduced its sterling resources, which were increased by legislation in July 1937.[101] The growth in the reserves eased the problems of the day-to-day management of sterling and led to a suggestion from the Bank of England in 1936 that the exchange rate be allowed to rise, which the Treasury rejected. Meanwhile the current account moved into deficit after 1935, because of vigour of the domestic revival from the depression. In each of the three following years there was a deficit on current account of about £50 million, but the reserves rose from £493 million at the end of 1935 to £825 millon at the end of 1937 because of the continuing gold inflow.

The situation changed as a result of the persistent decline of the franc, leading to its stabilization at a low level in May 1938. Sterling now looked overvalued in relation to both the dollar and the franc. Its weakness was

[99] Sayers (1976) p. 458 and pp. 464–68.
[100] Sayers (1976) p. 467.
[101] Ibid p. 471 and pp. 483–85.

confirmed when an outflow of funds began in May 1938 and continued during the Munich crisis.[102] As the fears of impending war mounted, it appeared to the British authorities that no change in the exchange rate would check the outflow of funds from Britain to the United States. The EEA let the sterling/dollar rate decline to $4.62 at the end of November and intervened in the forward market to protect the pound. Sterling was allowed to depreciate, provided it did not provoke criticism and possible retaliation from other countries, in particular the United States. The defence of the pound led to a fall in the reserves of £268 million in 1938 so that much of the gain of the previous three years was reversed. As a result the gold holdings of the EEA became depleted, and £350 million of gold was transferred to it from the Issue Department of the Bank of England in January 1939, so concentrating the country's reserves under Treasury Control and removing the statutory link between gold and the note issue.[103] The account was then able to hold the pound at $4.68 until August 1939, despite the heavy cost in reserves.

This brief account of exchange rate management after the suspension of the gold standard confirms that there was extensive intervention by the British authorities in the foreign exchange market. The large changes in reserves from year to year confirm that the float was far from being clean. As Howson (1980) has pointed out, the intervention was mainly the outcome of a policy of 'leaning into the wind' and of not resisting strong trends in the market. It appears, however, that in some years, such as 1932 and 1936, intervention went beyond the smoothing of market fluctuations and that a deliberate attempt was made to prevent the appreciation of sterling. Similarly, in the second half of 1938 and in 1939 the authorities intervened to support the sterling/dollar exchange as funds moved to the United States. There were smaller changes in the reserves in the years before 1935 than in those that followed, which is to be explained by the greater volatility of short-term capital in the later period rather than by a conscious attempt of the authorities to exercise greater control over the exchange rate. [see Chart 1 Page 312].

Competitiveness and the balance of payments 1932–1938

The wide fluctuation in exchange rates during the 1930s suggests that some form of weighted average exchange rate would be a better indicator of the behaviour of sterling than a single rate, such as the sterling/dollar rate. A measure of the average exchange rate of sterling against the currencies of competing industrial economies is given in Table 9.

Because of the weighting of currencies by shares of world trade in manufactures, a large weight is attached to European economies. The average exchange rate for sterling lies between the European currencies,

[102] Ibid pp. 562–67.
[103] Ibid pp. 488–90.

TABLE 9
Sterling exchange rates 1931–38

| | Indices 1929 = 100 annual averages | | | | | 1929–30 = 100 |
| | 1 | 2 | 3 | 4 | 5 | 6 |
	Sterling/ dollar	Sterling/ French franc	Sterling/ mark	Sterling average exchange rate	Sterling real exchange rate	Sterling effective exchange rate
1931	93.3	93.2	93.8	93.7	94.2	100.1
1932	72.1	71.9	72.3	75.2	81.4	86.7
1933	86.8	68.2	68.5	77.0	82.8	91.3
1934	103.8	62.0	62.7	75.4	81.7	95.9
1935	100.9	59.9	59.7	74.5	81.8	95.4
1936	102.3	66.9	60.4	77.7	86.1	97.5
1937	101.8	100.5	60.2	84.7	91.9	100.8
1938	100.7	137.6	59.7	86.9	91.8	105.1

Sources:
1–5 As for Table 3.
6 Redmond (1980) appendix composite index.

such as the French franc and the German mark, on one side and the sterling/dollar rate on the other. The average rate falls to a low point of 75 in 1935 (1929 = 100) and then rises to 87 in 1938. Redmond (1980) has calculated an effective exchange rate for sterling against a basket of 28 currencies, weighted by shares in bilateral and multilateral trade. The effective exchange rate includes the currencies of countries exporting mainly primary products, whereas the average rate is strongly orientated towards trade in manufactured goods. It lies closer to the sterling/dollar rate than the average exchange rate, which is strongly influenced by European currencies.

The question to be considered is whether the depreciation of the pound in the 1930s increased Britain's competitiveness. The real exchange rate, shown in Table 9, is the average exchange rate adjusted for the movement of retail prices in Britain relative to those in competing economies. The tentative index declines to 81 in 1932 with 1929 = 100 and then rises to 92 by 1938. U.K. relative export prices in current dollars are shown in Table 10. Relative export prices declined by 14% between 1931 and 1932, but by 1937 the improvement in competitiveness had been eroded. According to Maizels' index of unit values of exports of manufactures,[35] shown in Table 5, British export prices of manufactures fell by 10% between 1929 and 1937 compared with a decline of 6% in the prices of all major exporters. The pattern of price movements measured in current dollars varies among countries because of the wide fluctuations in exchange rates. UK competitiveness increased against Germany and Switzerland and to a lesser extent against Belgium and France. There was little change against the United

States but British manufactures became less competitive against those of
India and Japan.

Unit labour costs in current dollars are compared for Britain, the U.S. and
Germany in Table 10. Britain's advantage obtained in 1932 was offset by
the depreciation of the dollar in 1933–34, but after 1934 unit labour costs
rose faster in the US. Britain retained its advantage over Germany in unit
labour costs throughout the period following the departure from the gold
standard, because of the high valuation of the mark against sterling.

The measures of competitiveness which have been discussed give differing
results but all suggest that British exports became more competitive in 1932,
although they differ on the extent to which this advantage was retained in
subsequent years. The increase in competitiveness is reflected in the improvement in Britain's trade performance in the 1930s. According to
Maizels' estimates, the UK's share of world trade declined from 22.4% in
1929 to 20.9% in 1937, which is a considerable improvement on the
experience between 1913 and 1929. Increased competitiveness did not,
however, lead to a major revival of British exports because of the limited
growth of world trade during the 1930s. According to Maizels' estimates,
world trade in manufactures fell by 17.5% between 1929 and 1937. The
volume of British exports of goods rose by 29% between 1932 and their
peak in 1937, before declining by 12% under the influence of the world
recession of 1938. Even in 1937, exports were 20% less in volume than in
1929. While the improved competitiveness of British exports in the 1930s
did not result in export-led expansion, the suspension of the gold standard
had other important implications for domestic recovery by allowing changes
in monetary policy.

On the import side it is difficult to separate the impact of exchange
depreciation from the effects of the general tariff introduced in February

TABLE 10
Measures of competitiveness and the terms of trade 1931–1938
1929 = 100

	1	2	3	4	5
	UK relative export unit values	Unit labour costs in current dollars			Terms of trade
		UK	US	Germany	
1931	106	89	87	96	120
1932	91	68	80	80	121
1933	98	80	72	95	124
1934	98	92	83	124	121
1935	98	85	80	121	119
1936	101	85	79	121	116
1937	103	87	88	119	109
1938	109	91	91	122	119

Sources: As for Table 6.

1932. Both acted to reduce the volume of imports of goods, which rose by 20.6% between 1932 and 1937 compared with a rise in real G.D.P. of 23.3% over the same period. Richardson (1967) has examined the sectoral impact of protection and has concluded that the effects on imports were not substantial and that the employment effects were negligible. Capie (1978) has calculated effective rates of protection under the 1932 Tariff and shown that its impact on industry differs considerably from the impression created by looking at nominal rates of duty. In particular, protection hindered the building industry, which was a major contributor to recovery from the depression.

The combination of protection and exchange depreciation led to a decline in the imports of manufactures of 17.6% between 1929 and 1937. This reduction is in sharp contrast to the increase of 65.7% in imports of manufactures between 1920 and 1929 according to Scott's estimates (1963). In the import demand equation estimated by Thomas (1975) the effect of the tariff is allowed for by a dummy variable introduced for the years 1932 to 1938, which has a negative coefficient that is statistically significant. The effect of exchange depreciation on aggregate imports is relatively modest because of the low value obtained for the price elasticity of demand for imports (−0.5). Scott, using a disaggregated approach, derives price elasticities ranging from −7 for imported manufactures to −0.20 for imports of materials. To conclude, the relative effects of the tariff and the depreciation of sterling on imports remains unsettled and requires further investigation.

The suspension of the gold standard did not lead to an improvement in the current account of the balance of payments. The average annual deficit for 1932 to 1938 was £37 million compared with an average surplus of £22 million for 1925 to 1931.[104] Control of the outflow of long-term capital to non-sterling countries was a factor easing pressure on the pound in the 1930s. Overseas issues were prohibited on the suspension of the gold standard and remained subject to control in subsequent years.[105] In that the Treasury wished to see a lower value for sterling, one way of achieving this would have been to liberalize the restrictions on the outflow of long-term capital. The exchange rate was also pushed up by the tariff, which reduced the demand for imports. It does not appear that the effects of commercial policy and the restriction of capital issues on exchange rate policy were adequately appreciated by the authorities.

Exchange depreciation did not lead to a deterioration in the terms of trade, which had improved by 20% between 1929 and 1931, because of the collapse of world prices of primary products in the depression. From 1932 to 1938 there was little change in the terms of trade, apart from a deterioration in the world recovery of 1936–37, which was reversed in the recession of the following year. The terms of trade remained at a highly favourable level by

---

[104] Sayers (1976) Appendix 32.
[105] Ibid pp. 491–2 and Appendix 30.

historical standards. The increase in real incomes due to the low level of import prices was a major factor maintaining consumption during the depression and so offsetting the contractionary effect of the reduction in the volume of British exports.

Domestic monetary policy 1932–1938

If the exchange rate had been allowed to float freely, the money supply could have been insulated from external influences. In fact there was extensive intervention by the authorities in the foreign exchange market and purchases and sales of foreign currencies had domestic monetary effects. The Exchange Equalisation Account, set up in July 1932, served to insulate bankers' balances at the Bank of England from changes in the reserves, since purchases and sales of foreign exchange by the Account varied the amount of Treasury Bills available to the money market but did not affect the stock of high-powered money.

When in the first half of 1932 confidence in sterling revived and there was an inflow of funds, the Treasury was unwilling to let the exchange rate appreciate. The EEA was not yet in operation so that purchases of foreign exchange by the Bank of England increased bankers' balances, which were not fully offset by open market sales of securities. The rise in the banks' reserves led to a decline in short-term interest rates, enabling Bank Rate to be reduced by stages to 2% and bank deposits rose by 12.8% from end 1931 to end 1932. The authorities took advantage of the decline in short-term interest rates to announce the massive conversion of 5% War Loan at the end of July and the yield on Consols fell from 4.40% in 1931 to 3.39% in 1933. In this way cheap money was introduced.[106] It was intended both to encourage recovery from the depression and to reduce the cost of debt management.

The banks increased their holdings of gilt-edged securities, since the demand for loans and advances was depressed by the low level of economic activity, the proportion of investments in the portfolios of UK banks rising from 21.2% at the end of 1931 to 32.7% at the end of 1933.[107] They then became unwilling to add to their holdings of bonds, possibly because of the risk of capital loss if interest rates should rise. They would have preferred to increase their bill holdings, pending a recovery in the demand for advances.[108] However, the supply of market Treasury Bills was reduced in 1933 and 1934 as a result of deliberate action by the authorities. The release of Treasury Bills, due to the acquisition of gold by the EEA, was offset by increased holdings by government departments and the Issue Department of the Bank of England.[109] The response of the banks to the shortage

[106] Sayes (1976) pp. 436–47, Howson (1975) pp. 71–75 and pp. 88–9.
[107] Sheppard (1971) Table A (1–6).
[108] Nevin (1955) pp. 133–7.
[109] Ibid pp. 119–133, Johnson (1951), Howson (1975) pp. 95–103 and Appendix 2, Sayers (1976) pp. 492–5.

of bills was to bid up their price,[110] and to increase holdings of cash. Thus the deposit/reserve ratio declined in 1933 and 1934 and bank deposits declined by 1.6% between 1932 and 1933 on a year end basis.[111]

As the economy recovered, there was a revival in the demand for advances, but it did not rise to the level of the 1920s. Bank deposits grew by 16.2% from end 1933 to 1937 and the proportion of advances in total assets rose from 32.7% to 36.1%. Monetary growth was again interrupted in 1938, when bank deposits declined by 2.7%, under the influence of the recession on bank advances and a renewed shortage of Treasury Bills due to the debt management policy of the Treasury and the outflow of reserves from the E.E.A.[112]

Monetary growth was also restricted after 1935 by a shortage of bank reserves. The Bank of England took no further steps to raise bankers' balances, following the initial expansion in 1932.[113,114] Growth in high-powered money was in the form of currency, more of which might have found its way into bank reserves but for the rise in the currency/deposit ratio. Between 1933 and 1938 average non-bank currency holdings rose by 25%, due partly to currency hoarding by foreigners, compared with a growth in average deposits of 13.5% and in the money supply of 15.1% over the same period.[115,116] As the recovery proceeded, the growth of nominal income exceeded the growth in the money supply, the income velocity of circulation rising from 1.52 in 1933 to 1.73 in 1938. Long-term interest rates continued to fall until 1935, when the yield on Consols averaged 2.89%. In 1936 and 1937 the banks could only increase advances by selling bonds, leading to a rise in long-term interest rates, as the yield on Consols increased to 3.38% in 1938.[117] Bank Rate remained at 2% and the yield on Treasury Bills averaged only 0.6% because of the continuing shortage of bills in the money market. (See Table 11)

A peculiar feature of the cheap money policy was the official attitude to the floating debt. The massive increase in reserves from 1935 to 1937 did not lead to an increased issue of market Treasury Bills because of official funding policies. Howson (1975) emphasizes the continuing funding complex of the Treasury and the determination of both the Bank of England and Treasury to reduce the floating debt as a result of their traumatic experience with Treasury Bill finance in 1920.[118] They did not alter their priorities in the changed conditions of the 1930s. Norman saw the control of market

---

[110] Balogh (1947) pp. 177–82 and Howson (1975) p. 101 on decline in supply of commercial bills.
[111] Sheppard (1971) Tables (A) 1–1 and (A) 1–6.
[112] Nevin (1955) p. 137, Howson (1975) pp. 134–5.
[113] Ibid p. 103.
[114] Sheppard (1971) Table (A) 1–12.
[115] Howson (1975) p. 102.
[116] Sheppard (1971) Table 3–3.
[117] Nevin (1955) pp. 154–9.
[118] Howson (1976) pp. 95–99.

TABLE 11
Money supply, velocity and interest rates 1931–1938

	£ million		$3 = \frac{2}{1}$	Yield % annual average			
	1	2	3	4	5	6	7
			Income			Yield	Fed. Reserve
	Net	GDP at	velocity		Treasury	on	Bank of N.Y.
	money	current	of	Bank	Bill	$2\frac{1}{2}\%$	discount
	supply	prices	circulation	Rate	rate	Consols	rate
1931	2,606	4,359	1.67	3.93	3.59	4.40	2.25
1932	2,666	4,276	1.60	3.00	1.49	3.75	3.00
1933	2,805	4,259	1.52	2.00	0.59	3.39	2.75
1934	2,813	4,513	1.60	2.00	0.73	3.10	1.75
1935	2,913	4,721	1.62	2.00	0.55	2.89	1.50
1936	3,099	4,905	1.58	2.00	0.58	2.93	1.50
1937	3,244	5,289	1.63	2.00	0.56	3.28	1.25
1938	3,228	5,572	1.73	2.00	0.61	3.38	1.00

Sources: As for Table 6.

Treasury Bills as a way of keeping down short-term interest rates without making credit abundant.[119] The Bank did not attribute the rise in long-term rates after 1935 to funding policy but regarded it as the normal tendency for interest rates to rise in a period of strong economic recovery. However, the Bank did undertake extensive open market operations in 1936–8, which were intended to keep down the yields on gilt-edged securities[120] and in 1938 there was an increase in bankers' deposits, which had been held constant since early in 1933.

The impact of cheap money 1932–38

The decline in interest rates in the early 1930s was associated with a reduction in the cost of industrial borrowing. The yield on industrial debentures fell to a low point in 1936 and then rose as the price of gilt-edged securities fell. Nevin (1955) has shown that between 1932 and 1936 the cost of borrowing on debentures fell by 25% compared with a rise in the price of consols of 29%.[121] The recovery in share prices of 66% during the same period reflected the revival of economic activity and business confidence as well as the decline in interest rates. There was a revival of new issues which was concentrated on home non-financial issues, overseas issues being kept down by the restrictions on foreign investment. The proportion of issues made by small firms increased and companies took advantage of lower interest rates to repay bank borrowing by issue of debentures and to raise funds for investment by sales of gilt-edged securities. The financial con-

[119] Ibid p. 103.
[120] Sayers (1976) pp. 495–7.
[121] Nevin (1955) p. 217.

straints of the 1920s were relaxed during the 1930s and industrial investment rose as economic recovery proceeded.[122] The revival in non-housing
investment took place mainly after 1934; it rose by only 15.1% between
1932 and 1934, and then by 38.7% between 1934 and 1938. By contrast,
housing investment increased by 47.3% between 1932 and 1934 and then
fell back by 12.4% to 1938.[123]

Changed monetary and financial conditions created a favourable background for the growth of industrial investment but direct evidence of the
influence of financial factors on non-housing investment is lacking. In their
study of private sector non-housing capital formation in the interwar period,
Lund and Holden (1968) used a capital stock adjustment version of the
acceleration principle. They did not find significant interest rate effects,
partly, it may be suspected, because periods of relatively strong investment
demand, such as 1927–29 and 1935–37 were also periods of rising interest
rates on bonds. They did, however, find some influence of share prices on
investment. Smyth and Briscoe (1971) did not include financial variables in
the capacity version of the accelerator which they fitted to interwar data.
Thomas (1975) reports that non-housing investment was not sensitive to
interest rates in the interwar period. These studies seem, therefore, to
confirm the negative results of the Oxford survey on the effect of interest rates
on investment decisions (1938).

The main impact of cheap money was on investment in private housing.
MacIntosh (1951) has calculated that the weekly carrying charge of a new
house based on the average new mortgage loans of all building societies
declined by 9% between 1931 and 1933. Howson (1975) has shown, using
data from Stolper (1941), that private unsubsidised house building revived
in the half year September 1932 to March 1933, when the number of houses
built rose by 27% compared with the previous six months.[124] This timing fits
in well with the decline in short-term interest rates in the first half of 1932,
followed by the widely anticipated conversion of War Loan at the end of
July. MacIntosh (1951) argued that the reduction of interest rates in the
money market led to an influx of funds into the building societies, while the
demand for mortgages from prospective house buyers was stimulated by the
reduction in carrying charges.[125] The recovery of investment began in this
sector reaching a peak in 1934.

There is some empirical evidence of the sensitivity of investment in
private housebuilding to interest rates in Thomas (1975) and also in earlier
studies of the determinants of building, such as Tinbergen (1939)[126] and

[122] Ibid pp. 218–67.

[123] Feinstein (1972) Table 40.

[124] Howson (1975) p. 115, Richardson and Aldcroft (1968) emphasize the fall in building
costs p. 204.

[125] Bellman (1938) shows that the proportion of mortgages granted to wage earners rose
from 31% in 1932 to 51% in 1936, cited in Nevin pp. 294–5.

[126] Tinbergen (1939) pp. 95–108.

Robinson (1939).[127] The importance of financial variables in affecting investment in private housing is indicated by postwar studies, such as Vipond (1969) and Whitehead (1974).

In his survey of the channels by which monetary measures affect the postwar U.K. economy, Savage (1978) shows that there is stronger evidence for interest rate effects on housing than on investment by industry. This brief survey of the impact of monetary variables in the interwar period points to the same conclusion. It suggests that cheap money contributed to the revival of the British economy from the depression of the early 1930s, through its impact on private housebuilding. The improvement in the general financial position of British industry, associated with the reduction in interest rates, is also likely to have been important in ensuring that industrial investment would expand, once domestic recovery got under way and profit prospects had become more favourable. The overall effect of monetary changes on the economy is indicated in the money multiplier approach used by Walters (1977) and Sheppard (1971).[128] In both studies, changes in the money stock have lagged effects on real output and prices, but the process by which money is influencing the economy is not made clear.

Fiscal policy may have played a significant role in the recovery through the contribution of the orthodoxy of a balanced budget to business confidence. This is necessarily rather a speculative argument, since the effect of balancing the budget at a low level of economic activity was deflationary. Middleton (1981) has calculated a constant employment budget balance for the 1930s, showing that there was a surplus of 3–4% of Gross Domestic Product from 1931 to 1934 on a constant employment basis. The stance of fiscal policy then became more expansionary, so that the constant employment budget surplus had been eliminated by 1937, to be followed by deficits as expenditure on rearmament gathered pace.

The general features of the recovery from 1932 to 1937 are summarised in Table 12. While the revival of exports was limited for reasons which have already been discussed, investment showed a marked increase, due partly to the cheap money policy. Consumers' expenditure did not show a large increase in this period, its main effect had been in sustaining the economy in the recession years [see Table 7]. The rise in public current expenditure on goods and services came mainly after 1935, as defence expenditure expanded rapidly. Whatever the misgivings of the authorities about public works in the late 1920s and early 1930s, they were prepared to undertake substantial public spending to meet defence needs in the late 1930s and this expenditure moderated the impact on the economy of the world recession of 1938.[129]

The recovery of economic activity was associated with increases in money

---

[127] Robinson (1939) pp. 133–152.
[128] Sheppard (1971) pp. 73–101.
[129] The Treasury were concerned about the effect of defence spending on the balance of the budget. Howson (1975) pp. 120–6.

TABLE 12
General developments in the British economy 1932–37

Constant prices	Percentage change 1932–37
1. Gross domestic product	+23.3
2. Gross fixed investment	+47.4
3. Consumers' expenditure	+13.5
4. Exports of goods and services	+21.1
5. Public current expenditure on goods and services	+34.6
6. Imports of goods and services	+16.5
7. G.D.P. Deflator	+3.0
8. Weekly wage rates	+5.9
9. Real earnings	−0.2
10. Unemployment %*	17.0–8.5
11. Money stock	+21.7
12. Sterling/Dollar exchange rate	+41.2
13. Terms of trade	−9.7
14. Average balance on current account £ million	−33

* Percentage unemployment among employees in first and last years.
Sources: As for Table 1.

wages, although unemployment remained relatively high by historical standards, even in the peak year of 1937. The rise in wages[130] reflected the desire of wage earners to obtain compensation for the rise in the cost of living, due mainly to the upturn of world prices of primary products after 1934. Real earnings fell slightly over the period 1932–37, following their marked increase during the recession. Lipsey (1960) noted that wage increases after 1934 were greater than the predictions from his wage equation. This observation is consistent with the view that there may have been some increase in the underlying natural rate of unemployment during the 1930s.

The causes of unemployment

According to the Keynesian view, the high rate of unemployment in interwar Britain was caused by deficient aggregate demand, due mainly to the low level of exports. In the late 1920s exports were depressed by the overvaluation of the exchange rate and by the structural problems of the staple industries. In addition, domestic investment was hindered by high interest rates. During the 1930s the demand for exports suffered as a result of the world depression of 1931–2 after which only a limited recovery was possible because of the restricted growth of world trade. There was, however, a revival of investment and consumption, attributable to the cheap money policy and the effect of the favourable movement in the terms of

[130] Routh (1960) pp. 123–7.

trade on real incomes. Official policy can be blamed for both the overvaluation of sterling in the 1920s and the refusal to use public expenditure to
stimulate the economy, prior to the rise in defence spending near the end of
the period.

An alternative view has been advanced by Benjamin and Kochin (1979a),
who suggest that the persistence of high unemployment should be attributed
to a shift in the aggregate labour supply curve. They argue that the wider
availability of unemployment benefits after 1920 and the subsequent rise in
the ratio of benefits to wages led to an increase in voluntary unemployment.
The effect of benefits was to increase the amount of measured unemployment, since workers were encouraged to enter the labour force to register as
unemployed, in addition to the greater incentive to substitute leisure and job
searching for work. Benjamin and Kochin admit that cyclical factors caused
unemployment in the depressions of 1921–22 and 1930–32, but argue that
benefit induced unemployment was the cause of unemployment which
persisted even at cyclical peaks, such as 1929 and 1937. In their basic
equation, unemployment is regressed on the deviation of output from trend
and the ratio of benefits to wages. The coefficients of both variables have the
expected signs and are statistically significant.

A similar argument has been advanced by Maki and Spindler (1975), who
seek to explain the rise in unemployment in Britain since the mid-1960s by
the rise in the ratio of social security benefits to wages. However, Cubbin
and Foley (1977) argue that permanent income should be included as an
additional explanatory variable for sound theoretical reasons. If this is done,
the benefit/wage ratio ceases to be statistically significant. A similar objection applies to Benjamin and Kochin's equation, since Irish (1980) has
shown that the inclusion of a trended variable, such as population or output
per head, makes the coefficient of the benefit/wage ratio no longer statistically significant. Hatton (1980) has seriously criticised Benjamin and
Kochin's statistical procedures and in addition cast doubt on their cross-
section argument. They claim that the lower incidence of unemployment
among juveniles and women can be explained by the lower benefits available to these groups relative to their wages and stricter conditions governing
eligibility for benefit (1979b). Hatton points out that the unemployment rate
among juveniles was lower than for adult men before 1913, and, therefore,
pre-dated the general provision of state unemployment benefits.[131]

While the arguments advanced by Benjamin and Kochin must be qualified
in the light of these criticisms, it does not follow that they should be
dismissed. The Pilgrim Trust (1938) concluded from its study of long-term
unemployment that up to 20% of families supported by unemployment
benefits were at least as well off as they would have been if working.[132] In
'The Theory of Wages', Hicks (1932) observed that unemployment insur-

---

[131] These arguments are usefully discussed by Broadberry (1980) Chapter 4.
[132] Constantine (1980) pp. 28–30.

ance may have kept up wages, since refusal to accept employment at wages below the rates negotiated by trade unions did not provide grounds for disqualifying a worker from benefit.[133] The continuation of rent restriction after the First World War served to discourage the mobility of labour. As explained by Bowley (1945), from 1923 rent restrictions ceased when a sitting tenant quit.[134] Workers benefiting from controlled rents, therefore, had a reduced incentive to move in search of employment, because this might entail a substantial increase in rent.

The concentration of unemployment among workers in the staple export industries, such as textiles, coal mining and shipbuilding, which had severe problems of overcapacity, suggests that contraction of demand was the main cause of the unemployment. However, Benjamin and Kochin argue that the regional and industrial pattern of unemployment can be explained by variations in the benefit/wage ratio. This is a question which requires further investigation.

There are a variety of factors which may have raised the natural rate of unemployment in the interwar period compared with the years before 1914. However, the supply side explanation does not exclude the view that demand factors were also important. Unemployment may have risen because of a shift to the left in the aggregate labour supply schedule as well as a leftward shift of aggregate demand. International influences acted to depress demand, while government policy acted on aggregate supply. What is lacking is a satisfactory quantitative measure of their relative importance.

Conclusion and Comparisons with the current situation

Keynes was right in arguing that sterling was overvalued on the return to the gold standard in 1925, but it is questionable whether the extent of overvaluation was 10% as he claimed. A slightly lower exchange rate of about $4.40 would not have made much difference to Britain's difficulties in the 1920s. The decline in exports compared with 1913 reflected the failure of the British economy to adjust to postwar conditions. Structural adaptation was bound to take time and much progress was made during the interwar period in bringing about the necessary changes. In the late 1920s Britain's competitiveness might have been increased by a large devaluation or even severe deflation. The difficulty with both these policies would have been the inflexibility of real wages, particularly in the unsheltered sectors of the economy. One possible remedy for real wage inflexibility would have been the introduction of wage subsidies to raise employment. In fact, the tendency of economic policy was to subsidise unemployment rather than employment.

The reduction in costs after 1925 was not sufficient to enable the British economy to participate fully in the boom of the late 1920s, but preliminary

[133] Hicks (1932) p. 177.
[134] Bowley (1945) pp. 82–3.

calculations on the real exchange rate suggest that some progress was made in reducing costs during this period. There was a notable increase in competitiveness after the floating of the pound in the autumn of 1931, which was partly eroded by the subsequent devaluations of the dollar and the French franc. Britain achieved a better performance in international markets for manufactures during the 1930s, although the wide variation in exchange rates makes comparisons of competitiveness subject to considerable qualification.

There is sufficient evidence on the monetary transmission process in interwar Britain to support the view that the cheap money policy made an important contribution to the recovery of the economy. For the same reasons it may be argued that progress in the 1920s was impeded by the tight financial policies necessary to achieve and maintain the gold standard.

The persistence of high unemployment throughout the period after 1920 can be mainly attributed to deficient aggregate demand. This conclusion must, however, be qualified by the possibility of an increase in the natural rate of unemployment for reasons suggested by Benjamin and Kochin. It is not surprising that official policies, which subsidised unemployment, should have had some effect in raising the rate of unemployment. This does not mean that unemployment could not have been reduced by the choice of a lower exchange rate in 1925 and by more appropriate fiscal policies throughout much of the interwar period. The effectiveness of exchange depreciation in stimulating exports was limited in the 1930s because of the devaluation of other major currencies and the decline in world trade. During the 1920s a lower value of the pound would have had stronger effects. Demand might also have been increased by fiscal expansion but its scope would have been limited by the potential conflict with low interest rates. Such a conflict was beginning to appear in the late 1930s with the rise in borrowing to finance expenditure on rearmament.

Britain's interwar experience has some bearing on the current problems of the economy. At the end of 1980 sterling was more seriously overvalued in relation to competing currencies on a purchasing parity basis than during the 1920s. Export prices of U.K. manufacturers rose by about 25% relative to those of other industrial economies between 1978 and 1980. The Bank of England has calculated that relative U.K. labour costs per unit of output, cyclically adjusted, rose by nearly 40% between 1975 and the third quarter of 1980 and has commented that 'such a deterioration has no parallel in recent history, either in this country or among its major competitors' (Bank of England 1980). In the 1920s the overvaluation of sterling aggravated the underlying problem of the inappropriate industrial structure, due to excessive concentration on the staple industries, a legacy of the pre-1914 economy and the First World War (Clay 1929). In both cases a decline in the exchange rate would have increased industrial competitiveness, but the scope for adjustment could be restricted by the downward inflexibility of real wages. Britain was better placed to make the adjustment in the interwar period because of the reasonably satisfactory rate of growth of productivity in both new and old industries. Competitiveness could, therefore, have been increased in the 1920s, if the growth of real wages had been reduced.

The recent rise in sterling is partly the response of a floating exchange rate to the strengthening of Britain's trading position, as a result of the development of North Sea oil. In the 1920s problems arose from the weakening of Britain's balance of payments, combined with the choice of too high a parity for the fixed exchange rate. In both cases the result has been increasing competitive pressures on British industry, but the cause of the strength of the exchange rate was quite different. In particular, it may be noted that the balance of trade in fuels, which was positive before 1913, because of the strong overseas demand for British coal, was approximately in balance during the late 1920s, because of reduced coal exports and growing imports of petroleum. Excessive capital exports aggravated Britain's difficulties under the restored gold standard, as pointed out by Keynes in 'A Treatise on Money' (1930).[135] In the 1980s a capital outflow provides a useful way of keeping the exchange rate down and of building up invisible earnings in anticipation of the exhaustion of Britain's oil reserves.

During the 1930s Britain took advantage of the favourable shift in the terms of trade to move resources into the production of non-traded goods, such as housing and services. This reallocation of resources was assisted by the reduction of interest rates, permitted by the floating of the pound in 1931. A similar shift towards the output of non-traded goods should be made in the 1980s to benefit from the contribution of oil to the balance of payments. Since North Sea oil will eventually be depleted, consideration should also be given to the appropriate time profile of oil production, which has implications for the adjustments required of British industry. A faster expansion of oil exports will tend to increase the loss of industrial competitiveness and also bring forward the time when Britain will rely predominantly on non-oil exports. Interwar experience suggests that such structural adaptation is slow and painful, and that there is therefore a need to consider the impact of oil production on traditional export industries, such as engineering.

Interwar monetary policy has some lessons for the current situation. The deflationary policy of the early 1920s shows what control of the monetary base, through regulation of the note issue, can achieve if maintained for a number of years. It also shows that restriction of the monetary base is feasible, even though there are simultaneous problems of debt management, provided that there is sufficient flexibility of short-term interest rates. The lessons of this episode should not be overlooked in the current discussions on the introduction of monetary base control (Bank of England 1979). There were, of course, special features of the depression of 1921–22, which brought about a rapid decline in wages and prices. But the sustained

[135] Keynes (1930) Vol II pp. 184–9.

deflationary policy of 1920–25 may be a better indicator of the results to be expected from such a policy than the indecisive outcome of monetary policy under the restored gold standard. It has been argued that from 1925 to 1931 monetary and debt management policies tended to depress domestic activity, particularly after 1928, but that no serious attempt was made to reduce domestic costs in these years and that the banking system offset contractionary influences on the monetary base.

In the 1930s economic recovery took place with a combination of low interest rates and an approximately balanced budget. A similar combination of fiscal moderation and reduced interest rates could provide a basis for British recovery in the 1980s. A reduction of interest rates could reverse the recent effects of a positive interest differential in raising the exchange rate. Domestic recovery should also act to keep down sterling, because of the weakening of the current account of the balance of payments. British experience in the 1930s suggests that a policy of moderate monetary expansion, combined with an unpegged exchange rate, can be an effective way of bringing about recovery from a severe recession. The change in expectations at the time of the conversion of War Loan in July 1932 was a crucial factor in this revival. The general expectation of a permanent reduction in the rate of inflation and of the maintenance of stable financial conditions could have similar effects in the current situation.

REFERENCES

ALDCROFT, D. H. (1970), *The Inter-War Economy: Britain, 1919–39*, Batsford, London.
——, (1977), *From Versailles to Wall Street 1919–1929*, Allen Lane, London.
ALFORD, B. W. E. (1972), *Depression and Recovery? British Economic Growth 1919–1939*, Macmillan, London.
ARCHIBALD, G. C., KEMMIS, R. and PERKINS, J. W. (1974), Excess demand for labour, unemployment and the Phillips Curve in *Inflation and Labour Markets* edited by D. Laidler and D. L. Purdy, Manchester University Press, Manchester.
ASHWORTH, W. (1960), *An Economic History of England*, Methuen, London.
BALOGH, T. (1947) *Studies in Financial Organization*, Cambridge University Press, Cambridge.
Bank of England (1968), The Exchange Equalisation Account: its origins and development. *Bank of England Quarterly Bulletin*. December.
——, (1970), The Bank of England's holdings of gold and foreign exchange 1924–31. *Bank of England Quarterly Bulletin*, March Supplement.
——, (1972), The Balance of Payments in the Inter-war Period. *Bank of England Quarterly Bulletin*. September.
——, (1974), The Balance of Payments in the Inter-war Period: Further Details, *Bank of England Quarerly Bulletin*, March.
——, (1979) Monetary Base Control. *Bank of England Quarterly Bulletin*, June.
——, (1980) Economic Commentary. *Bank of England Quarterly Bulletin*, December.
BELLMAN, SIR H. (1938), The Building Trades in *Britain in Recovery*, British Association, Pitman, London.
BENJAMIN, D. K. and KOCHIN, L. A. (1979a), Searching for an Explanation of Unemployment in Inter-war Britain, *Journal of Political Economy*, June.
——, (1979b), What went right with Juvenile Unemployment Policy between the Wars: A Comment, *Economic History Review*, November.
BOWLEY, M. (1945), *Housing and the State, 1914–1944*, Allen and Unwin, London.

BROADBERRY, S. (1980), Unemployment and Consumption in Inter-war Britain: A Macro Model with Quantity Rationing. M.Phil. thesis, mimeo.

CAPIE, F. (1978), The British Tariff and Industrial Protection in the late 1930's, *Economic History Review*, August.

CHANG, T. C. (1951), *Cyclical Movements in the Balance of Payments*, Cambridge University Press, Cambridge.

CLARKE, S. V. O. (1967), *Central Bank Cooperation 1924–31*, Federal Reserve Bank of New York, New York.

——, (1977), *Exchange-Rate Stabilization in the Mid-1930's: Negotiating the Tripartite Agreement*, Princeton University, Princeton.

CLAY, H. (1929), *The Post-War Unemployment Problem*, Macmillan, London.

——, (1957), *Lord Norman*, Macmillan, London.

Committee on Currency and Foreign Exchanges after the War (Cunliffe Committee) *First Interim Report* (1918), Cd. 9182, H.M.S.O. London. *Final Report* (1919) Cmd. 464 H.M.S.O. London.

Committee on the Currency and Bank of England Note Issues (Chamberlain-Bradbury Committee) *Report* (1925), Cmd 2392, H.M.S.O. London.

Committee on Finance and Industry (Macmillan Committee) *Report* (1931), H.M.S.O. London.

——, *Minutes of Evidence* (1931) H.M.S.O. London.

CORNER, D. C. (1958), Exports and the British Trade Cycle: 1929, *The Manchester School*.

CONSTANTINE, S. (1980), *Unemployment in Britain between the Wars*, Longmans, London.

CUBBIN, J. S. and FOLEY, K. (1977), The Extent of Benefit Induced Unemployment in Great Britain: Some New Evidence, *Oxford Economic Papers*, March.

DRAYSON, S. J. (1978), British Exchange Rate Policy: From the Abandonment of Gold to the Tripartite Agreement, mimeo.

FEINSTEIN, C. H. (1965), *Domestic Capital Formation in the United Kingdom 1920–38*, Cambridge University Press, Cambridge.

——, (1972), *National Income, Expenditure and Output of the United Kingdom 1855–1965*, Cambridge University Press, Cambridge.

FRIEDMAN, M. and SCHWARTZ, A. J. (1963). *A Monetary History of the United States 1867–1960*, Princeton University Press, Princeton.

GOODWIN, R. M. (1941), The Supply of Bank Money in England and Wales, *Oxford Economic Papers*, June.

GILBERT, B. B. (1970), *British Social Policy 1914–1939*, Batsford, London.

GRANT, A. T. K. (1937), *A Study of the Capital Market in Post-War Britain*, Macmillan, London.

GREGORY, T. E. (1926), *The First Year of the Gold Standard*, King, London.

HATTON, T. J. (1980), Unemployment in Britain between the World Wars: A Role for the Dole, *University of Essex Discussion Paper No. 139*.

HICKS, J. R. (1932), *The Theory of Wages*, Macmillan, London.

HODGSON, J. S. (1972), An Analysis of Floating Exchange Rates: The Dollar Sterling Rate 1919–1925, *Southern Economic Journal*, October.

HOWSON, S. (1973), 'A Dear Money Man?' Keynes on Monetary Policy, 1920 *Economic Journal*, June.

——, (1974), The Origins of Dear Money, 1919–1920, *Economic History Review*, February.

——, (1975), *Domestic Monetary Management in Britain 1919–1938*. Cambridge University Press, Cambridge.

——, (1976), The Managed Floating Pound 1932–39, *The Banker*, March.

——, (1980), The Management of Sterling 1932–1939, *Journal of Economic History*, March.

HOWSON, S. and WINCH, D. (1976), *The Economic Advisory Council 1930–1939*, Cambridge University Press, Cambridge.

IRISH, M. (1980), Unemployment in Inter-war Britain: A Note, mimeo.

JOHNSON, H. G. (1951), Clearing Bank Holdings of Public Debt 1930–50, *London and Cambridge Economic Service Bulletin*, November.

——, (1975), Keynes and British Economics in *Essays on John Maynard Keynes* edited by W. M. Keynes, Cambridge University Press, Cambridge.

——, (1976), The Monetary Approach to Balance of Payments Theory in *The Monetary Approach to the Balance of Payments*, edited by J. A. Frenkel and H. G. Johnson, Allen and Unwin, London.

KEYNES, J. M. (1923), *A Tract on Monetary Reform* (J.M.K. Vol. IV) Macmillan London 1971.

——, (1930), *A Treatise on Money* (J.M.K. Vols. V & VI), Macmillan, London, 1971.

——, (1931), *Essays in Persuasion* (J.M.K. Vol. IX) Macmillan, London, 1972.

KENDRICK, J. W. (1961), *Productivity Trends in the United States*, Princeton University Press, Princeton.

KINDLEBERGER, C. P. (1973), *The World in Depression* 1929–1939, Allen Lane, London.

LEWIS, W. A. (1949), *Economic Survey* 1919–1939, Allen and Unwin, London.

LIPSEY, R. G. (1960), The Relation between Unemployment and the Rate of Change in Money Wages in the United Kingdom, 1862–1957. A Further Analysis. *Economica*, February.

London and Cambridge Economic Service, *The British Economy: Key Statistics* 1900–1970, Times Newspapers, London. n.d.

LUND, P. J. and HOLDEN, K. (1968), An Econometric Study of Private Sector Gross Fixed Capital Formation in the United Kingdom 1923–1938, *Oxford Economic Papers*, March.

MACDOUGALL, G. D. A. (1938), General Survey 1929–1937 in *Britain in Recovery*. British Association, Pitman, London.

MACINTOSH, T. A. (1951), A Note on Cheap Money and the British Housing Boom, *Economic Journal*, March.

MADDISON, A. (1962), Growth and Fluctuations in the World Economy 1870–1960 Banca Nazionale del Lavoro Quarterly Review, June.

MAIZELS, A. (1963), *Industrial Growth and World Trade*, Cambridge University Press, Cambridge.

MAKI, D. and SPINDLER, Z. A. (1975), The Effects of Unemployment Compensation on the Rate of Unemployment in G.B. *Oxford Economic Papers*, October.

MEADE J. and ANDREWS, P. W. S. (1938), Summary of Replies to Questions on the Effects of Interest Rates, *Oxford Economic Papers*, October.

MIDDLETON, R. A. H. (1981), The Constant Employment Budget Balance and British Budgetary Policy 1929–1939, *Economic History Review*, May.

MITCHELL, B. R. and DEANE, P. M. (1962), *Abstract of British Historical Statistics*, Cambridge University, Cambridge.

MOGGRIDGE, D. E. (1969), *The Return to Gold*, 1925. Cambridge University Press, Cambridge.

——, (1972), *British Monetary Policy: The Norman Conquest of* $4.86. Cambridge University, Cambridge.

——, (1971), British Controls on Long term Capital Movements 1924–31 in *Essays on a Mature Economy: Britain after* 1840, edited by D. N. McCloskey, Methuen, London.

MORGAN, E. V. (1952), *Studies in British Financial Policy* 1914–1925, Macmillan, London.

NEILD, R. R. (1979), Managed Trade Between Industrial Economies and Comment by D. Lal in R. L. Major ed. *Britain's Trade and Exchange Rate Policy*, Heinemann, London.

NEVIN, E. T. (1955), *The Mechanism of Cheap Money: A Study of British Monetary Policy* 1931–1939, University of Wales Press, Cardiff.

NURKSE, R. (1944), *International Currency Experience*, League of Nations.

OPPENHEIMER, P. M. (1966), Monetary Movements and the International Position of Sterling. *Scottish Journal of Policital Economy*, February.

PHELPS BROWN, E. H. and SHACKLE, G. L. S. (1939), British Economic Fluctuations 1924–1938, *Oxford Economic Papers*, May.

PHELPS BROWN, E. H. and BROWNE, M. H. (1968), *A Century of Pay*, Macmillan, London.

PHILLIPS, A. W. (1958), The Relation between Unemployment and the Rate of Change of Money Wages in the United Kingdom 1861–1957. *Economica*, November.

PIGOU, A. C. (1947), *Aspects of British Economic History* 1918–1925, Macmillan, London.

Pilgrim Trust (1938), *Men Without Work*, Cambridge University Press, Cambridge.

POLLARD, S. (1962), *Development of the British Economy* 1914–1950, Arnold, London.

—— (ed.) (1970), *The Gold Standard and Employment Policies between the Wars*. Methuen, London.

REDDAWAY, W. B. (1970), Was $4.86 Inevitable in 1925? *Lloyds Bank Review*, April.

REDMOND, J. (1980), An Indicator of the Effective Exchange Rate of the Pound in the Nineteen-Thirties, *Economic History Review*, February.

RICHARDSON, H. W. (1967), *Economic Recovery in Britain* 1932–9, Weidenfeld and Nicholson, London.

RICHARDSON, H. W. and ALDCROFT, D. H. (1968), *Building in the British Economy between the Wars*, Allen and Unwin, London.

ROBINSON, H. W. (1939), *The Economics of Building*, P. S. King, London.

ROUTH, G. (1960), *Occupation and Pay in Great Britain* 1906–1960, Cambridge University Press. Cambridge.

SAVAGE, D. (1978), The Channels of Monetary Influence: A Survey of the Empirical Evidence, *National Institute Economic Review*, February.

SAYERS, R. S. (1938), *Modern Banking*, 1st edition, Clarendon Press, Oxford.

——, (1957), Central Banking after Bagehot, Clarendon Press, Oxford.

——, (1970), The Return to Gold 1925 in Pollard (ed.), *The Gold Standard and Employment Policies between the Wars*.

——, (1967), *A History of Economic Change in England* 1880–1939, Oxford University Press, Oxford.

——, (1976), *The Bank of England* 1891–1944, Volumes 1 and 2 and Appendices, Cambridge University Press, Cambridge.

SCOTT, M. FG. (1963), *A Study of United Kingdom Imports*, Cambridge University Press, Cambridge.

SHEPPARD, D. K. (1971), *The Growth and Role of UK Financial Institutions* 1880–1962, Methuen, London.

SMYTH, D. J. and BRISCOE, G. (1971), Investment and Capacity Utilization in the United Kingdom 1923–1966, Oxford Economic Papers, March.

STOLPER, W. F. (1941), British Monetary Policy and the Housing Boom, *Quarterly Journal of Economics*, November.

——, (1948), Purchasing Power Parity and the Pound Sterling from 1919–1925, *Kyklos* (3).

SVENNILSON, I. (1954), *Growth and Stagnation in the European Economy*, United Nations, Geneva.

TINBERGEN, J. (1939), *Statistical Testing of Business Cycle Theories: A Method and its Application to Investment Activity*, League of Nations, Geneva.

THOMAS, L. B. (1973), Behaviour of Flexible Exchange Rates: Additional Tests from the Post World War I Episode. *Southern Economic* Journal, October.

THOMAS, T. J. (1975), Aspects of UK Macroeconomic Policy during the Inter-war period: A Study in Econometric History, Cambridge University Ph.D. thesis mimeo.

VIPOND, M. J. (1969), Fluctuations in Private Housebuilding in the UK 1950–1966, *Scottish Journal of Political Economy*, 16.

WAIGHT, L. (1939), *The History and Mechanism of the Exchange Equalization Account*, Cambridge University Press, Cambridge.

WALTERS, A. A. (1966), Monetary Multipliers in the UK, *Oxford Economic Papers*, November.

WINCH, D. (1969), *Economics and Policy: A Historical Study*, Hodder and Stoughton, London.

WHITEHEAD, C. M. E. (1974), *The UK Housing Market: An Econometric Model*, Saxon House, Farnborough.

YOUNGSON, A. J. (1960), *The British Economy* 1920–1957, Allen and Unwin, London.

ZELDER, R. E. (1958), Estimates of Elasticities of Demand for Exports of the United Kingdom and the United States 1921–1938, *Manchester School*, January.

SOME CONCLUDING COMMENTS

By P. J. N. SINCLAIR

THE first of six questions asked by the Editors of *Oxford Economic Papers* (to which this symposium is in large part a response) was, "How strong is the line of argument which suggests that tight monetary conditions will produce a rising exchange rate?" An excess demand for domestic money causes the exchange rate to appreciate if two propositions hold. One is that an excess demand for domestic money must imply a surplus on overall external payments, at the current exchange rate; the other, that such a surplus must induce appreciation. Both propositions are valid.

The essence of the story may be set out simply. Let us suppose that each country has an exogenous supply of *nominal* money, and an exogenous demand for *real* money. Suppose that the nominal money supply grows over time at a trend rate of m_h in the home country, and that the demand for real money grows at a trend rate of g_h at home. Both the supply of and demand for money may be subject to random influences. But this has no effects on the trends. Probably g_h will be close to the growth rate of real income at home, although it does not matter for the argument if it is not. Let us assume initially that the country is completely closed to international trade and to capital movements. In this case, it must be the domestic price level which absorbs directly the effects of any mismatch between the supply of money and the demand for it. If p_h is the rate of inflation, the demand for nominal money will grow at a rate of $p_h + g_h$, random disturbances aside. If the supply and demand for money are to stay in continuous balance, $m_h = p_h + g_h$ with the result that the trend rate of inflation must equal $m_h - g_h$. When the supply of money grows faster than the real demand for it, prices have to rise to bring up the demand for nominal money in line with its supply. When the opposite is true, inflation will be negative.

Now introduce international trade, between the home country and a foreign country (which could represent the rest of the world), denoted by subscript f. International trade will mean that countries' price indices cannot move independently, at least when the exchange rate between them is fixed. Under fixed rates, perfect arbitrage in goods will imply a common rate of inflation denominated in internationally traded commodities. But if the exchange rate is floating, inflation rates can differ. This difference will simply equal the rate at which the higher-inflation country's exchange rate depreciates in terms of the other country's currency. A country's relative *external* depreciation (against another currency) equals its relative *internal* depreciation (against goods). If the money markets are to clear in both countries, we must have $p_h = m_h - g_h$ and $p_f = m_f - g_f$. Hence relative domestic inflation, $p_h - p_f$, will equal $m_h - g_h - m_f + g_f$. But $p_h - p_f$ must equal the trend rate of depreciation of the exchange rate. Consequently the trend in the exchange rate will be $m_h - g_h - m_f + g_f$. This shows that there is a one-to-one relation between the rate of domestic monetary expansion, and the movement of the exchange rate. The formula will hold for any pair of countries in a many-country world. It will even survive the introduction of tariff barriers, taxes and non-traded goods, provided that trade barriers, and the relative prices of traded to non-traded goods, display no trend.

This basic picture can easily be elaborated by extending perfect international arbitrage from goods and currencies to assets, nominal and real, and to forward exchange. International nominal interest rate differentials will simply reflect expected exchange rate changes and forecasts of inflation differentials. If i represents the nominal rate of interest, $i_h - i_f$ should equal expected values of $m_h - g_h - m_f + g_f$. Expected real interest rates should be equalized between countries, aside from random disturbances. A high value of i_h is an indication of expectations of inflation and depreciation, rather than a lever set by the authorities to attract overseas capital and thereby cause appreciation. In conditions of imperfect international capital mobility, on the other hand, i_h could be held above its equilibrium level for a while; and that could induce an initial, temporary capital inflow with transient, but possibly powerful, upward pressure on the exchange rate.

If we return to the analysis based on long-run equilibrium relationships and perfect mobility of capital between countries, we notice that money is both neutral and 'super-neutral'. Real variables (such as profits and unemployment) are independent of the level and the rate of growth of the money supply. The exchange rate, which is just the price ratio between two countries' moneys, has no real effects either: neither its level, not its rate of change, can affect any real variable. Any tendency to persistent unemployment, for instance, must be ascribed to other factors: the high level of unemployment benefits, as in Professor Minford's article; or to trade union monopoly power; or to deficiencies in information in the labour market.

Most contributions to the volume take this overall picture as a starting point, or as a description of long-run relationships. Where they differ is chiefly in the extent and nature of the qualifications imposed upon it. Two papers (those from the London Business School, and from Mr. Hacche and Mr. Townend) subject it, and numerous variants, to the arduous task of explaining the record of sterling since 1972. The basic hypothesis that the change in the exchange rate equals $g_f - g_h + m_h - m_f$ (where g_h and g_f are now defined as the growth rates of real income) is far from confirmed, even in more sophisticated versions, perhaps because the relevant expectational variables cannot be observed.

One variant on the basic theme common to most papers is the introduction of a negative dependence of the demand for money upon the nominal interest rate. This makes the velocity of circulation of money vary with the rate of depreciation. The faster the rates of depreciation and inflation, the more quickly money circulates. The transition from one monetary expansion rate to another now causes the exchange rate to overshoot. The overshooting occurs because reducing the rate of growth of the money supply tends to raise the demand for money, once inflation expectations drop. This rise in the demand for money acts like a fall in its supply. It induces the exchange rate to appreciate, relative to trend. If expectations of inflation and exchange rate changes were formed adaptively on the basis of experience, a serious threat of instability could emerge. If expectations displayed little inertia, and the demand for money was sufficiently interest elastic, the exchange rate will not be stable. Expectations are, however, for the most part assumed to be formed rationally, on the basis of presumed universal knowledge of the model proposed. But rational expectations do not dispose of the stability issue. They merely alter the conditions required.

Another point of departure from the basic model is the treatment of aggregate output. There is wide agreement that it is not affected much, if at all, by *predicted* changes in the supply of money or the exchange rate. Unexpected changes, however, can exert important if temporary effects. Professors Buiter and Miller, Professor Corden and Mr. Scott all present analyses where the labour market adjusts sluggishly in the face of disequilibrium. Money wage rates are temporarily locked (Corden, Scott). Alternatively, their rate of change varies with the rate of monetary expansion, and the gap between actual and natural output (Buiter–Miller). Professor Artis and Dr. Currie employ a cost-mark-up model for pricing; while the London Business School builds upon an extension of the Lucas 'surprise supply function': this allows for subnatural levels of output and employment if and only if inflation is unexpectedly slow. Several contributors augment the demand for money function with a negative dependence of expenditure upon real or nominal interest rates, and a pricing equation that introduces less than perfect price flexibility in goods and labour markets. Most contributors discuss the structural composition of output, but their formal analysis is restricted to a one-good framework. Only Professor Corden and Professor Minford adopt a specifically two-sector approach, with separate treatment of traded and non-traded goods.

These and other modifications do not, however, serve to undermine the affirmative answer to the first question. All contributors are agreed that monetary stringency will generally cause the exchange rate to rise, other things equal. The slower the growth of the supply of money, the more slowly the exchange rate will depreciate (or the faster it will appreciate). The greater the reduction in the growth rate of the money supply, the bigger the jump in the exchange rate towards its new trend path. Admission of some interest-sensitivity in the demand for money, and tardiness in the adjustment of goods and labour markets when out of equilibrium, both lead the exchange rate to overshoot.[1]

The second of the Editors' questions was: "Are there satisfactory techni-

---

[1] The analysis of overshooting was first explored systematically by Dornbusch (2). The paper by Professors Buiter and Miller has a most interesting analysis of the factors governing the size of the phenomenon.

cal means by which a competitive exchange rate can be maintained while the authorities are simultaneously pursuing tight monetary policies?" This question received much less attention than the first. Many contributors base their argument on models where holding the exchange rate below equilibrium is incompatible with tight controls upon the supply of money. Mr. Scott, on the other hand, argues forcefully that this is false. Provided that payments surpluses are sterilized by official sales of bonds, he maintains, money supply targets are quite compatible with intervention in the foreign exchange markets. Indeed, for over 45 years from April 1932, British monetary policy was conducted in the light of the belief that some control over the exchange rate could be combined with an independent monetary policy. The newly fashionable view that they are incompatible, which Mr. Scott attacks, is based partly on Britain's experience of September and October 1977. Short-term capital inflows in these two months exceeded the total reserve assets of the British banking system; and banking statistics soon revealed that sterilization had been incomplete. Exchange rate intervention was abandoned in favour of a renewed attempt to adhere to monetary targets. Professor Artis and Dr. Currie draw attention to similar dilemmas confronting the monetary authorities in Germany and Switzerland; but in these cases, it was the monetary targets that were modified or removed (they go on to provide an interesting and closely argued general case for exchange rate targets in lieu of monetary targets). The difference between Mr. Scott and other contributors is of degree, not kind. Mr. Scott is right to insist that offsetting open market operations could in principle sterilize the entire monetary effects of payments surpluses, at least in tranquil conditions when the exchange rate is pegged reasonably close to equilibrium. But the historical record shows that sterilization has rarely been complete, whether conducted by open-market operations or by stringent reserve requirements on non-residents' bank deposits. Furthermore, November 1967, June 1972 and (arguably) October 1977 provide instances when the British authorities could not hold the exchange rate in the face of massive capital flows.

Another device which could reconcile tight monetary policy with a sub-equilibrium exchange rate is an interest equalization tax. This is considered specifically by Professors Buiter and Miller, and by Professor Artis and Dr. Currie. Its effect is to drive a wedge between the uncovered interest differential and the discount on forward foreign exchange. However, it is analysed in the framework of a simple model, without any scrutiny of the factors affecting its practicability. If put into practice, it would probably behave not unlike the two-tier exchange rates operated at various times by Belgium, France and Italy; and it would presumably suffer (as these have done) from the increasing difficulties faced by monetary authorities in enforcing a workable distinction between trade flows and capital flows.

Yet another possible way of preserving a low exchange rate during a phase of restrictive monetary policy is to buy foreign currency in the forward markets. By depressing the home currency's forward exchange rate, this will tend to create,· or increase, an unfavourable covered interest margin, and thereby stimulate an outflow of short-term capital. Domestic interest rates would tend to rise, and the spot exchange rate would drop, if forward foreign exchange purchases were conducted on a sufficiently large scale. The major drawback with such a policy is that it could lead to heavy losses, if the future spot exchange rates turned out to exceed the rates at which the forward contracts were entered upon. It may also be questioned whether Central Banks are likely to have greater forecasting abilities for exchange rates than other market participants. The Bank of England's £350 million losses on forward contracts maturing in 1967 and 1968 are a disagreeable reminder of this.

The most appealing negative answer to the second question, however, is Mr. Scott's. He argues that tight monetary policy can be combined with measures to prevent the exchange rate from rising, but that it is in fact *more desirable* to allow the exchange rate to float up. Permitting this appreciation enables the economy to enjoy the fruits of a transient, but otherwise absent, terms of trade improvement. It also means, he argues, that domestic price inflation is contained more quickly than under other policy mixes involving a lower exchange rate, the same monetary targets, and tighter fiscal policy.

The third question was "Are profitability and employment closely associated with international competitiveness?" Three contributions are addressed (in part) directly to this question: Those by Professor Corden, by Mr. Brech and Professor Stout, and by Mr. Hay and Dr. Morris. All papers testify to a robust if complicated and temporary association, Professor Corden by theoretical analysis, and the latter articles by empirical evidence on quality, volume and price responses to exchange rate changes. The theory suggests that an anticipated exchange rate change has no real effects, whether on competitiveness, real profits or employment, if all prices are fully flexible. An unexpected change in the exchange rate can produce large transitory windfall effects on profits and competitiveness; and also upon employment and output in the traded industries, when these are characterized by a 'surprise supply function' of the kind proposed by Lucas (4). If wage rates remain locked, on the other hand, in units of domestic currency, and firms are in full competitive equilibrium, the rise in profits and employment in tradables industries that will follow a devaluation is permanent. In these circumstances, the discovery of mineral wealth and a restrictive monetary policy (both of which lead to appreciation of a floating exchange rate) cause a once-and-for-all cut in profits and employment in traded industries, which Profesor Corden labels 'the tradables squeeze'. How long-lived the tradables squeeze proves to be in the British case will depend in part on how money wage rates respond. This is governed, in turn, by the characteristics of the Phillips curves that connect money wage rate changes to unemployment and expectations of inflation, and on how expectations of inflation are formed. If expectations are formed rationally, new information is transmitted instantaneously and wage contracts are continually renegotiable the unemployment 'cost' of appreciation is trivial: the Phillips curve will be vertical. But this will surely not be so if expectations of inflation are altered slowly and in the light of experience. In this connection Professors Buiter and Miller give a particularly interesting account of what happens when announcements of restrictive monetary targets are not effective; in these circumstances, the unemployment cost of reducing the growth in the money supply will be aggravated. Of the many empirical results obtained by Mr. Hay and Dr. Morris comes the most interesting finding that exchange rate appreciation of 20% may at least initially cut total company earnings by only 2% although as much as 40% may be lost on exports. Mr. Brech and Professor Stout find that appreciation has raised the average value of U.K. exports.

The fourth question was "By what means should any possible tendency of North Sea oil to raise the exchange rate be neutralized, if this tends to reduce the profitability of the rest of the economy?" Mr. Worswick's final plea for incomes policy, and the exploration of the effects of a tax on capital inflows by Professors Buiter and Miller, and Professor Artis and Dr. Currie, attract attention to devices which might shield profits in non-oil industries (at least temporarily) from the adverse effects of North Sea oil, by limiting the extent of the appreciation it induces. But it is Professor Corden's paper which presents a comprehensive treatment of how North Sea oil's effects on the exchange rate might be qualified or neutralized by different governmental policy measures.

In a short-run framework where money wage rates and either money expenditure or the money supply are assumed to be given Professor Corden considers three effects. Foreign capital flows in to finance North Sea oil development; there may be speculative inflows, anticipating appreciation; and the revenues from the oil itself increase the Government's tax receipts. Although all three combine to raise the exchange rate in the short run, depreciation could eventually ensue if the last effect leads to cuts in other taxes or the retiral of part of the National Debt.

In the longer run, Professor Corden argues, if total employment is kept constant, North Sea oil will tend to transfer output and employment from tradable to non-tradable industries. Profits will fall in tradables, and *rise* in non-tradables. But in Professor Corden's view this process could be stopped completely if the authorities hold the exchange rate constant and keep buying foreign exchange. (This assumes that sterilizing can be completely effective.) This would, however, call for a sacrifice in real absorption, and if the real rather than the money wage rate were given, could require a fall in total employment as well. Professor Corden eschews a normative conclusion. But he implies that protecting the tradables sector from the effect of North Sea oil could prove unacceptably expensive.

This tentative conclusion may be reached by other routes. In a world of flexible prices, for instance, the sudden discovery of mineral wealth should lead to an excess demand for both money and non-traded goods (and also to an excess supply of traded goods, if we take the flow of mineral output to be tradable). The first and third of these effects will drive up the exchange rate. Incidentally, an international comparison of price indices will then reveal a large increase in home prices measured in foreign exchange, since appreciation will be compounded by a rise in the domestic price of non-traded goods. Hence North Sea oil entails a change in the sterling exchange rate which is inconsistent with purchasing power parity considerations. This failure of purchasing power parity to explain exchange rates will be made still worse if countries importing this mineral (e.g. the U.S.A.) hold down its internal price: this will lead to even greater depreciation of their own currencies. Yet a further factor that helps to explain sterling's sharp appreciation in 1979–80, despite rapid inflation, is the near-doubling of V.A.T. in July 1979. As Professors Buiter and Miller suggest, this may have raised the domestic demand for money, and thereby exerted upward pressure on the exchange rate. But to return to the question of the desirability of restoring previous levels of production of other traded goods we may note that any attempt to do so will be equivalent (when all prices are flexible) to levying a tax on non-traded industries. If all other conditions are ideal, this new distortion can only reduce welfare potential. There may be a case for a temporary tax of this kind, to ease the costs of transition; but there is certainly no 'first-best' argument for it in the long run.

The fifth question was "Were Britain's relatively high unemployment and labour difficulties in the 1920s attributable, as Keynes believed, to the overvaluation of sterling, and were the relatively favourable developments in the later 1930s attributable to the lower exchange rate?" The contributions of Mr. Dimsdale and Mr. Wright are concerned with these. Mr. Wright concludes that the rise in unemployment caused by the return to gold in 1925 was modest if not negligible, and short-lived. Mr. Dimsdale considers it to have been more serious. Neither author concurs with neither Benjamin and Kochin (who argue that British unemployment in the 1920s was attributable almost exclusively to unemployment benefits), and Mr. Wright dissents somewhat from the traditional view proposed originally by Keynes and defended by Moggridge, that the return to gold was a major error. Mr Wright believes that it was only one of several factors that serve to explain the depression of the 1920s. He is also not convinced that measures to reduce unemployment would have led to a faster rate of growth. Furthermore, he considers that the prosperity of the later 1930s owed nothing to the exchange rate policies pursued at the time.

Surveying the evidence, Mr. Dimsdale concludes that exchange rates *did* affect competitiveness (at least in the short run) however this is measured. Unemployment *was* influenced by exchange rates and by aggregate demand. From 1932, through operations on the Exchange Equalization Account, the authorities *did* manage to combine some insulation of domestic interest rates and the domestic money supply from external conditions, with some degree of control over the exchange rate. A policy of cutting the supply of

Treasury Bills kept down bill rates, while long-term rates were reduced by the successful conversion of War Loan in 1932. Weak as the effects of this may have been on manufacturing investment, Mr. Dimsdale argues the evidence does point to its having contributed to the revival of private housebuilding in 1932–3. The balanced budget policy applied in the early 1930s could also have helped to keep investment up, through its effects on confidence in the maintenance of orderly financial conditions. It is also perhaps worth noting that a rise in government spending in such circumstances could have led to a rise in interest rates for any one of three reasons: first, the increase in real demand would have raised the demand for money, the supply of which might well not have been raised in step; second, if carried out on a very large scale, it might have inflamed fears of runaway depreciation and inflation; third, a consequential budget deficit would have entailed continuing increases in the supply of government debt. It is widely thought that equilibrium in the market of bonds implies that a budget deficit financed by selling bonds must bring continuing upward pressure on interest rates. But this will be true only if the demand for bonds fails to grow in step. In the conditions of the 1930s, a rise in government spending would have expanded the private sector, which might well have increased its net acquisition of financial assets, so its willingness to absorb bonds might also have risen.

The sixth of the Editors' questions was on inferences to be drawn from other countries' experience. One interesting fact which emerged was the decision by the Swiss in late 1978 to abandon their regime of monetary targets, and opt instead for an exchange rate target. It is still too early to say whether the Swiss experience proves that an exchange rate "policy" in Professor Minford's sense is feasible, desirable, or superior to a regime of monetary targets. What is certain is that these papers will serve to inform and illuminate debate upon critical issues of economic policy. They are of vital significance, not only for Britain, but for any other country which adopts similar monetary policies. Will efforts to reduce the United States' inflation rate substantially below 10 per cent, which may be made in 1981–5, raise the dollar in the manner that restrictive monetary policies have raised sterling?

REFERENCES

1. BENJAMIN, D. K. and L. A. KOCHIN (1979): 'Searching for an Explanation of Unemployment in Interwar Britain', *Journal of Political Economy* LXXXVII, 441–78.
2. DORNBUSCH, R. (1976): 'Expectations and Exchange Rate Dynamics', *Journal of Political Economy* LXXXIV.
3. KEYNES, J. M. (1925): *The Economic Consequences of Mr Churchill*, London.
4. LUCAS, R. E. (1973): 'Some International Evidence on Output-Inflation Tradeoffs, *American Economic Review* LXIII 326–34.
5. MOGGRIDGE, D. E. (1969): *The Return to Gold 1925, the Formulation of Policy and its Critics*, Cambridge.
6. MOGGRIDGE, D. E. (1972): *British Monetary Policy, 1924–1931, and the Norman Conquest of $4.86*, Cambridge.

AUTHOR INDEX

SUBJECT INDEX